VALUING LIVES, HEALING EARTH:
RELIGION, GENDER, AND LIFE ON EARTH

ESWTR Studies in Religion

Published *sub aegis* of the European Society of Women in Theological Research

Edited by Gertraud Ladner (Innsbruck, Austria), Teresa Toldy (Coimbra, Portugal), and Kristin De Troyer (Salzburg, Austria)

Advisory Board:
Elzbieta Adamiak (Koblenz – Landau, Germany), Carmen Bernabé Ubieta (Bilbao, Spain), Isa Breitmaier (Karlsruhe, Germany), Athalya Brenner-Idan (Haifa, Israel), Judith Gruber (Leuven, Belgium), Maaike de Haardt (Tilburg, The Netherlands), Ann Heirman (Gent, Belgium), Anne Koch (Linz, Austria), Silvia Martínez Cano (Madrid, Spain), Zhiru Ng (Claremont, California, USA), Susan Roll (Buffalo, NY; Ottawa, Canada), Lena Roos (Uppsala, Sweden), Mona Siddiqui (Edinburgh, UK), Agnethe Siquans (Vienna, Austria), Nicola Slee (Birmingham, UK; Amsterdam, NL), Najeeba Syeed-Miller (Claremont, California, USA), Mariecke van den Berg (Nijmegen, The Netherlands), and Mireia Vidal Quintero (Madrid, Spain).

1. Julie Hopkins, *'The Wings of the Spirit'—Exploring Feminine Symbolism in Early Pneumatology: A Reassessment of a Key Metaphor in the Spiritual Teachings of the* Marcarian Homilies *in the Light of Early Syriac Christian Tradition*, Louvain: Peeters, 2020.
2. Antonina Wozna, *Némesis: modelo de justicia de Mary Daly*, Louvain: Peeters, 2021.
3. Theresa Yugar, Lilian Dube, Teresia Mbari Hinga, and Sarah Robinson (eds.), *Valuing Lives, Healing Earth. Religion, Gender, and Life on Earth*, Louvain: Peeters 2021.

VALUING LIVES, HEALING EARTH: RELIGION, GENDER, AND LIFE ON EARTH

Edited by

Theresa A. Yugar
Sarah E. Robinson
Lilian Dube
Teresia Mbari Hinga

PEETERS
LEUVEN – PARIS – BRISTOL, CT
2021

ISBN 978-90-429-4385-8
eISBN 978-90-429-4386-5
D/2021/0602/23

A catalogue record for this book is available from the Library of Congress.

© 2021, Peeters, Bondgenotenlaan 153, B-3000 Leuven, Belgium

No part of this book may be reproduced in any form or by any electronic or mechanical means, including information storage or retrieval devices or systems, without prior written permission from the publisher, except the quotation of brief passages for review purposes.

CONTENTS

Dedication VII
Acknowledgements IX
Poem: Bone Blessing, Sarah E. Robinson XI
Foreword: Whitney A. Bauman XIII

Chapter 1: Sarah E. Robinson, Theresa A. Yugar, Lilian Dube, and Teresia Mbari Hinga: Editors' Introduction: Amplifying Voices, Disinfecting Sunshine, and Mutual Solidarity 1

I. KNOWLEDGE

Chapter 2: Ivone Gebara: Real Life and Ecological Solidarity: Garbaging the Environment, Women, and Ourselves 13

Chapter 3: Lilian Dube: Land Justice for Broken Women Healing Earth: Colonization to COVID-19 25

Chapter 4: Jea Sophia Oh: *Salim*, Women, and *Oikos*: A Planetary Expansion of Family 47

Chapter 5: Alyssa Moore: "Solidarity Among Creatures": Catholic Exegetical Grounds for Fellowship with Nonhuman Creation ... 57

Chapter 6: Yuria Celidwen: Women Weaver-of-Worlds: Earth-based *Mythopoesis* in Restorative Indigenous Narratives 69

II. RITUAL

Chapter 7: Rebecca Berru Davis: *Picturing Paradise*: Peruvian Women's Art and a "New Creation" 85

Chapter 8: Mary Judith Ress: Ecofeminism's Cry: Let's Remember Who We Are — Earth's Children! 101

Chapter 9: Frédérique Apffel-Marglin: The Enclosure of the Psyche in Modernity: Healing the Internal and External Landscape ... 113

Chapter 10: Sylvia Marcos: Healing and Valuing Women's Medical Pluri-verse (in Mexico) 125

III. Activism

Chapter 11: Aruna Gnanadason: Indian Women: Nurturing the Earth, Protecting Life 135

Chapter 12: Rosemary Radford Ruether: Wangari Maathai and African Environmental Reform 149

Chapter 13: Rosalind Flynn Hinton: Environmental Racism and Reflective Democracy: Louisiana and Cancer Alley 155

Chapter 14: Pamela K. Brubaker: Indigenous Women Act to Defend Mother Earth: Empowerment and Solidarity 167

IV. Food

Chapter 15: Adrienne Krone: Humans and Honey Bees: Bee-Human Relations, Sacred Space, and Environmental Sustainability at Shoresh Jewish Environmental Programs 187

Chapter 16: Kelsey Ryan-Simkins and Elaine Nogueira-Godsey: Tangible Actions Toward Solidarity: An Ecofeminist Analysis of Women's Participation in Food Justice 203

Chapter 17: Juan A. Tavárez: The *Tianguis*: A Mexican Model of a Green Ideology and Philosophy 223

Chapter 18: Laurel Marshall Potter: *Campesina* School: Popular Agroecological Education in Ecclesial Base Communities in El Salvador 235

Bibliography 249

Contributor and Editor Biographies 267

Index 275

DEDICATION

With this volume, we celebrate
Rosemary Radford Ruether's ecofeminist legacy,
plus other allies and women who likewise
listen and learn,
champion and labor,
reflect and contribute to
religious, economic, and ecological
justice and healing
from the local family
to the regional community
to the national conversation
to the global web of interrelations,
all of which can be renewed
toward wholeness through
valuing lives,
particularly those most marginalized and oppressed,
and healing the earth,
giving most attention and care to
suffering siblings in the human family
in order to right wrongs of the past
and endeavor to live into
a world renewed with justice and kindness
health and prosperity
peace and wellbeing for all living.

We honor the memory of precious ancestors including departed family, who taught us to pay attention to the rhythms of our land and whose dedication to love and justice lives on in us: Nelson Chipoka Dube (1917-2003) and Esther Siziba Dube (1927-1999), Robert P. (Skip) Robinson (1939-2018), and Jeanne Marie Yugar (1968-2021).

ACKNOWLEDGEMENTS

The *Valuing Lives, Healing Earth* volume editors offer this collection of essays in celebration of formidable ecofeminist theologian, professor, and scholar-activist Rosemary Radford Ruether. Her moral clarity and leadership have translated into the practical work of human-to-human and human-to-other-than-human solidarity, justice, liberation, and healing in the face of profound human suffering and systemic injustices, as well as environmental harm. The editors celebrate Ruether's dedication to solidarity, expressed with people she encounters from around the world and across history, particularly women and other vulnerable people, whose daily struggles to meet basic needs connect to disparities in regional, social and ecological systems. Our justice-building way is made easier and more joyful in the substantial wake of formidable scholars like Ruether and others like her, some of whom are participants in this volume.

This volume's authors embody commitments to healing the earth and valuing lives rendered vulnerable by problematic social systems. The authors demonstrate their work of solidarity, despite varying vulnerabilities of authors and study participants, knowing their liberations are inseparable. The volume's variety of voices does not represent a unified, singular, homogenous methodology or singular solution to human and ecological problems. Instead, our authors share space to develop collaborative, coalitional vision toward dynamic, healing, refreshed earthly existence. Despite serious generational conundrums, such as climate and racial injustices, these participants do not sit back, waiting for an external saving force. Neither do they throw up their hands to give up on the renewability of life, even amidst intense suffering personal and collective. Instead, they remember themselves in their aliveness, rendering new their living capacity to see clearly, not merely to know, but to renew earth and work together in solidarity and beneficial hope. Despite tantalizing powers of Anthropocentric solace or Anthropocene technologized escape, these authors assert a thoroughly human renewal in community and in relation with those who share this earthly living place, sacralized by our every breath.

The task of creating this cohesive, inclusive volume required extensive time, effort, and collaboration. In the process, the editors encountered personal to global issues, which needed timely attention toward resolution and healing. The collaborative vision was realized through communication, care-driven understanding, mutual solidarity, and "patient passion" steering us forward toward the goal.¹ Without these tools of community resilience, this volume would not be possible.

In this spirit, the *Valuing Lives, Healing Earth* book project editorial team offer profound gratitude to our families, friends, and colleagues. We thank the eyes that offered editing insights, and contributing authors, whose patience, commitments, and shared vision gave life to this intention. We offer sincere and profound gratitude to copy editor Genevieve Beenen and Nathalie op de Beeck for their attentive proofreading. Their assistance renders this volume much stronger.

We would also like to thank our colleague in Women's Studies in Religion, Diane Ward, for proofreading drafts at all stages of its publication. And, Juan A. Tavárez, for giving graciously of his time to comment, clarify, and finally to aid in the administrative aspects of this project. As well, to Elisabeth Hernitscheck at Peeters Publishing for her steadfast enthusiasm in helping us complete this important manuscript. And, finally to Paul Peeters for making our dream possible.

The editors wish to especially thank Kristin De Troyer for her gracious welcome as President of the European Society of Women in Theological Research (ESWTR) to publish this international volume through the ESWTR publishing venue, Peeters Publishing. As the volume developed, Dr. De Troyer shared our deep respect for Ruether's legacy and sense of urgency to provide opportunities for solidarity among people seeking justice from complex Global South and North locations. We thank Karen Jo Torjesen for her transnational feminist vision and leadership at Claremont Graduate University.

Most importantly, we want to thank our mentor, colleague, professor, and friend Rosemary Radford Ruether for her steadfast commitment to social and ecological justice. Ruether's work is widely recognized and celebrated, we believe, because she lived out her theoretical commitments for a more just world for all. Our ultimate hope for this book is to demonstrate Ruether's vision and passion to embody and enable social and ecological justice, which lives on in all who step forward in honest intention and practical ways to value vulnerable lives and heal the earth. The editors and authors share this intellectual stream with multitudes, past, present, and future, who endeavor together to live into a more just and healthy living community.

What else might the face of Love look like on Earth?

August 2020

---

1. "Being rooted in love for our real communities of life and for our common mother, Gaia, can teach us patient passion, a passion that is not burnt out in a season, but can be renewed season after season." Rosemary Radford Ruether, *Gaia and God: An Ecofeminist Theology of Earth Healing* (New York: Harper Collins, 1992), 273.

Bone Blessing, Sarah E. Robinson

Our bones
legacy remnants
of long passed travelers who
like us breathed this air
the same blood pulsed
through tissues now turned to dust

We now are living dust
living bones
living waters
singing the same mystery song
without answers
we breathe and sing
dance through sorrow
rise in righteous fierceness
caress in gentle forgiveness
delight in celebration

These bones
return to the Wellspring
pulsing life through every tissue
every idea
every moment
Gratitude for healing
for the passing of life from body to body
breath to breath
bone to bone

Blessed are the living and the dead
blessed are the bodies and the lives yet to come
for whom we are ancient ancestors
May we prepare this ground here for them
soften their steps with petals
protect them with canopies of leaves
save seeds for their harvest
May we honor this moment here
these hands here
working this precious ground here
beloved bone dust
cushioning our bones as we step forward
from here

FOREWORD

Rosemary Radford Ruether: A Prophet of the Planetary

Whitney A. Bauman

In many ways, Rosemary Radford Ruether was an intersectional scholar and activist before "intersectional" even existed.[1] From participating in Freedom Rides, and her first academic position at Howard University,[2] to her first books addressing *Sexism and God Talk*, and her early books *New Woman: New Earth* and *Gaia and God*, Ruether has understood that the systems of anthropocentric, racist, ethnocentric, hetero-patriarchy will not be undone by addressing just one of its oppressive logics alone. They must be understood and deconstructed together. The book *Valuing Lives, Healing Earth* gives witness to her life and work devoted to unraveling the economic, political, and institutional "isms" that support the logic of domination. The volume gives witness to the belief that new, different, planetary possibilities can change our world for the better. However, such changes will, as the books' different sections suggest, take both knowledge and action: knowledge that arises from engaged scholarship, and action that is informed. Likewise, this volume is a reminder that it will take re-embodying ideas and actions to recognize our embeddedness in planetary systems with other earth bodies through new rituals and in thinking about our food and other consumptive practices.

Filled with the voices of scholars and activists all over the world, and from many different cultural, biological, ecological, geographical and social locations, this volume does much to highlight and carry on Ruether's legacy. As one of the lucky people in this world who have been privileged to study with her, I would like to offer some of the key highlights of how she has dealt with the twin phenomena that mark the 20th and 21st centuries: globalization (or more aptly described by Derrida as globalatinization)[3]

---

1. Kimberlé Crenshaw, "Demarginalizing the Intersection of Race and Sex: A Black Feminist Critique of Antidiscrimination Doctrine, Feminist Theory and Antiracist Politics," in *University of Chicago Legal Forum*, Vol. 1989: Issue 1, Article 8.
2. Rosemary Radford Ruether, *My Quests for Hope and Meaning: An Autobiography* (Eugene, OR: Wipf and Stock, 2013).
3. Jacques Derrida, "Faith and Knowledge: The Two Sources of 'Religion' at the Limits of Reason Alone," in *Religion*, edited by Jacques Derrida and Gianni Vattimo (Stanford, CA: Stanford University Press, 1998), 1-78.

and climate change (or what I, following a modification of Amory Lovins, call climate weirding).[4] These two phenomena affect different humans and earth others differently, depending upon one's embodiment and specific location, but to be sure, no place or body is unaffected.

When I use the term globalization, I mean it in both an economic and a socio-cultural sense. It is the period since World War II that some sociologists refer to as "the great acceleration," when fossil-fueled communication, transportation, and production technologies have sped up the daily lives of most "western" folk, and made the world much smaller.[5] This has been an unequal process affecting people differently based upon class, race, gender, sex, sexuality, and geographical location. Ruether's work on globalization and ecofeminism reveals her awareness of this process and the unequal distribution of goods and ills brought about by the globalization of neo-liberal capitalism and modern, western technologies.[6]

In addition, the globalization of information and culture is not an even process. For example, I spend some time teaching in Jogjakarta, Indonesia, at the University of Gadja Mada. When I ask students there who the president of the United States is, they all know. When I ask my students in Miami who the president of Indonesia is, none of them know and in fact most could not point to Indonesia on a map. Western exceptionalism,[7] gender and sex roles,[8] and monotheistic values of western, Christian cultures have been imposed by the so-called "Modern West" upon the rest of the world.[9] This is so-much the case that Derrida referred to the process as "globalatinization." That is, globalization is not an equal process everywhere but the enforcing of western economics, cultures, and ideals over the face of the globe. Ruether has a deep understanding of this process and connects the contemporary process of American exceptionalism and domination to ancient patriarchal empires and earlier forms of European colonization. This uneven cultural exchange is paralleled by an unequal economic exchange with resources and benefits going to the wealthiest,

---

4. Thomas Friedman, "The People We Have Been Waiting For," in *The New York Times* (December 2, 2007): https://www.nytimes.com/2007/12/02/opinion/02friedman.html?_r=1.
5. J.R. McNeill and Peter Engelke, *The Great Acceleration: An Environmental History of the Anthropocene since 1945* (Cambridge, MA: Harvard University Press, 2014).
6. See, eg. Rosemary Radford Ruether, *Integrating Ecofeminism, Globalization and World Religions* (Lanham, MD: Rowman and Littlefield, 2005).
7. Rosemary Radford Ruether, *America, Amerikkka: Elect Nation and Imperial Violence* (New York, NY: Routledge, 2014 edition).
8. Rosemary Radford Ruether, *Sexism and God Talk: Toward a Feminist Theology* (Boston, MA: Beacon Press, 1983).
9. Rosemary Radford Ruether, *Christianity and the Making of the Modern Family* (Boston, MA: Beacon Press, 2000).

while the ecological and social costs of global neoliberal capitalism are felt disproportionately by the poor. Colonization, Enlightenment, and Development in the name of "progress" should always face the question, "progress for whom and toward what end?" Ruether's work in regards to racism, sexism, and anthropocentrism has been instrumental in sifting through the detritus of history to uncover the "dark" side of modernity and progress.[10]

One of the consequences of fossil-fueled globalization is that we are literally living at a pace that is beyond the regenerative capacities of the planet. Climate change, and all that goes with it, is one of the negative consequences of pumping fossil fuels into the veins of humanity. Ruether's work, from *New Woman, New Earth* to *Gaia and God* among others,[11] has addressed the problems of this fast-paced living, even when other theologians were not. Her understanding of the web of life and her relational ontology recognize that humans, as part of the rest of the natural world, cannot control and manage the rest of the natural world and that attempts to do so will end up causing problems. Instead, humans ought to work with and support the flourishing of the planetary community and all bodies therein.

In addition, Ruether recognizes that relationality also means vulnerability: something we are all very aware of as the climate changes and as pandemics spread across the globe. Furthermore, just as the effects of globalization are not distributed equally, she understands that we need not just climate activism, but climate justice that pays attention to how poor women, children, and people of color around the world experience the ill effects of climate change more so than the wealthy humans who contributed most to the problems of climate change. The unequal distribution of costs and benefits is, again, due to the underlying, systemic structures of racism, sexism, classism, and other disparities that persist in the modern world.

This volume, like Ruether's corpus, helps us to re-attune to issues of planetary justice, ecological degradation, and animal welfare through keeping our eyes on the ways in which the "least of these" are affected by current neo-liberal, capitalist systems. Whether Gebara's method of thinking with "garbage," Dube's focus on the unequal effects of COVID-19

---

10. Walter Mignolo, *The Darker Side of Western Modernity: Global Future, Decolonial Options* (Durham, NC: Duke University Press, 2011).

11. Rosemary Radford Ruether, ed., *New Woman, New Earth* (New York: Seabury Press, 1975); *Women Healing Earth: Third World Women on Ecology, Feminism, and Religion* (Maryknoll, NY: Orbis, 1996); and Rosemary Radford Ruether, *Gaia and God: An Ecofeminist Theology of Earth Healing* (New York, NY: HarperCollins, 1992).

due to continued forces of colonization, Gnanadason's focus on women in India, Ruether on the work of Maathai, Hinton's work on Cancer Alley and the aftermath of Hurricane Katrina, or Brubaker's work on Indigenous and farmer activists in Peru, Honduras, Guatemala, and Costa Rica; each of these essays starts reflections from the grounded, embodied experience of those most affected by the forces of globalatinization and climate weirding. Furthermore, they do not simply critique the violence done to bodies by these two forces and name the injustices perpetuated, but rather many of the essays begin to offer new visions. Sophia Oh's vision of the planetary family, Moore's solidarity among creatures, Berru Davis's vision of new creation from the *testimonios* of Peruvian women, the green economic model of Tavárez's "green marketplace," the *Tianguis*, and the agro-ecological educational model of Marshall Potter's *Campesina*; these are all visions of new possible worlds being co-created toward a more just and flourishing planetary community.

In conclusion, the ways in which Ruether deals with globalization and climate change in an intersectional and interrelated way, which is reflected in this volume, suggests that she has what I might call a planetary environmental ethic.[12] Such an ethic understands that humans are deeply embedded in evolutionary and ecological processes, and that we are first and foremost, citizens of the planet. From the perspective of a planetary ethic, the ideal and the real (god and gaia) exist on an immanent plane within this planet. Our ideas matter for the world around us, and the world gives birth to our ideas. However, relationality does not mean we are all the same. Different bodies experience the world differently based upon race, class, sex, gender, sexuality, and ability (among other identity markers) precisely because we co-construct worlds that favor certain ways of being and becoming over others. This book, and Ruether's planetary ethic in general, are a call to critically attune to the worlds in which we live, all of which make up the planetary at any given moment, in order that we might co-construct worlds that bring about more justice and more flourishing for the entire planetary community.

---

12. Whitney A. Bauman, *Religion and Ecology: Developing a Planetary Ethic* (New York, NY: Columbia University Press, 2014).

CHAPTER 1

EDITORS' INTRODUCTION: AMPLIFYING VOICES, DISINFECTING SUNSHINE, AND MUTUAL SOLIDARITY

Sarah E. Robinson, Theresa A. Yugar, Lilian Dube,
and Teresia Mbari Hinga

> when you learn to think
> no matter where you may be
> you can find the stars
> — Sarah E. Robinson

1.1. Introduction

This book goes to print in 2020-21, a time when the Earth's people shudder and cry for breath in a global pandemic[1] and economic downturn, alongside a burgeoning awakening to the horrors of racial injustice. Healing the earth requires responding with empirical clarity, creative reflection, and moral acuity to these issues, such as inherited inequities amplified in climate disruptions and health crisis circumstances, compounding existing injustices and disenfranchisement. The authors join multitudes, who seek to cast disinfecting sunshine on all forms of oppression, corruption, and misuse of privilege and power, while inviting others to live in renewed living communities. Such renewal is most effectively expressed with a moral priority for those who suffer most.

In this way, solidarity is not abstract, but rather emerges through life-giving activities, which mend the fabric of life. In order to facilitate connection, directed assistance, and understanding, solidarity requires strategic questions such as:

> Whose decisions shape a community, and how does community cohesion and democratic participation relate to resilience?

---

1. The medical term for coronavirus is severe acute respiratory syndrome coronavirus 2 (SARS-CoV-2), the virus causing novel coronavirus disease, or COVID-19. World Health Organization, "Naming the coronavirus disease (COVID-19) and the virus that causes it," Web resource: https://www.who.int/emergencies/diseases/novel-coronavirus-2019/technical-guidance/naming-the-coronavirus-disease-(covid-2019)-and-the-virus-that-causes-it (accessed May 25, 2020).

Whose voices must be heard more clearly in order to attend to crucial, moral tasks of earth, climate, and inclusive community care?
How can community responsiveness be timely and locally appropriate?
Can solidarity facilitate relationships of mutual wellbeing?
Solidarity with whom? By whom? For whom?
Whose voices are "we" as scholars and people of integrity leaning in to hear? Can "we" represent others' voices? If so, how can allies represent responsibly?
How can greater wholeness and wholesomeness be cultivated among people who find themselves grounded in different social and environmental locations from each other, yet committed in common to empathetic understanding and coalition building?
How can people participate in health-giving or "healing" activities in home places, among real people in real environments, on issues that range and complexly intersect in local to global, personal to political, vulnerable to powerful, social to environmental issues and spaces?

Each author in this volume provides a unique lens through which readers may recognize the full humanity of people, many of whom experience marginalization and nevertheless involve themselves in repairing their local ecology and asserting their communities' value.

1.2. Origins of the Project

This volume provides a timely revisiting of themes from Rosemary Radford Ruether's book *Women Healing Earth* (Orbis Books, 1996) among feminist scholar-activists, who, like Ruether, seek to embody and integrate social and ecological justice. In 2017, the editorial team emerged from a panel at the Catholic Theological Society of America (CTSA) conference, which met in Albuquerque, New Mexico. Scholar of comparative religions Teresia Mbari Hinga of Kenya (Santa Clara University) organized and moderated an invited panel, entitled "Women Healing Earth: Revisiting Rosemary Radford Ruether's Work on Moral Agency and Ecological Ethics among Women of the Global South." The panel presenters were Lilian Dube (University of San Francisco), Sarah E. Robinson (also, Robinson-Bertoni; Santa Clara University, Pacific Lutheran University), and Theresa A. Yugar (California State University, Los Angeles).

These panelists built on Ruether's legacy, highlighting the critical importance of theological, ethical, ecological insights of women in the Global South, who — despite dangers from multiple intersecting crises related to ecological degradation — exercise moral agency toward a world where all can flourish. The panel encouraged listening to new ecological, feminist, and ecofeminist voices and mapped best practices to leverage women's agency and cross-border solidarity in the global quest for just sustainability. Those present at the CTSA panel expressed interest in a larger project, also fueling interest in this volume's collaboration. Through the panel and this volume, the editors aim to 1) amplify key, marginalized voices who participate in and encourage integral ecology, and 2) facilitate local, cross-regional, and global engagement in mutually fruitful dialogue on ecological meaning and social solidarity in ethical praxis, combining ethical ideas and actions.

Following the conference, Hinga, Dube, Robinson, and Yugar agreed to embark on editing a volume to revisit themes of feminism, ecology, and religion for a twenty-first century context. Sharing a common commitment with Ruether to enact global ecological healing and local human wellbeing, the editorial team envisioned highlighting specific lives committed to and intertwined with healing the earth. Through collected articles, the volume highlights a dynamic balance of epistemology and activism, writing and actions, intangible concepts and tangible efforts. Further, the editors sought to provide critical-constructive assessments that take into account interlinked and increasing risks to climate, biodiversity, and human diversity. For example, climate disruptions impact traditional knowledge systems, including traditional environmental knowledge of indigenous people and intimate, experience-based understanding of local places, such as local women who daily carry water and collect fuel for a cookfire, supporting sustenance. Environmental crises intensify urgent needs for structural changes to reduce suffering and promote health for marginalized people and biological systems worldwide. In this spirit, the editors sought essays that envision a renewed future and report on integrated, intersectional work toward ecological and human community wholeness in specific, local landscapes. The *Valuing Lives, Healing Earth* volume builds on foundations forged by Ruether, a foremother who uplifted dialogue among global voices committed to social and ecological health. Ruether's 1996 edited volume *Women Healing Earth* enabled solidarity, facilitated communication across divides, and amplified marginalized voices. In parallel with *Women Healing Earth*, this volume gathers a variety of voices, amplifies experiences of vulnerability, adds disinfecting sunshine to situations of injustice, and facilitates mutual relations of solidarity among a variety of people, whose eyes are open to their embeddedness in local living systems.

1.3. Why Religion, Gender, and Life on Earth?

Valuing Lives, Healing Earth develops the central insight of ecofeminist scholars — that working closer to the earth does not necessarily reflect a divinely ordained social location, but rather enables a uniquely informed vantage point for addressing local ecological issues. In 1983, Ruether asserts that ecofeminists discern "a symbolic and a structural connection between the mistreatment of women and the mistreatment of nature."[2] In 1996, Ruether presents:

> What connects these essays is not a conscious use of a particular ideology of how women and nature are connected but rather a complex reality of how women and nature have been exploited both by their own societies as well as by colonizing powers, how women function as the mediators of nature's benefits for their families, and in this context, as caretakers of nature.[3]

Similarly, in *Valuing Lives, Healing Earth*, the authors do not represent a singular ideology, but instead identify problematic patterns faced in divergent locations, which people respond to with life-affirming power.

Through their chapters, authors seek to understand how real people face burdens, beauties, and vulnerabilities in living interdependently with local biosystems, waterways, and landscapes, all of which (including humans) are impacted by changing weather patterns, the privatization of the commons, and interlinked losses to biodiversity and human diversity. Thus, the volume editors seek to highlight strategies employed by local communities to bring about interconnected social equity and ecological health.

The editors intended for the volume to facilitate leadership to amplify varied voices for community and environmental wellbeing. Authors acknowledge traditional ecological knowledge, held particularly by women and marginalized others in a variety of social and environmental locations where daily work is tied to an awareness of ecological wellness or degradation. Further, theoretical frameworks or analysis emerge from particular communities engaged in environmentally significant work with moral leadership from various marginal voices to community decision making. Our intent is to highlight work "on the ground," which brings renewed focus to intertwined environmental and social issues.

1.4. Sections and Book Chapter Overview

Valuing Lives, Healing Earth contributing authors represent diverse contexts and methodologies, religions and locations, which coalesce into four sections: Knowledge, Ritual, Activism, and Food. Each chapter interacts

---

2. Rosemary Radford Ruether, *Sexism and God-Talk: Toward a Feminist Theology* (Boston: Beacon Press, 1983), xv.
3. Rosemary Radford Ruether, "Introduction," *Women Healing Earth: Third World Women on Ecology, Feminism, and Religion* (Maryknoll, N.Y.: Orbis Books, 1996), 2.

with feminism, religion, and ecology in situated ways, highlighting what is most relevant in context. Thus, the editors invite readers to endeavor to listen to each voice on its own terms. The volume combines seasoned and emerging voices, representing decolonial, postcolonial, indigenous, and ecofeminist perspectives. For further details on each author, see Contributor and Editor Biographies.

The editors intentionally invited scholars of color, indigenous scholars, and scholar-activists of colonial European descent, whose work enacts ecological solidarity and coalitional thinking. Valuing coalitions, these scholars work to ensure that, for example, those people alive today whose ancestors enslaved other human beings or participated in indigenous decimation, whose families have benefited from light-skin, economic, linguistic, and other types of privilege, such inheritors of a dubious past fully participate in generating accountability in contemporary structures of power. In other words, inheritors of abusive power structures may participate in liberation in conversation with those who live with legacies from ancestral and contemporary oppression. Despite ancestral and recent horrors, contemporary people of a variety of backgrounds can work together to remake a more humane, just, and life-giving world.

The book's four themes — Knowledge, Ritual, Activism, and Food — reflect dimensions of meaning, which emerged organically from authors' goals. The first section, Knowledge, retrieves indigenous knowledge about the three pillars of sustainability: economy, environment, and society, while recognizing unsettling realities and identifying means toward integrity and restoration. The second section, Ritual, focuses on how ritual themes and activities engage in embodied earth healing, or more specifically, healing relations with local, beloved places as activities of remembering and recovering wholeness. Section three, Activism, provides reflections on power, gender, race, colonialism, indigeneity, and grassroots movements for self-determination, democracy, solidarity, and protecting life on earth. Section four focuses on Food, recognizing daily experiences of food procurement, which interconnect with cultural inheritance, innovations, and relations with other-than-human lives through the intimate act of eating. Thus, the four sections provide structure for understanding dimensions of ecological and social life in which people seek wellbeing, justice, and solidarity.

The volume begins with Knowledge. In the essay "Real Life and Ecological Solidarity: Garbaging the Environment, Women and Ourselves," Ivone Gebara recognizes how impoverished Black women, who do the dirty work of collecting and sorting trash in Recife, Brazil, become identified as trash themselves in a dual denigration of racialized human beings and discarded land. In "Land Justice for Broken Women Healing Earth: Colonization to COVID-19," Lilian Dube draws connections between Zimbabwean and African American community relationships with slave lynching trees, the Black Lives Matter Movement, and negative impacts of the COVID-19 epidemic. Dube approaches her subjects through poetic, narrative, historical, and theological means. She draws on experience in Zimbabwe's independence movement and qualitative research on painful histories commemorated in the continued presence of historically significant trees known as markers of lives lost. Dube artfully addresses unique ways that trees figure in contemporary African and diaspora cultural conscience, relating to racial and earth healing justices. Jea Sophia Oh's essay, "A Planetary Expansion of Family," offers an ecofeminist liberationist approach to earth healing drawing on Korean history, key terms and concepts. She integrates household metaphors rooted in the term *oikos*, revising patriarchal inheritance. Allysa Moore's article "Fellowship with Non-Humans," presents a textual analysis of the Roman Catholic Church's catechism, enlarging on Catholic understanding of God's relationship to both human and non-human creation. In "Women Weavers of Worlds," Yuria Celidwen resists language-culture extinction through conservation and revival of Mexican indigenous storytelling traditions, asserting cultural identity and continuity by centering the voice of her grandmother as storyteller, medicine woman, and accountability partner.

The section on Ritual begins with Rebecca Berru Davis' chapter, "Picturing Paradise, Peruvian Women's Art and a 'New Creation.'" Her work reclaims the *testimonios* (testimonies) of women who live in Shantytowns of Lima, Peru. Their *testimonios* are in the form of *cuadros*, or fabric pictures, which communicate their relationship to the land on a day-to-day basis. Like Ruether, she leverages her privilege to offer a reflective space for women in Pamplona Alta to articulate their *sabiduria* (wisdom) in relationship to the environment, as well as Pope Francis' call for ecological conversion for Catholics and non-Catholics alike. Frédérique Apffel-Marglin, founder of the *Sachamama* Center for BioCultural Regeneration in Peru, presents her chapter "The Enclosure of the Psyche in Modernity" on Peruvian Upper Amazon indigenous shamanic practices, weaving theory with decades of lived experience. She describes Yanomami healing practices, which involve integrative community experiences of human, natural, and spirit realms, describing rituals in contradistinction to psychological isolations woven into colonial modernity. From Chile, Mary Judith Ress writes "Ecofeminism's Cry: Let's Remember Who We Are — Earth's Children!," which celebrates and charts over twenty years of the foremost ecofeminist collective of women in Latin America, called *Con-spirando*. Ress describes their work to decolonize minds and bodies from patriarchal Christian doctrine and cultural social codes for women in Latin America, finishing with an epic poem on the cosmic, creative dance of life. Sylvia Marcos' article, "Healing and Valuing Women's Medical Pluri-verse (in Mexico)" identifies the centrality of women in indigenous medical practices. Distinctive from institutional medical paradigms, Nahua indigenous knowledge systems and body healing practices practiced by women doctors and *curanderas* emphasize balance, wellbeing, wholeness, and healing, which is intimately connected to a cosmological worldview. Marcos' pluri-verse offers a decolonial cosmology in which contemporary healing practices nest in ancestral knowledge systems.

The Activism section presents Aruna Gnanadason's article, "Indian Women: Nurturing the Earth, Protecting Life." Gnanadason critiques policies of industrial development, which contaminate rivers, forests, land, and people's health. Envisioning human and earth flourishing, she resists these violations and calls for an ecofeminist theology that supports an "eco-just" movement aimed at a subjective, relational, and personalized God of compassion. Ruether's chapter, "Wangari Maathai and African Environmental Reform," situates the pioneering activist work of 2004 Nobel Peace Prize winner Wangari Maathai and her Green Belt Movement within the historical context of colonial powers, past and present, that appropriated and impoverished both the economy and land in the region. Ruether highlights tree planting interconnected with access to food, fresh water, and democracy, all situated in politics of land use in postcolonial Kenya. The essay completes with recognizing Maathai's historic Nobel Peace Prize as a means to amplify these issues, empowering those who share her commitments. Rosalind Hinton's article, "Women Rising in St. James Parish, Louisiana's Cancer Alley," maps the pre- and post-crisis U.S. environmental injustices exacerbated by Hurricane Katrina in 2006. Cancer-causing toxins occupy the intersection of systemic racism and environmental crisis. Hinton celebrates solidarity gestures by a local Catholic church. In "Indigenous Women Act to Defend Mother Earth: Empowerment and Solidarity," Pamela K. Brubaker reports from The People's Climate Summit in Lima, Peru, in 2014. She amplifies voices of Indigenous, union, farming, and other social activists in Peru, Honduras, Guatemala, and Costa Rica. These activists work to protect lands and natural resources from transnational corporations, which are more focused on profit than community well-being. Like Ruether, Brubaker's research and activist work fosters transnational feminist solidarity, spanning and strengthening ties of solidarity between the Global North and South.

In the final section on Food, Adrienne Krone's essay "Humans and Honey Bees: Bee-Human Relations, Sacred Space, and Environmental Sustainability at Shoresh Jewish Environmental Programs" introduces a call to attend to pollinator health as a deep-rooted Jewish tradition which resounds among Canadian Jewish sustainable agriculture leaders. Based in Toronto, Canada, Krone's research integrates Jewish ethical tenets in "Community Supported Beekeeping" spaces, which directly support honey bees and pollinators, as well as local Jewish communities, toward greater flourishing. In the article "Tangible Actions Toward Solidarity: An Ecofeminist Analysis of Women's Participation in Food Justice," Kelsey Ryan-Simkins and Elaine Nogueira-Godsey engage in qualitative research with urban garden projects in Columbus, Ohio, U.S., analyzing intersections of solidarity and food justice with women's agricultural work in the Global South. Juan A. Tavárez's article "*Tianguis*: A Model of a Green Ideology and Philosophy," reclaims a pre-Columbian communal sacred space in Mexico, the *tianguis*. In 1994, the North American Free Trade Agreement, or NAFTA, resulted in the commercialization of the *tianguis*, a modern-day swapmeet. Tavárez asserts that there were no inherent race or class distinctions in pre-Hispanic *tianguises*, where "green" marketplace dynamics rooted in traditions of ecological and social significance. Laurel Marshall Potter's chapter "*Campesina* School: Popular Agroecological Education in Ecclesial Base Communities in El Salvador" focuses on an agroecological curriculum in El Salvador, which centers on community ritual, civic engagement, and food justice. Marshall Potter names the driving forces in rural life, sun, rain, and seasonal dependability, which in their absence fuel migration from Central American rural locations. Emphasizing the importance of *Campesina* Schools, Marshall Potter's chapter completes the book with attention to the importance of trust in local knowledge, particularly among those with less formal education, to create a meaningful educational project that affirms "*otro mundo posible*" or "*otros mundos posibles*." Other worlds, worldviews, and perspectives are not only possible, but already here, welcome, and formative of agroecological education. In a forward-looking spirit, the book completes with the last word of Marshall Potter's chapter: "*Adelante*," Spanish for "Onwards!"

1.5. Conclusion

This volume provides some answers to questions posed at the start of this chapter, though not through a monolingual enterprise in abstract scholarship. Instead, these voices together represent a variety of distinct methods in active, engaged scholarship, which interweaves with and for solidarity in real communities of people and other-than-human living beings in real places in real time, the early decades of the twenty-first century. The volume *Valuing Lives, Healing Earth* builds on a foundation strengthened by Ruether's scholarship, particularly her edited volume *Women Healing Earth*, which provided a similar space for conversation across differences and geographies, among people who largely recognize ecological and social justice as life-giving and connected to religious integrity. This volume fulfills a need to bring greater attention to local and global, interconnected projects, which connect ecological thinking and action, root in religious and feminist commitments, and produce community wellbeing in real, beloved places. Combining attentive scholarship, poetry and artistic reflection, and community engagement, these projects vary in methods, but share a commitment to a healthy future, a shared sense of wholeness and wholesomeness, and a common home in the living earth community.

In addition to fostering global South-North and South-South partnerships, this volume expands on Ruether's vision by offering an additional focus on North American North-North relations of solidarity across differences. The people of North America cannot be reduced to a unitary, monolithic, homogenous group, despite formidable and apt critiques of North American hegemony and problematic memes of a unitary "American-ness."[4] Therefore, this volume of scholarship provides a means to renew texturing of a feminist scholarly canvas, integrating a fuller understanding of globally inclusive projects in a biodiverse and culturally diverse landscape of meaning-making. Therefore, contributors represent inclusive scholarly methods in their respective communities, valuing lives rendered vulnerable by problematic social systems and healing the earth that they know and love.

---

4. Also see Rosemary Radford Ruether, *America Amerikkka: Elect Nation and Imperial Violence* (New York: Acumen Publishing, 2007).

I

KNOWLEDGE

CHAPTER 2

REAL LIFE AND ECOLOGICAL SOLIDARITY: GARBAGING THE ENVIRONMENT, WOMEN, AND OURSELVES

Ivone Gebara

This text is meant to be a tribute to Rosemary Radford Ruether, a theologian and friend of many years who has always challenged the ecclesiastical and political establishment, seeking justice and rights for women and respect for different forms of Life.

2.1. Introduction

Ecological theories surrounding the destructive actions of the planet are innumerable, and typically come from male sources. Despite their importance, they at times create collective warnings and fears without provoking effective action. These theorists also organize important discussions, international symposia, and various publications in a language that is difficult for the general public to access. As such, we can see how simple and local social actions, especially those headed by women, do not seem to have much social recognition on the part of ecological theorists. Often we have the impression that scientific theories seem very far from the everyday practices of everyday people and thus create distances that can be insurmountable between one world and the other. It is as if we speak two different languages that are inaccessible to one another, while living in different worlds.

In an attempt to overcome this distance I would like to reflect on a common practice among poor women, the recycling of garbage, especially in larger cities of Latin America. Within this activity, we see several contradictions between ecological theory and everyday practice, economic theory and survival practice, as well as paid work and labor, without labor rights. Incredible as it may seem, recycling yields only a small profit to waste pickers and a large amount of money for industries that recycle materials and sell them, saving time and money. The recycling industry feeds the capitalist market in yet another way and does not always open up options for a new way of living and caring for the Earth as our habitat and common body. The recycling industry appears to continue the same exploitative practices, while giving a propagandist impression that they are recycling and taking care of the planet. For this reason, I want to focus my reflection on the effects of recycling on women's lives and show the near impossibility of overcoming the ecological, economic, political and social contradictions at the present moment in our history. These contradictions are revealed in the disastrous exploitation of the planet, its inhabitants, and especially women.

If, on the one hand, recycling expands solidarity and forms of survival, on the other hand, it also increases the exploitation of the labor force of the poor, especially that of women, in favor of large enterprises that keep up a facade of caring for the world. This directly feeds a savage capitalism that uses recycled garbage produced by capitalism itself for its own benefit. But whose hands work in this garbage? Are they recognized for what they are worth?

The contradiction and complexity of our actions show that everything connects with everything else. As such, recycling alone does not lead to a change in the consumerist and destructive logic of this hierarchical and exclusive capitalist system in which we live. Recycling may be a necessary immediate action, but it does require further reflection and concomitant action on a global scale. It also requires another understanding of human beings in their intimate interdependence with our planet as a whole. We need, therefore, collective actions that announce alternatives in the different spaces of our life. We need to talk more about the diversity of our languages and actions, and above all, we need to learn to listen to ourselves and to other forms of life. I believe that this is a method for rebuilding relationships with all expressions of this Common Body called EARTH.

It is in this simple, yet complex context, that the present text discusses the impasses of real life and ecological solidarity in our times.

2.2. The Real Life of Women Who Recycle Trash

To speak of real life seems on the one hand something very simple and on the other hand rather audacious in the face of life's complexity. What is the real, the reality of life? I dare to say that the real is in the first place that which appears to us, what we perceive, feel and that which touches our existence closely. It has several faces, situations, emotions, and interpretations. In this reflection, I will limit it to the need for human survival of women who work with garbage. This is a means for them to guarantee their need for housing, food, health and child care. It signifies their desire to 'live well' in the midst of the 'bad living' that is imposed upon them.

To talk about the real life of women who recycle garbage is first and foremost to talk about women who survive because of this difficult task. They need it to have their daily bread, since they cannot find another way to support themselves. Many women form co-ops and are indirectly linked to some larger company that reuses various materials. Although they are the first subject of this reflection, I also want to call to mind the many recyclers of domestic waste, those who in their daily lives are inhabited by a cause, a reason, a love for the greater life on the planet. It is the housewives, the cooks, the mothers of the family who have this work and who feel just how urgent it is to embrace this cause everyday. Many are aware of the importance of not polluting land, rivers, and seas, and do so in Latin America in increasing percentage. It seems that cleaning the house and the planet has been and continues to be a practical task for women! And among them, I particularly reflect on those who have assumed the work of recycling garbage as a source of survival. They are poor women, poorly schooled, and have difficulty finding work to support themselves and their families. Many are single mothers, some are married to garbage collectors, and all have to face hard work in taking care of their homes and families as well as financially guaranteeing their subsistence. They have a double working day. In other words, a quasi-restless journey. Depending on the day, many go out at night to collect garbage, especially on weekends, alongside bars and street parties. They look first at the beer and soda cans that are the most valuable because of the aluminum that goes into a circular process of production and reuse. In the background these women are 'ghost' workers in the packaging industries, and they do not know it. They are invisible and exploited workers. The can and packaging industries do not pay for their work because they only buy the product from intermediaries who in turn pay a minimum price to the collectors. And this minimum is still proudly valued by the women themselves, who with their labor manage to get off the streets and find substandard housing for their family to live. These women have been able to transform some of their lives by recycling garbage of various kinds and organizing it for sale.

Some of these women manage to develop an ecological conscience like Teresa Felipe Costa, who lives on the east side of São Paulo and founded the National Collectors Movement.[1] She has said many times with great pride that she was living and helping the environment to live as well. She denounces waste and the wastefulness of packaging. She also denounces the precarious situations, which face the women who take on recycling as work. This social awareness of both Teresa and many others does not

---

1. Bulletin from ABES-SP. "The Feminine Force of Recycling", March, 2014.

guarantee them social or labor rights. They continue to be exposed not only to precarious situations related to their workers' rights, but also to health risks as they deal with debris from multiple sources without due protection. Furthermore, they end up promoting the profits of business owners, who do not pay for the labor of many recyclers.

Thus, a hierarchy of poverty is created. The poorest ones who are exposed to the biggest amount of waste are the ones that receive the least amount of payment. At the same time that they talk about the importance of cleaning the streets and the planet, they also realize that they need garbage to survive and that this same trash is a source of maintaining their lives. The production of garbage thus becomes a source of survival in an interdependent cycle of life and death.

The evils of environmental destruction by the unbridled initiative of capitalism are transferred to the poorest, in this case, to women. It is these women who do the cleaning, getting their hands dirty in order to live, and in turn benefit the bigger system of capitalism. While indirectly cleaning the planet, they are also forced to live in the dirt and deal with poor sanitary conditions. Currently in Brazil, seventy-five percent of poor people who work in recycling everyday are women.[2]

Undoubtedly, there has been a growth in the ecological awareness of many, but at the same time, and to a much larger degree, we have seen a growth in the production of garbage accompanied by an increase in human poverty. Thus, the poorest remain the greatest victims of environmental degradation at least in its immediate consequences. It is the poor who live in the unhealthiest places, who have no drinking water in their homes and no proper sewage systems in their neighborhoods. They cleanse the planet in local ways, but they do not benefit from a healthy living space. In this environment, women take on the task of recycling to live, but are unable to escape a life surrounded by garbage. They recycle garbage to survive on garbage and in turn help the increasingly differentiated production of new forms of garbage.

In addition to their social condition of poverty, the great majority of women trash collectors and recyclers are black, especially in Brazil. This introduces us to the complex problem of the racial identity of poverty within gender and class issues. We are invited to think about the relationship between the production of garbage, the many human lives that produce it and, above all, those who live in direct contact with it.

---

2. Maira Fernandes, "Mulheres são a maioria entre catadores e catadoras de materiais recicláveis," *Centro de Estudios e Apoio ao Desenvolvimento, Emprego, e Cidadania*, 17 October 2016. Web resource: http://www.ceadec.org.br/noticias/mulheres-sao-a-maioria-entre-catadores-e-catadoras-de-materiais-reciclaveis. Accessed 2 July 2019.

2.3. Working with Garbage as the Poor

All living things in one way or another produce garbage. Trash is a part of us and what we consume that we do not deem necessary to our life. Therefore, we dispose of it or use it in some other way deemed less worthy. We can give what we do not want to other humans, animals or just simply throw it in the trash can.

Each culture and language give a specific connotation to the word garbage. We could even make a list of meanings in Portuguese, specific to these Brazilian women, that could also be found in other languages, despite different nuances. My intention is only to show the relation between the meanings of the word trash and its correlations to certain human lives that are disdained or considered to be located within the lowest level of humanity. I refer to the most despised people in society – the people who count less on the social scale. Those who are considered almost trash themselves, contradictorily, are the ones who work to bring life to trash. This is a fascinating contradiction that we are not always aware of.

The Spanish philosopher Adela Cortina in her recent book, talks about *aporophobia*.[3] The word comes from *aporos* meaning poor in Greek and *phobia* that indicates our various fears. Our society is afraid of the poor, expels them from social life, wants them to be invisible or exploits them to the fullest. There is, therefore, in the line in which I am reflecting, an anthropological correlation of meanings and places of social recognition between garbage and garbage cleaners. In general, the word garbage is associated with debris, ashes, waste, filth. It is also associated with the word scrap, as that which comes out of something, the part of a material no longer needed, some minor residue that must be thrown away. But thrown away from what? And who deems it as such? No doubt it is thrown away from the valuable part, that which is recognized as important and necessary. And those who throw it out are those who do not need it for the work they are doing.

This disdained trash, which the rich do not lay hands on, is often symbolically projected on marginalized people, who are also considered the trash or junk of society. This is also called the "precarious condition of life" according to philosopher Judith Butler. "The precarious condition refers to the politically induced condition in which certain populations suffer from deficient social and economic support networks and are exposed differently to rape, violence and death."[4]

---

3. Adela Cortina, "Aporophobia, the Rejection of the Poor" (Barcelona-Buenos Aires-México: Paidós Estado y Sociedad, 2017).
4. Judith Butler, *Pictures of War: When Life is Mournful* (Rio de Janeiro: Civilização Brasileira, 2015), 46. (Translated)

The precarious condition of women garbage collectors has several expressions, frameworks and relationships with different social instances regarding the precariousness of their lives and their necessary protection. For example, they seek the protection of the police, but find themselves attacked by the same police. They seek hospital care, but it is often denied. They seek help in the churches, but often the alms they receive are accompanied by judgments and moral lessons that diminish them. Their situation produces a series of stereotypes and social behaviors that exclude them from the value of human dignity.

In the world of garbage or in the complex world of waste, depending on its materiality, a **bad smell** is intensely and persistently present. It penetrates the nostrils and incorporates itself into the skin and clothes of garbage collectors. People outside the circle of garbage assimilate the bad smell to the person who collects it and exclude them from their coexistence as quickly as possible.

The stench from which one wants to escape probably comes from something that was once good and even smelled good. The same body that delights in flavors and odors repudiates the smell of garbage and excrement transformed into dirt. This stench is also symbolically transferred to the poor and to those who work with garbage, people who have become socially disposable just like trash itself. They not only work with garbage and clean the city and the planet, but many live near open-air garbage dumps from which they derive their livelihood. They share food with other animals and birds and expose their health to various inconveniences. They blend their odors with a myriad of others so that their scent becomes a mark of their existence and social presence.

People are in fact producers of many kinds of trash. There is garbage produced by industries, as well as daily household garbage. There are also many types of garbage produced on a large scale by our world, such as e-waste, atomic waste, and space junk, and we still do not know what their fate will be. Trash is a problem because whoever produces it leaves it for others to take care of and this task is usually given to women and especially to the poor.

In spite of the immensely diverse production of garbage, Brazilian women collectors deal with specific garbage, the daily trash of homes, businesses, and the streets. This collected trash belongs to a different and distant world from that of big garbage producers. Their access to goods that were once part of glittering and expensive products that were bought and sold is reduced to goods transformed into waste that women select and resell.

I want to invite us to think about our relationship with what we consider disposable, with what we consider unnecessary or useless. Whoever takes care of that which is disposable or considered garbage becomes socially disposable in our societies of abundance and waste.

An astounding contradiction is before us. Those who collect garbage reveal more and more the visibility of new ways of exploiting the poor, and marginalized women of color in particular. Without a specific professional identity, people who live from garbage are only 'garbage collectors', and are not employees of a particular company that collects trash in the city. As I have already said, they have no labor rights or fixed wages. They become, in a sense, almost trash to this garbage-producing society that needs them and at the same time refuses them a dignified life. This observation reveals the ambiguity of the discourses about the necessary cleanliness of the planet, the economy of natural sources, and various types of recycling in comparison with the real situation of women who survive on garbage. It also reveals the contradiction that inhabits us when we give poor women the responsibility of cleaning up the dirt that we ourselves produce. And what is worse, we maintain this work for them as their only access to a life of mere survival.

2.4. Environmental Injustice and the Sexual Division of Labor in the Everyday Lives of Women Who Collect Recyclable Materials

The perception and analysis of environmental injustice issues are closely linked to the social division of labor and the precariousness of lives threatened by environmentally and economically exploitative projects. This is not a new insight. Since the Chernobyl Power Plant explosion in the Ukraine (1986), many women have reported the maximum workload placed on their shoulders. This has been a major complaint from ecofeminists in many parts of the world.

Similarly, the author of the book published in 1997, *Voices of Chernobyl*, Svetlana Aleksievich (winner of the Nobel Prize for Literature in 2015), used first hand reports to bring to the public's attention the suffering of victims far beyond what had previously been released. In these reports, women have a particular testimony. As we know in the early hours of April 26, 1986, a nuclear reactor at the plant exploded during a safety check. During 10 days nuclear fuel burned, releasing a great amount of toxic clouds into the atmosphere. Moscow tried to hide the accident that happened in the former Soviet Republic and authorities waited until the next day to evacuate the 48,000 inhabitants of Pripyat, which is only three kilometers from the plant. Gasses infiltrated everything, especially food and air, which became a major problem, especially for women who were caring for, breastfeeding or preparing food for their children. The devastating consequences for numerous people's lives and their future generations are widely known.

Similar situations have taken place throughout the world. Environmental disasters have occurred frequently because many human lives are considered disposable in the face of an uncontrollable thirst for profit. Along these lines, although in a different way, I also want to situate the suffering of women who collect garbage. They expose their lives and the lives of their families to dangerous situations that present a possible risk of death. They deal with toxic gasses and polluted dirt that produces diseases in their skin and eyes. Many voices of women garbage collectors today denounce the precarious conditions of their work, but are not heard by those who hold political and economic power, those who have a thousand different ways to hide their deeds as well as the reasons for the proliferation of environmental garbage and injustice.

In this logic, we observe that the individuals who gain the least from the production of recycled products appear to be the most exposed to environmental degradation and risks detrimental to their health. In the case of women garbage collectors, the more demobilized, disorganized and in need they are, the more exposed they become to present social injustices. As a result, they have less freedom of choice in their housing, food, clothing, health, and percentage of profit. They are, therefore, forced to live in unsafe places and cannot reject the installation of polluting industries or the dumping of waste in their communities. In addition, they are forced to accept the price offered by the recycled material, which is the fruit of their daily work. As environmental economist Henri Acserald says: "As long as environmental ills can be transferred to the poorest, the general pressure on the environment will not cease."[5]

This means that environmental injustice cannot be separated from social injustice, nor can social injustice be separated from the current injustice of gender and ethnicity. These injustices are interconnected and one is generating the other in a world where the profit and exploitation of others seems to be the daily bread of the world economy. This is the logic of the capitalist environmental economy.

Thus, environmental economics are linked to environmental injustice that exploits the workforce of the poorest. This is why the idea of taking

---

5. Henri Acserald, "Environmental justice and the dynamics of socio-environmental struggles in Brazil- an introduction," in *Justiça Ambiental e Cidadania*, eds. Henri Acserald, S. Herculano and J. Padua (Rio de Janeiro: Ed. Relume-Dumará, 2004), 147.

care of nature and the planet by utilizing recycling practices that exploit women is wrong and unfair. In other words, it is sustained by the cruelty of exploitation that characterizes the capitalist system present in many countries, especially the countries of Latin America. It makes recycling both a source of salvation and a source of perdition for those who work with it. This is why we talk about environmental social inequality, especially when we refer to the living spaces occupied by those who 'clean' the environment. Environmental social inequality can be understood as the unequal distribution of the parts of an environment that has been unfairly divided and exploited; and its mechanisms of injustice are similar to the mechanisms that produce social inequality. In this line, environmental protection is also unequal when it comes to approving public policies. For some, there is financial help, for others, there is not. Aid, thus, becomes oblivious and limited for the poorest who actually need it. It often generates intentional long-term and short-term environmental risks for the most vulnerable populations. According to some authors, recycling in Brazil only became possible, on a large scale, when the screening of the material proved to be a low-cost task, carried out by unemployed workers who became simple collectors of trash, accepting low wages. As such, the exploitation of classes and particularly of the people considered 'junk' persists in different ways in urban environments, which allows for few investments in technologies for the emergence of reproduction of the recycled material.[6] So once again, capital appropriates the poverty of these workers with the intention of making it profitable for those who own the means of production. And, in addition, it appropriates the discourse of environmental protection and uses the media to advertise their service, value and care for the environment, exalting certain figures, especially women, who are dedicated to recycling. In this frequently perverse line of thinking, garbage collectors are called 'environmental protection agents', presenting them with an identity and social status that is highly valued. Unfortunately, as people who need support and appreciation, we welcome these praises as trophies of glory and do not perceive the hidden traps amid complacent, but often deceitful, speeches.

As such, the ambiguity of policies becomes abundantly clear when it comes to garbage and the work of women. On the one hand, we consider the character of resisting the poverty and misery that is imposed on these women and the positive reaction of many collectors who are worthily seeking to survive and sustain themselves. On the other hand, we see the

---

6. Antônio De Pádua Bosi, "Urban Reform and Class Struggle" (São Paulo: Ed. Xamã, 2004).

exploitation and appropriation of the collectors' work being used to reinforce companies that feed on the leftovers of a society of consumption and reinforce the capitalist accumulation. This accumulation does not liberate people, especially not poor women or the environment.

In the face of this picture we seem to be in a seemingly hopeless situation. But it is only apparent, because the signs of a growing consciousness, despite the necessity of survival, have provoked an intense social movement and a growing solidarity among different social groups.

2.5. Conclusion: The Responsibility of the Church Towards the Exploitation of Women

I believe that it is of utmost importance at the conclusion of this reflection to recall something of the work of Christian churches in the face of environmental crises and the exploitation of women.

It is undeniable that many Christian churches have raised their voices in favor of the defense of the planet and against the environmental destruction made by big mining and other companies.[7] However, there is a kind of internal censorship in churches when it comes to favoring the defense of female victims or the leadership of women with regard to various initiatives. It is as if a strange sense of shame were present in a majority of religious leaders preventing them from publicly assuming the defense of women, especially those who are the sole leaders of their families and even of some social movements. I speak of shame, but I believe that the issue is much more complex and encompasses the need for a new philosophical anthropology to preside over our Christian ethical tradition in a more plural and inclusive way that better represents our diversity.

In recent years, many Christian Churches and the World Council of Churches have addressed, by means of gatherings and publications, issues relating to the planet's sustainability, inviting its faithful to work in line with a humanism that includes the lives of all beings that make up the planet. However, in these same texts the human being is spoken of in a generic way, of the universal human, without actually explaining the identities of the subjects involved, without making clear the social hierarchy of the victims and the *aporophobia* present in our society. It may be too much to expect major changes in Christian churches, as they are undoubtedly not yet freed from the excesses of power and a male metaphysical order

---

7. For example, the Pastoral Letter "*Laudato Si'* — on care of the common house" by Pope Francis, published in 2015.

that continues to prioritize the male in so-called ecclesiastical structures. It should also be remembered that ever since the 1970s, when feminism was already taking hold in Latin America, Christian churches have never seen this movement with fond eyes. Some have accepted a soft juxtaposition of the issue of women embracing ecofeminism, but they emphasize the dignity of the planet more so than justice to women. They integrated women in line with the old metaphor that considers nature feminine. On the one hand, she is a Mother who nourishes her children and on the other hand, an uncontrollable force capable of subverting the harmony of nature through storms, violent winds or endless, often unexpected, droughts.

I dare take this second image as an almost comic metaphor for the consideration of feminism by Christian churches. Feminism has been accused of many evils, especially of being the disruptor or transgressor of the natural, familiar and sexual order desired by God.

We have assiduously denounced the use of these limited images, but they still seem to subsist in many ways in the religious culture of our times. As we criticize them, it is clear that some church leaders save the image of the **earth** as a generous and protective Mother, while at the same time crucifying the **earth** as a tempting, bold and disobedient woman. They divide the female body into opposing symbologies according to its ideology and the need to safeguard its power. However, beyond this symbology, it must be said that Christian theology needs to be reviewed and reaffirmed in inclusive ethical and anthropological terms, and no longer from a hierarchical and excluding metaphysics.

The hierarchy of churches and some believers may even praise the work of women garbage collectors, but they do not touch their real condition 'outside the religious order', that is, poor women, single mothers, separated, lesbians with children from several partners, transsexuals, bisexuals ... Plural women whose real life is concealed and wronged, but who effectively reveal an incredible daily fighting force. They are faced with a wide range of situations and relationships and only subsist because many embrace the many forms of immediate love and justice that flourish in their lives. They have a faith that believes more in the unexpected designs of life than in pre-established orders, even though some continue to sporadically attend their home churches. New plural theologies need space to be born and to develop, and in this particular space, the theological work of Rosemary Radford Ruether remains a worldwide reference for commitment to justice and a loving inspiration for the work of many women.

CHAPTER 3

LAND JUSTICE FOR BROKEN WOMEN HEALING EARTH: COLONIZATION TO COVID-19

Lilian Dube

3.1. Introduction

As we celebrate Rosemary Radford Ruether's prophetic witness in the world, we memorialize African green legends like Maathai Wangaari who inspired countless grassroots women and scholars in their fight to bring about restorative justice by healing earth. In her classic, *Women Healing Earth*, Ruether persuaded us to meaningfully engage in conversations about real experiences of poverty and environmental degradation and how women rise and flourish.[1] This view is corroborated by the environmental justice pioneer Carl Anthony, whose masterpiece, *The Earth, the City and the Hidden Narrative of Race*, is packed with suspicions of healing-the-earth ceremonies that demand we hear only the voice of Earth in non-human nature crying out in pain.[2] By focusing on painful symbols like the slave tree of Zambia, the lynching tree of Zimbabwe and other trees of pain like the 'forgetful tree' of the Democratic Republic of Congo, the chapter unpacks the real struggles of people arising from slavery, colonization and neo-colonization. It inspires the reading of messages on painful trees. Therefore, the chapter privileges land-deprived people in the fight for earth justice and correlates the 'war of trees' with their 'land ownership woes' in order to humanize the theoretical environmental frameworks for earth-healing endeavours. Examples in Kenya and Zimbabwe show the paradox of 'broken women' healing earth, exemplified by *Mau Mau*[3] women as active combatants and supporters and *Chimurenga*[4]

---

1. Rosemary Radford Ruether, *Women Healing Earth*, 1996.
2. Carl Anthony, *The Earth the City and the Hidden Narrative of Race*, 2017.
3. Teresia Hinga, "The Gikuyu Theology of Land and Environmental Justice," In Rosemary Radford Ruether, ed., *Women Healing Earth*, 1996, 177-8.
4. *Chimurenga* means revolution or uprising in the Shona language spoken by two thirds of people in the Southern African country of Zimbabwe. In Ndebele, the second largest population in Zimbabwe, the synonym for revolution is *Umvukela*. The Shona and Ndebele warriors revolted against the British colonial rule in 1896-1887, the First *Chimurenga*.

women war heroes[5] hanging from trees, who inspired women's ecological activism in 'green wars.' Tumani Mutasa Nyajeka's discussion of 'Shona Women and the Mutupo Principle' is grounded in the cosmology of the Shona and Ndebele people of Zimbabwe who evoked the Mwari cult to resist land invasions by Britain in 1896 to 1897. The first *Chimurenga* war of liberation was led by Nehanda Nyakasikana, a female fertility spirit medium who was hanged by the British colonial authorities. To dialogue with Nyajeka is, therefore, to be grounded in the cosmology of the Shona/Ndebele people inspired by the spirit behind the multiple revolutions invoked in this chapter.[6]

3.2. Singing Grass Fiction

Doris Lessing preserves the environmental history of Zimbabwe, a Southern African country formerly called Rhodesia, through novels that depict the natural vegetation from the onset of colonization to post independence. Her vivid descriptions of poverty, land erosion, wildlife destruction, and AIDS on one hand and the majestic beauty of Zimbabwe together present the irony of independence. Through vivid nostalgic wit, Lessing exposes the ugly inequalities of black and white lives under the Rhodesian racist colour bar. Her memoirs give a captivating land narrative of a community going through radical socio-political transitions. She captures this painful history through graphic autobiographical fiction that puts her on the wrong side of history. Without losing sight of the natural rhythms of seasonality, landscape, and wildlife, she pens the most readable herstory of the contested land that spans her lifetime seen through her white eyes.

A few years after independence, I was reading Lessing's novel *The Grass is Singing*[7] for an English course at the University of Zimbabwe. Our analytical tools derived from dialogue with post-independence pan-African literature that flooded our curriculum for the first time in a century. Thus, we found Doris Lessing's description of our land provocative. Her presentation of land as a private commodity for commercial use and enjoyment by the settler community was as disturbing as her captivating description of land beauty, which created a century of struggle for us. Her story described prime land grabbing that cramped

---

5. Tumani Mutasa Nyajeka, "Shona Women and the Mutupo Principle", In Rosemary Radford Ruether, ed., *Women Healing Earth*, 1996, 135-6.
6. A story-telling method equips me with words and insights drawn from lived experiences, songs and bubbles of free verse punctuate this chapter.
7. Doris Lessing, *The Grass is Singing*, 1950.

us into tsetse-fly infested semi-arid Tribal Trust Lands (TTL) as a simple matter of fact, not as a gross injustice. It also omitted our desperate search for food in the land of plenty and talked about the singing grass. Just what songs was the grass in Lessing's novel singing to a nation that was so racially divided? She invoked our chagrin and fury for land justice. The same quest for land justice had driven youth, then at my age to the war that led to our liberation from colonial rule, a war recently ended, yet without really liberating the land.

3.3. Land Education

Colonial education was not only segregated, it tamed the harsh realities of land dispossession through propaganda that side-tracked us from focusing on the prevailing land injustices responsible for land wars in Zimbabwe. At best, school education made us curious about life in foreign lands abroad, but distorted the harsh turmoil of our contested land mainly through songs. Exploiting our childhood naiveté, colonial songs created phantasmagorical euphoria that polluted youthful conscience and disguised landless poverty as we proudly sang songs that were tightly wrapped in the dry irony of dispossession. Adapted from the American folk song that fostered patriotism, *This Land is Your Land*[8], we in racist Rhodesia, were singing the antithesis of our lived realities.

> *This land is my land*
> *This land is your land*
> *From the Zambezi*
> *To the Limpopo*
> *Rhodesia was made for you and me*

This song and its refrain in community conscience undermined the trauma of over one hundred thousand natives evicted from their ancestral lands to make room for about twenty-two thousand white settlers, mostly post-war emigrants from the United Kingdom between 1945 and 1960.[9] The natives were condemned to derelict Tribal Trust Lands for a century. While we belted happy songs about the shared landscape, our grandparents sang myriad versions of landless blues to their early graves after the first uprisings were thwarted and their war heroes lynched, among them Nehanda,[10] whose lynching tree is now an urban shrine.

---

8. Woody Guthrie, *This Land is Your Land*, 1940.
9. Robin Palmer and Isobel Birch, *Zimbabwe: A Land Divided*, 2010.
10. Ibid. Prominent woman rebel leader of the first *Chimurenga*, war of liberation, waged by natives against colonial rule in Rhodesia from 1890-1896.

3.4. *Chimurenga 2*, War of Liberation (1966-1979)

Inspired by the tenacious spirit of Nehanda, we had quickly learned new songs that supported the struggle for the contested land, prophetic songs that decolonized our minds and prepared us for the second *Chimurenga*, a protracted war that ended white minority rule in 1980. We sang freedom songs that weaved past and present to a liberated future, or so we thought. We danced our freedom dreams into reality and celebrated the legendary warrior Nehanda Nyakasikana, who became both an old rebel and current guerrilla fighter. The image of a victim of war is revoked by her actions as a crafty warrior, who mobilized her community to revolt as she wore the noose and died prophesying about her bones that would raise freedom. She inspired us to sing with conviction and anticipation for radical change and true freedom of the land.

> *Mbuya Nehanda Kufa Vachitaura*
> '*Kuti Zvino Ndofirawo Nyika*'
> *Shoko Rimwe Ravakandiudza*
> '*Tora Gidi Uzvitonge*'
>
> *Mbuya Nehanda truly dies wondering*
> '*How shall we take (back) this land?*'
> *The one word she told us was*
> '*Seize the gun and liberate yourself*'

3.5. Strange Fruit

An exploration of ecological symbols of pain and power in Africa uncover a sacred environment defiled by the noose and slave chains. This chapter discusses the landscape seen through an indigenous spiritual lens to establish parameters for justice. It examines lynching and the slave trade engrained in Southern African trees by systems that sought to erase their victims from living memory through punishment and human trade.

In Zimbabwean tradition, the tree that a person commits suicide from, like the animal that preys on human life, is destroyed because it embodies anti-life curses. The tree is cut down very close to the ground, chopped up and burnt to intercept the cycle of death by suicide. The common belief is that the tree can be manipulated by witches to cause more people to commit suicide. Even if it hangs with fruit, its power to nourish life is intercepted as it rubs with death. The tree (and forest) is not only desacralized by death, it invites more suicide and has the capacity to taint the whole forest with negative energy without subsequent cleansing rituals. Considering there are thousands who commit suicide in the global North, a few lessons could be drawn from suicide prevention practices derived from an appreciation of the sacredness of life in Africa to create more rituals of healing earth and valuing life in the North.

Deep forests in the southern states of North American, though, had witnessed more lynching than suicides. Lynching presents dynamics that differ from the ecological belief systems discussed above. The lynch master and slave master who hang black lives on trees violated communities and defiled the forests in the strongest imagery in Billie Holiday's song below.

"Strange Fruit": Song[11]

> *Southern trees bear a strange fruit*
> *Blood on the leaves and blood at the roots*
> *Black bodies swinging in the Southern breeze*
> *Strange fruit hanging from the poplar trees*
>
> *Pastoral scenes of the gallant South*
> *The bulging eyes and the twisted mouth*
> *Scent of magnolias sweet and fresh*
> *Then the sudden smell of burning flesh*
>
> *Here is a fruit for the crows to pluck*
> *For the rain to gather*
> *For the wind to suck*
> *For the sun to rot*
> *For the trees to drop*
> *Here is a strange and bitter crop*

Lynching was rampantly used to stamp revolt from the colonized and oppressed black people in Africa and North America, especially in the Southern states. Thus, slavery and colonialism complicated the relationship of people, God, and the earth. Lynching and chaining on trees violated taboos and desacralized life. Yet, the Shona people also believe that without guided appeasement of the aggrieved spirits (of people and nature), the angry spirits *Ngozi*[12] would wreak havoc on the culprits, haunting them from multiple fronts down generations. Thus, these culprits may have invited anti-life curses manifest inhumanly through madness like the 'knee on neck'[13] that has scandalized human consciences in modern history. Massive demonstrations ensued and the life of George Floyd (May 26, 2020) was memorialized by murals and shrines that erupted across the earth.

---

11. Song by Billie Holiday recorded in 1939, written by Abel Meeropol, 1937.
12. Michael Gelfand, *Shona Religion*, 1962, 162.
13. On 25 May, 2020, Minneapolis Police Officer Derek Chauvin was captured on video kneeling on the neck of George Floyd in handcuffs for eight minutes, three minutes of which he had stopped breathing. This ignited world-wide protest against police brutality and an outcry for racial justice.

A revolution was born, a movement for justice that drew rage from the strange fruit in Billie Holiday's protest song against the lynching of Black Americans in the Southern United States at the turn of the twentieth century.[14] Clearly, these protests issued a cry for justice for black women, men, and the environment, for healing earth and valuing lives.

3.6. Memorial Shrines

Most 'death trees', lynching trees and slave trees discussed below were never felled. Instead, they are endeared to and memorialized by people because these trees are synonymous with the legends sacrificed thereon. The trees that grounded rich treasures of oral traditional history into the African soil revived by this chapter are dotted along the African coastlines, and the less known deep interior like Zambia and Zimbabwe discussed below.

3.7. Nehanda's Lynching Tree[15]

Although the uprising was thwarted by the British colonial authorities and Nehanda was 'lynched on a *Musasa* tree', seeds of the second Chimurenga sprouted a hundred years later when men and women inspired by the spirit of Nehanda waged a war that ended colonial rule by Rhodesia's white minority in 1980. At Independence, the century-old *Msasa* tree became the buoyant 'green shrine' in the city that introduced traditional conservation taboos, *marambatemwa*, into urban spaces. On 8 December, 2011, the tree met its fate at the intersection of two busy city roads when a Harare City Council truck rammed it down and ignited national panic, grief, confusion, and subsequent cleansing rituals by a nation facing socio-economic and political destabilization decades after independence. The ominous demise of the iconic 200-year old tree inspired eco-feminist conversions and eco-justice stories initiated by Rosemary Radford Ruether.

Nehanda's memory was not marked by flowers or gifts. There wasn't even her picture or statue, just a big green *Musasa* tree and the invincible presence of her spirit passing down through generations. In the absence of the physical tree, both her spirit and the tree spirit live in the memory of the living. This transformation justifies the convergence of oral history with different powerful literary rivers (narrative, poems and songs) to strengthen the national storage memory. There was neither a fence to protect the

---

14. Gunnar Myrdal, *An American Dilemma*, 1944, 561.
15. http://www.telegraph.co.uk/news/worldnews/africaandindiaocean/zimbabwe/8944988/Zimbabwe-sacred-Hanging-Tree-is-felled.html "Sacred 'Hanging Tree' Felled", *The Telegraph*. June 23, 2020.

Nehanda tree from the known nor a plaque to chronicle the history of her fate for visitors like my students and myself at the Ndola tree. Its open coexistence with massive exotic Jacaranda trees dwarfing it, is as ironic as it is telling a story of preservation of the sacred in their natural state. Thus, the tree sheltered birds in the concrete desert, guarded by exotic Jacarandas. October heralds the Harare Jacaranda festival which seemed to mock and jeer at the lonely indigenous *Musasa*. Yet she stood there uncompromisingly watching over our history as her name was invoked in every *Chimurenga* to save the earth and value lives singing the Mbuya Nehanda song in this chapter. The tree, therefore, became a symbol of powerful history deliberately lodged in the memory of the living, grafting the history of evil, and the victory of her-story in a city tree.

At one point, it did not exactly matter which leaves dripped the blood that watered the earth and vanished deep down to nourish roots that sprouted massive revolutions, since *Chimurenga* is inconceivable without the spirit of Nehanda. When the memory of such events is so poignantly lodged in the survivors' psyches, the plaque is not only mobile, it snowballs into a massive collective reminder of earth legends that they inscribe on city street signs, lakes, and rivers shedding off colonial names. Thus, the nation carries a collective plaque of Nehanda Nyakasikana.

The erection of a statue befitting Nehanda in Harare was recently announced.[16] This will settle her in the public space of power where she belongs with other women fighting for land justice, but will never replace the tree that had become such a formidable green presence in the city, where concrete invaded *kopjes* (hills), choking rivers and streams. The rationale for the proposed statue site far from the hanging tree site is, 'the place that she used to rest and drink water from a river'. Yet the river is invisible, sealed off below. This stretches the imagination and brings critical history of only one hundred twenty-five years closer to fiction.

Nehanda's tree is more than a reminder and history marker. After all, her remains are believed to be among countless trophy skulls still on display in Westminster Abbey and the National History museum in Britain.[17] The allegory of her countless leaf-eyes falling to the ground before raising multiple revolutions after every rough season to demand new justice in spring, personifies Nehanda Nyakasikana's driving force behind *Chimurenga* 2, 3, 4 and more to come. Through seasonal change, Nehanda's tree presents a spirit of unbreakable resistance in the face of adversity

---

16. https://www.herald.co.zw/work-on0mbuya-nehanda-memorial-statue-begins/. "Mbuya Nehanda Memorial Statue Begins", *The Herald*. August 13, 2020.

17. http://www.thepatriot.co.zw/ol_posts/bring-back-our-heroes/ "Bring Back Our Heroes", *The Patriot*. March 3, 2020.

and a vision larger than an individual. Thus, the tree of the shrine is a persona. Sacred spaces, like the shrine of Nehanda's tree, need to multiply a million times the green vision planted by Wangari Maathai and Marthinus Daneel, who renamed himself after the *Muchakatatree* (an evergreen tropic food and medicinal tree of Africa found in Zimbabwe also known as *Parinari Curatellifolia*).[18] James Cone and Billie Holiday present dry satire through bleeding trees, which water the soil that yields sons and daughters raging for racial justice in global Chimurenga, screaming "Black Lives Matter!" in all shades of fall colours. In order to liberate not only the trees, but all of the endangered people threatened by poverty, starvation, and the multiple injustices, the seeds for healing earth and valuing lives are packed in this book and ready to crack.

3.8. Ndola 'Slave Trees'[19]

Ndola, Zambia, has two slave trees. One is an ancient pod mahogany or *Mushuku*, which stood gallantly on the island between the Ndola-Kitwe dual carriageway. When it fell to its demise during a powerful storm, the community responded with cleansing and enshrining the dead tree. The other slave tree is a fig tree or *Mupapa*, which was fenced out near the city center, also a national memorial to those killed in the slave trade. Under the shadow of these trees, Swahili traders discussed gruesome transactions and sold inland captives to Arab slave traders. An undated memorial tree plaque reads:

> This plate has been placed upon this Mupapa
> tree to commemorate the passing of
> the days when, under this shade, the last of
> the Swahili traders, who warred upon and enslaved
> the people of the surrounding country, used
> to celebrate their victories and share out
> their spoils.[20]

For five years, my students and I paid tribute to the broken lives who caught their breath in chains under these shady trees. We blocked our ears from the discordant jubilee of the spoilers who have now retreated into oblivion. We prayed for our own healing from the burden of the trauma and community guilt shared in the sin of slavery. The experiences of my students and me were surreal.

---

18. https://en.wikipedia.org/wiki/Parinari_curatellifolia.
19. https://www.zambiawatchdog.com/the-ndola-slave-tree/, *Zambia Watchdog*, 15 March, 2019.
20. https://www.atlasobscura.com/places/ndola-slave-tree, *Atlas Obscura*.

Such green symbols prevail all over African communities where they signify collective memories of history and unfinished business. The painful memories rooted in slavery and in colonial history of humiliation and exploitation of communities and natural resources led to collective measures to counter obliteration of green evidence of crimes committed against humanity. The enshrined crime scenes, slave trees and the lynching trees, are strong reminders of how Africa was pauperized and dehumanized by the 'First World' and are, therefore, a call for restitution, reparation, and vindication. Besides, these green symbols can be a powerful source of national unity around a green revolution by harnessing religion for ecological reverence and conservation. The urgency to capture these lessons is precipitated by the rot and accident with Nehanda's tree discussed above, needless to mention how the lynching trees in the USA continue to be documented to ensure history is not pushed into oblivion. Literary shrines like James Cone's work are highly commendable.[21] These stories have to be told, and enshrined in art, songs, dance, ritual, picture, and literature. They inspire wars for justice and change.

3.9. *Chimurenga 3*, War of Trees (1990-2000)

Earth healing stories of women reclaiming gullies to feed their desperate families and heal from post-war trauma still inspire this chapter. They are drawn from my last extensive field research in Zimbabwe a few miles from the village where I grew up in colonial Rhodesia, which was ravished by multiple liberation wars described in this chapter. It was exciting to return 'home' as a researcher under the guidance of a world-renowned scholar of religion and earth-healing, Professor Marthinus Daneel.

My research experience in South Chivi villages was enriched by personal lessons from ZIRRCON Interfaith Earth Care and Dialogue. We danced the welcoming chorus with jubilation while exchanging warm embraces before we sat down for introductions. The simple chorus had only two lines, so I quickly joined the fun.

ZIRRCON ndoidiniko?
Ndoita yokubereka

What shall I do for ZIRRCON?
I will carry it on my back (like a baby)

---

21. Cone, *The Cross and the Lynching Tree*, 2011.

3.10. Church Gift Story

As soon as I introduced myself, their local daughter of the soil and Nelson Chipoka Dube, their attitude changed for reasons I was yet to crudely discover because they were meticulous at covering up their shock. Their reaction confused me as they led the way up where a small church dominated the hill. I was puzzled when we stood in a circle outside and did not go inside even though the doors were wide open. I was more confused when they announced that we were going to pray for my parents while standing outside. Fear gripped my wild imagination about all the sins my parents could possibly have committed in that place now hindering my research. I started cursing in my heart, angry about the embarrassment to my profession, then focused on possible forgiveness. After all, our earth healing day started with a forgiveness prayer to the trees and the environment we savage wantonly. I was lost in shame when a voice quivering with emotion startled me. She was pointing upwards, so I closed my eyes ready for the cleansing ritual for whatever my parents did, but was interrupted by showers of praise for them. This was followed by the beautiful story of the gift my parents, Esther and Nelson Dube, had donated to this church. A huge brown church bell mounted up a high tower has been calling people to church since 1957. I raised watery eyes, dry mouth wide open as the women started to sing and dance again to the 'gong-gong' salute. I bowed to my generous parents who kept this gift top secret in their hearts. Armed with the story of selfless giving that brought healing to the community for generations, we prayed for the trees and ourselves before we went to reclaim the gully down below.

Thus, in this section, I draw from memory the songs of women reclaiming gullies by planting grass and trees, and dances after creating flourishing oases of food for their communities from gardens. I also draw from memory of the new songs of green liberation inspired by ZIRRCON,[22] a unique green movement founded by Marthinus L. Daneel and African Initiated Churches in Southern Zimbabwe to wage the third *Chimurenga*, a war of trees that mobilized indigenous communities at the grassroots level.[23] The animated songs women created for the trees and themselves while reclaiming gullies won the war of trees as they adopted trees' identities and cared for the environment they were rooted

---

22. Zimbabwean Institute for Religious Research and Ecological Conservation in the Masvingo province was one of the largest movements for environmental reform in Southern Africa responsible for the planting twelve to fifteen million trees in several thousand woodlots a decade after Zimbabwe liberation wars.

23. Marthinus L. Daneel, *African Earthkeepers. Volume 1 & 2*, 1998 and 1999.

in. When Bishop Moses, leading by example, adopted the name *Muchakata,* it meant that Professor Inus Daneel became that green giant tree that feeds people and animals with nutritional *hacha* fruit and provides them with sheltered respite from the Southern summer scourge. Therefore, cutting down trees became a taboo similar to wanton killing of kin - witchcraft or suicide. Both sins are taboos capable of unleashing evil, drought and pandemics like AIDS, COVID-19, and other pestilences according to Shona traditional beliefs strongly shared by African Independent Churches.

My field research of 2001 gives fascinating insights on how to dream healing earth with others through religion, culture, sustainable ways to reduce poverty, and women's active approach to environmental knowledge. Many scholars have dealt with issues concerning the ecological crisis in a variety of ways. A lot has also been written about poverty and women in their struggle for survival, especially in developing nations. There are also bountiful sources of African religion and cultures available in libraries. What makes this research fascinating is the way in which it manages to bring together three very important disciplines and merge them into a unified whole. The research offers a valuable contribution to knowledge and life by bringing together 1) aspects of religion and culture, both old and new; 2) poverty alleviation strategies in the form of sustainable development projects; and 3) shows how women actively participate in combating the ecological crisis pervading their environment and livelihoods. The research highlights rays of hope ushered through ZIRRCON development projects to rural village women and their families in Masvingo Province. The correlation of ecological crisis and poverty, with religion and ethics is exposed. It goes further to illustrate just how ZIRRCON manages to involve women in the alleviation of both the ecological crises and poverty and how they actually take centre stage in the development of conservation projects. ZIRRCON also demonstrates how the role of religion, both the old and the new in the concretization and motivation processes, cannot be underestimated in this holistic African Eco-feminist study. Although famed as one of the most innovative indigenous green movements in the Two-Thirds World,[24] ironically, it was crippled by the political upheaval of the fourth *Chimurenga,* the contentious war of land retribution in the 2000s described below. However, the ZIRRCON model remains one of the best tried methods of earth-healing and valuing lives.

---

24. Catherine Tucker, ed., *Nature, Science, and Religion,* 2012, 193.

3.11. *Chimurenga 4*, War of Land Restitution (2000-2019)

Twenty years after independence, our land remained in the same white hands who formed only 2% of the entire population. Natives remained lodged in the same arid Tribal Trust Lands without restitution for colonization or land to feed themselves. What a senseless war and grotesque ridicule of the prophetic vision of land justice. As disillusioned youths, we registered our anger and frustration with fake freedoms that buckled down economic liberties and prohibited self-reliance unleashed by the land. Confronted with this sordid reality, we refused to sing new songs of the liberated and demanded justice in the land of the free.

Politically motivated land-grabs of 2001were chaotic. Backtracking the barbaric colonial invasions unleashed social and economic doldrums as activists and economists predicted a gory bleak ending of the nation's golden glory. We helplessly watched the dangerous maneuvers that left Zimbabwe bleeding profusely. The madness of violent reverse land dispossession from whites to blacks inspired no new songs worth noting. The grass was singing mournful songs as veld fires ravaged the countryside, clearing the way for floods to destroy dotted settlement on wetlands that create massive poverty just as COVID-19 grips the world and suffocates the hungry poor in impossible lockdowns with no escape routes. From slavery to colonization, the exploitation of Africa has prepared a perfect storm for Africa's demise from pandemics like HIV/AIDS, COVID-19, or any future storm for that matter.

Desolate

Desolate Landscape
Barren drylands
Bleeding trees
Bruised mountains
Smoldering grass
Jostling winds
Twirling smoke
Whirling winds
Children choke
Gasp for air
Lung bursting
COVID-19

Desolate Landscape
Ravished wetlands
Ruffled riverbeds,
Silted rivers
Bursting banks
Flooding plains,

Floating houses,
Women and children
Livestock too,
Wiping clean
Villages
Fields and graves

Desolate Landscape
Girls dotted
Highways selling
Tender thighs
Baby breasts
Unscrupulous dealers
Trading humans
Unsheltered land
Shelters not
Humans roaming
Clueless gazes
COVID-19

3.12. War Dreams

Mirirai (pseudonym) was a very smart teacher I met in Britain, and we became good friends. She packed her bags to leave England forever when I joined the school where she was teaching in 2002. I cautioned her against repatriation at a time when another war had erupted in Zimbabwe. White farms were invaded by the hungry landless black peasants incited and supported by politicians. This precipitated international sanctions that crippled the country with economic doldrums still reverberating twenty years later in the Southern African country. Nothing distracted Mirirai from her master plan to return, farm, and feed the nation. So, she left to fulfill her patriotic dream, and I never heard from this wife of an Anglican priest and her family again after she returned to Zimbabwe where their gifts and ministry were needed most. After all, three wars[25] had been violently fought for this dream, all in her absence.

At independence in 1980, Mirirai was safely studying abroad in Britain. I had survived the war with a full cachet of the horror. A giant 'sale-out' (disdainful term for a black soldier who served the Rhodesian army during the liberation war) had landed a thunderous slap across my face yelling. *'aripi magandanga!'* where are the terrorists! (a term used for freedom fighters by the Rhodesian Front army). Everything happened very

---

25. The first *Chimurenga*, war of liberation from 1890-1896 the second *Chimurenga* from July 1964-1979, the third *Chimurenga*, Land Invasions of 2000 onward.

quickly. Before I could answer, I was reeling on the ground rapidly mouthing thoughtless defences about how I had never seen a *gandanga* because I was a Catholic, just returned from boarding school. With that miracle life-line, another giant white soldier jumped to my rescue without smiling. I scrambled up and ran a marathon to warn the guerrillas to leave the base they had just settled in and summoned us for food. They scurried off within seconds, taking us with them unbeknown to our parents. From across the river, under cover of trees and bushes, we watched a tense single file of soldiers intermingled with adult civilians. They had captured human shields as they disappeared beyond the eerie grooves. I was a war child that saved our three villages from a barrage of guns and bombs, caught in the crossfire that marked the Rhodesian bush war for the same contentious land of Zimbabwe. Yet I stood there feeling like a sell out for walking away from the historical restitution of land stolen from our ancestors by British invaders at the turn of the 19th century to hide and dream of other ways of saving lives a world away.

Several efforts to resolve the Zimbabwe land issue amicably had been hampered by corrupt land grabbing local elites[26] and the Labour Party's arrogant revocation of the 1979 Lancaster Agreement where Britain had committed to provide funding to facilitate smoother land transfer on a 'willing buyer, willing seller' basis.[27] Once ignited, Chimurenga 4 seemed unstoppable. Did it swallow up Mirirai? Did she survive and leave like me or was she farming organically like she had dreamt till the day she left? Seventeen years passed without a word from her until we were connected by a call across the deep Atlantic while in COVID-19 quarantine worlds apart. I was desperate to hear about the merge of her feminist dreams that made her sacrifice the familiar luxuries of England and live on the farm. Was it like Doris Lessing described in "The Grass is Singing," or were there more intimate tunes from the grass? Did she tame and harness the rushing rivers that blocked the trout or just watched them freely rush off to sea? Is organic just for the labels, or does she let nature nourish its own without chemical cohesion and bleach? Do the giant trees form intimidating jungles where birds hide from flying arrows as we did from guns and bombs, or do the loaded hunters own the sacred forests for sporting fame? We agreed to enjoy the moment of finding each other and savour the synchronicity without words. After we calmed down, we would slowly peel the onion layers and dream as broken women healing earth and each other.

26. J. L. Fisher, *Pioneers, Settlers, Aliens, Exiles: The Decolonisation of White Identity in Zimbabwe*, 2010, 159-65.
27. Matthew Preston, *Ending Civil War: Rhodesia and Lebanon in Perspective*, 2004, 25.

3.13. The COVID-19 Poor

What started as an "ethnic" virus in Fall of 2019 snowballed into an unstoppable human catastrophe. The North was ablaze and gods, raving mad. COVID-19 targeted everyone everywhere. The viral storm relentlessly polluted the earth in a tsunami-like air wave that wreaked havoc in Asia, ripped through Europe and America before it headed South. As untold panic ripped through the earth's central nervous system, scientists prescribed stringent quarantine that closed economies of the developed nations in unprecedented bitter blows. Without warning, the world was no longer a global village. Back to zero.

> **Flash**
> *Forced*
> *Closures*
> *Ground Airlines*
> *Cruises Ship*
> *Stranded Wanderers*
> *Roam Wild*
> *World Shrinking*
> *Fast*
> *Measures*
> *Strict Borders*
> *Freed Spaces*
> *Share*

Chaotic scenes at the hospitals without key equipment identified for COVID-19 response created panic, anxiety, infections and loss of life in the developing world. The scarcity of ventilators, PPE, masks and testing kits displayed shocking shortcomings only a few could associate with North America. Scientists seemed clueless and clearly powerless when medicine was collapsed into the politics of masks and cure pivoted on saving the economy and/or people still raging. The efficacy of facial masks was debated until they were mandatory in most public spaces and even bandanas were deemed essential. The side effects of ventilators were exposed as numerous patterns of COVID-19 chattered in a slew of information dazzling to the general public.

With healthcare in shambles and desolate economies, Africa prayed COVID-19 away and hoped that a delayed onslaught would extend their begging time. So, while Northern scientists scrambled to fix the world with 'one size fits all' measures to stop COVID-19, the South plagiarized 'survival scripts' that left them stranded. These developing countries were clueless on how to feed the quarantined poor without social security funds and ventilate collapsed lungs without oxygen machines or nurse to health or dignified deaths and burials of COVID-19 victims without PPE. For many in slums, even the basic hygiene of washing hands with soap was challenged by lack of clean water or shelter. The mask dance remained too sophisticated for populations that still cannot afford condoms, the life-saving prophylactic device prescribed decades ago to reduce exposure to HIV. Imagine 'ghetto social distancing' and 'quarantine' in one sentence that collapses 'shack sleeping shifts' into one long nightmare, especially for women and children.

The virus preys on masses in crowded places who live without clean water or sanitary basics, that cannot hoard food or avoid massive contacts with the infected as they hassle and tussle for daily bread. It preys on the poor whose healthcare systems were in shambles well before COVID-19 invasions. The virus preys on children huddled around trusted private teachers, where there are no virtual classrooms, electricity or technology. Their whole academic years were scrapped off the school calendars and critical exams cancelled indefinitely. COVID-19 preys on essential healthcare workers, even those who brave the sting with break room dance, prayer and stubborn resilience and have a huge price to pay for saving lives. In Africa, these brave martyrs hold the fort unfortified. In delivery rooms, theatres and emergency rooms, they man the frontlines without PPE or remuneration. COVID preys on massive mobs chanting 'Black Lives Matter!', on riled citizens demanding basic rights desperate for better lives, including COVID-equipped hospitals. COVID is relentless to the hungry, who are scavenging food that is now scarce in dump-heaps where waste materials are not just dirty, but contaminated with the dreaded virus in human waste and even dead bodies. Where there is widespread starvation, COVID-19 prevails. The situation is dire in quarantine.

3.14. Quarantine

Quarantine became the buzzword that some world leaders have latched onto like religion for repression and looting without the checks and balances of quarantined masses. COVID laws are created on the go without much push back, research, or debate. Even universities have aggressively tackled unions with premature pay cuts, furloughs, and layoffs because of speculative reduction in student revenue. While there is a direct correlation between quarantine and COVID control, quarantine also typifies terrifying restrictions, confinement, silencing, and careless denials. Those who escaped to work risk COVID-19 infections in hospitals and care facilities, grocery shops, construction sites, transport networks and food production frontlines, needless to mention the forces and firefighters. In some African countries, enforced quarantine leaves essential workers packed into buses and tense police officers riddled with fear of the sleek virus sternly restricting non-essential movement. For the poor masses, ghetto quarantine means awaiting nothing in particular. They are trapped in crowded rooms where the frail cries of starving children invoke violent jostling that endangers the mothers till they muffle these innocent alarms with bleeding breasts. Women and children take the hell heat of COVID-19, hungry and paralyzed with fear quarantined in stinking corridors. Pope Francis sums up the visibility of poverty through a COVID-19 prism.

Zero

stinking cities,
thick gray pollution
plastic burning
chemicals
teargas fumes
vendors hopeless
running battles
police-army
packing shacks
mock quarantine
trapped
family distance
Zero

stinking sewer
contaminating
trickling water
rusty taps dry
desperate faces
long lines form
shallow wells
puddles
hoards share
muddy juices rare
social distance
Zero

3.15. *Chimurenga 5:* Food Justice (2020 onward)

So, at the end of this journey, when I see swinging nooses, people in chains from AIDS to COVID, and extreme poverty, exploited inside out, I also see a revolution that is green. I feel *Chimurenga* 5 rising from multiple fronts. I hear thunder from the diaspora as clouds herald rain after severe drought, for plants with roots that dug deeper in search for rivers connecting the maze beneath fake boundaries raised by colonization, crumpled by globalization, and now tightly erected in gloomy concrete walls of COVID-19. *Chimurenga* 5 is the economic revolution fought with inexhaustible weaponry of the awakened. This chapter advocates for virtual farming designed to crumple the wedges between black and white, rich and poor, men and women as well as inhuman wedges created by sexual orientation or religion. This is the context of *Chimurenga* 5 forged from strange fruits of profiling, exclusions and knee killings of the North where bountiful resources can be channelled into sustainable agricultural partnerships with communities of accountability in the South.

3.16. Collaborators

In Spring 2019, my dream to raise a *Chimurenga for racial justice* resulted in a conference I organized in partnership with colleagues at the University of San Francisco (USF). The 'Black Theology and Racial Justice' conference was dedicated to the memory of James H. Cone and Katie G. Cannon, the visionaries and founding members of Black Theology and Womanist Theology respectively. A blueprint for racial justice was crafted by a collaboration of my African Theology students, scholars, activists and religious leaders grounded in race, gender, sexuality, and green justice. I am honored to place a plaque of the luminaries who screamed 'Black Lives Matter' at USF in Spring 2019, prophesying to the wind!

> Susan Abraham
> Simon-Mary Aihiokhai
> Jorge A. Aquino
> Karen Baker-Fletcher
> Erin Brigham
> Sharon Sanderlin Cheek
> Stan Chu Ilo
> Shawn Copeland
> George Cummings
> Lilian Dube
> Julia Anne Dowd
> Candice Harrison
> Teresia Mbari Hinga
> Rhonda V. Magee
> Bryan N. Massingale
> Tana Roseboro
> James Lance Taylor
> Shamann Walton
> Mary J. Wardell-Ghirarduzzi

The vision of Pope Francis to retrieve humanity from the doldrums of stinking poverty exposed by COVID[28] motivates my farming mission that has been both challenging and exciting. My rural background was helpful in the conceptualization of the project in the countryside. My experience in designing a star global study abroad program rooted in the Service-Learning methodology, the Zambia Today Program, was a training ground for my vision. Thus, the privilege to open new frontiers and act outside the box was less intimidating. The virtual farming project shares the momentum of the global Service-Learning program I designed and became the sole faculty in charge of from 2009 to 2014.

3.17. The Farming Poor

Farming is a delicate skill that is so complicated and alienating to many scholars and people in different professions. A farmer is synonymous with dirt and back-breaking work, which can leave you broke and depressed like the characters in Doris Lessing's epic novel discussed in this chapter. Even when they were equipped with the land, servants, and the privileged colour white in a British colony, her characters, Mary and Dick Turner, are trapped in vicious poverty, depression, desperation and ultimately death. This story forms a bridge across experience and fiction. It is a classic example to illustrate the intricacies of commercial farming that made *Chimurenga 4* largely a dismal disaster in some sectors.

Zimbabwe farm invasions were violent land take-overs to redress the violence of colonial native displacement that crushed the earth and stumbled upon lives, preparing a perfect storm for COVID-19. Hence the urgency of this final reflection on the perceived emergency response to a critical humanitarian crisis which is inseparable from the bleeding environment. This crisis was precipitated by myriad factors including the violation of the Lancaster Agreement by Britain in 1986 and corruption of politicians who amassed land for themselves while pretending to act on behalf of the landless poor. Additionally, lack of farming skill or training for poor peasant black families resettled on new lands without adequate support such as starting capital or fair trade settings for their produce. The systematic exclusion of Zimbabweans in the diaspora from subsequent land reform programs if addressed could rescue starving masses on vast tracts of land that have been degraded and stripped to the bare bones. Trees have been recklessly cut and sacred woodland cleared; from Cecil

---

28. Web resource: https://www.bbc.com/news/world-53055220 "Pope Francis Warn the Poor Have Become Part of the Landscape". *BBC News*. June 22, 2020.

the lion to the smallest rabbit, animals have been poached. Hellish winter veldt fires burn grass to the roots and the scorched bare soil gives way to rushing floods. Without irrigation facilities, rivers choke with siltation from survival river-bank cultivation that flourishes for a short while. Without a vibrant export market for their produce, these new farmers are doomed because of subtle sanctions that have left Zimbabwe foreign trade in shambles. Reduced to desperate vendors, the rest desperately wait by roadside crowded markets for reluctant buyers till their produce rots or are forced to surrender their produce at compromised prices that keep them orbiting in circles that eventually knock them out of business.

This chapter is, therefore, concerned about healing earth and valuing lives in the COVID-19 pandemic lock-down, a crisis fully described above. It appeals to the African Diaspora network of partnerships with locals on farming projects to feed the desperate nation, create employment with fair working conditions, plant trees and reclaim gullies as before. With an agrarian economy and a religious community, the tested model of Professor Marthinus Daneel can certainly be re-adopted for the rural communities. I strongly advocate for the landless urban dwellers equipped with financial resources, the African diaspora, gainfully employed to be accommodated in land reform programs intended to heal the earth and dignify lives. I introduce into this matrix virtual farming.

3.18. Virtual Farming Model

Being prophetic moves communities beyond routine cash handouts that trickle to the endless bottom eroded by hyperinflation and mocks cash. Connected with the land through women healing earth, feeding themselves and others, I am currently locked in virtual horticulture and open grain farming. Using the small resources at my disposal, I have set up a satellite horticulture project and open field under irrigation just under 5 hectares; employed women and youth to assist in the work and management for the small-scale farming project. My family has been generous with their time virtually and physically. A network of farmers speaks daily online freely advising each other on a variety of subjects. The surrounding farming community looks out to alert and assist in resolving simple challenges; 'you learn as you go', they firmly advise. Finally, government officers at the rural council level are involved and reassuring with skills within their means. There is support at the grassroots of commercial farming. There is also a solid community desperate for partners to revive the economy, heal the land and restore the dignity of people in the country together. Food production, gully reclamation, and land restoration requires respectful dialogue and a strong desire to heal the nation. It is a patriotic gesture more than it is economic, especially during COVID-19 challenges. If the government could facilitate land reform dialogue that is inclusive and progressive without corruption, Zimbabwe will be restored as the breadbasket of Africa, and our land will be healed. These unimaginable dreams are achieved through collective effort that will erupt the grass we planted along runoffs into victory songs of true liberation for all.

3.19.1. *Conclusion*

The prophetic voice of Rosemary Radford Ruether reverberates in the buzz of voices from the global South and North condensed into *Valuing Lives, Healing Earth,* the 2021 sequel of her masterpiece, *Women Healing Earth: Third World Women on Ecology, Feminism, and Religion* (1996). In conclusion, the snippet below provides an inconclusive source of theoretical frameworks for empirical research and material for dialogue.

3.19.2. *Theoretical Frameworks for Dialogue*

Evaluating the findings of this research against the work of Ruether's *Women Healing Earth*, and discussing the contribution of 'Third World' women to ecology, feminism, and religion provide a broader framework relevant for valuing lives and healing earth for women in Third World and African contexts. The prophetic voices of Teresia Hinga and Tumani Nyajeka are particularly relevant to this chapter. The work by Eleanor Rae, 1994: *Women, the Earth, the Divine* also provides critical comparative expression of the divine and various feminist expressions thereof. It sheds some light on the evaluation of the role of religion in this study. The dialogue between environmentalists and scholars of religion is clearly expounded by John Carmody, 1983: *Ecology and Religion*. Although the book is heavy with Christian overtones, it has interesting insights. Leonardo Boff and Virgilio P. Elizondo (eds.), 1995: *Ecology and Poverty* bring in one of the major issues in this chapter, the connection between the two crises and the alleviation strategies adopted by Marthinus Daneel's ideal vision of ZIRRCON and discussed in Chimurenga 3 above. There is also the realization of women as the poorest of the poor, which justifies ZIRRCON's focus on the poverty alleviation scheme. Additionally, Bart Johnson and Kristina Hill, 2002: *Ecology and Design*, make vital connections in the area of Christian faith and the environment. Informed by Hebrew and Christian Scripture and spirituality, they make inroads into the feminist agenda of ecology.

CHAPTER 4

SALIM, WOMEN, AND OIKOS: A PLANETARY EXPANSION OF FAMILY

Jea Sophia Oh

4.1.

As a political and economic system, capitalism affects all aspects of life in the places that are subject to it. Neo-liberal capitalism's profit-oriented development has brought human crisis to such an alarming level of inequality and ecological crisis that we cannot but not be paying attention. In this regard, economy and ecology have been employed as disciplinary matrices in a seeming representation of opposing concerns. Nevertheless, both ecology and economy, as disciplinary matrices find a common etymological home in the Greek word *oikos* meaning "household." There are some patriarchal dangers of course to be countenanced in using such household metaphors within feminist studies due to the western myth of universal patriarchy and the hegemony of a transcendent male monotheistic God that have justified males as heads of the ordinary or mundane household. Despite destructive effects of these dangerous household metaphors, some ecofeminist scholars such as Sallie McFague reconstruct the term *oikos* to mean "the whole earth" as God's flourishing household in which we are all called to live. *Salim* is a Korean term, literally meaning "enlivening." However, both *salim* and women have been inferiotized as women's household tasks by housewives although they both are most fundamental entities for living in an ecologically enlivening way. This paper suggests a planetary expansion of family (eco-family) intimating an interconnected ecosystem and an extended meaning of *salim* as all diverse activities aimed at enlivening a sustainable, planetary symbiosis. This holistic conception of *oikos* not only combines ecology and economy as a sustainable living of a planetary home but also recognizes women who work for *salim* activities as "ecofamilists" such that the mutual victimization of women and naturalization of neo-liberal capitalism will be thoroughly deconstructed.

4.2. Korean Women in the Confucian Family

For Korean women, the meaning of family is a complex matter. Throughout the history, women's status in Korean households has been highly complicated and at least double-sided within *Joseon* dynasty (1392–1910) identity politics as well as within the 21st century lived reality of Korea. It is wrong and careless to judge that both Confucianism and Korean patriarchal society are extremely misogynic in terms of victimizing women within the Confucian family. Women's role(s) in the Confucian family should be re-imagined from multiple angles. Recognizing Korean women in the category of "Asian women" from the western eyes as so-called the "submissive China doll," the "exotic geisha," the "good cook," the "compliant wife," etc. is highly fetishized and Orientalized which is even worse than recognizing Korean women as mere victims of the Confucian household.

Unlike general assumptions that Korean society has been described as an extreme form of patriarchy since *Joseon* dynasty, Korean women's role in the Confucian family is predominant and even more powerful than women in the western family on some points. For instance, Korean women do not change their surnames even after getting married since *Goguryeo* dynasty (BCE 37 ~ 668). Another evidence for reverence toward women in the traditional Korean society can be found in the traditional wedding custom in *Goguryeo* named *seo-ok-jae* (壻屋制, son-in-law's flat system) which means that the bridegroom lives with the bride's family in a separate flat in his parent-in-laws' house until his children grow to maturity. In *Joseon* dynasty, the well-known Confucian scholar Yi I (pen name Yulgok) also was born and raised in his mother Sin Saimdang's hometown *Gangneung* with his maternal grandparents. Until the age of nuclear family by which wedding customs have been westernized, in order to marry, commonly the bridegroom needed to arrive at the bride's parents' house for having the wedding ceremony. Even today *Seo-ok-jae* remains in the current Korean marriage customs given that the bride and the groom stay in the bride's parents' house for some nights after their honeymoon trip before starting their own married life. Also, an evidence of *Seo-ok-jae* can be found in the Korean expression, *jangga-deunda* (丈家 장가든다, "going to bride's house") for "getting married."

A most powerful factor of women's power in traditional Korean households was that the wife had substantial economic control of the household property. During the *Goryeo* dynasty (918-1392), compared to *Joseon* dynasty, women had relatively great economic and social powers and freedoms. It might be true to say that, historically speaking, Confucianism

Shin-hang (新行, wedding trip), Joseon dynasty folk art by Danwon (pen name), Kim Hong-do (1745-1806?)[1]

has contributed to gender inequalities and oppression of women in Korea. However, Korean women have not been merely submissive participants in terms of household management and agency. In the *Joseon* dynasty, only the wife has the key to the family property barn (곳간 *gotgan*), which is like a family bank account and transfers the key to her daughter-in-law from generation to generation. Even today in a typical Korean household the wife manages all the household money and the husband receives an allowance from his wife.[1]

The homogeneous aspects of seeing Korean women as merely passive victims of Korean history and Confucianism as an extremely misogynous, patriarchal ideology throughout the history are pessimistic as well as destructive for the future of Asian feminism because these aspects Orientalize Asian philosophies as well as feminize women. I am not trying to

---

1. Kim Hong-do's *Shin-hang* illustrates the wedding customs in *Joseon* dynasty. *Shin-hang* means the wedding ritual that the bridegroom takes a journey to have a wedding ceremony in the bride's house. After the ceremony the bride and bridegroom stay in the bride's house usually for three days (or many years in some cases) before starting their own living as a new family.

romanticize Korean women's gender roles in the traditional Korean Confucian households. If so, it becomes a denial of women's oppression in the patriarchal history of Korea. In spite of the general history of women's oppression, it is extremely crucial to excavate unspotlighted stories of women's active roles and to discover women's bio-power (the power from "below" or from the "margins") in order to deconstruct the traditional male/female dichotomy that has been normalized as a fixed, natural, and unchanging natural duality.

4.3. *Oikos* and *Salim*

> A different kind of economy is the *oikos*, the household. To discover who we are (what the world is) we see ourselves within God in Christ. We are the body of God. We are God spread out, we are God incarnated. We (the universe) come from God and return to God. We all together make up the body of God – God going out, God enfleshed, God becomes matter.[2]

The Greek term *oikos* refers to household in a narrow sense and to the universe in a broad sense. McFague uses the concept of *oikos* to recognize the universe as a whole organic unity, the body of God. Unlike the human household, the key points of McFague's analogy are to overcome the anthropocentric and patriarchal culture and to transform them into cosmocentric and ecocentric ones. When she mentions the word "we," it does not refer to humankind only but the entirety of the universe. All life viewed as an interconnected cosmic body, including inorganic things, and not focusing exclusively on human beings, can be considered as a community of family. Using an analogy of *oikonomene* to explain the interconnectedness and interdependency of every entity of the earth, the whole pluriversal cosmos can be interpreted as a dynamically holographic web of interpenetrating microcosmic and macrocosmic family resemblances. We live in this divine household with our fellow creatures as God's family (*familia Dei*).

There are some obstacles to use the term *oikos* (household) to understand the entirety of our planetary living. Firstly, the dichotomy of economy and ecology in the neo-liberal capitalistic structure has inferiorized ecology (earth) to economy (money). Both economy and ecology are derived from the Greek, *oikos*. Nonetheless, *oikonomene* has been used to refer to the human inhabited world of the cosmos in an anthropocentric sense. Secondly, using this household concept we cannot avoid the conventional patriarchal structure in which the father is almost always the

---

2. Sallie McFague, *Life Abundant: Rethinking Theology and Economy for a Planet in Peril* (Minneapolis: Fortress Press, 2001), 183.

head of the household. As long as the Christian Church conceptually genderizes God as only Father (male), the patriarchalization of God legitimates various forms of patriarchal violence by cosmically ordaining a husband as the natural head of a human household. Such a patriarchally reified conceptual pattern justifies a destructive human hierarchy as if it were the divine order of God, man, woman, animals, and all of nature. In order to avoid this problem, God has to be called "She" or "He" as neither man nor woman or both. The Christian Church and theology should be free from this old anthropomorphic Father God and keep calling "Mother God" more often along with all other metaphorical names. Therefore, the pronouns of God should be "She" as well as "He" or "They."

Both the concepts of household (*oikos*) and family have been employed by patriarchal systems of oppression in Eastern and Western cultures to subordinate women. The patriarchal dimensions of household management serve to promote male members of families as the heads of the household and maintain primary power and predominance in roles of political leadership, moral authority, social privilege and control and distribution of family property. In East Asian Confucian societies there is a legacy of traditionally patrilineal family order, by which titles and rituals are inherited by male family lineage. The central Confucian virtues of family are filial piety (*xiao* 孝) and family harmony (*jiahe* 家和), but these have been historically misogynistically practiced. In such a gender hierarchy, a woman's roles in a family are at various times conceived to be subordinated to her father, husband, and also male siblings.

The patriarchal system on the head of family (戶主制 *Hojujae*, family headship system) had been a legal system since 1923 by the Japanese Government General of Korea and finally abolished in 2005 by the efforts of feminist activists. The abolition of *Hojujae* was accomplished by Korea Women's Associations United, Korean National Council of Women, and Korean Legal Aid Center for Family Relations. Korea's family register system is disadvantageous to women and often required registration of family relations that differ from actual situations because Korea continues to rely on a male-dominant paternal kinship system for determining family relations. According to *Hojujae,* when a husband dies, instead of his wife, her male child regardless of his age had to be the head of the household. This male-oriented system strengthened a patriarchal society in which women are relegated to playing a subjugated role to men. Moreover, *Hojujae* did not originate from the Korean traditional family system, which is much more egalitarian than *Hojujae* such as *Seo-ok-jae*, the wedding custom (as discussed) since *Goguryeo* dynasty but in large part was rooted in the Japanese ideology of imperial clan hierarchy, which was introduced to Korea following the Japanese invasion of Korea. Therefore, it was not just a patriarchal but also a colonial imperialistic system. Many liberated women in Korea who were opposed to this misogynic system had to postpone to register their marriage certificates until the abolition of *Hojujae*.[3]

As I mentioned above, a wife's leadership role in a typical Korean household has indeed been much greater than it has been characteristically misunderstood as in terms of the Orientalized and misogynized 'submissive wife'. *Oikonomos* (managing a household) is called *salim* in Korea. *Salim*, in a narrow and traditional sense refers to women's everyday embodied tasks such as cooking, educating children, cultivating gardens, and managing household economics and affairs. *Salim*, in a broad sense, can also include all diverse ecological activities that enliven and sustain all the eco-flourishing, planetary living. Although *salim* has been gendered and degraded as exclusively women's tasks in Korea, due to the traditionally oppressive gender roles, the power of *salim* is not merely of women, but in everything (more than humans), including male gendered persons as well.

Beyond managing a household, for keeping a sustainable living of this planet, Korean women have been always at the frontline of Korean ecological movements which are referenced as *salim* movements. The Korean *salim* (enlivening) movements, ongoing since 1997, — emerged as a collective of ecological resistance movements initiated as a result of the destructive consequences of the International Monetary Fund (IMF)-imposed crisis. When the International Monetary Fund (IMF) and South Korea negotiated the largest IMF rescue package in early December 1997, of approximately US $57 billion, it came as a shock to most Koreans. The situation became popularly known as the IMF crisis. Confronting the IMF crisis, the *salim* movement has been predominantly carried out by Korean women in the everyday practice of caring for their homes. The *salim* movement in Korea is a recycling movement that engages in the practices of *an-na-ba-da*. *An-na-ba-da* stands for saving (*ah*), sharing (*na*), exchanging (*ba*), and reusing (*da*). The *salim* movement functions as an ecological movement in saving the economy and ecology as a valuable *oikos*, our living organism, and the household.[4] Beyond a narrow meaning

---

3. For example, Jin Seon-mi who was nominated as the Minister of Women's Affairs and Family Affairs of the second government of Moon Jae-in government, postponed to register her marriage after a *de facto* marriage for 19 years until the abolition of *Hojujae* was accomplished.

4. Jea Sophia Oh, *A Postcolonial Theology of Life: Planetarity East and West* (Upland, CA: Sopher Press, 2011), 36.

of *salim* as women's household tasks, a concept that could be easily degraded along with women, *salim* in a broad sense means all activities that are directed towards sustainable planetary living including recycling, recovering, reconciliation, repentance, and responsibility.

4.4. Ecofamilism: Planetary Expansion of Family

> Heaven is my father and Earth is my mother, and even such a small creature as I find an intimate place in their midst. Therefore, that which fills the universe I regard as my body and that which directs the universe I consider as my nature. All people are my brothers and sisters and all things are my companions. — 張載 Zhangzai[5]

The neo-Confucian scholar Zhangzai (1022-1077) identified himself with the whole cosmos. Zhangzai expanded the category of family beyond a set of biological ties that may restrict and limit the process of expansion of our love and compassion to the myriad things in the cosmos. Zhangzai's horizontal expansion of family, as the whole cosmos beyond both a biological family and an exclusive anthropocentrism, deconstructs the pseudo-biological boundaries and patriarchal obstacles of "family" conceived of as an ecological model of sustainable living that overcomes the pitfalls and limitations of a narrowly humanistic orientation of a certain brand of environmental ethics.

As McFague argues that a non-patriarchal economy is implicit in the *oikos*, the *household* of which we are part of the living body of God, Bron Taylor also uses the home as metaphor for the earth: "Earth is our home and home to all living beings. Earth itself is alive. We are a part of an evolving universe. Human beings are members of an interdependent community of life with a magnificent diversity of life forms and cultures."[6] I would emphasize our bodily connection to all things in the whole universe as one living body as a homelike organism. A living subject cannot completely distance herself from the other living subjects as well as from non-organic things. This symbiotic perspective of living can be called "ecofamilism."

The term ecofamilism was first offered by a Taiwanese ecofamilist Wan-Li Ho as a theoretical platform for thinking through environmental movements. Instead of using the western theoretical models of ecofeminism, Ho uses traditional Confucian family values as her conceptual framework

---

5. Wingtsit Chan, *A Source Book in Chinese Philosophy* (Princeton: Princeton University Press, 1963), 467.
6. Bron Taylor, *Dark Green Religion: Nature, Spirituality, and the Planetary Future* (Berkeley: University of California Press, 2010), 203.

to construct her new theoretical framework of ecofamilism. Ho emphasizes filial piety (*xiao* 孝) and benevolence (*ren* 仁) as virtues of ecofamilism that should be extended to familial care, to strangers and even enemies. Her expansive notion of family overcomes gender dichotomies and deconstructs anthropocentric boundaries with the goal of realizing a flourishing planetary macrocosm by recognizing humans as a part of the web of life and the entirety of humanity as an integrated body, drawing upon Zhangzai's cosmology: "That which fills the universe I regard as my body and that which directs the universe I consider as my nature."[7] According to Ho's research of the Taiwanese environmental movements, as the *salim* movement has been carried out by Korean women, unlike patriarchal families, the members of Taiwanese environmental activist groups are predominantly housewives who are the leaders of their communities. Ho conceives of the role of "activist housewives" as expanding "the boundaries of home and family to include the ecological environment, broadening the scope of traditional familial duties along the lines of ecofamilism."[8] In this regard, the term "family" is not a patriarchal system but this planet and our planetary living as an extended family and as an open-ended, dynamic system processing over generations and evolving over time. This "planet as an extended eco-family" can be possible by practicing our compassion with others who are unfamiliar to us beyond our biological families, political parties, sexual orientations, countries, religious upbringings, and human species, which I call *salim* (enlivening) ecology.

As an Asian ecofeminist scholar, I strongly maintain that it is extremely important to discover our distinctive cultural elements and resources in order to envision a more sustainable ethic of living wisely. I feel responsible to find more constructive cultural alternatives from my Korean culture which can challenge the Eurocentric dominance of the area of ecofeminism and environmental ethics in academia. Although the term feminism cannot be identified solely with white feminism, it has historically been predominantly a white-dominated discourse throughout the three long waves of feminist movements. Many iterations of Western feminisms have been criticized for taking into account only white, middle class, and college-educated perspectives. For this reason, Ho refuses to use the term feminism then and presents her own distinctively Taiwanese version of "ecofamilism."

---

7. Wan-Li Ho, *Ecofamilism: Women, Religion, and Environmental Protection in Taiwan* (St. Petersburg: Three Pines Press, 2016), 27.

8. Ibid., 90.

Despite destructive practices of patriarchal family around the world, I would like to borrow the term "ecofamilism" as an alternative sustainable ethic for this expanded planetary family. In 1996, Rosemary Radford Ruether offered the anthology *Women Healing Earth* as a collection of women's voices from Latin America, Asia, and Africa on religion, ecology and feminism for presenting an effort at cross-cultural communication and solidarity between women throughout the world struggling against the effects of Western colonization.[9] In the anthology *Ecofeminism*, Vandana Shiva and Maria Mies recognize that ecofeminism has always driven women's efforts to save their livelihood and make their communities safe, as we have seen such movement like *Chipko* in the 1970s which was led primarily by women who embraced trees to protect them from being cut by loggers and struggled to create life-affirming societies.[10] Indeed, non-western ecofeminism significantly predates the emergence of North American ecofeminism. It is crucial to turn to contributions from non-western ecofeminist scholars as well as to contextual and cultural elements from other parts of the world that explore the intersections between postcolonial and ecological concerns. With this purpose, in my first book, *A Postcolonial Theology of Life: Planetarity East and West* (2011), I introduced *salim* as a postcolonial ecofeminist movement. Indeed, I named my work "postcolonial ecofeminist theology" for which I bridged postcolonialism and ecotheology with the use of *salim* as the philosophical underpinning for the argument that all forms of life are equal and divine. Many current thinkers working in the field of postcolonial ecofeminism are not only talking about non-western feminism, but also developing critical theoretical tools and strategies to better address the task of decolonizing nature from humans' destructive neoliberal capitalist colonization in the Anthropocene epoch. By all means, then, we need to hear more women's voices, especially non-western and marginalized voices, aimed at decolonizing this planet. Called by many names—ecofeminism, postcolonial ecofeminism, ecofamilism, and so on—ecologically healing women's movements are more vitally important than ever before as we stand on the brink of climate catastrophe and ethically hoping for viable futures.

---

9. Rosemary Radford Ruether, *Women Healing Earth: Third World Women on Ecology, Feminism, and Religion* (New York: Orbis Books, 1996), 1.

10. Vandana Shiva had been a participant in the *Chipko* Movement of the 1970s, and has been particular about emphasizing the connection of women with the environment to their daily interaction and economies. See Maria Mies and Vandana Shiva, eds., *Ecofeminism* (London and New York: Zed Books, 2014).

CHAPTER 5

"SOLIDARITY AMONG CREATURES": CATHOLIC EXEGETICAL GROUNDS FOR FELLOWSHIP WITH NONHUMAN CREATION

Alyssa Moore

"There is a solidarity among all creatures arising from the fact that all have the same Creator and are all ordered to his glory."
The Catechism of the Catholic Church

5.1. Introduction

This chapter and its conclusions rely almost entirely on two sources: Holy Scripture (that is, the Bible, in *New Revised Standard Version*) and *The Catechism of the Catholic Church*, specifically the edition edited by Cardinal Joseph Ratzinger and promulgated by Pope Saint John Paul II. Because of the potentially controversial nature of my study, I deliberately chose to use only these two most foundational Catholic texts, as well as more conservative, pre-Vatican II church documents, where needed, to enhance my understanding of a given passage. I believe that the authority of the Scriptures speaks for itself, as does that of the Catechism, "a sure and authentic reference text for teaching Catholic doctrine and [...] preparing local catechisms," and of the two celebrated traditionalist theologians and Vicars of Christ who refined this particular edition.[1] All findings are either (1) summaries and discussions of explicitly stated principles and mandates from these sources, or (2) conclusions that can be logically inferred from them.

For the purpose of clarity and comprehension, I separate these biblical and catechetical teachings on nonhuman creation into four general categories: first, nonhuman creation as *imago Dei*, the "image of God," and thus as living revelation; second, nonhuman creation as "willed in its own being," purposefully created, designed, and sustained by God; third, the Trinitarian destiny of nonhuman creation, which it shares in common with humankind; and fourth, the most *essential* and most *excellent* aspects

---

1. CCC, 6.

and uses of nonhuman creation, borrowing this terminology from the eminent theologian Father Bernard Lonergan, SJ.[2]

In an effort to avoid any confusion or inconsistency resulting from shifts in terminology, I will make use of the expression "nonhuman creation" as an umbrella term encapsulating animals, plants, the physical environment, etc. — in short, all of nature, living and inanimate, with the exception of human beings.[3] The latter part of the term is intentionally chosen, since this essay is intrinsically founded upon the Catholic Christian premise that God "creates and conserves all things" outside of Godself.[4] However, more specific wording will be used as appropriate, whether to preserve the original meaning and implications of a source text or when a point is relevant only (or at least primarily) to a particular sector of nonhuman creation.

One such crucial distinction lies between sentient and non-sentient creation, i.e. nonhuman creation that is capable of sensation, of perception, of feeling, or even of self-awareness, versus nonhuman creation that does not possess these faculties. Though this essay seeks to inform human interaction with nonhuman creation in general, different considerations will necessarily govern our relationships with different categories of creation: for example, a sentient creature must be acknowledged to "*participate in Being itself*" at a different level than an insensible object, and therefore merits to be treated with an additional amount of caution and care.[5] This statement is not intended to suggest the existence of an ontological hierarchy in which certain members of creation are somehow "closer" to God, as other theologians have proposed, but rather to qualify that the specific needs, rights, and basic nature of individual classes of nonhuman creation should be taken into account as we shape and examine our Christian relationship with them.[6]

---

2. CCC 339.
3. The Oxford Dictionary defines "nature" as "the phenomena of the physical world collectively, including plants, animals, the landscape, and other features and products of the earth, *as opposed to humans or human creations*" (emphasis added).
4. CCC 54, 290.
5. CCC 34 (emphasis added).
6. In *The Darkness of God: Negativity in Christian Mysticism*, for example, Denys Turner summarizes the position of early theologian Denys the Areopagite, who argues that God is present to God's various works at different levels of "immediacy," with angels and human beings enjoying the most intimate connection with their Creator. However, this concept is ultimately flawed, since all of creation only exists or *is real* insofar as it is in and with God. According to Denys' principle, created things with which God has "less" immediacy would therefore be "less real," which cannot be accepted as true. Furthermore, arguments along these lines can be seen to encourage a short-sighted anthropocentrism with disastrous consequences for all of creation.

5.2. Nonhuman Creation as Imago Dei

The Catechism repeatedly proclaims that "all creatures," not just humankind, "bear a certain resemblance to God"; humankind, in truth, ultimately represents "but a small part of [God's] creation."[7] Each individual being and species is said to possess "its own particular goodness and perfection," which "radiate[s] in different ways" the "one goodness of God."[8] Even nonliving creation — the earth, the sea, the sky — is in itself what St. Augustine calls "a profession [*confessio*]" which reflects the beauty and constancy of its Creator.[9] Biblical language about God and God's plan is thus frequently based upon the myriad desirable characteristics that nonhuman creation manifests. The kingdom of heaven is likened to a mustard seed, sown small but ultimately prodigious; Christ in his meekness and purity is "the Lamb of God"; God is compared to a stable rock or fearsome lion in God's steadfastness, and so on.[10]

Nonhuman creation, however, serves not only as a manifestation of the *characteristics* of God, but as a kind of witness to the eternal *presence* of God, as a continual declaration or revelation. Rather poetically, the Catechism states that "when he listens to the message of creation and to the voice of conscience, man can arrive at certainty about the existence of God, the cause and end of everything," since "God has left traces of his Trinitarian being" in created things.[11] It even goes so far as to argue that "we can name God only by taking creatures as our starting point," illustrating the indispensable nature of "the great book of creation."[12] This in itself is a manifestation of God's beneficence. The Catechism quotes St. Bonaventure in support of this idea: "God created all things 'not to increase his glory, but to show it forth and to communicate it'" for our sake.[13] The following section will briefly explore the means and motivations by which God establishes and animates creation, human and nonhuman alike.

5.3. Nonhuman Creation as "Willed in Its Own Being"

The Priestly narrative of Creation found in Genesis, in which God "calls everything from nothingness into existence," points explicitly to the goodness of created things and the divine intentionality that brought about

---

7. CCC 41, 30.
8. CCC 339, 970.
9. CCC 32, quoting St. Augustine, *Sermo* 241, 2: PL 38, 1134.
10. Matthew 13:31-32, John 1:36 (cf. Is 53:7; this is of course in addition to Christ's culturally symbolic role as the Passover lamb, sacrificed that others might live).
11. CCC 237.
12. CCC 46, 40, 2705.
13. CCC 293, quoting St. Bonaventure, *In II Sent.* I, 2, 2, 1.

their existence.[14] Over the course of six days God fashions night, day, sky, land, oceans, stars, sun, moon, vegetation, birds, sea creatures, wild and tame animals, and finally humankind; each is brought into being by God's command, "let there be," and of each it is said that "God saw that it was good."[15] The Catechism affirms that this work "proceeds from God's free will," with "no other reason [...] than his love and goodness."[16] Additionally, it is a work in which all three Persons of the Trinity can properly be seen to participate, for "the Word of God and his Breath" — the Son and Holy Spirit — "are at the origin of the being and life of every creature."[17] This is especially true of the Spirit, who "being God [...] preserves creation in the Father through the Son."[18]

As the previous quotation suggests, God's creative power is not an isolated action or choice, but a *continuous* one: "God does not abandon his creatures to themselves [...] but also, and at every moment, upholds and sustains them in being, enables them to act and brings them to their final end."[19] God "cares for all his creatures" with a "parental tenderness," "pouring out his heavenly gifts on all things without exception," and "his compassion is over all that he has made."[20] Christ himself speaks movingly of this truth in conversation with the disciples, illustrating that God prizes nonhuman creation far above human estimation; speaking of the intimacy and the omnipotence of God, Jesus asks: "Are not five sparrows sold for two pennies? Yet not one of them is forgotten in God's sight."[21] The Catechism affirms that, just as Christians pray for God to "give us this day our daily bread," God "gives to *all* the living 'their food in due season,'" and this since the dawn of Creation, bestowing on human and nonhuman

---

14. CCC 2566.
15. Genesis 1:1-31. Jesus seems to affirm the almost unfathomable beauty of creation in Matthew 6:26-30, taking "the lilies" or "the grass of the field" as an example: despite the fact that they are short-lived, "alive today and tomorrow [...] thrown into the oven," "even Solomon in all his glory was not clothed like one of these."
16. CCC 295, 293. This appears to contradict the Yahwist narrative of Creation in Genesis 2:4-20, in which God makes nonhuman creation as a kind of afterthought, to relieve the first man's solitude and give him "a helper as his partner" (v. 18-19).
17. CCC 1988; cf. John 1:1-14.
18. CCC 703. This in itself has interesting implications about the value of nonhuman creation, given that "those in whom the Spirit dwells are divinized" (CCC 1988, quoting St. Athanasius, *Ep. Serap.* 1, 24: PG 26, 585 and 588).
19. CCC 301.
20. CCC 309, 239, 1050, 295 (quoting Ps 145:9).
21. Luke 12:6; cf. Matthew 29. In subsequent verses, Jesus exhorts his disciples not to fear, since they "are worth more than many sparrows" (Lk 12:7; cf. Mt 31) — a statement which might indeed seem to minimize the worth of nonhuman creatures in God's sight, despite God's immanent connection with them. However, I would suggest that since God is the source and foundation of love and goodness itself, even the smallest measure of God's attention or affection would be a gift too infinite for our understanding to grasp.

creation alike fruits, plants, and grass to eat, that they might be sustained while still living in harmony with one another.[22]

Though it is God alone who can grant the gift of life, it is important to note that this "providential care" is not a unilateral project.[23] God also wills that creatures participate in caring for and upholding themselves and one another, and consequently "grants [them] not only their existence, but also the dignity of acting on their own, of being causes and principles for each other, and thus of cooperating in the accomplishment of his plan."[24] The Catechism testifies to the fact that God even grants all of creation a participation in the divine life: "that his creatures should share in his truth, goodness, and beauty — that is the glory for which God created them."[25]

As the next section will discuss, there is a considerable amount of evidence in both the Bible and the Catechism to suggest that this loving, intimate relationship continues on beyond the temporal reality, even unto resurrection and eternal life.

5.4. The Trinitarian Ends of Nonhuman Creation

In the Book of Ecclesiastes, the narrating teacher, Qohelet, "the son of David," poses the following question:

> I said in my heart with regard to human beings that God is testing them to show that they are but animals. For the fate of humans and the fate of animals is the same; as one dies, so dies the other. They all have the same breath, and humans have no advantage over the animals; for all is vanity. All go to one place; all are from the dust, and all turn to dust again. Who knows whether the human spirit goes upward and the spirit of animals goes downward to the earth?[26]

Similarly, the Catechism asserts that "God, who alone made heaven and earth, can alone impart true knowledge of every created thing in relation to himself," including and especially their eschatological fate.[27] However,

---

22. Matthew 6:11 (cf. Luke 11:3); CCC 2828, emphasis added; Genesis 1:29-30. In God's post-flood covenant with Noah, his family, and all surviving nonhuman creation, God allows humans to begin using "every moving thing that lives" for food (Gen 9:3); the writer seems to see this not so much as God's own desire as a concession God makes after concluding that "the inclination of the human heart is evil from youth" (Gen 8:21).
23. CCC 2416. The manner in which this partnership should proceed will be discussed in sections to follow.
24. CCC 306.
25. CCC 319.
26. Ecclesiastes 1:1, 4:18-21.
27. CCC 216.

both the Bible and the Catechism also clearly suggest that nonhuman creation shares a common destiny with humankind — that "the ultimate end of the whole divine economy" is in fact "the entry of God's creatures into the perfect unity of the Blessed Trinity."[28]

Much as humankind yearns for the fulfillment of the kingdom of God, "the universe was created 'in a state of journeying' (*in statu viae*) toward an ultimate perfection yet to be attained, to which God has destined it."[29] Paul's Letter to the Romans describes all creation as "groaning in labor pains," "in hope that the creation itself will be set free from its bondage to decay and will obtain the freedom of the glory of the children of God."[30] Surprisingly, the Church, through the Catechism, seems to argue that nonhuman creation, alongside humankind, is justified in this hope. This is visible in several of its statements on the resurrection and the new creation, in which — given the almost extreme specificity in much of the rest of the text - the wording appears intentionally broad and inclusive.

> Creation is the foundation of 'all God's saving plans,' the 'beginning of the history of salvation' that culminates in Christ. Conversely, the mystery of Christ casts conclusive light on the mystery of creation and reveals the end for which 'in the beginning God created the heavens and the earth': from the beginning, God envisaged the glory of the new creation in Christ.[31]

Drawing from Tertullian, the Catechism elaborates on the meaning of the "definitive sabbath rest for which he created heaven and earth," in what could be considered equally expansive language: "We believe in God who is the creator of the flesh; we believe in the Word made flesh in order to redeem the flesh; we believe in the resurrection of the flesh, the fulfillment of both the creation and the redemption of the flesh."[32] It is important to note that "flesh" is not exclusive to human beings; according to the Bible, each living being, in its own particular incarnation — "one flesh for human beings, another for animals, another for birds, and another for fish," "perhaps [one] of wheat or of some other grain" — is sown perishable, but raised imperishable.[33] For God "is God not of the dead, but of the living."[34]

---

28. CCC 260.
29. CCC 302.
30. Romans 8:22, 20-21.
31. CCC 280.
32. CCC 314, 1015.
33. 1 Corinthians 15:35-54.
34. Matthew 22:32.

5.5. Most Essential and Most Excellent Uses of Nonhuman Creation

Heretofore the Bible and the Catechism have proved remarkably consistent in their outlook on nonhuman creation, at least in reference to the three concepts previously discussed. They provide some very illuminating statements on these topics that, once collated and summarized, present what I hope is a clearer framework for understanding. On the following subject, however, the Bible and the Catechism seem to contradict themselves and one another, and thus my exegetical work is necessarily somewhat more speculative.

To begin with, the Catechism itself states that when reading the Bible, "the reader must take into account the conditions of [biblical authors'] time and culture, the literary genres in use at that time, and the modes of feeling, speaking, and narrating then current" — for the purposes of this chapter, meaning that any historical, religious, or cultural uses of nonhuman creation demonstrated therein do not necessarily remain appropriate in a modern context.[35] Therefore, it is critical to reexamine such practices in light of the many hundreds of years of biblical scholarship and theological refinement which have followed.

To that end, I would like to borrow from the work of Father Bernard Lonergan, SJ CC, who writes that all created things "are part of a dynamic whole in which [...each] level of being or activity subserves another" through either their most "essential" or most "excellent" aspects — that is, either their most basic or material aspects or their higher, most divine or "supernatural" ones.[36] For example, "the essential end of oxygen is to perform the offices of oxygen as oxygen; but its more excellent end is its contribution to the maintenance of human life."[37] I believe that, within this context, the Catechism's claim that God "destined all material creatures for the good of the human race" can perhaps be more fruitfully understood.[38]

For example, having established that nonhuman creation is in itself a revelation of God's presence, goodness, and splendor, it is reasonable to say this "good" is intended to be spiritual as much as purely material, perhaps even more so. The ability of nonhuman creation to serve as an object of reflection, and ultimately a means of bringing ourselves closer to God, would therefore be its most excellent function or aspect, while the consumption of nonhuman creation, for food, shelter, etc., would

---

35. CCC 110.
36. Lonergan, Bernard. *Collected Works of Bernard Lonergan* (Toronto, University of Toronto Press, 1993), 482.
37. Lonergan, 482-3.
38. CCC 353. Cf. Augustine's *On Christian Doctrine* and Ignatius of Loyola's *Spiritual Exercises*.

remain its most basic or essential. Along these lines, the Catechism holds that an implication of faith in God "*means making good use of created things:* faith in God, the only One, leads us to use everything that is not God only insofar as it brings us closer to him and to detach ourselves from it insofar as it turns us away from him."[39]

Consequently, human beings must "therefore respect the particular goodness of every creature, to avoid any disordered use of things which would be in contempt of the Creator and would bring disastrous consequences."[40] This passage demonstrates the inherent dignity of the created order — all of its parts as parts related to each other in an ordered, harmonious whole. It also necessarily entails reverence for nonhuman creation's revelatory nature, considered unselfishly, apart from its benefit to humankind, as well as the "submission of man's intellect and will."[41] I would venture to suggest that humankind's treatment of nonhuman creation generally fails to demonstrate such respect.

To make a comparison that I hope will not be viewed as impertinent: the physical books comprised of paper and ink that we call "the Bible" are not directly or immediately the revelation of God. The Bible's revelation is mediated through the words and ideas it contains; the paper and ink serve merely to house them. And yet a Catholic Christian would rightfully be appalled to intentionally desecrate or destroy a copy of the Bible, understanding it to be an act of disrespect. Why then does humankind find it acceptable to mar and destroy nonhuman creation and the bodies of nonhuman beings, which we now know are *in themselves* revelations of God's presence, willed and sustained by God, fellow creatures with whom God has established an eternal covenant?[42]

Echoing this, the Catechism declares that nonhuman "*animals*" in particular "are God's creatures. He surrounds them with his providential care. By their mere existence they bless him and give him glory. Thus men owe them kindness," and "should recall the gentleness with which saints like

---

39. CCC 226.
40. CCC 339.
41. CCC 341. Elsewhere the Catechism notes that the freedom of humankind (in thought, action, etc..) "does not imply a right to say or do everything. It is false to maintain that man, 'the subject of this freedom,' is 'an individual who is fully self-sufficient and whose finality is the satisfaction of his own interests in the enjoyment of earthly goods" (CCC 1740). Rather, people must work to "subordinate the 'material and instinctual dimensions to interior and spiritual ones," prioritizing what is right and just over what is attractive or desirable (CCC 2223). Therefore, humans' conduct toward nonhuman creation should be guided by respect for their common Creator rather than by appetites alone.
42. Cf. Genesis 9:9-17.

St. Francis of Assisi or St. Philip Neri treated animals."[43] The Catechism continues on to state that it is therefore "contrary to human dignity to cause animals to suffer or die needlessly," even as the Church cautions against "direct[ing] to them the affection due only to persons."[44] This emphatic statement has an explicitly scriptural basis, for "the first commandment enjoins us to love God above everything and all creatures for him and because of him."[45]

The above mandate, understood in its full meaning and richness, calls into question any interpretation which claims that the Catechism allows for nonhuman creatures to be legitimately or unconditionally used for food, clothing, and medical and scientific experimentation, at the whim of their human stewards.[46] Additionally, and necessarily, it should spur a prayerful reexamination of not only our individual morality, but the broader economic and social structures which we create and in which we participate — structures which too often have been founded upon the commodification and exploitation for profit of human and nonhuman creation alike. For the Catechism also states that "to love is to will the good of another," even at the expense of one's own desires.[47] I would argue, then, that any exploitative use of nonhuman creation, particularly sentient creation, which is motivated by matters of taste, desire, or mere convenience rather than actual need cannot be said to be based in such love, and thus is in contradiction to God's commandments.[48] This is especially true given that "God did not make death, and he does not delight in the death of the living"; to borrow Christ's words, "it is not the will of your Father in heaven that one of these little ones should be lost."[49] The Catechism also warns that "God alone is the Lord of life from its beginning

---

43. CCC 2416. St. Francis is popularly known for preaching the gospel to nonhuman creatures, exhorting "all birds, all animals, all reptiles, and also insensible creatures, to praise and love the creator" (Thomas of Celano, I Celano XXI); St. Philip Neri is believed to have been a vegetarian, out of concern for animals rather than as a form of religious self-mortification, and to have insisted that small animals such as birds, mice, and flies be freed from capture rather than allowing them to be killed.
44. CCC 2418.
45. CCC 2093; cf. Deut 6:4-5, Mt 22:36-40.
46. CCC 2417. The only caveat presented here is that such experimentation must remain "within reasonable limits," with no clarification as to what those limits might be. Another passage affirming that animals "may be used to serve the just satisfaction of man's needs" remains likewise unexplained (CCC 2457).
47. CCC 1766, quoting St. Thomas Aquinas, STh I-II, 26, 4, corp. art.
48. Cf. CCC 2541, which notes that "the God of the promises always warned man against seduction by what from the beginning has seemed 'good for food.'"
49. Wisdom 1:13, Matthew 18:14.

to its end," and that "we are stewards, not owners of the life God has entrusted to us. *It is not ours to dispose of.*"[50]

The Catholic faithful should seek to be continually mindful of this edict, not only in the interest of their own temporal well-being, in that of the whole of creation, and because of their moral responsibility toward the myriad "generations to come," but because of the aforementioned promise of the new and total resurrection of creation.[51] "God created everything for man, but man in turn was created to serve and love God and to offer all creation back to him"; according to the parables of Christ, the Creator's gifts should be offered back to the Creator not in the same number or state as they were bestowed, and certainly not in worse condition, but multiplied, perfected, insofar as humankind is able.[52]

This mission, while not to be underestimated, should be understood as a gift in itself rather than a cause for anxiety, for "the sign of man's *familiarity* with God is that God places him in the garden. There he lives 'to till it and keep it,' [in a] collaboration of man and woman with God in perfecting the visible creation."[53] Humankind is intrinsically called to live "in friendship with his Creator and in harmony with himself and with the creation around him," "to share in [God's] providence toward other creatures" — a vocation to which God never ceases to invite us.

5.6. Conclusion

By the above standards it is clear that humankind "has broken the right order that should reign within himself as well as between himself and other men and all creatures," and therefore acted in contradiction to God's loving will.[54] The Catechism, however, offers a hopeful outlook, testifying that "the order of creation persists, though seriously disturbed. To heal the wounds of sin, man and woman need the help of the grace that God in his infinite mercy never refuses them."[55] This healing reconciliation with nonhuman creation is a journey that will require prayer, humility, and dialogue, as well as an awareness of the grace which God has already shared with us through the continuous revelation of all of creation and the promise of its redemption — of our redemption. Meanwhile, our Mother Church promises to accompany us and all her children in this

---

50. CCC 2258, 2280 (emphasis added).
51. CCC 2456.
52. CCC 358.
53. CCC 378 (emphasis added).
54. CCC 401, quoting *GS* 13.
55. CCC 1608.

task: "until everything is subject to him" who is eternal, "until there be realized new heavens and a new earth in which justice dwells, the pilgrim Church, in her sacraments and institutions, which belong to this present age, carries the mark of this world which will pass, and she herself takes her place among the creatures which groan and travail yet and await the revelation of the sons of God."[56]

Ours is a liberative project which will necessarily take diverse forms in different cultural, social, and religious contexts, but which, with an increasingly rigorous theological framework, can hopefully take shape as a unified Christian effort toward right relationship with God and with all of creation, "on earth as it is in heaven."[57]

---

56. CCC 671, quoting *LG* 48.
57. Matthew 6:10.

CHAPTER 6

WOMEN WEAVER-OF-WORLDS
EARTH-BASED MYTHOPOESIS IN RESTORATIVE
INDIGENOUS NARRATIVES

Yuria Celidwen

Cantsil[1]

Cantsil, amid the buzzing earth
hummingbirds of wonder glow|
licking within your brilliant flow
into the moisture of your core

Cantsil, whispers in the water
carry upon the secrets waves
the pulsing tale that echo tells
sounding in the womb of caves

Cantsil, in the crackling fire
burning honey, sweetened glory
combs of hundred thousand bees
light the sparks of lightning stories

Cantsil, petrichor in the air
wakes the smell of incense flair
blessed smoke of spirits flowing
vibrant birds in prayer blowing

Cantsil, the eternal cosmic space
heal our wounds with patient light
eased by time and sacred humming
vastness... opens in the heart!

I grew up in *El Paraíso*, the second valley of Ocosingo, Chiapas, Mexico. For seven generations, this was the family ranch until it was expropriated in the civil uprising of 1994. Our home was in the *yashal te 'tiquil k'inal* or "forest in the clouds". It was the greenest, most fertile land in the highlands. It was prime land for tending maize, coffee beans, and dreams. Evening rituals with my grandparents were full of moonlight and stories. The whole space took an aroma of roasted sunset and the taste of cornbread.

---

1. *Cantsil,* "my darling", is an endearing epithet used in direct address to a loved one in the Indigenous Tseltal language of the highlands of my motherland in Chiapas.

Entire worlds sprouted from my grandma's words. As a medicine woman, she knew the time of the trees, the voice of the wind, the whims of seasons' breaks, the gossip of the birds. She taught me to dig my roots into the boundless earth, where lays the medicine for the sorrows of the world. She used to say that the secret to happiness is to love. Indeed, she filled my childhood with love. She opened me up through her expansive and fluid language of the heart, the language of the earth. Since then, every night enthralled in a lucid quest, I sense my verges break into the soil beneath my feet and above to reach the stars. In that space, I am no more. There is only the vastness of the world, and at its core are our stories.

Our Stories

Cantsil, from the stories we hear
and that we tell
we weave our world.
From the intention of the star
to the chills of wind
and the lightning's wrath,
we weave our land
with stories.

Cantsil, nourished by
and bound with others
we become the world
through stories.

This chapter investigates the process of *mythopoesis*—the act of creating stories—as an Indigenous way of resistance. It engages with Indigenous storytelling as a voice against social, political, and economic oppression. Specifically, I refer to the action of creating contemporary cosmogonies or stories of origin as a process that I find crucial to reclaim, preserve, and transmit the Indigenous identity. Although cosmogonies in the classical sense imply narratives that tell how the world and culture are created, they are also essential paths to understand how human perception and identity are generated.

This tapestry of ideas is weaved with the threads of the Indigenous wisdom ways of narrative and the Western humanities and social sciences of mythology and psychology (depth, personality, and social). I bridge these two ways of knowing through three core narratives: personal, communal, and cultural stories.

In the Indigenous perspective, personal narratives revolve around an individual's experience of the world, the challenges, struggles, and development of a sense of responsibility to the community. These stories enhance a sense of belonging. In reality, personal narratives are never solely about the individual's identity, but always in relation to the environment.

Communal narratives are sources of moral transmission. They emphasize the ethical aspects of social behavior that enhance values and transmit them through generations. They intend to instruct on the ways to cultivate harmonious relationships. Cultural narratives are generally mythic stories that involve a suspended sense of time and space. They are foundational stories. These are stories that connect the people with the land and the ancestors that inhabited it. Naturally, these narratives evoke a sense of reverence. These sacred narratives are transmitted through the family line and by initiation.

These three different kinds of narratives—personal, communal, and cultural—elicit insightful self-awareness and have pedagogical content. They are vessels to establish a sense of purpose, belonging, and responsibility to self, community, and environment. Therefore, it is possible to say that Indigenous narratives are ethical and ecological narratives.

Other Indigenous relatives have elaborated on the classification of stories. Marlene Castellano (Mohawk) says stories are personal, orally transmitted, experiential, and holistic.[2] Maggie Kovach (Cree) mentions two kinds of narratives: personal-anecdotal and mythical-cultural.[3] Elder Tom McCallum (Cree) elaborates that mythical stories are considered a revelation, believed to have been given by spirits; therefore, they are considered sacred; thus, they should never be changed when orally transmitted.[4] Shane Wilson (Opaskwayak) suggests yet another kind of story, the legend.[5] Agreeing with Kovach, McCallum, and Wilson, Judy Iseke (Métis) adds that personal stories are pedagogical, frequently used as resources for individual counseling.[6] Gregory Cajete (Tewa) pointedly says: "The human mind as an extension of nature and as Creator of story becomes the fertile ground where myth, science, and our human perception of reality meet."[7]

---

2. Castellano, M. B. "Updating Aboriginal Traditions of Knowledge." In G. J. S. Dei, B. L. Hall, and D. G. Rosenburg (eds), *Indigenous Knowledges in Global Contexts* (Toronto: University of Toronto Press, 2000).

3. Kovach, M. *Indigenous Methodologies: Characteristics, Conversations, and Contexts* (Toronto: University of Toronto Press, 2009).

4. Iseke, J., and Brennus, B. "Learning life lessons from Indigenous storytelling with Tom McCallum." In G. J. S. Dei (ed.), *Indigenous Philosophies and Critical Education* (New York: Peter Lang. 2011), 245-261.

5. Wilson, S. *Research is Ceremony: Indigenous Research Methods* (Halifax, NS: Fernwood, 2008).

6. Iseke, J. "Indigenous Storytelling as Research." *International Review of Qualitative Research*, vol. 6, no. 4, 2013, 559-577.

7. Cajete, G. *Native Science: Natural Laws of Interdependence* (Santa Fe, NM: Clear Light Publishers, 2000) 13.

One way the West studies narratives is through mythology. This interdisciplinary and multicultural field analyzes the social expressions of identity that manifest in the stories that establish a sense of identity of an individual to a group. Mythology delves into the human experience by the way of inquiry into the human imagination. It aims to explore and understand the ways of association and expression of the symbolic images generated by the mind. Mythical narratives mirror the mind's paradoxical qualities. As such, these narratives tend to be interpretative, ambiguous, and manifest the transformative ways of metaphor. It is through these images that we make sense of the complexity of the natural cycles and human societies.

In mythology, a narrative can be expressed as a story, ritual, religious belief, literature, and art. Since narratives excite the imagination, they engender a powerful impulse for creation. Through the study of story, it is possible to attain a granular and dynamic comprehension within and between cultures, precisely because narratives aim to situate the individual within the society and the world.

The role of narratives in human cognition, emotion, and behavior has been studied by western psychology through different viewpoints, among them are: depth, personality, and social psychology. Depth psychology affirms that myths are the creative expression of the human unconscious, imagination, inspiration, and customs, as they are presented in symbolic, archetypal form.[8] This approach affirms that knowledge is shared in metaphorical ways that guide moral imperatives, self-discovery, and growth. Thus, it offers a way of analyzing and interpreting these metaphors. It brings light to the social conditioning and psychological adaptations embedded in culture. This reflective and interpretative system examines the role of the unconscious in thought processes and behavior and its influence on the conscious self.[9]

Personality psychology constructs the different aspects of experience into an integrated sense of identity. From this perspective, the creation of a life narrative is an open-ended process of construction and deconstruction. It encompasses adaptation, revision, expansion, and transformation. Thus, life stories are inherently relative,[10] a view that is shared by

---

8. Jung, C. G. "Personality Types." In *The Collected Works of C.G. Jung: Complete Digital Edition.* CW 6 (Princeton: Princeton University Press, 2014).

9. Jung, C. G. "Archetypes and the Collective Unconscious." In *The Collected Works of C.G. Jung: Complete Digital Edition.* CW 9, part 1, (Princeton: Princeton University Press, 2014).

10. Josselson, R. "On becoming the narrator of one's own life." In A. Lieblich, D. P. McAdams, and R. Josselson (eds), *Healing Plots: The Narrative Basis of Psychotherapy* (Washington, DC: American Psychological Association, 2004), 111-127.

Indigenous communities. We emphasize our relational bond with everything that exists with the well-known motto "We Are All Related." Finally, social psychology explains how narrative styles and narrative formulations influence our well-being and our choices in life in terms of our relationships with the environment.[11]

The three different narratives—personal, communal, and cultural—are intertwined and in many ways mirror each other. From the micro to the macro they present similar patterns of adaptation and change. All of them are sources of meaning and purpose as containers of place, holders of the natural and cultural system that we inhabit. Personality psychologist Dan McAdams observes:

> If you want to know me, then you must know my story, for my story defines who I am. And if I want to know myself, to gain insight into the meaning of my own life, then I, too, must come to know my own story.[12]

Personal narratives are life stories that start in youth. They help us reflect on our place in a group, in the world, and the environment as we grow into adulthood. At this stage we develop relationships on our own, so we question what is our role. Rites of passage and coming of age stories are essential in the human developmental process. Constant changes and rearrangements of the personal story unfold as people deal with life events, according to whatever goals, determinations, and changes we experience.[13] The past is retold with modifications to a life story to better make sense of the emotional state of a person. Personal myths are acts of an integrated imagination.[14] McAdams continues:

> A personal myth is a story that we naturally construct to bring the different aspects of our self and scattered experiences into a purposeful whole. It has a beginning, middle, and end, defined according to the development of plot and character. Our personal myth is an act of imagination, integrating our remembered past, perceived present and anticipated future.[15]

According to depth psychology, the purpose of a life story is to generate psychological integration, which it calls "individuation". This is the process

---

11. Boyd, B. *On the origin of stories: evolution, cognition, and fiction* (New York: Harvard University Press, 2009).
12. McAdams, D. P. *Stories We Live By: Personal Myths and the Making of the Self* (New York: William Morrow and Company, Inc., 1993), 11.
13. McAdams, *Stories We Live By*.
14. McAdams, *Stories We Live By*, 12.
15. McAdams, D. P. *Unity and Purpose in Human Lives: The Emergence of Identity as a Life Story* (New York: Springer Publishing Co., 1992). McAdams, *Stories We Live By*. Parry, A. "Why We Tell Stories: The Narrative Construction of Reality". Transactional Analysis Journal, 27 (2) (1997), 118-127.

by which a person becomes an indivisible unity or whole.[16] It assumes that consciousness is the completion of the psychological individual. Rather than defining consciousness, depth psychology aims to symbolize it by an image of the conciliation of apparent opposites. In this metaphor, opposites come together in a dynamic harmonic adaptation. A sense of meaning is represented as the dialogue between the ego and the Self.[17] A personal story weaves the threads of life experiences put together by the individual within a cultural context.

The performative capacity of personal stories travels into community narratives in the way of politics. It is from narratives that a social and political sense arises and, with it, the accountability that defines our sense of ethics. Stuart Hall identifies this process as the poetics and the politics of representations.[18] Politics is informed by how identity produced by narratives connects to power, regulates conduct, shakes up subjectivities, and defines representation.[19] Poetics is the art of creating that involves the power of language for meaning-making. It weaves experiences and perceptions into a coherent developing story. So, we have that personal and communal stories are the grounds in which we construct and give meaning to our culture and institutions.

Te 'tiquil
(Our First Mother)

To know your story, *Cantsil*,
you must first know our people
because their kindness led to you.

You bow to the quetzal in the rainbow,
the jaguar in the star,
and those that were before you,
to whom you will return.
Know this, *Cantsil*,
trees and rivers you'll become.

Ask the *Te 'tiquil*, our First Mother,
the greenest mother forest,
for Her guidance.
She will speak to you, if you come in service.
Offer Her your heart.

---

16. Jung, C. G. "Conscious, Unconscious and Individuation." In *The Collected Works of C.G. Jung: Complete Digital Edition*. CW 9, part 1-IV (Princeton: Princeton University Press, 2014), parr. 490.

17. Edinger, E. F. *Anatomy of the Psyche: Alchemical Symbolism in Psychotherapy* (Chicago: Open Court, 1985), 218.

18. Hall, St. *Representation: Cultural Representations and Signifying Practices* (London: Sage, 1997), 6.

19. Hall. *Representation: Cultural Representations and Signifying Practices*, 6.

Indigenous ways of knowing aim for an adaptive harmony. Our wisdom traditions teach of a dynamic impulse, an indivisible life force—a unity—that holds all of existence together. We call it Spirit. Stories tell of the different ways in which Spirit manifests relationships. They guide us on the ways to cultivate successful interactions as adaptable, flexible members of our communities. Thus, personal and cultural stories develop an awareness of interconnected ethics based on Spirit. Life stories are intertwined with mythic creation stories because stories are pathways to an integrated reverential social order. Elder Joseph Marshall III (Lakota) explains:

> Stories entertain and inform, but, of course, this is only their obvious purpose. Tales and allegories told by Lakota elders very directly enable an entire culture to survive because they carry the culture within them. [...] By providing both knowledge and inspiration, stories continue to strengthen Lakota society and enable us to cope with our world and the times we live in. Stories of virtue are at the core of cultural renewal for each new generation. [...] Each story has a teaching essence enfolded in it.[20]

This system of integration is achieved through purpose and associations. I call this system *Ethics of Belonging*. It is the responsibility of caring for the community and the environment by its commitment to interrelationships for the greater good. Its aim is a state of adaptation that is based on a cohesive, relational unity. The awareness of the constant changes in balance helps to adapt to larger natural patterns of change. In other words, this ethos develops a social-ecological responsibility in a cooperative, cognitive, emotional, and social *state of being and becoming* in an active, dynamic process. Philosophically, it manifests an ontology of integration (body, heart, mind, and Spirit). Symbolically, it gives expression to the unfathomable web of relations apart from which nothing could exist. Metaphorically, it gives rise to a collective cosmic Spirit in a boundless system of becoming.

For Indigenous cultures, the perception of self and world is preserved and transmitted through storytelling. Narratives have been the preferred means to share our cosmovision and traditional wisdom.[21] Storytelling

---

20. Marshall III, J. M. *The Lakota Way: Stories and Lessons for Living* (New York: Penguin Compass, 2002), i-xiv.

21. See for example Cajete, G. "American Indian Epistemologies." *New Directions for Student Services*, 109, 2005, 69-78. Denzin, N. K., and Lincoln, Y. S. (eds). *The Sage Handbook of Qualitative Research* (Fifth Edition. Thousand Oaks, CA: Sage Publ., 2017). Also see the work of Cree scholar Kovach, M. "Doing Indigenous Methodologies. A Letter to a Research Class." In Denzin and Lincoln (eds), *The Sage Handbook*, 214-234. And Smith, L. T. *Decolonizing Methodologies: Research and Indigenous Peoples* (Second Edition. London: Zed Books, 2013).

has become a method in itself in the research of Indigenous epistemologies.[22] This has been adopted as an alternative methodology in recent initiatives for social and environmental justice.[23] Stories are at the core of the repositioning of Native pedagogies, science, philosophy, and spirituality.[24] Judy Iseke (Métis) explains:

> Story is a practice in Indigenous cultures that sustains communities, validates experiences and epistemologies, expresses experiences of Indigenous peoples, and nurtures relationships and the sharing of knowledge. [...] Elders' stories inform discussions of (a) storytelling types (mythical, personal, and sacred), (b) storytelling as pedagogical tools for learning about life, (c) storytelling as witnessing and remembering, and (d) sharing stories of spirituality as sources of strength.[25]

Culturally, the stories that elicit a most powerful sense of belonging and purpose are cosmogonies (*kosmos*: order, *genesis*: origin). They are the narrative seeds of culture and the world. Cosmogonic myths "set forth a tone and style for the modes of perception, the organizing principles, and provide the basis for all creative activities in the cultural life."[26] They are narratives of how culture comes to be.[27]

---

22. Archibald, J. A. *Indigenous Storywork: Educating the Heart, Mind, Body, and Spirit* (Vancouver: UBC Press, 2008). Kovach, M. *Indigenous Methodologies: Characteristics, Conversations, and Contexts*. Iseke, J. "Indigenous Storytelling as Research.", 559-577.

23. In terms of storytelling as a vehicle for social justice see Caxaj, C. S. "Indigenous Storytelling and Participatory Action Research: Allies Toward Decolonization? Reflections From the Peoples' International Health Tribunal." *Global Qualitative Nursing Research,* vol. 2, 2015. For Indigenous participation for social justice and political protection see Kraft, S. E., and Johnson, G. "Protective Occupation, Emergent Networks, Rituals of Solidarity: Comparing Alta (Sápmi), Mauna Kea (Hawaii), and Standing Rock (North Dakota)." In L. Hogbood and W. Bauman (eds). *The Bloomsbury Handbook of Religion and Nature* (London – New York: Bloomsbury, 2018). For the power of stories for environmental and conservation initiatives see Datta, R. "Traditional Storytelling: An Effective Indigenous Research Methodology and Its Implications for Environmental Research." *AlterNative: An International Journal of Indigenous Peoples*, vol. 14, no. 1, Mar. 2018, 35-44. Fernández-Llamazares, Á., and Cabeza, M. "Rediscovering the Potential of Indigenous Storytelling for Conservation Practice." In *Conservation Letters*, 11: e12398. doi:10.1111/conl.12398).

24. For storytelling as therapeutic method for well-being see Hodge, F. S., Pasqua, A., Marquez, C. A., and Geishirt-Cantrell, B. "Utilizing Traditional Storytelling to Promote Wellness in American Indian Communities." *Journal of Transcultural Nursing*, 13, no. 1, 2002, 6-11.

25. See her influential work on storytelling as a methodology for research in Iseke, J. "Indigenous Storytelling as Research.", 559-577.

26. Long, Ch. H. "Cosmogony." In L. Jones (ed.). *Encyclopedia of Religion. Vol. 3* (Second Edition. London: Macmillan, 2005), 1985-1991.

27. Leeming, D. A. "Introduction." In *Creation Myths of the World: An Encyclopedia*, vol. 1: Parts I-II (Second Edition. Gale Virtual Reference Library. ABC-CLIO, 2010), xvii-xx. http://link.galegroup.com/apps/doc/CX2440800008/GVRL?u=carp39441&sid=GVRL&xid=1f8a9048. Accessed 4 Oct., 2018.

Cosmogonies help to achieve an understanding of a cultural environment, along with the social conventions construed around it. These origin stories are windows to subjective and collective experiences. Everyday interactions are made of these narratives. As noted earlier, stories are the vessels where our identities are created. Hence, cultures base their understanding of group-identity both on personal narratives and cosmogonies. The nature of Indigenous knowledge is dynamic. Through oral narrative, ethical codes and prosocial behaviors are passed through generations. They are tools for moral learning.[28] Marlene Castellano (Mohawk) clarifies:

> [Storytelling is a way] of engaging with reality rather than an artifact surviving from the past. Indigenous knowledge is specific to place and rooted in history, described in some traditions as reaching back seven generations and looking forward seven generations. It is holistic, involving body, mind, feelings and spirit. It emerges in dialogue and is acquired over time. Indigenous knowledge is expressed in symbols, arts, ceremonial and everyday practices, narratives, and (especially) relationships. A recurring theme in Indigenous knowledge of diverse peoples is relationship with the land as a living entity that reveals the way of right living.[29]

Cosmogonies explicitly generate a sense of balance within the natural environment. We celebrate how humans are weaved into nature. Our Indigenous traditional wisdom is based on emergence stories that emphasize the human relational capacity, dependence, and belonging to nature.[30] Hence, self-awareness is only as profound as our relationship to the earth.

As vessels of spirit, cosmogonies awaken a sense of urgency for environmental action. They follow the impulse to integrate with the natural environment, to protect it, and regenerate it. As a source of encouragement,

---

28. Castellano, M. B. "Updating Aboriginal traditions of knowledge." In Dei, Hall, and Rosenburg (eds), *Indigenous Knowledges in Global Contexts*.

29. Castellano, M. B. "Indigenous Research." In L.M. Given (ed.). *The Sage Encyclopedia of Qualitative Research Methods* (Thousand Oaks, CA: SAGE publications, 2008), 425.

30. See Kawagley, A. O., and Barnhardt, R. "Education Indigenous to Place: Western Science Meets Native Reality." In G. A. Smith and D. R. Williams (eds). *Ecological Education in Action: On Weaving Education, Culture, and the Environment* (Albany, NY: SUNY Press, 1999), 117-140. And the research on Indigenous education in Canadian case studies by H. J. Michell in Cree communities in Canada, especially "*Nehithawak* of Reindeer Lake, Canada: Worldview, Epistemology and Relationships with the Natural World." *Australian Journal of Indigenous Education*, 2005, 33-43. And their doctoral dissertation *Nihithewak Ithiniwak, Nihithewatisiwin and Science Education: An Exploratory Narrative Study Examining Indigenous-based Science Education in K-12 Classrooms from the Perspectives of Teachers in Woodlands Cree Community Contexts* (University of Regina, SK, Canada, 2007). And Battiste, M. "Maintaining Aboriginal Identity, Language, and Culture in Modern Society." In M. Battiste (ed.), *Reclaiming Indigenous Voice and Vision* (Vancouver: UBC Press, 2000), 192-208. And *Indigenous Knowledge and Pedagogy in First Nations Education: A Literature Review with Recommendations* (National Working Group on Education and the Minister of Indian Affairs, Indian and Northern Affairs Canada (INAC), 2002).

empowerment, and persistence cosmogonies are earth stories. Vine Deloria Jr. (Sioux) strongly suggests:

> The future of humankind lies waiting for those who will come to understand their lives and take up their responsibilities to all living things. Who will listen to the trees, the animals and birds, the voices of the places of the land? As the long forgotten peoples of the respective continents rise and begin to reclaim their ancient heritage, they will discover the meaning of the lands of their ancestors.[31]

Earth-based Indigenous narratives elicit collaborative social qualities. They focus on conservation efforts, sustainability, and biodiversity from their emphasis on the role of animals in the generation of order.[32] These narratives elicit awareness of the interdependence of beings and the role of each in the generation of balance. These earth stories engage humans with the environment through a rewilding process.

How the Earth Was Made

It is said, *Cantsil*, that Our *Muk'-ul Nan*[33]
created Our *Ajaw Choj*[34] to look after the Earth,
the waters, and all the living beings.
She made It first of clay and left it in a sacred cave.
But It felt too soft and grew tired of the dark,
so Our *Muk'-ul Nan* took it to the Sun.
But It got too hard and grew tired of the light,
so Our *Muk'-ul Nan* took a lock from her long black hair
and weaved a web of darkness and of day,
and made the Earth.
She took the *Ajaw Choj* and placed it there,
and left the darkness, sun, and stars forever on Its pelt.
That's how the Earth was made,
and why Our *Ajaw Choj* roams at night and day
in mountains, caves, and lakes.

Purpose, meaning, and belonging are weaved in cultural stories. All that exists has a place and purpose, and it is interrelated. This is a shared foundational perspective to the cosmovision of Indigenous peoples around the globe. Cajete celebrates it as a dynamic reflection of the Indigenous way of knowing:

> Cosmology is the contextual foundation for philosophy, a grand guiding story, by nature speculative, in that it tries to explain the universe, its origin, characteristics, and essential nature. A cosmology gives rise to philosophy,

---

31. Deloria Jr., V. *God Is Red: a Native View of Religion. 30th Anniversary Edition* (Third Edition. Wheat Ridge, CO: Fulcrum Publishing, 2003), 295.
32. Leeming, D. A. *Creation Myths of the World: An Encyclopedia. Vol. 1: Parts I-II* (Second Edition. Santa Barbara, CA: ABC-CLIO, 2010), 24-29.
33. Great Mother.
34. Jaguar God.

values, and action, which in turn form the foundation of a society's guiding institutions.[35]

Giving birth to the world is a constant metaphor in origin stories.[36] Indigenous cosmogonies recognize women's creativity and our ability for establishing community by giving the feminine divine the principal role in the creation, generation, and order of the world. By attaching to land and culture women build the strength, resilience, and preservation of a community's vitality and wellbeing. Women are the keepers of cultural identity as much as the traditional caretakers of the natural environment.[37]

Indigenous women's reality is very different from the mythic ideal. Women are discriminated against by oppressive systems that do not recognize the feminine creative and regenerative power. We are frequently denied rights and opportunities in favor of political and economic policies. Indigenous girls and women are much more vulnerable to extreme forms of violence, as our vulnerability includes not only gender but also race and ethnicity. It is known that violence against women is a cultural direct product of colonization:

> For indigenous women gender-based violence is shaped not only by gender discrimination within indigenous and non-indigenous arenas, but by a context of ongoing colonization, militarism, racism and social exclusion, and poverty inducing economic and 'development' policies. These phenomena are interactive and mutually reinforcing, as are the various aspects of identity that shape women's experience of violence, and their strategies of resistance.[38]

The marginalization of Indigenous women is extreme. Of all ethnic groups, Indigenous women have the least access to health, education, housing, dignified work, and safety from crime.[39] Under these conditions, the reality is that long-term intergenerational psychological trauma will remain for generations. So a way to counteract and re-empower women's place as creators of community and culture is through stories. Research suggests that indeed storytelling and journaling are effective ways to deal

---

35. Cajete. *Native Science: Natural Laws of Interdependence.*
36. Idem, 29.
37. Capobianco, L. *Community Safety and Indigenous Peoples: Sharing Knowledge, Insights and Action* (Montreal: International Centre for the Prevention of Crime, 2010), 13.
38. *Mairin Iwanka Raya—New Beginnings—Indigenous Women Stand against Violence.* FIMI Companion Report to the UN Secretary General's Study on Violence against Women. Executive Summary, 6.
39. UNDP. *Social Justice? The Challenge of Intersecting Inequalities* (New York: United Nations, 2010). And Hall, G. H. and Patrinos, H. A. *Indigenous Peoples, Poverty and Development* (New York: Cambridge University Press, 2012).

with trauma.[40] These practices are also a way to demand a reckoning of the long-standing systems of abuse. But voices are still absent from the conversation. Proma Tagore warns:

> The writings and testimonies of women of color, Indigenous women, and Third World women not only find themselves regularly absent from Western liberal and/or colonial traditions of literature but also from the canons of white Western feminist thought and criticism as well as from the mainstream scholarship on race and postcoloniality, which has typically failed to address many of the details around the complex, inextricable, and intimate relations between gender and colonization.[41]

It continues to this day that the voices of Indigenous peoples and Indigenous women, in particular, lack access to platforms of influence in the decision-making process that affect us and our communities. Therefore, stories become the way to resist the systems of subjugation. Cultural narratives become the semiotic vessels to redefine our culture. Women create new cosmogonies as a way to develop a new identity within a new worldview. We use stories as sources of freedom and as agents of power:

> While indigenous forms of knowledge drawn from experience traditionally have been passed on for purposes of understanding nature and ways of being in the world, this knowledge can also be understood as articulating a cosmology that contradicts forms of domination such as patriarchy, racism, militarism, scientific and economic colonialism, and imperialism.[42]

Stories become how women establish a new identity, one that is empowered and resilient. Stories become pathways to justice.[43] Therefore, the regained sense of identity that comes from stories offers a new status and a repositioning of Indigenous women and culture in the global scope. The creative aspect of narratives offers an encouraging tool to deconstruct oppression. A shift to an identity of empowerment challenges the dominant culture of oppression and establishes narratives based on common values.

It is by strengthening the collective identity that we challenge the social structures of domination. Stories become an act of resistance to the establishment of colonial storylines. The reestablishment of personal, communal, and cultural stories offers the possibility for recovering strength, com-

---

40. Pennebaker, J. *Writing to Heal: A Guided Journal for Recovering from Trauma & Emotional Upheaval* (Oakland, CA: New Harbinger Publications, Inc., 2004).

41. Tagore P., *Shapes of Silence: Writing by Women of Colour and the Politics of Testimony* (Kingston, ON: McGill-Queen's Press, 2009), 141.

42. Dei, Hall, and Rosenberg (eds), *Indigenous Knowledges in Global Contexts: Multiple Readings of Our World*, 87.

43. Deloria Jr., V. *Custer Died for Your Sins: An Indian Manifesto* (Norman, OK: University of Oklahoma Press, 1969).

munity, solidarity, and hope. These are the seeds of consciousness that we choose to sow. These are the threads we weave for a society of courage, dignity, inclusiveness, and freedom.

C'a'teshil Q'uinal
(Fertile Ground)

To know the wind is to know your words, *Cantsil*.
It is to know you are made of silence and of songs
that from the kindest words the healing comes
of tempests and of foes.

To know the rivers is to know your forms, *Cantsil*.
It is to know you are made of fish and waves,
that day and night they come and go
in constant restless games.

To know the sky is to know your mind, *Cantsil*.
It is to know you are made of suns and stars
that in the darkness dreams
give tender moonlight gleams.

To know the earth is to know your heart, *Cantsil*.
It is to know you are made of seeds and soil
that within your web of roots bliss flows
to nourish life, to rest in love!

II

RITUAL

CHAPTER 7

PICTURING PARADISE: PERUVIAN WOMEN'S ART AND A "NEW CREATION"

Rebecca Berru Davis

7.1.

In his 2015 encyclical *Laudato Si'*, Pope Francis states, "If we are truly concerned to develop an ecology, capable of remedying the damage we have done, no branch of the sciences and no form of wisdom can be left out, and that includes religion and the language particular to it."[1] Clearly, the insights that emerge from science, religion and the theological communities provide deeper understandings of our common home. However, it is Francis' assertion that "no form of wisdom should be left out" that caught my attention. I believe, as many in this volume do, that it is the experience of women, and in particular those who know the global inequities of environmental degradation and social decay first hand, that have something significant to contribute to the conversation about healing the earth. I further believe, as do others, that it is necessary that we widen the

---

1. *Laudato Si'*, 63. See Francis. "Laudato Si'. On Care for Our Home." 25 May, 2015 http://www.vatican.va/content/francesco/en/encyclicals/documents/papa-francesco_20150524_enciclica-laudato-si.html. In the 2020 encyclical *Fratelli Tutti*, Pope Francis underscores the importance of including those on the peripheries of life "for they have another way of looking at things." See Francis. "Fratelli Tutti." The Holy See, 3 October, 2020, 215 http://www.vatican.va/content/francesco/en/encyclicals/documents/papa-francesco_20201003_enciclica-fratelli-tutti.html.

scope and consider the varied ways that wisdom is communicated.² One such way that is worth attending to is the arts. In this chapter, I describe a project that shines a light on Peruvian women and their *sabiduría* (wisdom) communicated through their art. Their convictions about environmental well-being and hope for achieving this goal are depicted in their fabric pictures, called *cuadros*. Their insights stitched into cloth are visual testimonies of their reality and the better world they envision. I assert that if we are to expand our understanding of ways to heal and renew the earth and establish a "New Creation," then we must pay attention to the wisdom of women, which is very evident in their artistic endeavors. Their art is an important contribution, not to be overlooked.³

My research as a third-generation Hispanic woman living in the United States, has centered on art, faith, and justice as a way to understand the spiritual and religious expressions of those located on the margins of society. This project embraces my interest in women and their creative activity evidenced in the home, the church and the community. Moreover, this is a project that links the global North and South. Over time, I have come to realize that, for me, this effort at activist research is a way to expand and deepen the dialogue about the environment through art. In this chapter, I begin by introducing the reader to the women artists of Pamplona Alta, their context and a particular project they undertook. I then turn to

---

2. Theologian María Clara Bingemer asserts that "women's historical testimonies and research on their lives and experiences and thoughts" need to be retrieved. She continues, "Rather than a theology of texts, a theology of testimonies can become a rich challenge for Latin American feminist theology in its attempt to rescue and empower women, who have been marginalized and muted by every social institution." In Maria Clara Bingemer, *Latin American Theology: Roots and Branches* (New York: Orbis Books, 2016), 83-84. Jon Sobrino maintains the conviction that if the Kingdom of God is Good News, its recipients, the poor, will fundamentally help in clarifying its content. In Jon Sobrino, *Jesus the Liberator: A Historical-Theological Reading of Jesus of Nazareth* (Maryknoll: Orbis, 1993), 79. Clodovis Boff states that what is needed is "a more emotive methodology that draws on images and feelings." Boff goes on to explain, "We have to value beauty, which signals the transcendence of the human, over necessity. This is very linked with ecology and with the feminine." In Mev Puleo, *The Struggle is One: Voices and Visions of Liberation* (Albany, New York: State University of New York Press, 1994), 154-156. Maria Pilar Aquino and Maria José Rosado-Nuñes, eds, *Feminist Intercultural Theology: Latina Explorations for a Just World* (New York: Orbis Books, 2007), 25. In her chapter, "Feminist Intercultural Theology: Toward a Shared Vision of Justice," María Pilar Aquino makes reference to Uma Narayan's assertion of the importance of opening up places so that the socially marginalized and powerless "may become active participants in articulating their interests, commitments and visions of justice." I would add, how important it is to consider alternative "spaces" such as art, where these interests and visions are expressed.

3. In *Laudato Si'*, Chapter 2 "The Gospel of Creation," Pope Francis establishes the importance of reclaiming our faith convictions to commit to the care of creation. He provides the biblical foundations, referencing the anthropological and individual side of participating in the renewal of creation.

the exhibition that emerged and how it has become an avenue for awareness and encounter between two distinct communities inspiring a sense of connection and solidarity between two hemispheres. I then return to the women's art underscoring the importance of imagination in envisioning and illuminating a "New Creation."

7.2. The Women Artists

> *I sensed we were nearing the periphery of the city of Lima and entering Pamplona Alta. From the combi window, I noticed the activity on the streets increasing — women and men carrying bundles and pushing carts laden with everything from fruit to recycled metals. The red and yellow micro taxis buzzed about like insects. Everything that emerged from the sandy, treeless hills was a monotone grey matching the overcast sky. Weary looking stalks of dusty green emerged here and there in the landscape; evidence that their effort to survive was not an easy task. Rebar rods extending from the tops of unfinished concrete buildings, reaching vertically into the sky, with the expectation and hope that further construction will resume. We made a turn onto the Pisto Nuevo where the billboard advertised the canned milk "Gloria" and I knew exactly where we were.*[4]
>
> Rebecca Berru Davis, Pamplona Alta

Nowhere in the world does one encounter more fully the stark realities of life on the margins and the economic challenges faced by humanity than in the shantytowns that encircle most large cities in the developing world. Whether in Asia, Africa or Latin America, increasing numbers of *desplazadas* (displaced persons) migrate to the cities in search of better opportunities. They reside in makeshift communities and struggle daily with the challenges of making do. Pamplona Alta is one such shantytown located on the southern edge of the capital city of Lima, Peru. These shantytowns are home to over 35 percent of the population of Lima.[5] Many of these residents migrated to Lima after their lives in the countryside were disrupted by the brutal terrorism of *Sendero Luminoso* (The Shining Path) that assaulted them throughout the last quarter of the twentieth century.[6]

---

4. Field notes, July 2008.
5. Lima's 2018 population is now estimated at 10,419,000 (Peru's total population is 32,726,000). Lima comprises 30 districts that are within the city and 13 outer districts. http://worldpopulationreview.com/world-cities/lima-population/. For more information about poverty in Lima, Peru, see https://borgenproject.org/top-10-facts-about-poverty-in-lima-peru/. In 2017 San Juan de Miraflores, one of the districts located in the Southern Cone of the city, population was calculated at 355,219. The shantytown of Pamplona Alta is located in the district of San Juan de Miraflores. https://www.citypopulation.de/php/peru-limametro.php?cityid=150133.
6. *Sendero Luminoso* (The Shining Path) was founded in 1970 by Abimael Guzmán, a philosophy teacher inspired by the writings of Peruvian Marxist, José Carlos Mariátegui. The Shining Path utilized guerrilla tactics in their attempt to overthrow the government

However, migration to the capital city continues. Environmental devastation caused by deforestation, illegal mining and the disruption of seasonal patterns of agriculture or fishing, brought about by climate change, leave fewer options for sustaining a livelihood in the countryside.[7] In search of new prospects, these internal migrants move to the peripheries of major cities in order to build new lives.

In these *pueblos jóvenes* (young towns) countless residents engage where countless residents engage in the informal job market as construction workers, taxi cab drivers, and street vendors. However, for many women, particularly those with children, working close to home is preferred. New mothers desire to nurse their babies, accompany their school-age children to and from school, and provide a hot meal, midday. Thus, procuring work in neighborhood art cooperatives is opportune in that it provides the flexibility needed to be available to their children, while earning modest incomes. Two such cooperatives in Pamplona Alta are *Manos Ancashinas* and *Compacto Humano*.[8] They are home to a group of approximately twenty Peruvian women artists who daily stitch together *cuadros* to sell in the tourist market locally and abroad. In their fabric pictures they create pictures of their past life on the coast, the countryside, the *altiplano* (high plains), or the jungle, places where they previously lived or know well (Fig. 1). These lush landscapes look nothing like the stark landscapes of their current homes in the shantytowns. The memories of their previous lives inform their art and their imagination inspires their vision of a verdant world where all life flourishes and life is celebrated.

---

during this period of terrorism. According to the final report assembled by the Peruvian Truth and Reconciliation Commission (2001-2003), it is estimated that the total number of Peruvians who died during this period was between 61,007 and 77,552, in addition to hundreds of thousands of displaced persons. See the United States Institute of Peace for the proceedings https://www.usip.org/publications/2001/07/truth-commission-peru-01.

For more information see *Lugar de la Memoria* (Place of Memory), a museum located in Lima, Peru and founded in 2015 whose aim is to provide a public space dedicated to the critical examination of the terrorism that took place and an effort to promote tolerance through education. https://lum.cultura.pe.

7. For more information about deforestation (some, the result of illegal logging); overgrazing of the slopes of the coast and mountains leading to soil erosion; desertification; air pollution in Lima; pollution of rivers and coastal waters from municipal and mining wastes, see CIA World Fact Book https://www.cia.gov/library/publications/the-world-factbook/geos/pe.html.

8. Throughout the shantytowns, a number of women's cooperatives exist with similar intentions to contribute in varied ways to their family's income. *Manos Ancashinas* (Hands from Ancash) made up of women primarily from the Department of Ancash and *Compacto Humano* (Human Compact) are two I have maintained a relationship with since 2006.

My first visit to Pamplona Alta in 2006 was as an art historian. My intention then was to survey, document, and contextualize the *cuadros*. However, in the process, I became increasingly interested in understanding how the women worked together to create art. These pictures not only served as a means to secure a livelihood, they were also an avenue of self-expression, and a tangible way to create visual narratives of the experiences that impact their lives.[9] As I sat around the tables, watching them piece together their fabric pictures, I was particularly struck by the contrast of their brilliant palette against the reality of the shantytown's very grey world (Fig. 2). It seemed that stitching these vibrant worlds onto fabric was a way for the women to imagine life different from their present realities. The questions emerged: How is it that beauty and hope persist even in the harshest conditions? And what better world for themselves and their families do these women envision? This is how the first project emerged. With special funds set aside to commission some art from them and in an effort to better understand how the women perceived their current lives and imagined their future, I proposed a project that I knew could be completed within a short time without disrupting the pattern of their daily operation. I asked the women to each create a small *cuadro* (10"x10") illustrating their hopes and dreams. I purposely framed the task to be as open-ended as possible and left it to the women to visually express their ideas. The resulting *cuadros* revealed very personal wishes as well as universal aspirations. There were dreams of permanent homes with roofs, improved employment opportunities for themselves or their family members, and places where their children could play without fear of violence or environmental contamination. Their utopian visions were as uniquely defined as anticipating the birth of another child, meeting the "man of their dreams," and as all-encompassing as living in a world where all persons, regardless of race or social status, lived together in peace. Their images reflected their resilience, imagination and hope-filled responses to the dire reality of their daily lives. For example, Isabel said:

> My dream is to live in a place where my children can live without worries or fear of violence. In this cuadro you can see there is no smog and pollution like

---

9. Ivone Gebara notes, "Resistance is also expressed in collective ways of working at various crafts, sharing responsibility for production and selling and also sharing the profits. This becomes more than a work initiative because these small organizations become cells for personal communal change. Within these cells women dare to talk about themselves, about social and political organization or disorganization. They have the freedom to reflect, agree or disagree and then their consciousness, lulled by the clatter of plates and pans, begins to awaken. It finds words and feels the urge to reorganize this world differently." Ivone Gebara, "Option for the Poor as an Option for the Poor Women," in *Concilium 194 Women, Work, and Poverty*, Elisabeth Schüssler-Fiorenza, ed. (Edinburgh: T&T Clark, 1987), 110-117.

> in the city. I would love to live in a forest where there are trees and a lagoon with a lot of ducks. Here my two children are playing soccer. My husband and I are harvesting fruit from the trees. We would be able to live together in a quieter place in tranquility. (Fig. 3)

Enma described her world:

> In this garden of many flowers, my husband and I are embracing as we await the arrival of our second baby. Here you can see my little daughter playing with a ball. My brother Javier, who I love like a son, because I have known him since he was a baby, is swimming in the river with an inner *tube*. Notice the butterflies fluttering about and my well-built two-story house. This is my dream. (Fig. 4)

And Lucy explained,

> This cuadro depicts a dream that may only come true if there is a world without wars. This would be a world like Paradise. My dream is to have people of different classes and different races live together. In this cuadro there are people of all colors and animals of all kinds. If there weren't wars, racism, and violence we could live together with people from different countries. We would be able to live together with our animals, because animals represent everything that is beautiful in the world. The tree that I have made here represents heaven on earth. We are all together and sharing. (Fig. 5)

Throughout this initial project, I was (and continue to be), very conscious of my position as outsider and the prickly issues related to ethnography, power, subjectivity and voice. Acknowledging the "complexities, confusions, and unexpected turns" embedded in this work, this methodology begins with the women's experience, as the best way to get at meaning, and bringing to light the women's sensibilities, understandings and perceptions.[10]

In this first visit, my initial concerns about interfering with their work and the value of the project were put to rest by Julia, one of the women who shared with me and with the group, "Thank you for this opportunity. I had never thought of sharing my dreams with anyone, because no one ever asked us about our dreams." The project thus served to make manifest what was otherwise imperceptible, as well as contributed to the women's sense of self-awareness. I carried Julia's words with me when I left

---

10. Ethnographer and author, Karen McCarthy Brown makes explicit the challenges and ambiguities of ethnography. She says, "Ethnographic research is a social art form and therefore subject to all the complexities and confusions (and unexpected turns) of human relationships in general. In research sites, as well as every other life arena, narratives are contextual and so slippery, practices are easily misapprehended — sometimes with intention — and shared meaning is always approximate," 133. In "Writing about 'The Other' Revisited." In *Personal Knowledge and Beyond: Reshaping the Ethnography of Religion*, James V. Spickard, et al., eds (New York: New York University Press, 2002).

Pamplona Alta that year, struck by the way in which their art served to make manifest and affirm the women's visions for a better world. Their dreams, visually constructed with their hands, depict a different social order. The transformation of a society begins with imagination and the capacity to envision a better future. For these women, art helps to make tangible their implicit hopes and dreams.

7.3. Picturing Paradise: The Exhibit

For fifteen years, I have remained committed and accountable to the women and to this project. I return to Pamplona Alta almost annually, maintaining communication with the women, noting their growing children, and with them celebrating the arrival of new grandchildren. When in Peru, I continue to accompany the women on the ground, in their homes, and at their tables.[11] In the process I become not merely "researcher-observer," but "witness" to their challenges and joys.[12] Moreover, I have become interlocutor and advocate. Shortly after the completion of the first project, their hopes and dreams and other works of art, along with the women's photos, words, and testimonies were assembled into an exhibit called *Picturing Paradise*. This continues to be a collaborative endeavor as we have determined that juxtaposing their brightly stitched visual narratives with their photos and the contextual photos of the shantytowns is most effective. Over the past fifteen years this exhibition has circulated throughout the United States and abroad (twice in Lima) as a way to draw attention to the lives of these women, the challenges they endure, and the beauty that persists despite the

---

11. Theologian Ada María Isasi-Díaz, asserts, "The purpose in doing "translations" for *mujerista* theology is to discover the themes that are important rom the women, the ones about which they feel the strongest, which move them, which motivate them. In *mujerista* theology we refer to these themes as generative words. They emerge from the world of Hispanic Women and express the situations they have to grapple with as well as their understanding of themselves in those situations. These generative words of themes are not only those "with existential meaning, and, therefore, with greatest emotional content, but they are also typical of the people" (70). In Ada María Isasi-Díaz, *En La Lucha: Elaborating a Mujerista Theology* (Minneapolis: Fortress Press, 1993). In Chapter 3, Isasi-Díaz outlines "ethnomethodology," a strategy for understanding and the procedures she employs in shaping a *mujerista* theology (62-80). For this work, I draw on her methodology employing an approach that interlaces art, cultural and gender studies and theology focused on what Ada María Isasi-Díaz named, *lo cotidiano*, everyday life.

12. I thank Dr. Joanne Doi, M.M. for this insight. Doi develops this notion of "witness" in a theological sense as opposed to participant/observer in her dissertation, *Bridge to Compassion: Theological Pilgrimage to Tule Lake and Manzanar* (Unpublished Dissertation: Graduate Theological Union, Berkeley, CA, 2007), 23-27.

harsh condition of their lives.[13] Notably, the exhibit is a space for women who are virtually invisible to the world, to speak about their current realities and the hopes they hold for their families and all creation. In addition to the compelling works of art, a brief description of the piece in the artist's own words underscores the woman's unique voice. Accompanying each piece, a photograph of the woman at work or with her children draws the viewer into a personal encounter with each artist.

The exhibition project continues to serve a purpose as it underscores that art is a powerful and effective means of communication and an expression of wisdom not to be dismissed. Moreover, the artistic "authority" and postures for reflection ascribed by gallery and museum spaces prompt engagement from viewers. The women's dreams about a healthy and verdant world resonate with the shared aspirations of their audience. Thus, despite differences in culture, class, or geographic distance, there is a felt connection. In the process, additional works of art are sold, and the project helps to support the women and their families.

As *Picturing Paradise* travels to various venues, I become aware that the exhibition serves another important purpose as it initiates an "encounter." While the stories and images may resonate with their viewers, they are also effective prompts to move beyond a culture of indifference and toward a "culture of encounter" — to take that decisive step toward relationship, solidarity, and justice.[14] Thus, the representation and reception of the work is an important function and a crucial link between two distinct hemispheric communities — the global North and South — in ways that "move the human heart."[15]

7.4. Paradise as a "New Creation"

Recently, I spent time in Pamplona Alta with the women to revisit with each of them the hopes and dreams they identified in 2006. For some, their dreams had been realized. Vero had met the "man of her dreams."

---

13. Since 2006, *Picturing Paradise* has been exhibited in over thirty university galleries and museums throughout the United States, twice in Lima (2009 and 2016) and in Cochabamba, Bolivia (2012) and Barcelona, Spain (2012 and 2014).

14. Pope Francis, on a regular basis has spoken of a "Culture of Encounter" as a goal for human society. A society that espouses a Culture of Encounter instead of exclusion, facilitates right relationships among humans and involves a spirituality that emphasizes a relationship with God, who first encounters us in love, and thus moves us toward solidarity with one another. See *Joy of the Gospel* (2013). For more on "Encounter" see Pope Francis' "First Pentecost Homily," Vatican City, May 19, 2013.

15. Alejandro García-Rivera, *A Wounded Innocence: Sketches for a Theology of Art* (Collegeville, MN: The Liturgical Press, 2003), ix.

Enma had a second child. But for others, steady employment for a husband was still out of reach or constructing a home for a growing family was far from accomplished.

Among the *cuadros* created in 2006 was one by Mirtha Aliaga. Mirtha's cuadro revealed her convictions and hopes for a safe and sustainable environment for her children, for Pamplona Alta, and for the world.

> *In this cuadro I depict a dream that I have always hoped for. In order to make the world better, we must preserve sea life so that the whales, dolphins, sea wolfs, and fish do not become extinct. We must protect and care for all the animals and plants that are running the danger of extinction.* (Fig. 6)

Mirtha's first hope and dream for her daughters was for a better environment. Almost ten years later, she noted the environment is worse and they now have to buy water. Mirtha explained, "What good is it to accumulate things? It does not make sense if you do not have an earth."[16] She described her new *cuadro* with these words:

> *This cuadro is a continuation of a dream that I hope will become reality. People are conscious when they hurt the seals that live on our planet. Many times, we encounter an animal badly wounded and we leave it to die on the beach without even realizing that we have hurt its habitat. It is for this reason that we must help these seals rather than doing nothing. We are the ones who have altered the sea and their way of life, fishing in places that are prohibited. It is for this reason that you see persons who are helping these seals that need healing by cleaning the environment since we are the ones who have altered the environment. God is in every person that expresses this love and care for the animals that we all need.*[17]

For Mirtha, her dream of a world where all creation can flourish had not been realized. Instead, Mirtha's new *cuadro* depicted her conviction of how we should treat our environment, including its most vulnerable creatures. Mirtha illuminates her concerns and advocates for ecological virtues, prompting response and solidarity from all who view her art.

Ivone Gebara notes that her ecofeminism "is pregnant with health: not health as we understood it in the past, but the health of a future that promises deeper communion between human beings and all other living things." She explains further, "My ecofeminism is shot through with the staunch conviction that beauty is important in healing people."[18] Gebara suggests that "[we] must return the poetic dimension of human life to theology, since the deepest meaning in the human being is expressed only through analogy;

---

16. Interview, Mirtha Aliaga, May 17, 2017.
17. Descriptive words that accompanied Mirtha's 2015 *cuadro*.
18. Ivone Gebara, *Longing for Running Water: Ecofeminism and Liberation* (Minneapolis: Fortress Press, 1999), vii.

mystery is voiced only in poetry, and what is gratuitous is expressed only through symbols."[19]

Picturing Paradise continues to be a work in progress. It reclaims art and beauty as a significant means of expressing the vital concerns of human existence and of communicating in ways deeply felt. It is a project that seeks to bring to light the lives and creativity of women as social poets living on the margins of society, counting their art and their perspectives as important contributions to our understanding of environmental well-being.

In this chapter I have presented a way in which art, its making, and its reception, holds potential for creative transformation. The project I have described highlights the resilience, ingenuity, and beauty that persist among these Peruvian women artists despite the dire challenges they face. It draws attention to their creativity and their insights while asserting that visual art created by ordinary people is a creative activity worthy of being examined. Conveyed in their art are the women's hopes and dreams that anticipate a "New Creation." They describe what this "New Creation" looks like and suggest how one participates in it. The resulting exhibition attempts to engage individuals and communities with the women and their lives, thus initiating an experience of encounter and solidarity. Indeed, the way in which the women picture "Paradise" makes evident God's abiding presence.

---

19. Ivone Gebara, 'Women Doing Theology in Latin America." in *Through Her Eyes: Women's Theology from Latin America*, Elsa Támez, ed. (Maryknoll: Orbis Books, 1989), 45.

Figure 1: Cosecha (Harvest)
Betty Rojas, *n.d.*
17" × 19"

Figure 2: Botanica (Flower Garden) contrasted with Pamplona Alta

Figure 3: Isabel Principe Liñan
Hope and Dreams, 2006

Figure 4: Enma Principe Liñan
Hopes and Dreams, 2006

Figure 5: Lucy García Corahua
Hopes and Dreams, 2006

Figure 6: Mirtha Aliaga's Hope and Dream for an Improved Environment
2006 and 2015

Detail – Cosecha (Harvest)

Sewing Botanica

CHAPTER 8

ECOFEMINISM'S CRY: LET'S REMEMBER WHO WE ARE — EARTH'S CHILDREN!

Mary Judith Ress

8.1.

Con-spirando began in the early 1990s when, as just a smattering of women in Santiago, Chile, we began to gather to hold our own rituals. We were nuns, ex-nuns, missionaries, academics, and NGO workers of various stripes. All of us were feminists committed to the empowerment of women. We were just recovering from 17 years of dictatorship under the Pinochet regime and needed to find our own space to celebrate the joys and sorrows we were experiencing. We were frustrated that neither our churches nor the feminist movement was providing this "safe space" where we could feel a sense of belonging. We were hungry for community, for a chance to share our experiences, explore our *mestizo* roots, our history as women. We needed to MOVE — to dance, leap, and chant together — and to keen together when our hearts were heavy. We were a nomad group until we finally found an old *conventillo* to rent in downtown Santiago. Our ritual time together grew into gatherings of like-minded women with whom we could talk about our beliefs and experiences of the Holy in our lives. In the closing circle of one of these gatherings, someone said, *estamos con-spirando* — we are con-spiring together, breathing together in one great breath of life. And so we were named.

Con-spirando has become a women's collective working in the areas of ecofeminism, theology and spirituality. I am a founding member. From 1993 to 2009 we published 60 issues of *Con-spirando: Revista latinoamericana de ecofeminismo, espiritualidad y teología*, a journal exploring themes as diverse as images of the divine (God, Mary, Jesus, the *Pachamama*), violence against women, money, sexuality, sustainable communities, the goddess traditions as related to archetypal patterns of behavior, the black Madonna — to name just a few.[1] We have held workshops, seminars and an annual School on ecofeminist theology, spirituality and

---

1. The entire collection is now available on www.conspirando.cl.

ethics, and offer a yearly cycle of rituals. In our journal's first issue, we set out our purpose, which more than 25 years later, still very much defines what we are about:

> In the patriarchal culture in which we live, women's contributions are not taken seriously. This is particularly true in the area of theology. Our lives, our everyday religious practices and our spirituality are simply not present in current theological reflection. Absent, too, are our experiences of suffering, joy and solidarity — our experiences of the Sacred. Besides expressing our criticism of patriarchal culture, we also seek to contribute to the creation of a culture that allows theological reflection to flower from our bodies, our spirits — in short, our experiences as women.
>
> We seek theologies that take account of the differences of class, race and gender that so mark Latin America. We hope to open new spaces where women can dig deeply into our own life experiences without fear. These experiences are often negative, even traumatic, in terms of the religious formation we have received. We seek spaces where women can experience new ways of being in community; where we can celebrate our faith more authentically and creatively; where we can rediscover and value our roots, our history and our traditions — in short, to engage in an interreligious dialogue that helps us to recover the essential task of theology, which is to search out and raise the questions of ultimate meaning.
>
> We are convinced that, to bring about relationships marked by justice and equality, we must celebrate our differences and work toward a greater pluralism worldwide. To this end, we need theologies that unmask the hierarchies in which we live, theologies that, rather than seeking to mediate Mystery, celebrate and explore the Holy without reductionisms or universalisms. We call for theologies that question anthropocentrism and that promote the transformation of relationships based on dominance of one race, nationality, gender or age group over another and of the human over other forms of life. Such theologies will have profound political consequences.
>
> Such a feminist perspective based on our diversity of class, race, age and culture must also take up our love as well as our anguish for all life on the planet that we feel is so threatened today. We call this posture ecofeminism. It is within this perspective that we seek a spirituality that will both heal and liberate, that will nourish our Christian tradition as well as take up the long-repressed roots of the original peoples of this continent. We want to explore the liberating dimensions of our experience and imagination of the Holy. To do this, we *"con-spirar juntas."*[2]

Over the years, the *Con-spirando* team has discovered that naming and reflecting upon our own experience of the Holy is essential in the process of speaking one's own theological word. Offering new images of the Sacred — out of which evolve both new ethical demands as well as new spiritual practices — has been part of *Con-spirando*'s work since its

---

2. *Con-spirando: Revista latinoamericana de ecofeminismo, espiritualidad y teología* (Santiago de Chile) No. 1. March, 1992, 2-5.

beginnings. In our workshops and rituals we try to empower women to rename the Sacred according to their own experiences and insights. The starting point here has been listening to our bodies, which includes staying profoundly connected to dreams, intuitions, emotions, sensations, and the wisdom surfacing in our women's rituals. We espouse an embodied theology holding up women's bodies as "sacred text."

Many who belong to the *Con-spirando* network have been trained in the *concientización* methodology of Brazilian educator Paulo Freire by which oppressed groups, concentrating on their own experience, engage in social analysis for change (*praxis*).[3] We have learned that our women's bodies are social and cultural constructs, that our history of violence and pain as well as of joy and pleasure is stored in our bodies' memory. The body, then, becomes our theological starting point to counteract the patriarchal mindset that a woman's body is the source of evil. We strive to heal the dualistic split between body and spirit, and to learn to love ourselves as embodied "temples" of the Holy.

Our yearly cycle of rituals follows the seasonal changes. We relate these changes to our own lives: In March (Southern hemisphere), we celebrate the Earth's harvest — and our own. Then, we prepare for winter. In late June, we celebrate the winter solstice, which is also the Mapuche and Aymara New Year. The fire is key here, as we gather to wait for the moment when the sun begins its return journey to our hemisphere. Since it is cold, we often huddle together and drink warm wine and eat *sopaipillas* and tell stories. We prepare ourselves for the season of hibernation. "When the Earth rests, the people of the Earth must rest too," say the Mapuche. In September, we celebrate the arrival of Spring and the Earth's and our new life! Here in Chile, in September we commemorate our national independence day. But we also recall September 11, 1973, the anniversary of Chile's military coup. Finally, in December, at Christmas time, we celebrate the fullness of life, the fruits and flowers and passion of summertime! There are various moments to each ritual, which can include circle dancing, chanting or movements such as Tai Chi or Chi Kung. We always finish with an *Aptapi,* an Aymara word for "pot luck."

What has become clear during these rituals is that we remember who we are — daughters of a living Earth. We yearn to bond again with the *Pachamama* and to learn from our indigenous sisters how to honor her and live within her cycles.

---

3. Paolo Freire, *Pedagogy of the Oppressed* (New York: Herder & Herder, 1970).

8.2. Myths and their power over us

Besides ritual, *Con-spirando* has delved deeply into myths and their power over our collective psyche. In our workshops, when women shared their religious formation with regard to God and sin, many told traumatic stories of what could only be termed theological violence. In 1996 *Con-spirando*, WATER[4] and Brazilian theologian Ivone Gebara, gave birth to a program called the Shared Garden, an initiative to create a broad network of women to engage in theological reflection that would move beyond patriarchal theologies. It was also a space for ongoing self-formation. Three gatherings, which took place in 1997 and 1998 in Santiago, Washington and Recife, searched for pathways that would lead "Beyond Violence." Participants wanted to move beyond the barriers that separated women from one another, whether the women were Catholic, Protestant or agnostic, whether they were white, *mestizo* or black. Above all, they wanted to cross the divide between South and North America. More than 120 women experienced the richness and the difficulties of the participants' diversity and heterogeneity. They also discovered how the problem of violence penetrates all our relationships and is ingrained in our bodies and in the way we perceive the world.

Participants enacted and then analyzed the creation story of Adam and Eve found in Genesis 2, the foundational myth undergirding our current patriarchal Christian culture. We began to realize how much we had internalized this myth, which sustains both our cultures and our cosmologies and continues to operate within us at a very deep, although frequently unconscious level. As one woman from Brazil said, "Now I am not afraid to show how this myth is profoundly violent. This myth has basically destroyed women's lives. It has destroyed the possibility of friendship between men and women, between women, between religions and our relationship with the Earth."

After the Shared Garden experience, we felt the need to delve more deeply into how myths originate and how they operate to uphold patriarchy as "normal" or "God-given." We realized just how deeply patriarchal relationships affected us — they are not "outside," but inhabit us unconsciously, expressed in our bodies, language and imagination. This led to *Con-spirando*'s commitment to hold an annual School of Ecofeminist Spirituality and Ethics that would offer a contained space where women could ask their theological questions without fear. In deciding to study myths of origin and the image of the Sacred found within them, we found

---

4. WATER: Women's Alliance for Theology, Ethics and Ritual, founded by Mary Hunt and Diann Neu, based in Silver Spring, Maryland.

ourselves constantly shifting between different dimensions: the personal, the political, the cosmological and the religious, to name the four that were most evident.

One of the most exciting memories I have of these Schools is how, in studying the evolution of our god-images throughout our evolution as a species, we came to realize that there is no "one god" — our deities arise from our geography (our "gods of place") and what is happening in society at the time. We studied the earliest images of the holy — and found to our delight that the so-called "Venus figures" of the Paleolithic Era were wonderfully naked images of women whose bodies reflected the fertility of Mother Earth herself. We passionately adorned the walls of our meeting room with images of the Goddess of Willendorf (20,000 BCE), the Goddess of Laussel (20,000 BCE) and so many others from all over the planet as we realized that indeed, in the beginning, "god was a woman." By tracing the transformations to these images of the Sacred, we could see the development of patriarchy: first, there were images of pregnant women (Paleolithic and early Neolithic Eras): gradually these mother figures became paired with either a son or a lover (later Neolithic), such as the Sumerian myth of the Mother Goddess Inanna and her consort Dimuzi (where the Sacred Marriage ritual is depicted to "wake up" Mother Earth in springtime). Finally, in the Babylonian epic, *Enuma Elish* (1,700 BCE), we read of the assassination of the Mother God Tiamat by the young warrior God, Marduk. With the study of these creation myths under our belts, we could return to the Genesis myth and see traces of Marduk in the Hebrew god Yahweh. He now governs the Earth from above; he creates by his word, alone; he has no image, no lineage. As we continued to trace the evolution of our images of the divine, we saw how Yahweh eventually became "one God, the Father, the Almighty, Maker of all that is, seen and unseen" (Nicene Creed).

During the School in 2003, we asked ourselves, where is the female image of the deity today here in Latin America? The answer came shouting back at us: in the many images and feasts of the Virgin Mary! We suspected that buried within these Marian celebrations, lay older, suppressed pre-Colombian deities or legends where female figures were once powerful. We wanted to find out — not so much to prove the earlier existence of goddess figures in Latin America before the Conquest, but to show how images of the Sacred evolved according to the demands of society's dominant class. We also wanted to rehabilitate those female images of the Sacred held by our indigenous ancestors.

We formed local teams and set about researching some of Latin America's most famous shrines and festivals dedicated to Mary. We published our findings in *Vírgenes y diosas en América Latina: La resignificación de lo sagrado*.[5] What we knew in our innards proved to be true: the Spanish and Portuguese conquest displaced Latin America's indigenous cosmologies along with their deities and rituals, relegating them to clandestinity. Worship of the *Pachamama* hid behind the Andean Virgins of the Candelaria (Copacabana in Bolivia, and Puno in Peru), the Virgin of Quinche in Ecuador and Our Lady of Carmel in northern Chile. The ancient Aztec goddess, Tonantzin, has morphed into the powerful Our Lady of Guadalupe in Mexico. The African mother goddesses Iemanjá, Oshun and María Lionza became the Immaculate Conception in Brazil, the (impossible-to-hide sexy) Virgin of Charity in Cuba and the Good Shepherd in Venezuela. In Guatemala, the Mayan mother goddess Qana It'zam who gave her people the gift of corn hides behind the compassionate Our Lady of the Forsaken. When the teams participated in these Marian *fiestas*, they were struck by the passionate dancing and chanting present in the celebrations. There was no clear separation between devotion to Mary and an earlier deity who once inhabited the area.

A personal experience: One of the most famous Marian feasts here in Chile is the Feast of our Lady of Carmen on July 17th, better known as *La Tirana* (the tyrant), the name of a tiny village in the high Andean plateau in northern Chile. The village is named after an Inca princess, Huillac Ñusta, who — along with her uncle and a sizable army of soldiers — were forced to march from Cuzco to what would become Chile, by the Spanish conqueror Diego de Almagro. Along the way, she escapes with soldiers loyal to the Inca and eventually founds a resistance settlement, which bears her nickname, *La Tirana*. She earned the title for refusing to let any foreigner into the settlement. However, as legend has it, one day a handsome Portuguese soldier landed at her doorstep and she fell madly in love with him. Supposedly, he told her the beautiful story of Jesus and asked her to convert to Catholicism. Once he told her that they would be united forever — even after death — she consented to be baptized. But even before the water on her forehead was dry, two arrows fired by the Ñusta's loyal lieutenant found their mark and killed them both. And, as she lay dying, the Ñusta requested that a cross be placed on her grave. Years later, another missionary in the area discovered the cross, and built a chapel there in honor of Our Lady of Carmel, Chile's patron.

Why does this Marian *fiesta* convoke so many people? For a whole week, indigenous *campesinos* come down from the Andean highlands to

---

5. Verónica Cordero, et al., *coordinadoras, Vírgenes y diosas en América Latina: La resignificación de lo sagrado* (Santiago de Chile: Con-spirando y Red Latinoamericana de Católicas por el Derecho de Decidir, 2004).

dance passionately in front of the church. They put on ancient costumes and masks reflecting the *cofradía* they belong to, but you also have kids dancing in Batman or Mickey Mouse costumes as well. Even the seven dwarfs showed up. When I asked, "Who they were dancing for?", they always answered, "for the chinita". *La chinta* is a term of endearment — something like "for mommy".

Recently I met a young, indigenous woman from the North who told me that there are *fiestas* to lesser-known virgins all over the Andean highlands. She had just come from celebrating the feast of her local town. No, she answered, she was not dancing for the Virgin, but yes, she was dancing for her *chinita*. Even though she lives in Santiago, every year she goes to dance — because, she says, it gives her a feeling of belonging, of being held. In reflecting on what we learned from this study, we concluded that — despite the region's entrenched patriarchy — we cannot eradicate the feeling that we are earthlings. We come from Mother Earth and at the end of our days we will return to her womb. The many references to the feminine, symbolized by images of goddesses and virgins, are related to our primordial experience as humans. We yearn for a sense of belonging, of being protected, cared for and loved. Our genetic memory takes us back to our mother's womb — that primordial experience sought after again and again in "religious" experiences that convey a maternal tone of tenderness and dependency.

During the Schools, we spent time working on the four great feminine archetypes (Mother, Hetaira, Amazon, Medium) and how these energies have been present in the goddess images we unearthed and also how they are present in our own lives. These feminine archetypes offer four basic ways of expressing relationships. But the central feminine archetype is Mother Earth herself, teeming with possibilities. According to Jungian scholar Rachel Fitzgerald, who was often our guest lecturer at the Schools, "the feminine — both in its interior consciousness and in its external expression — is related to the living material world and to its sacred character and to our species' interaction with the natural world."[6]

We also confronted the shadow side of the Mother — she gives life, but promises a life that is finite. This contrasts with the idea of immortality, a foundational belief of patriarchal religion. On the collective level, we — who are her children — try to stifle our great fear that if we continue to destroy the planet we are destroying ourselves as a species.

---

6. Rachel Fitzgerald, *Feminine archetypes: Patterns of relationships* (translated into Spanish in: *Con-spirando*, No. 36, June, 2001, 4-11).

8.3. Conclusions

Because of *Con-spirando*'s work, women all over Latin America are creating their own rituals — and celebrating what they want to celebrate. Many are returning to their indigenous roots and, in so doing, they are reconnecting with the Pachamama in all her manifestations. We are remembering who we are.

Through our experience in ritual and in studying creation myths and the images of the Sacred contained within them, we conclude that there is a great longing in our hearts for belonging to something larger than ourselves. In the past, we have given names and images to this longing. Today, quantum physics shows that everything is interconnected in one great web, holons nesting in holons. New images of the sacred emerge: a mandala, a spiraling galaxy, a circle of people dancing, a spider's web. And new images will continue to bubble forth from our collective unconsciousness to shape and reshape who we are. Images of the Sacred are a key element in the very structure of human consciousness at every stage of our evolution as a species.

And finally, if the earth's journey continues — and oh how we pray that it will! — **you will be there and I will be there** in those beings who will come after us who will "reach out their hands and touch the stars." We will be in those forms of life that come after us, who without a doubt will be more complex than the human species and will discover ways of being more intimately in communion than we have known. New surprises in this cosmic dance of Surprise Without End.

8.4. Poem, "Surprise without end," Mary Judith Ress

The universe is full of surprises. Indeed, it is continuous creativity, surprise without end. And you and I form part of it all.

You were there and I was there when the universe burst forth some 15 billion years ago in one great flaring forth. Energy, fire, light and heat radiated in every direction creating the universe, time and space. All that one day would come into existence was present in that first flaring forth — the galaxies, stars, planets, oceans, mountains, trees, ants and elephants. Buddha, Jesus, Teresa of Ávila, Monteczuma, Sor Juana Inés de la Cruz, you and I — all were present in the energy of that first unimaginable first moment.

You were there and I was there during the following billions of years of fecund night when atoms joined together to become first hydrogen and then helium.

You were there and I was there when in an instant during that fecund night, the universe in another great burst of creativity birthed more than 100 billion galaxies — among them our own relatively insignificant Milky Way. Each galaxy had its own inner dynamics, each in its turn created millions and millions of stars.

You were there and I was there when some five billion years ago, in a corner of the Milky Way, our own star was born from the stardust of the explosion of a supernova. Once born, our sun demonstrated the same self-organizing principles present in the entire universe and created its own system of planets, including our own dear planet earth.

You were there and I was there when the earth mixed within its womb, minerals, gases and liquids from which was brought to birth, some four billion years later, the first tiny cell. With the passage of time, these cells learned to remember, to join together, to adapt. And in a great leap of creativity, they learned to "eat" the sun's energy! To reproduce themselves, they invented sex, and by learning to eat one another, they invented death.

You were there and I was there when some 600 million years ago, a fantastic array of multicellular organisms was born: worms, corals, insects, crabs, starfish, sponges, spiders, vertebrates of every sort! Worms learned to crawl while other beings developed wings. Some invented teeth while others invented shells.

You were there and I was there during the following millennium when ocean waves washed up some sea plants among the rocks. These plants learned to live along the seacoasts. Little by little, some of these plants became trees and soon the continents were roaring with green life.

You were there and I was there when the sea creatures followed the plants onto the land. During the next several millennia, amphibians, reptiles and insects of all kinds inhabited the continents, including the dinosaurs.

And you were there and I was there when some 67 million years ago, a great astronomic collision changed the earth's atmosphere to such a degree that almost all the forms of animal life had to reinvent themselves or disappear. This destruction also opened new possibilities: the birds and the mammals — which were not able to develop in the presence of the dinosaurs — now flourished as a result of this so-called disaster.

You were there and I was there when the mammals, now a permanent presence on earth, some 60 million years ago began to develop emotional sensitivity — a new ability of the nervous system to feel the universe in a new way. Beauty as well as terror of the world became deeply encrusted in the mammalian psyche, including that of the human. In some rare occasions, especially among the primates, this emotional sensitivity combined with the neural ability of consciousness to be conscious of itself — which was the case of the human animal.

You were there and I was there when some four million years ago, our ancestors stood up on two feet; when some two million years ago, we began to use our hands to mold tools from the earth and to harness fire; when some 35,000 years ago, we arrived at a new level of consciousness that we expressed in dance and music, in celebrating the changing seasons of the year, in burying our loved ones who died; when, some 20,000 years ago we began a cycle of domestication of plants and animals which also domesticated us. Slowly, we abandoned our hunting and gathering lifestyle of our tribes and clans and began to settle down and grow food.

You were there and I was there when with our food supply more secure, we began to live in villages. In this new context we were able to develop ceramics, weaving, architecture. We could build temples and perform rites to the Great Mother. Between 10,000 and 5,000 years ago, we created the structures of language, religion, cosmology and art that would define human civilization until the present time.

You were there and I was there when some 5,000 years ago, we began establishing the great urban civilizations as humanity's new centers of power. Babylon, Paris, Rome, Jerusalem, Athens, Cairo, Mecca, Delhi, Teotiatlan, Cusco. These great cities were characterized by their hierarchical relationships and by their emphasis on specialization and the division of labor. An era of many transformations: rivers and seas would now be navigated and used as trade routes; forests and minerals could be exploited as natural resources. In this stage, human civilization increased in number and in wealth; we built great cathedrals, palaces and temples. To defend this wealth, we developed military force with arms that became ever more sophisticated. War became chronic. The Great Mother of Neolithic times who was so identified with agriculture was replaced by a Father God who, like the king, ruled from on high.

You were there and I was there when during the 19th and 20th centuries, we have evolved the nation state with is mystique of nationalism, progress, democratic freedoms and individual rights to private property and economic gain. When we developed tremendous power in the areas of science, technology and economics to the point where — as a species — we can control the very process of the earth itself and use it for our own good.

You were there and I was there when only recently in the last few years we are discovering that the universe is not a "place," a backdrop for the stage upon which the human acts, but an evolutionary community continually birthing ever more complex life forms.

You are here and I am here when life itself is forcing us to remember what is stored in our body's memory, what our genes have always known: that nothing exists, or has existed or will exist for its own sake. Nothing exists without the rest. We are a link in a chain of DNA that is at every moment reshaping and transforming itself.

Let us remember well: **you were there and I was there** in the fireball at the beginning of the universe; then in the galaxies, then, in the planets, then in the wiggle of the worm, in the flight of the bird, in the broad-reaching branches of the Araucaria tree, in the first human who stood up on two feet and used her hands to start fire, then as a member of the tribe collecting fruit in the forest, then in the village taking part in the fertility rites to the Great Mother and then in the city dominated by the cathedral where we went to pray to God the Father.

And finally, if the earth's journey continues — and oh how we pray that it will! — **you will be there and I will be there** in those beings who will come after us who will "reach out their hands and touch the stars." We will be in those forms of life that come after us, who without a doubt will be more complex than the human species and will discover ways of being more intimately in communion than we have known. New surprises in this cosmic dance of Surprise Without End.

CHAPTER 9

THE ENCLOSURE OF THE PSYCHE IN MODERNITY: HEALING THE INTERNAL AND EXTERNAL LANDSCAPE

Frédérique Apffel-Marglin

Since the beginning of time, Omama [creator spirit/deity] has been the center of what the white people call **ecology**...*For the shamans, these have always been words that came from the spirits to defend the forest...In the forest, we human beings are the 'ecology'. But it is equally the xapiri [spirits], the game, the trees, the rivers, the fish, the sky, the rain, the wind, and the sun! It is everything that isn't surrounded by fences yet...*
If the forest were dead, we would be as dead as it is! But it is truly alive. The white people may not hear it complain, yet it feels pain just like we humans do.
Davi Kopenawa, *The Falling Sky*[1]

9.1. Integral Ecology

These words from a Yanomami shaman of the Brazilian Northwest Upper Amazon express a worldview that is common to most indigenous peoples and many other non-western cultures. It is a worldview where humans, non-humans and other than humans such as spirits are all part of the same world. Those worlds are not divided into a world of humans and their thoughts and artefacts (a 'cultural' world) on one side and the natural world on the other hand as well as separated from a 'supernatural world' of immaterial and invisible beings above nature. Such worldviews as the one articulated by Kopenawa have been named by Thomas Berry and his followers as 'integral', speaking of an 'integral ecology'.[2] Pope Francis' ecological encyclical *Laudato Si'* similarly speaks of an integral ecology where the "cry of the poor" and the "cry of the earth" are one. Such an integral

---

1. Davi Kopenawa and Bruce Albert, *The Falling Sky*, Tr. Nicholas Elliott & Alison Dundy (Cambridge, MA: The Belknap Press of Harvard University Press, 2013), 393, 382.
2. See Thomas Berry, *Evening Thoughts: Reflecting on Earth as Sacred Community* (San Francisco: Sierra Club Books, 2009); T. Berry and Brian Swimme, *The Universe Story* (San Francisco: Harper, 1992); B. Swimme, *The Hidden Heart of the Cosmos: Humanity and the New Story* (Maryknoll: Orbis Books, 1996); B. Swimme and Mary Evelyn Tucker, *Journey of the Universe* (New Haven: Yale University Press, 2011).

view of ecology has also been at the heart of the work of some scientists such as biologist Lynn Margulis and cosmologist Brian Swimme. However, not all scientists embrace the realm of spirits as pertaining to the materiality of the cosmos. Lynn Margulis for one remained careful to distance herself from the spiritual connotations of the name Gaia in her well-known 'Gaia Hypothesis' and always insisted that the name referred only to a self-regulating and living entity and *not* to a spiritual entity.[3]

Brian Swimme, however, does not shy away from spirituality; in fact, he insists that it is not only impossible not to recognize it in the new vista opened by the latest cosmological scientific discoveries, but that such a lack of recognition "is to live a life that is vulnerable to fundamental distortions."[4] He asserts that "we have identified a non-material realm suffusing not only the great macrocosm of the universe but suffusing the microcosm as well of the human and of every being of the Earth and universe."[5] Such an explicit recognition of the inseparability — or entanglement — of a material and a spiritual realm, although not unique, is much less frequent among scientists or just scholars in general, for that matter.[6]

9.2. Modernity's Anthropocentrism

The neo-Jungian archetypical psychologist James Hillman points out the totally human-centered, anthropocentric nature of the field of psychology. He points out that dictionaries of psychology and schools of psychology of all orientations agree that reality is of two kinds:

First, the word [reality] means the totality of existing material objects or the sum of conditions of the external world. Reality is public, objective, social, and usually physical. Second, there is a psychic reality, not extended in space, the realm of private experience that is interior, wishful, imaginational.[7]

Thus, the external world has no psyche, no soul and soul has migrated and shrunk to the interiority of human beings. Hillman is struck by the soul's sophistication he sees in his patients which he attributes to a

---

3. See the documentary: *Symbiotic Earth: How Lynn Margulis Rocked the Boat and Started a Scientific Revolution*; a film by John Feldman, Bullfrog Films, 2019.
4. Brian Swimme, *The Hidden Heart of the Cosmos: Humanity and the New Story* (New York: Orbis Books, 1996), 48.
5. Ibid., 104.
6. The signatories of the Post-Materialist Manifesto (2014) all adhere to such a view. See: http://www.opensciences.org/about/manifesto-for-a-post-materialist-science. However, the materialist position is still dominant in academia as in modern western culture generally and its global variants.
7. James Hillman, *The Thought of the Heart & the Soul of the World* (Dallas, Texas: Spring Publications, Inc., 1992), 95.

hundred years of psychoanalysis. He also notes that during those same one hundred years, psychology has become increasingly individuated and intra-subjective. When mental pathology made its appearance, the focus of psychology consisted in readjusting inner psychodynamics. As Hillman puts it: "Complexes, functions, structures, memories, emotions — the interior person needed realigning, releasing, developing."[8]

Hillman quickly reviews the more recent field of family and group therapy, where the problem was inter-subjective, located in the patient's close social relationships. Therapy then consists of improving inter-personal psychodynamics. However, the world remains 'external reality,' an objective backdrop to human action and subjectivity but one without its own subjectivity, its own psyche.

Hillman admits that the dynamics of psyche has been recognized to be influenced by a small social group around the patient but insists that it has never been seen by psychology as caused by the outside world. The outside world whether it be human-made or natural has no psyche itself. It does not suffer; it does not communicate with the individual human psyche. This of course strikingly contrasts with Davi Kopenawa's forest who feels pain when it is being aggressed. The built environment, such as cities, buildings, agriculture, mining and such are recognized in varieties of social psychiatry as possible objective causes of psychopathology but one without psyche. This is how Hillman phrases it:

> This was especially the American dream, an immigrant's dream: change the world and you change the subject. However, these societal determinants remain external conditions, economic, cultural, or social; *they are not themselves psychic or subjective.* The external may cause suffering but it does not itself suffer. For all its concern with the outer world, social psychiatry too works within the idea of the external world passed to us by Aquinas, Descartes, Locke, and Kant.[9] (emphasis added)

Social psychiatry recognizes the built environment as a possible cause of psychopathology but like the 'natural' environment, neither of them possesses subjectivity. In other words, *res extensa* — Descartes' 'extended thing,' whether built or natural, whether bodies or buildings — has no subjectivity, no psyche, no soul. This soulless *res extensa* therefore cannot be diagnosed with any sort of psychopathology of its own.

Of course, in transpersonal psychology associated with Carl Jung, Abraham Maslow, Stanislav Grof and others, this view has been profoundly challenged and the spiritual dimension of external — as well as

---

8. Ibid., 93.
9. Ibid., 94.

internal — reality affirmed. However, what Hillman writes describes the dominant cultural reality in the field of psychology and psychiatry and in western modernity in general.

Modernity is still overwhelmingly in the grip of this dead world, which is also a deadening, pathological world. Swimme thinks that "hoping for a consumer society without drug abuse is as pointless as hoping for a car without axle grease." In what follows he explains why:

> When humans find themselves surrounded by nothing but objects, the response is always one of loneliness… But isolation and alienation are profoundly false states of mind. We were born out of the Earth Community and its infinite creativity and delight and adventure. Our natural genetic inheritance presents us with the possibility of forming deeply bonded relationships throughout all ten million species of life as well as throughout the nonliving components of the universe. Any ultimate separation from this larger and enveloping community is impossible, and any ideology that proposes that the universe is nothing, but a collection of pre-consumer items is going to be maintained only at a terrible price.[10]

Today this ten million of species has been severely diminished with the largest extinction of species since the disappearance of the dinosaurs, and one caused by humans, giving our geologic era the label of the 'anthropocene.' We are all in deep mourning, depressed and bereft whether we are aware of it, or of its deeplying causes, or whether we have repressed all of this to our collective unconscious.

Swimme, along with Thomas Berry[11] and Mary Evelyn Tucker (2011), all assert that the cosmos and of course the earth and humans, are part of a living, evolving, sentient and sacred, numinous universe. Their worldview is a modern version of the kind of Amazonian worldview so eloquently articulated by Davi Kopenawa in his autobiography.[12]

Another one of the 'terrible prices' that Swimme refers to in the above citation is the alarmingly growing epidemic of addiction in the US. Besides environmental destruction and species extinction, the price is also paid by humans. And it is not only drug addiction that is rampant and rising but also all sort of mental illnesses as we shall see below. The deadening and destructive effect of this modern world view of an insentient, dead external world of objects affects both humans' internal world as well as the external world since these two are part of the same living, sentient, numinous cosmos.

---

10. Swimme, *The Hidden Heart of the Cosmos*, 33-34.
11. Thomas Berry, *The Thought of the Heart & the Soul of the World* (Dallas, Texas: Spring Publications, Inc., 1992).
12. See Kopenawa and Albert, *The Falling Sky*, 2013.

The work of psychologist Susan Miller of Columbia University has focused on the relationship between the lack of attention and seriousness given to lived spirituality, especially during the time of puberty and young adulthood in the US, and the risk of addiction and other mental issue among young people. Miller states that the escape and connection teens experience with drug use "needs to be understood as a spiritual quest, inherently good and important."[13]

Miller emphasizes the split that occurs early in children's development between "logic-based learning and direct experience and inner heart knowing."[14] She stresses modern culture's, particularly American culture's, lack of value given especially to children and adolescents' inner voices and inner wisdom as "not real... not scientific."[15]

Educational institutions from K through PhD overwhelmingly emphasize the rational, analytical mind, leaving to the arts such concerns pertaining to the creative imagination but not to 'reality.' She calls this inner wisdom 'heart knowing' and adds that "[d]ue to socialization in our current society, heart knowing is often blocked, denied, or disintegrated. This leads to enormous suffering, as we can become cut off from other people, our higher selves, and even our transcendent relationship."[16]

According to Miller children are born with a natural sense of being related to everything. Puberty not only unlocks the process of sexual maturity but also is a time of "a biologically primed tidal surge in natural spirituality."[17] She seems to conclude from her and others' studies that for spiritual individuation to successfully protect against the most destructive of behaviors, this process of individuating our natural spirituality must be successful in the sense that it eventuates in a lived, embodied, experienced spirituality highly meaningful to the adolescent or young adult. In the process she and her co-researchers found that *nobody has talked to them [the adolescents/young adults] about this experience.* "Without supported and guided spiritual awakening in adolescence, our teens are left to fend for themselves. The cost is high."[18] The cost she speaks of refers to the epidemic of drug addiction and mental illness in the US.

---

13. Susan Miller, *The Spiritual Child: The New Science on Parenting for Health and Lifelong Thriving* (New York: St. Martin's Press, 2015), 43.
14. Ibid., 169.
15. Ibid., 74.
16. Ibid., 78.
17. Ibid., 79.
18. Ibid., 71.

Such a view is also shared by Swimme, who writes that:

> It is simply not human finally to live a life sealed off from all conscious contact with those powers at work throughout the Earth and universe and within every one of our cells. So intolerable is this sense of being out of it, of being left out, of being without central meaning for the world, we will resort to any route to ease the pain. And the quick and mindless way... is to ingest mind-altering chemicals that dissolve the thin veneer of consumer culture... spiritually desiccated... [and] out of touch with the numinous powers pervading each being in the universe... Thus, if only for a moment, and sometimes at a horrible cost... one can be at home again in the great flood of beauty.[19]

So, it is not only the fencing of the Amazonian forest of which Davi Kopenawa speaks. The fencing of the Amazon rain forest is itself the contemporary expression of the century's old enclosure movement in Western Europe that fenced the commons: lands, forests, rivers, lakes and ponds where the elves, fairies and leprechauns frolicked, and the poor derived their sustenance and celebrated their gratitude to the non and other than human world with their May Pole festivities.[20] However, according to Davi Kopenawa, he asserts that during a visit to France to defend the rain forest he says: "Yet the spirits of this distant land are not dead. They still live in the mountains that *Omama* gave them for houses and they only come down from them for the shamans who are able to see them."[21] He claims that he himself saw those spirits in Europe.

9.3. A European Colonialist Mindset

The enclosure movements then and now, by turning the earth into a "natural resource" for the exclusive use of humans and everything into a commodity or a 'pre-manufactured consumer good' in Swimme's language, have transformed the spirits into imaginary figments of our modern minds. In other words, our minds, our consciousness themselves have become enclosed, fenced off from the numinous powers of the earth and the cosmos. Those numinous powers enable us humans to hear and communicate with the non-humans and other than humans. We have become blind and deaf, altogether insensible, to the psyche of the non-human world, to the Soul of the World known in Renaissance Europe as Anima Mundi.

---

19. Swimme, *The Hidden Heart*, 35.
20. See my *Subversive Spiritualities: How Rituals Enact the World* (New York: Oxford University Press, 2011), Chapter 3 which resulted in a disenchantment and a commodification of the land.
21. Kopenawa and Albert, *The Falling Sky*, 323.

In other words, the spirit world is *both* beyond the phenomenal world as well as integral with it, that is integral with materiality. This means that the spirit world is not spoken of as either a facet of the collective human unconscious *à la* Jung or as projections of the inner world of humans as many varieties of psychology maintain. Nor is the spirit world seen as somehow expressing some facets of the socio-cultural worlds of humans in the manner of much anthropology. Nor is the spirit world relegated to a realm above 'nature,' a *supernatural* realm as many religious traditions, especially the theistic ones, maintain. Rather, the spirit world is spoken of as an experienced tangible reality resonating beyond the world of the one experiencing the spirits.

The new cosmological and other scientific revelations of the late 20th and the 21st centuries impel us to leave behind our European colonialist mindset born with the destruction of the cosmovision of the European oral peasantry starting around the 15th century when the Pope declared 'witches' to be heretics.[22] Such destruction began before the exportation of this colonial enterprise at the turn of the 15th and 16th centuries with the slave trade and the invasion of the Americas. This exportation of a colonialist mind-set — that is the exportation of coloniality — cast the spirit worlds encountered in those continents as a mark of backwardness and inferiority since that is how the European slave traders and invaders saw the cosmovision of their own oral peasants. Such a mind-set was born from the murder of Anima Mundi in Europe and exported worldwide its view of the spirit world as an irrational, superstitious and backward mode of knowing. As the philosopher of science Isabelle Stengers put it:

> "We" on our side, presume to be the ones who have accepted the hard truth that we are alone in a mute, blind, yet knowable world — one that is our task to appropriate… Science, when taken in the singular and with a big S, may indeed be described as a general conquest bent on translating everything that exists into objective, rational knowledge…what is called Science, or the idea of a hegemonic scientific rationality, can be understood as itself the product of a colonization process.[23]

What Stengers — following Bruno Latour[24]– calls Science with a capital S has been called by others materialist reductionist science or simply Classical and/or Newtonian science. The label of 'post-materialist science' is meant to convey a transcendence of the dominant materialist reductionist

---

22. David Noble, A *World Without Women: The Christian Clerical Culture of Western Science* (Oxford: Oxford University Press, 1993), 206. Noble gives the date of 1484 for this papal decree.
23. Isabelle Stengers, "Reclaiming Animism," *e-flux Journal* 36 (July 2012).
24. Bruno Latour, *We Have Never Been Modern*, Tr. Catherine Porter (Cambridge, MA: Harvard University Press, 1995).

classical science paradigm and not a rejection of the relevance of matter. As Swimme and Berry put it so felicitously, the spirit world refers to those dimensions of nature beyond the phenomenal world but integral with materiality. In other words what they are saying is that although the spirit world is invisible, it is real since it is integral with materiality.

9.4. Words of an Upper Amazonian Peruvian Shaman

His name is Randy Chung Gonzales and I have known him since he was 15 years old; he is now 37 years old. He has been associated with my non-profit organization in this region for many years.[25] In June of 2016 he was initiated by disembodied spirits in an ayahuasca ceremony to which he did not want to go, and quite against his will. However, the spirits would not take no for an answer and he had to accept their initiation, which incidentally was incredibly painful and frightening. Ever since he has been on an intense and extraordinary shamanic learning journey where he has been given healing powers by a variety of spirits/deities and a disembodied indigenous master. People spontaneously began coming to him for healing even though he has not advertised at all locally and he has healed them, often achieving spectacular healings.

In the following I have translated what he has told me about his first encounter with the spirit of the mountain sacred to the local indigenous Kichwa-Lamistas, named Waman Wasi: The House of the Eagle. This encounter happened in February of 2018. The land outside of the town of Lamas where he has created a healing and integral ecology center faces this mountain.[26]

> Before this ayahuasca ceremony, I noticed that Waman Wasi [the sacred mountain] was totally clear, without clouds. At the end of the ceremony, around 1 am, I see the mountain from my seat and I mentally call it asking it to come to me. Immediately I enter a trance and experience myself at the foot of the mountain: flowers, trees, a fresh breeze. I knew it from up close for the first time. The mountain rose up near my feet; fragrances of flowers, a cool breeze… My elder companion told me that the mountain is asking for an offering. He advised me to buy mangos, grapes, pineapple, white roses, two bottles of red wine and caramels. Two days later we prepared for a ceremony devoted to the sacred mountain Waman Wasi.

---

25. My organization is: Sachamama Center for Biocultural Regeneration which I founded in 2009 on the outskirts of the small upper Amazonian Peruvian town of Lamas: www.asociacionsachamama.org.

26. We have named this center Urkumamanwasi: The Place of the Sacred Mountain: www.urkumamanwasi.com. It is dedicated to the healing of the internal and the external landscape.

> We prepared my altar with the fruits, roses; everything I had bought. I drank the cup of ayahuasca and offered it to my companion. Immediately I entered a trance, which surprised me for it was happening so quickly. I was a bit afraid. The trance was extremely strong, and I lowered my head. As I lift it and raise my eyes I see an eagle with its wings spread from door to door in the *maloca* [ceremonial lodge]… Later, I see coming towards me a kind of hand in the form of a serpent, offering me something. Involuntarily I join my hands to receive what the serpent was offering me, and it empties something in them. I took what it gave me and drank it. After drinking this I felt something so terribly powerful that my body, all my muscles felt like they were contorting and twisting. I said to my companion: "I can't withstand this any longer"; he told me: "You have to bear it. Bear it! It is Waman Wasi's *mariri* [shamanic power]."

This vivid evocation of the reality of the spirits — and I only translated here a very small part of the experiences that Randy has told me about — I think makes Davi Kopenawa's statements about the reality of the spirits dramatically real. In my own experience with ayahuasca for the past 24 years I have also understood that ayahuasca (among other psychedelics) opens the door to the reality of the spirit world.[27]

It is I believe relevant to note that Randy is not himself indigenous. His great-grand-father came from China and married an indigenous woman. His mother is *mestizo* and his father the grandson of the original Chinese ancestor and his indigenous wife. The Chinese ancestry marked the great-grand-father's male descendants. He was sent away by his mother sometimes in the late 1920s to avoid being jailed or worse by Chiang Kai-shek during the civil war with Mao Zedong from 1927 to 1949. The young man was pro-revolution and thus endangering his life. This leftist streak persisted in Randy's father who is a confirmed atheist and influenced Randy's mother who is equally atheist. This has meant that Randy grew up with no religious instruction or experience, never having set foot in the church in Lamas and ignorant of the Catholic saints, Virgins and such. As a *mestizo* himself, he was also only peripherally aware of the local indigenous spirits of the Kichwa-Lamistas and certainly did not believe in their reality.

All of this of course radically changed after his initiation and his many subsequent dramatic experiences not only in ayahuasca trance but at night in more than real visions or visitations with not only several indigenous spirits but also Catholic Saints and the Virgin of Guadalupe and a disembodied Ashaninca master shaman. Concerning the Virgin of Guadalupe,

---

27. The only psychedelic I have ingested is ayahuasca, but I am basing this assertion on both Pollan's and Kopenawa's books. Pollan's book is about mostly psylocibin and LSD. The Yanomami's yakoana is DMT-based, as is ayahuasca.

the first time she appeared to him, he had no idea who she was. However, since it happened in the presence of an elder shaman, this person was able to identify for him the apparition as that of the Virgin of Guadalupe.[28]

The kinds of maladies suffered by residents of Lamas and its indigenous quarter, Wayku, are overwhelmingly due to sorcery, which is rife especially in this town but quite common all over Peru. Most of the persons seeking Randy's help there suffer from the effects of some *daño*, i.e. sorcery. In my more than twenty years of yearly visits to Lamas I have realized the terrible efficacy of sorcery that can afflict physical or psychological harm as well as death. But Randy has also had the opportunity to heal persons coming from abroad suffering from more psychological problems. However, as we have seen in earlier sections of this essay, western modernity by separating the psyche from the non and other than human world, has created types of diseases of the psyche seen by the several authors mentioned above as emanating from such an enclosure of our psyches.

This western modern form of enclosure of the human psyche — separating it from the non-human world as well as from the other than human world — results in a hardening of those borders. Most saliently, modernity overwhelmingly holds the view that the non-human and other than human world do not possess psyche, a direct result of the murder during the Age of Reason of the world view of Anima Mundi, shared by both the occult philosophers and the oral peasantry.[29] The Age of Reason, a name given to the 16th and 17th centuries in Western Europe, refers to the time of the scientific revolution. But it is well to remember that the very same centuries are also called, especially by feminist historians, the Burning Times. That is due to the extermination of the worldview of Anima Mundi through the extermination by burning of the so-called witches and most of the occult philosophers.

9.5. Healing the Internal and External Landscape.

Michael Pollan's latest book on psychedelics *How to Change Your Mind* main contribution is to make the public in the US aware of the powerful therapeutic effects of psychedelics and the woeful inadequacy of existing

---

28. This Virgin first appeared in Mexico in 1531 to a Nahuatl peasant, later known as Juan Diego in Tepeyac, now within the city of Mexico. Randy and I visited Tepeyac in September 2018, accompanied by a Nahuatl guardian of the volcano Popocatepetl, Don Juan, who sang a song to her, calling her "Tonantzin Maria". Tonantzin represents the pre-Columbian earth mother who had a shrine at this place and is considered by indigenous Mexicans to be identical with the Virgin of Guadalupe.

29. The word 'psyche' in ancient Greek means soul/mind. On the murder of Anima Mundi, see my introduction in our book edited with S. Varese: *Contemporary Voices of Anima Mundi: A Reappraisal* (New York: Peter Lang Academic Press, 2020).

therapies in the field of addiction and mental illness. Pollan notes that the former director of the National Institute of Mental Health calls the mental health treatment in the US broken.[30] In the process, Pollan's work also makes us aware of the role that the dissolution of the ego effected by psychedelics plays in healing addictions, traumas, depression and other mental illnesses, all of them being on the rise in the US. Pollan's book is not about ecology, integral or otherwise. However, by comparing the role of psychedelics in his book and in Kopenawa's autobiography, I can make visible how healing the internal landscape is connected to the healing of the external landscape.

I will start with Pollan's unforgettable rendering of one of his own experience:

> 'I' now turned into a sheaf of little papers, no bigger than Post-its, and they were being scattered to the wind. But the 'I' talking in this seeming catastrophe had no desire to chase after the slips and pile my old self back together... And then I looked and saw myself out there again, but this time spread over the landscape like paint, or butter, thinly coating a wide expanse of the world with a substance I recognized as me.
>
> But who was this 'I' that was able to take in the scene of its own dissolution?... For what was observing the scene was a vantage and mode of awareness entirely distinct from my accustomed self; in fact I hesitate to use the 'I' to denote the presiding awareness, it was so different from my usual first person. Where that self had always been a subject encapsulated in this body, this one seemed unbounded by *any* body, even though I now had access to its perspective.... the 'personal' had been obliterated... I was present to reality but as something other than my self.[31]

It is interesting to note that Kopenawa speaks of taking the hallucinogenic used by the Yanomami — *yãkoana*, the resin of a tree prepared as a snuff containing DMT — as 'dying.' Throughout his autobiographical narrative as a shaman he — rather off-handedly — regularly refers to taking this psychedelic as a 'death.' However, he never dwells on this experience of dying or death but rather on the experience of seeing the *xapiris*, the spirits and what they do, that this 'death' act opens for him and others in his society.[32]

---

30. Michael Pollan, *How to Change Your Mind: What the New Science of Psychedelics Teaches Us About Consciousness, Dying, Addiction, Depression, and Transcendence* (New York: Penguin Press, 2018), 335.

31. Ibid., 263-4.

32. Kopenawa's narrative is translated into French from Yanomami by the anthropologist Bruce Albert who has worked with Kopenawa for some 30 years. Albert is masterfully able to at once preserve Kopenawa's manner of speaking, while at the same time making it understandable to a non-Yanomami readership.

The two books, Kopenawa's and Pollan's, are linked by the centrality of the role of psychedelics in both. There is also a huge difference in Kopenawa's central focus on the destruction of the rain forest by whites and the complete absence of the role or even existence of the spirits among them. The *xapiris* play a key role in the renewal, preservation and health of the forest and everything else. It is striking that their appearance, their reality, seems to be completely dependent on the ingestion of *yãkoana*, the Yanomami's traditional psychedelic. In both accounts, taking a psychedelic involves the death or dissolution of the ego. And in both accounts, this death of the ego opens one to a spirit-filled dimension of the world. Pollan emphasizes the therapeutic effect of this on the human ingester while Kopenawa's strong emphasis is on the whites' destruction of the forest — what I refer to as modernity's destruction of both the human's internal as well as external landscape and their refusal to see the spirits and their role in preserving the life of the forest, of humans and everything else.

It is for me extremely difficult to not see that the hardened boundaries of the ego in modernity — in other words the enclosure of the psyche — and the prohibition against ingesting psychedelics have made the spirits invisible and silent. The existence of the spirits has been relegated to the realm of imagination and to a credulous and superstitious past long ago superseded. The role of the spirits as our link to the sky, the air, the earth, the waters, the trees is invisible, even denied. These characteristics of modernity are directly correlated with the "white's" propensity to destroy the rain forest along with so much else in and around this earth. In Kopenawa's words:

> White people are surprised to look at us become spirits with the *yãkoana*. They think that we are losing our minds... Yet, if they understood our language and cared enough to ask... they might understand the words that the *xapiri* bring us from the edges of the earth, the sky's back, and the underworld they come from. But [...] white people prefer to remain deaf because they find themselves too clever with their paper skins, their machines, and their merchandise.[33]

Pollan's superb reportage on the dazzlingly positive therapeutic effects of the ego-dissolving ability of psychedelics must be paired with the horrifying effect of the enclosure of the psyche on all of reality, human, non-human and other than human.

---

33. Kopenawa and Albert, *The Falling Sky*, 418.

CHAPTER 10

HEALING AND VALUING WOMEN'S MEDICAL PLURI-VERSE (IN MEXICO)

Sylvia Marcos

> Doña Luz moves her arm around me with sweeping motions. In her hand, she has a bunch of herbs that fill the air with a pungent smell. Standing in front of her, I feel a freshness as she blows on my back, my face, my entire body. Finally, she stops. "You're well now, *Señorita*. The bad spirits that were clinging to you have left. Tonight, when you go to bed, place a white flower on your night table and drink a tea of white zapote leaves boiled with three lemons cut in the form of a cross...."

10.1.

Cognitive frameworks pervade our thinking, influence our conceptions of causality and guide our sensory perceptions. At all times, we are immersed in a knowledge "episteme" that organizes the way we conceptualize the material world around us to fit this cognitive system. When we are immersed in the world of indigenous and traditional medicines, we can discern — if we are perceptive enough — that underlying this, there is a knowledge system intimately bound to a cosmology. In the overall pattern of medical practices in Mexico today there is a contrasting interplay between the institutional medical paradigm and the indigenous one. Indigenous medicine has its own classification system, its special categories, its medical tools, its particular connections between illness and health and its concepts of bodies and wellbeing. Some curing and healing practices characteristic of popular medicine will be mentioned.[1]

---

1. My methodology is Medical Anthropology. It is connected to a decolonial research perspective involved in recuperating and respecting the ancestral and spiritual beliefs and practices of the wise women that are contemporary healers. Searching to focus on clarifying epistemic spiritual particularities for deep comprehension. There are also some references to primary historical sources which are brought to today in the contemporary practices of those women healers. The research was done mainly in surrounding boroughs of Cuernavaca Morelos, through participant observation and interviews.

10.2. Similarity and Proximity: Epistemic Healing Tools

Let's start with the example of Doña Maria, a *curandera*, a healer from the spiritualist temple of the Sixth Seal. A patient consults her because he feels ill and thinks he is suffering from "bad air," a *mal aire*, as we say in Spanish. Doña Maria first rubs a whole raw egg over the patient's body in order to absorb the bad "air." If the patient wishes, Doña Maria then takes a look at the egg, breaking it into a glass of water. Air bubbles, long filaments and spirals appear in the egg white. Eventually, solid particles will also appear. If these impurities penetrate the egg yolk, Doña Maria will diagnose that the illness is taking root because it has entered the body. An analysis of this curative practice reveals no strict frontier between the diagnosis and treatment: healing. The egg enables the disease to be diagnosed and then cures it.

First, the diagnosis provides the healer with a vision of connections manifest in "similarities": the similarity of the bubbles with eyes, the materialization of pathological entities in material forms, the analogy of the divide between egg white and yolk with the chasm between the body and its immediate environment. Then, after grasping the connections of which the illness is an expression, the healer sees in them the means for undoing the evil knots. Frequently, the session ends with the patient being given some herbal medicine or a special object as protection.

Another procedure, equally common in popular medicine, is the *limpia*, "cleansing." In the cleansing, the *curandera* — in the Nahuatl language of the Mexican Altiplano, *curanderas* or healers were called *titici* — sweeps the patient's entire body with a bundle of aromatic plants made into a brush that is capable of absorbing the disease. This brush is destroyed after the cleansing ends, usually by burning. This technique is an example of the principle of "proximity."

On other occasions the healer will breathe on the patient's head, hands or wherever there is pain, other times she will chew the herbs which she will then rub on the affected body part. Also, very common is the practice of curing with the hands by touching the patient or in other instances forcefully shaking him or her. We will review here below some further classic "illnesses" as conceptualized (diagnosed) within the complex set of epistemic Mesoamerican definitions for health and illness.

10.3. Cosmic Concepts of the Body

Let's analyze some further meanings of these bodily curing practices. The body is conceptualized as the focus of fluid animic (non-material) entities. According to traditional indigenous medicine, the body is porous, permeable and open to the great cosmic currents. It is not a package of blood, viscera and bones enclosed in a sack of skin like the one which, according to modern medicine, the individual "has." Nor can the body be the inert terrain of modern anatomical charts. What must be read in the body are the signs of a relationship with other beings in the universe. Inversely, the external world — the macrocosm — is rich in signals which relate it with the small universe — the microcosm — which is the body. Diagnosis is frequently based on the observation of entities penetrating the body or, inversely, of the motions of various entities leaving it. In this last respect, one of the most frequent diagnoses is the loss of the soul, *la perdida del alma*, as we say in Spanish. Viewed through the lenses of the medical profession science and even theology, this pathological category must clearly be discarded as superstitious, ignorant and backward. How can one suffer soul loss and continue to live? Yet today "soul loss," *perdida del alma*, is still one of the main diagnostic categories within the Mexican indigenous healing practices.

Several ethnographic field studies describe and analyze multiple variations of soul loss.[2] The diagnosis of "soul loss" means literally that the soul is lost, a prisoner of another being or that it is wandering around. However, the soul here is not the unitary soul. This Mesoamerican concept of "soul" is formed by a multiplicity of invisible and psychic entities that inhabit the body. In his studies on the influence of black (African) medicine in Mexico, Gonzalo Aguirre Beltrán, a researcher well-known for his classic study *Medicina y Magia*,[3] affirms the existence, among the population in a region of Mexico, of four psychic and material components of the self. One is the dream soul, another is the breath soul, still another is the shadow soul and finally the mortal body. Another researcher, Evon Vogt in his studies on Zinacantan, a community in Chiapas, a Maya region south east of Mexico, points out that the *c'hulel*, (the Maya soul) has up to thirteen components. Some of these components can become independent of the body and interact with the supernatural world.

In ancient Aztec Mexico, the entities that animated the body, as Alfredo López Austin affirms[4], are invisible and that some could leave the body at various moments in life. He describes specially *Ihiyotl, Tonalli, Teyolia* as the main areas of focus of non-material entities within the body.

---

2. Evon Z. Vogt, "*Zinacanteco* 'Souls'" (London: Man, 1965). Bernardo Baytelman, "Jardin Ethnobotánico en el Estado de Morelos" (Mexico: DEP-INAH, 1986).
3. Gonzalo Aguirre Beltrán, *Medicina y Magia: El Proceso de Aculturación en el Estructura Colonial* (México: Instituto Nacional Indigenista-SEP, 1980).
4. Alfredo López Austin, *Cuerpo Humano e Ideología*. 2 volumes (Mexico: UNAM, 1984).

For example, *ihiyotl*, whose principal dwelling was the liver, could at times produce emanations harmful to people. Some individuals could produce them at will, others involuntarily. These concepts of harmful emanations are the origin of the diagnosis of *mal de ojo*, or evil eye in Spanish, and occasionally of envy as a pathogenic factor.

The *tonalli*, whose principal dwelling was considered to be the head, travelled at night during dreams. In these journeys, it ventures on the path of the supernatural beings. It is believed to be able to leave the body during coitus and sometimes during an unexpected experience. Until today the *perdida del alma* or loss of the *tonalli* is frequently seen as an outcome of an unexpected situation, not necessarily negative. When it is negative, such a condition is now called *susto*, fright, an event reputed to cause loss of soul or loss of the shadow. Due to an inadequate identification of the *tonalli* with the Christian concept of a unitary soul, there have been many hermeneutical distortions. These misinterpretations have had their impulse since the early primary sources of the history of colonisation in Mexico, among them Sahagún, Ruiz de Alarcón etc. The misunderstandings and colonizing epistemic religious impositions on the part of the colonizers has left its imprint on today's elite and the Mexican population that shares a belief in the absolute superiority of hegemonic medicine. These sectors of Mexican society judge as ignorance and superstition any way of conceptualizing the body and its healing other than by its traditional wellbeing rituals.

The third psychic entity that accumulated non-material energy was the *teyolía*. It was centered principally in the heart. It was considered the seat of reason, of intelligence, knowledge and memory. This was the only entity which, when it abandoned the body, caused death. It is interesting to point out that in divine possession among the Aztecs, the divinity possessed the *teyolía*, and not the head. The head is usually conceptualized as the receiver of divine possession within several Afro-American religions like Candomblé, Santeria and Voodoo.

Recently a medical doctor doing social service in a town bordering the jungle in south east Mexico reported how his patients expressed their symptoms: "Doctor I have a pain here" (he touched his heart) …" but it is moving here" (and then he touched his neck)… "and also moves around here (and he pointed to his legs…)." These contemporary reports express the fluidity of those animic entities which have a preferential location in the body but not a fixed static center.

In Mesoamerican traditions, the body's characteristics are different from the ones that we find in the concepts of the anatomical body of modern medicine. For instance, interior and exterior are not separated by the hermetic barrier of the skin. Between interior and exterior, there is a continuous exchange that conventional modern medicine does not understand. Moreover, the material and non-material are not considered as mutually exclusive opposites but rather as complementary poles on a spectrum of continuously interacting and mutually redefining fluid entities or shades. It is in this interaction that pathologic entities and the corresponding healing practices take shape. This polarity of complementary opposites is a recurrent feature of Mexican epistemic characteristics and it gives Mesoamerican philosophy its coherence. The complementary poles that constitute dualities — like up and down, exterior and interior, masculine and feminine, day and night, life and death — structure the whole cosmos in such a way that every primary duality is reproduced into an infinity of dual forms.

10.4. Symbolic Action

Within such a cognitive framework, it is not surprising to discover that sickness, an abstract and immaterial entity, takes on material form. One of the therapeutic practices that more clearly shows this is curing by sucking, which consists of extracting the illness from the body by sucking it out. Women healers who work this way say that they extract insects, worms, even frogs and snakes but the terms that they use reveal the symbolic aspect of this process. They express that things "like" worms came out, "like" little frogs and snakes. These terms reveal the symbolic aspect of what they do. The word "like" shows that, symbolically, what came out was the illness "materialized," that is "like" one of those animal forms. These procedures have been defined by scholars and researchers[5] as healing practices that have effects by "symbolic action." Within this medical paradigm, what we call "objective" reality is not as important as the chain of symbolic meanings. The materialization of an illness as an object — a frog, a worm, a snake or yet a piece of bone, glass or hair, for example — means that it may be destroyed, burned or thrown out. It indicates also that the immaterial illness flows towards the material pole and transforms itself into matter.

Wellbeing, wholeness, health depends thus on the balance of the material and the immaterial flow between the body and its environment. In this flow, the beings that move between the interior and the exterior do not perform only on a spectrum from the material to the immaterial but also on a symbolic basis. This is more crucial than the often emphasized

---

5. Beltrán, *Medicina y Magia*, 1980. Vogt, "*Zinacanteco* 'Souls," 1965.

chemical similarities between modern medical remedies and the potions prescribed by *curanderas*.

Information on the healing practices from the early stages of colonization in Mexico (we are speaking of the 16th century)[6] confirms that we are, today, in presence of persistent formations of Mexican indigenous medicine. The conquest was barely over when Fray Bernardino de Sahagún — a Franciscan friar and one of the first and more celebrated chroniclers of the Aztec traditions with his *Historia de las Cosas de la Nueva*[7] described the different practices of the *titici* or Aztec women doctors. Among those various practices in healing, he describes *titici* as:

> ... those who extract something from someone: first they chews absinthe and then sprinkles and rubs the patient with this. Then they massage with their hands. From the places that they massage, they take out things such as pieces of flint or obsidian, paper, splinters of pine or other things... When something has been extracted the patient recovers....[8]

He describes the woman healer as one who:

> knows well the properties of herbs, roots, trees and rocks. She has a great deal of experience with them and likewise knows many medical secrets. She who is a good doctor knows how to cure the sick, and, for the good which she does them, practically brings the dead back to life, making them get better or recover with the cures she uses. She knows how to bleed, to give purges, administer medicine and apply ointments to the body, to soften lumps in the body by massage, set bones, lance and cure wounds and the gout, cut away bad flesh and cure the evil eye. ... [By] blowing on the sick, subtly tying and untying cords, looking into water, throwing the large grains of corn customarily used in divination...she learns about and understands illnesses....[9]

This citation is from one of the foremost chroniclers in historical primary sources. Sahagún documents his experiences with the practices and knowledges of ancient women healers during the early years of colonial México.

Not long ago, I was invited to do a workshop with indigenous Mayan Zapatista women (members of an indigenous political autonomic project) *promotoras de salud*, in English "promoters of health." This term refers to the medical practitioners in regions of the State of Chiapas, in Southern

---

6. Fray Bernardino de Sahagún, *Historia General de las Cosas de Nueva España* (México: Porrua, 1982).
7. Ibid., 1577.
8. Ibid., 1540.
9. Fray Bernardino de Sahagún, *Florentine Codex: General History of the Things of New Spain*. Book X, Chapter XIII (Salt Lake City: School of American Research and University of Utah, 1974).

Mexico. When I mentioned Sahagún's XVIth century descriptions of the ancient healing practices, these women were amazed. They started sharing their own recipes, with all of us in this workshop, while emphasizing the similarity of their healing rituals with Sahagún's descriptions. It was my turn to be surprised by the continuity and permanence of these traditions, albeit refunctionalized,[10] through the centuries. These contemporary women were their communities' healers, the medical doctors, the *titici* of the Zapatistas. We spent the next hours sharing the equivalences, differences, and permanences between early and contemporary healing practices, ritual procedures and herbal potions.

This is an example of a culture of resistance to colonization. Resistance, in this case, to the invasion and imposition of European medical and Christian paradigms.

We have reviewed here a few of the indigenous healing practices of the women healers in Mexico today. We can notice that there is always a coherent reason for their medical and ritual practices. That is so, if you keep in mind to review them within their own epistemic references, their alternative "rationality" and their particular way of perceiving, conceiving and constructing the body, wellbeing and health. It is a coherence that is efficient and escapes the dominant, colonized, medical, modern mentality. Let's not debase them by our own ignorance, calling them backward and primitive beliefs and practices.

10.5. Concluding Remarks

The main difficulty for acknowledging the contributions of indigenous medical practices and the prominence of women within these beliefs and practices lies in accepting as only valid definitions by the hegemonic medical and political establishment of who we are and how we ought to be. Demands for an open and alternative "pluriverse" can open the possibility of respecting the plurality of conceptions that goes beyond accepting only one "universal" medical paradigm. This brief review shows how we can approach indigenous medicine, respecting and appreciating it within its own complex epistemic universe of interconnection, interdependence and symbolic action. Let's claim our right to put the world together, to conceive of health and illness and in a variety of ways to incorporate women's spiritual and ritual domain as part of our wellbeing.

---

10. López Austin, *Cuerpo Humano e Ideología*, 1984.

III

ACTIVISM

CHAPTER 11

INDIAN WOMEN: NURTURING THE EARTH, PROTECTING LIFE

Aruna Gnanadason

> For us, the rivers, the forests, and our land
> are the basis of our existence,
> This earth is our mother.
> No one can snatch her away from us.
> No one has the right
> to take away our land from us.
> We therefore take an oath today
> that we will always protect
> our land and rivers.
> Large dams being built in this area
> are drowning our forests,
> our mountains and our land.
> We pledge never to let this happen.
> **A solemn pledge by the people in a mass gathering against
> the Subarnarekha dam project.**[1]

11.1.

India is walking swiftly on the competitive road to becoming a "developed" nation — this is the ideology, the ambition that drives every policy, every political program in this country. To aspire to possess a "bullet" train (even if millions still have to walk great distances or depend on ill-equipped and fragile public transport systems); to build the tallest statue in the world (even if Indigenous Peoples are displaced, many cultivated lands inundated, many trees decimated and waterways disturbed to give way for it); to have more and more industrial production (even if it leaves India as one of the most polluted countries in the world). All these and more onslaughts on the earth and on the life of the poor of the earth,

---

1. People in a mass gathering against the Subarnarekha dam project in Jharkhand (former South Bihar), *Voices of the Adivasis/Indigenous Peoples of India*, ed. Sarini (Delhi, India: All India Co-ordinating Forum of the Adivasis/Indigenous Peoples, 2001), 65. Quoted by Aruna Gnanadason, *Listen to the Women: Listen to the Earth* (Geneva: Risk Book, WCC Publications, 2005), 1.

challenge the flourishing of life and a sustainable future. The powers-that-be focus on the desires and needs of the middle and upper classes so as to persuade them into believing that this so-called "development" is what will give them a better life. All this in a bid to ensure that they who rule are voted back to power, even if they are corrupt and however anti-poor, short-sighted, or lopsided their policies may be. For example, the demand is for faster and faster internet connectivity (even if it means destroying small publicly owned networks and lining the pockets of the biggest business houses in India), while millions still live with little or no electricity even — the list could go on. The denuding of the forests, destroying green stretches, digging into the mountains and the earth, polluting the waters at an absolutely unsustainable pace, and eroding the life, livelihood and dignity of millions of people seems to be the only way to ensure the "development" of the nation for the benefit of a privileged minority. The lives of millions of the poor seem to have no value at all!

An icon of this so called "development" is the controversy that rages in India just now — the building of a statue of Vallabhai Patel, a leader of the Indian freedom movement who, in 1948, was Deputy Prime Minister of newly Independent India, after 200 or so years of British rule. At that critical moment in 1948, Patel was charged with the responsibility to bring together the many petty existing kingdoms so as to forge a united India. And now some 70 years later, the present government has decided to build a statue to honor Patel and appropriately to call it the Statue of Unity. However, is this a befitting way to honor a leader or is it a ploy to gain a political edge? That has been the question raised by many. The statue has been built in the state of Gujarat on the River Narmada, a few kilometers away from the Sardar Sarovar Dam (this major dam is one of the many on the river Narmada that flows through four states of India). A strong resistance was underway, since 1985, with massive participation of Indigenous women to "Save the River Narmada" or *Narmada Bachao Andolan*, from a project of several dams on the river. The protest did force the World Bank to withdraw from the project. Yes! But the Indian government went ahead with alternate funding. The non-violent struggle of largely Indigenous peoples continues today. One method they use is for women and men protesters to stand in the river, waist-high, for days on end, defying the threats of being drowned by the waters from the opened sluices of the dams.

And now they face a new threat. Construction related to this statue, at a cost of roughly US$ 440 million (according to a BBC report[2]), has

---

2. British Broadcasting Corporation, "World News: Asia: India," 31 October, 2018, Accessed on 11 November, 2018: https://www.bbc.com/news/world-asia-india.

already submerged large areas of land, including the land that had previously been cultivated by the Indigenous communities who live in the villages in that area. Just for the inauguration of this statue by the Prime Minister of the country, water was released from the dam, so that the dignitaries and other guests could enjoy the grandeur of the River Narmada in full swell. Forty acres of cultivated land were submerged on October 31, 2018, to allow for this — cultivated vegetables which were getting ready for harvest were inundated; to make matters worse the farmers were not warned that the water was being released. "We are witnessing the water level rise by the hour and land submerging gradually," Ambaben Poonabhai, a 60-year-old Indigenous woman, told a reporter. She lives in Navagam, one of those villages that will be submerged as water rises in the weir of the Narmada river.[3]

From here my narrative moves to the South of India to another largely women-led resistance movement.

11.2. "Women at the forefront of the anti-Sterlite protests" in the Headlines[4]

According to the people of Thoothukudi, a small town in South India, women were the ones who led the protests against the UK-based multinational Vedanta, which is setting up a copper smelting unit in Thoothukudi. The Sterlite Copper Smelting factory has been in the news since 2001 because from then the factory has been systematically opposed by the local residents for polluting their environment and causing a range of health problems. The unit has been subject to several closures, on the grounds of its violations of environmental norms. The National Environmental Research Institute (NEERI) and the TNPCB (Tamil Nadu Pollution Control Board) have found evidence that Sterlite contaminated the groundwater, air and soil with its effluents and also violated standards of operation.[5]

More than 60,000 people live in eight towns and 27 villages within a 10 km radius of the plant. Activists in the area have been accusing Sterlite

---

3. https://sabrangindia.in/article/tall-price-gujarats-tribals-are-paying-tallest-statue, Accessed 11 November, 2018.
4. https://www.livemint.com 27 May, 2018, Accessed 31 October, 2018. The smelter — Sterlite Copper is located within the State Industrial Promotion Corporation of Tamil Nadu (SIPCOT) complex in Thoothukudi in South India and has operated since 1997. Attached to the smelter, is a refinery, a phosphoric acid plant, a sulphuric acid plant, a copper rod plant and three captive power plants. Sterlite Copper is the Indian copper-producing unit, a subsidiary of Vedanta Resources, the UK-based mining company.
5. www.thehindu.com › News › States › Tamil Nadu, May 27, 2018. Accessed on 13 November, 2018.

of contaminating the water resources and also of causing air pollution. Many villagers alleged that pollutants from the Sterlite factory have caused breathing disorders, skin diseases, heart conditions, along with other health problems. Speaking to a reporter a resident named Baby said: "We could taste the pollutants in the water." She also reported that the people have completely stopped using groundwater.

In 2013, people had complained that they were facing a variety of health problems, nausea, throat infection, and difficulty in breathing, because of a gas leak from the Sterlite Industries plant. In 2013, the plant was ordered to be closed for a period based on the report of the Tamil Nadu Pollution Control Board. However, as a result of the company's pressure on the Central Government, the plant was reopened as ordered by the central government.

In March and April 2018, there were renewed mass-protests led by women against the company's plans of setting up a second smelting complex and demands were made for an entire shutdown of the smelting plants, because they were again blatantly violating environmental regulations.[6] On 22 May, 2018 the non-violent protests took a deadly turn as 14 people were killed and several others injured, following police shooting into the crowd, supposedly to quell the protests. Following this, mass protests occurred all over the State and nation and even in other parts of the world. On 28 May, 2018, the Government of Tamil Nadu was finally forced to order the permanent closure of the Sterlite plant in Thoothukudi.

The protest spread overseas when a section of the Indian diaspora in London held a demonstration at the home of Anil Agarwal, Vedanta's CEO. The protests have been consistently non-violent on the side of the aggrieved citizens. The Tamil Nadu Pollution Control Board submitted a report before a panel constituted by the National Green Tribunal to show that the ambient air quality has improved in the vicinity since the closure of Vedanta's Sterlite copper plant in Thoothukudi, and they warned that the plan of the Company to reopen a second smelting complex will once again lead to pollutants in the air.[7] This has been contested by the firm.[8] But currently the plant remains closed as ordered by the government of Tamil Nadu.

---

6. www.legalservicesindia.com/article/1926/Environmental-Laws-and-Constitutional-Provisions-In-India.html. Accessed 26 June, 2019.

7. https://www.thenewsminute.com/article/sterlite-here-s-proof-data-air-pollution-and-case-missing-trees-78841. April 5, 2018. Accessed on 11 November, 2018.

8. https://www.ibtimes.co.in/sterlite-plant-tamil-nadu-rejects-report-tuticorin-groundwater-contamination-citing-prejudice-780023. 9 September, 2018. Accessed 13 November, 2018.

From this presently successful struggle we move to a small town called Koodankulam, and to another women-led movement which had taken place a few years earlier!

11.3. Women Have Been Protesting against the Setting Up of a Nuclear Power Plant

The *Guardian* newspaper had reported that: "Women are leading protests in Tamil Nadu state against a nuclear power plant — yet few people in India know the village they're from, let alone support their cause." Since the late 1980's, when it was first proposed, a campaign has been mounted against the nuclear reactors being installed near their villages in the South Indian state of Tamil Nadu. Protests have increased in vehemence since 2011 when the first reactor was fueled. Celine, 73, was among the protestors who take it in turns to go without food. "Not a single government, not a single political party is willing to take up our cause," she says. "Only Mother Mary can save us now."[9]

The *Guardian*, quoted above, writes a moving testament to the women and their courage in this protest. As India "develops," its energy needs are growing rapidly. More than 300 million Indians are still without electricity. India consumes a whopping 872 million tons of oil equivalent for power; only China and the US use more. Its annual energy import bill is 120 billion dollars, which will grow to one trillion dollars by 2040. The Indian government presents nuclear energy as part of its "clean energy" solution to its looming energy crisis. The Nuclear Power Corporation of India was set up by the government and according, to its mission statement, it is to "produce nuclear power as a safe, environmentally benign and economically viable source of electrical energy to meet the increasing electricity needs of the country."[10] However, the women have become aware of the disasters caused by faulty reactors and leaks and the impact these have on the people. They know about the 1986 Chernobyl disaster and these reactors in Koodankulam being Russian has left them little comfort, as they confront these new threats to the lives of the people in their region.

Despite India's billions of dollars of investment in nuclear power, the latest figures from the Department of Atomic Energy (DAE) that were obtained by The *Guardian* suggest nuclear plants produced 37,456m units of electricity which covers just about 2% of the country's annual

---

9. https://www.theguardian.com/global-development/2016/jun/06/lonely-struggle-india-anti-nuclear-protesters-tamil-nadu-kudankulam-idinthakarai 6 June, 2016. Accessed 20 June, 2018.

10. indianpowersector.com/2010/09/npcil. Accessed 11 November, 2018.

consumption needs. And anyway, the people fear that the electricity produced is for industrial establishments and not for domestic use.

The *Guardian* reports that many countries have taken a slice of India's budding nuclear energy market: the UK, Canada, the US, Australia and Japan have all offered expertise and resources. Nuclear plants, backed by foreign governments, dot India's coastlines and central states. Yet foreign governments have shirked responsibility for the impact these units will have on the people living in the locations where they are set up. When President Barack Obama visited India a few years ago he signed a deal limiting the US's legal liability in the event of an accident at a nuclear plant.[11] The women know just how dangerous this is to the environment and to their lives and just how vulnerable they are and what little relief they will be given in case of an accident. Here their struggle did not end well as the reactor has continued to operate. These are among the examples of the many women-led movements in different parts of India demanding closure of so called "development projects" that are in fact death-dealing to people.

11.4. An Eco-feminist Approach and Theology from an Indian Christian

The history of the church in India shows examples of the negative role played by Christian missions in undermining the value and sacredness that Indigenous peoples attach to the earth. Colonialism and the desire to "develop" nations — which have led to conquest and occupation and the extraction of resources/wealth of colonized nations — were closely linked to a particular understanding of Christian theology. Such an ideology persists until today; it is therefore urgent that Christianity turn towards the earth and the people of the earth.

Ecofeminism in India recognizes that the protection of the earth is closely linked to other systems of injustice and discrimination — the issue of intentionally instituted poverty and other forms of discrimination, including the role of colonialism and neo-colonialism in the use and abuse of both women and the earth; social structures of injustice such as caste and ethnicity have also played a contributory role in denigrating women and the earth in India. Therefore, an ecofeminist vision is inspired by the knowledge of poor women in India, particularly Indigenous and Dalit women.

---

11. https://www.theguardian.com/global-development/2016/jun/06/lonely-struggle-india-anti-nuclear-protesters-tamil-nadu-kudankulam-idinthakarai 6 June, 2016. Accessed 20 June, 2018.

They represent hope as they carry within their life experiences the traditions of prudent care with which they have lived with the earth for centuries. Many Indigenous communities of women try to recover patterns of spirituality that connect them to their roots and to their traditional wisdom — often having to work against forces that attempt to stifle their histories, their knowledge systems, their lands. For many of them, destruction of the earth is destruction of life itself. Theirs is a different worldview, a different epistemology, a different analysis, and they offer unique spiritual resources that they are ready to contribute to the care of the earth.

Indigenous women of the Gond Peoples in Central India speak of the earth as mother, in a relational sense.[12] There is no space for romanticism here, as they too face violence in the domestic sphere, as mothers and as women. Therefore, one uses the motif of "motherhood" with caution because of the oppressive and dehumanizing ways in which motherhood has been appropriated by patriarchy. However, when Narango Puri, a Gond woman, refers to the selfless love that the earth as mother has for all her children, her language did not seem to have similar patriarchal overtones. Narango said in a very matter-of-fact-way that the: "Earth is like our mother, like a mother who cares for her children selflessly. As humans we go through the life cycle — we give birth, we nurture our young ones at the breast, we grow and we die. The earth will never die, but this requires that we as women who go through the same processes of birthing and caring for our children need to also nurture the earth."[13] She was also quite pragmatic in her response as to why they consider some groves and mountains to be sacred. "The sacred groves are seed banks — and have a diversity of plants. Therefore, we worship them with rituals and prayers. We never touch this life source but allow regeneration there. In this way the sustainability of the earth is protected. Narango ended our conversation by saying, "We may die, we may face death, but we will not leave the land — we will not be separated from our mother."

What can we as environmental feminists learn from Narango Puri and other Indigenous and Dalit women as we work to reclaim and redefine the relational and "sacrificial" value of motherhood, debunking it of the expectation patriarchy has imposed on it? From the context of the political engagement of Adivasi women in Orissa and in other parts of India,

---

12. This section is based on a conversation I had with Narango Puri and other women of the Deomali Women's Society in Semiliguda, Orissa in Central India, January 2003. They are Gonds, an indigenous group of people who face serious threats to their lives and their lands with the setting up of factories and other "development" projects on their ancestral lands.

13. Aruna Gnanadason, *Listen to the Women! Listen to the Earth!* (Geneva: RISK Book Series, WCC Publications, 2005), 17.

it is evident that motherhood is symbolic of political action for a healed earth — it cannot be reduced to a biological role as has been emphasized in patriarchal societies. It is this transformed image of motherhood that has inspired eco-feminist theological reflections on the image of the earth as the body of God and as the mothering womb of God.[14]

11.5. Protestant Christianity and Its Ambivalence about the Earth

This discussion becomes important if we consider the ambivalence of Protestant Christianity in India and some of the mistakes made in Christianity's mission history which had in some instances dismissed the customs, practices and spiritualities of Indigenous peoples in derogatory ways, labeling them as "pagan and animistic." In recent times, Indigenous theologians in India have begun to interrogate this history and some elements of Christianity that subvert environmental goals. Wati Longchar, an Indigenous theologian from Nagaland in North East India, writes:

> Creation is the first act of God's revelation. God cannot be perceived without water, wind, trees, vegetation, sky, light, darkness, animals or humans. It is the first act of revelation. God revealed himself/herself as *co-creator* with the earth... God is present in creation. The presence of God makes the earth sacred. That is why God entered into a covenantal relationship with all creatures... The major problem in theology is the articulation by faith of human history without taking into consideration all the members of the earth's family.[15]

No wonder then that Lynn White Jr. wrote more than four decades ago of the callous attitudes of Christianity towards the earth:

> In Antiquity every tree, every spring, every stream, every hill had its own genius loci, its guardian spirit ...... Before one cut a tree, mined a mountain, or dammed a brook, it was important to placate the spirit in charge of that particular situation and to keep it placated. By destroying pagan animism, Christianity made it possible to exploit nature in a mood of indifference to the feelings of natural objects.[16]

---

14. Ibid., 99–102.
15. Wati Longchar, "Indigenous Theology in Asia" in *Asian Theology on the Way: Christianity, Culture and Context*, ed. Peniel Jesudason Rufus Rajkumar (London: SPCK, 2012), 94.
16. Lynn White Jr., "The Historical Roots of Our Ecological Crisis," *Science*: 1967. Reprinted in Readings in *Ecology and Feminist Theology*, ed. Mary Heather MacKinnon and Moni McIntyre (Kansas City: Sheed and Ward, 1995), 31. See also Carolyn Merchant, *The Death of Nature* (San Francisco: Harper and Row, 1980); Rosemary Radford Ruether, *Gaia and God: An Ecofeminist Theology of Earth Healing* (San Francisco: Harper, 1994); Larry Rasmussen, *Earth Community* (New York: Orbis Books, 1996); John E. Carroll, Paul

In the face of the large-scale environmental damage in India, the urgency of this task cannot be underestimated. The question to be asked is whether feminist theologies and the theological gifts of Indigenous Peoples, Dalits and other subaltern communities have had any impact on the Christian understanding of creation theology. The epistemologies of women and other groups on the edges of the society can influence theological teaching and the churches in India — regrettably, this impact is minimal as Christianity is still immersed in inherited Christian theologies and has remained deeply entrenched in a Euro-centric missionary past and patriarchal worldview.

11.6. Earth Care: Some Ethical Values that Ecofeminism Offers

Towards a new way of relating with each other and with creation:

Christian faith, its theology and more particularly feminist theology, does contain the potential to provide a liberation ethic that would challenge all forms of oppression — between human beings and between humanity and the earth. For example, Letty Russell underlines the importance of feminist theology which "reaches for a new mode of relationship: neither a hierarchical model that diminishes the potential of the 'other' nor an 'equality' defined by a ruling norm drawn from the dominant group, but rather a mutuality that allows us to affirm different ways of being."[17] To eco-feminist criticism of anthropocentrism is related to the refusal of humanity to recognize the patriarchal fundamentals of the destructive way we live with the earth. Eco-feminists criticize the patriarchal systems and structures which have privileged those who plunder the earth for profit and fail to recognize the integrity of the earth and all life forms including the lives of those communities that live on the earth and nurture it. In this context it is important to acknowledge the work of eco-theologians such as George Zachariah, who stresses the importance of a form of anthropocentrism so as to reclaim the agency of people's movements in resisting development projects that destroy ecosystems. He calls this a "non-anthropocentric anthropology that affirms the being and becoming of a new humanity in the community of creation."[18] Therefore, when feminists in India would reject androcentrism (males as norms of

---

Brockelman et. al, *The Greening of Faith* (Hanover and London: University of New Hampshire Press, 1997).

17. Letty M. Russell, *Feminist Interpretation of the Bible* (Philadelphia: The Westminster Press, 1985), 116.

18. George Zachariah, *Alternatives Incorporated: Earth Ethics from the Grassroots* (London: Equinox, 2011), 123-124.

humanity) they have to take this a step further and be bold in rejecting all forms of domination and exclusive values between human beings. Additionally, what is required is an epistemological shift that respects the earth's integrity, as well as explores ways in which we listen to the wisdom of the earth and all the children of the earth.

11.7. The Ethic of Eco-justice as the Frame of Analysis

Both the poor and the earth cry out for justice. Nature can be seen as the new poor, "not the poor that crowds out the human poor, but the 'also' poor; and as such it demands our attention and care."[19] This requires political engagement to transform the injustice that is done both to the earth and to the poor — it calls for a merging of political activism with a spirituality of resistance. It calls for our engagement as theologians with people's movements such as the ongoing struggles referred to above, because "our participation in their struggles for liberation mediates our own liberation. In fact, it requires more than an intellectual reexamination of the way we have done theological ethics; it calls for a new discipleship journey — a detour in the way we live our faith."[20] In exploring with Indigenous women the depth of their ecological wisdom we can learn a new ethic of care. This is not to legitimize the language of biological determinism that presumes some kind of inherent link between women and nature. But Narango Puri said it well: "There is a radical relationship between the woman and the land" — to her it is about the relational character of humanity with the land. Women emphasize the interdependent character of the radical relationship[21] between the earth and humanity and the urgency of an ethic of care that women can offer to the earth in its distress.

11.8. Reclaiming Women's Ways of Knowing: Feminist Epistemologies

For eco-feminist theologians therefore, an alternative epistemology is based on a commitment to transform hierarchical structures of power and injustice so as to rediscover the liberative potential of Christianity. This implies social action that has the courage to question and resist unjust structures

---

19. Sallie McFague, *Super, Natural Christians: How We Should Love Nature* (Minneapolis: Fortress Press, 1997), 6.
20. George Zachariah, *Alternatives Incorporated*, Ibid., 9.
21. Sallie McFague, *Life Abundant: Rethinking Theology and Economy for a Planet in Peril* (Minneapolis: Fortress Press, 2000), 18. McFague explores the concept of the radical relationality reflective of the wisdom of Indigenous women such as Narango Puri in Orissa.

and systems of knowledge that are framed by centers of abusive power. Eco-feminist theologians call for an overcoming of dualistic and hierarchical ways of knowing and bringing center stage the wisdom and knowledge of subaltern communities. This is based on an understanding that in such knowledge we will find resources to reverse the ecological destruction that has been caused by dominant ways of knowing and so-called scientific forms of enquiry. This also demands new ethical judgments on what is good, just and sustainable. Vandana Shiva articulates this well:

> The intellectual heritage of ecological survival lies with those who are experts in survival. They have the knowledge and experience to extricate us from the ecological cul-de-sac that the Western masculinist mind has maneuvered us into. And while Third World women have privileged access to survival expertise, their knowledge is inclusive, not exclusive. The ecological categories with which they think and act can become the categories of liberation for all, for men as well as for women, for the West as well as for the non-West, for the human as well as the non-human elements of the earth.[22]

11.9.1. An Eco-feminist Vision in India Is, Therefore, an Eco-just Feminist Vision[23]

The crucial hyphenated word "eco-just" qualifies an Indian eco-feminist vision. Dominant ecological discourse has not adequately addressed the interconnections between the economic and ecological dimensions of life. Neither have they affirmed the spirituality of hope and resistance that lies in the wisdom of the people most affected by the earth's distress. The solutions lie not just in individual actions of care for the earth but in transformation of an unjust world order. There seems to be reluctance to relate with the political dimension of church and mission history, with regards to the conquest of nature and of the earth. These theologians do not address questions of unequal power relations in our world and the way this impacts the earth.

11.9.2. An Eco-feminist Vision Affirms More Compassionate Images of God

This calls for a new understanding and language for the image of God. God in India, from an eco-feminist liberation perspective, is in fact shaped by Indian cosmology, which affirms the interdependence of all

---

22. Vandana Shiva, *Staying Alive: Women, Ecology and Survival in India* (Delhi: Kali for Women, 1988), 224.
23. This formed the main focus of my D.Min. Thesis submitted to the San Francisco Theological Seminary, D.Min. in Feminist Theologies. It was adapted as a book and published by the World Council of Churches, Geneva. *Listen to the Women! Listen to the Earth*, 2005.

forms of life and the dialectical harmony between humanity and the divine, between human beings and the earth, and between the male and female principles.[24] God intervenes in a caring relationship not in a dominating way. But God is not reduced to the world because God transcends human understanding; therefore no one image would suffice.

The model of the world as God's body[25] encourages holistic attitudes of responsibility for the care of the earth and for the vulnerable and the oppressed; it is non-hierarchical. Both in God's immanence and transcendence, the image of a God is found within us and in all of creation. Kwok Pui Lan writes:

> We can come to know God through nature as well as through human history. There is no separation between 'special revelation' known through the specific Christian story and the so-called 'general revelation' known through nature and wisdom from other cultures.[26]

An earth-friendly God is a God of compassion, who has "profound reverence toward life, empathy towards those who suffer and concern for the flourishing of all beings."[27] The focus of such an understanding of God is not on human beings alone but on all of life. Eco-feminist theologians draw on God's reciprocal relationship with the earth and with humanity — interconnecting the spirit and matter. God's spirit is accessible to us only in the body, i.e., the world. The world is not just nature, the good creation, but also society, the way human beings interact with one another and with nature. Exploitation and violence are thus done to the body of God whenever we inflict violence on the earth and on the vulnerable ones on the earth.

Eco-feminist theologians therefore call for a shift from an implicitly dualistic, hierarchical, individualistic and utilitarian subject-object relationship with God and with the earth, to a subject-subject relationship which values the integrity and goodness of all of creation. This will naturally draw us into understanding our image of God anew in terms of relationality. God as the resisting, struggling poor woman — God as one who brooks no injustice and who protects the earth; God as community — emphasizing the inextricable link between the divine, humanity and all of the earth. God as a mothering, nurturing woman is perhaps the most crucial understanding for our times.

---

24. Aruna Gnanadason, "Toward a Feminist Eco-theology for India," *Women Healing Earth: Third World Women on Ecology, Feminism and Religion* (New York: Orbis Books, 1996), 74–81.

25. Sallie McFague, *Life Abundant* (Minneapolis, MN: Augsburg Fortress, 2001).

26. Kwok Pui Lan, *Introducing Asian Feminist Theology* (Sheffield, England: Sheffield Academic Press, 2000), 75–76.

27. Ibid., 7.

We face an urgent task of reversing the damage we have done to the earth in the last 200 years or so of industrial growth compounded by a more recent neo-liberal growth model of development. Many voices, many forms of wisdom are needed — among them the eco-feminist theological vision is offered with its commitment to prudent care and transformational ethics. Do we dare to not listen to the earth and to the women?

CHAPTER 12

WANGARI MAATHAI AND AFRICAN ENVIRONMENTAL REFORM

Rosemary Radford Ruether

12.1.

Africa was divided up between the European powers in the last decades of the nineteenth century. The period from the 1880s to the 1960s saw a rapid appropriation of African land, the marginalization of its people and the denigration of its traditional cultures and worldviews by the European colonialists. Although political independence came to many African nations in the 1960s, for others, such as Zimbabwe, the struggle for national liberation went on until 1980, for Namibia until 1990 and for South Africa until 1994. Patterns of land appropriation and economic domination created by colonial regimes were largely continued on by the new independent African regimes, many of which became one-party dictatorships. The trauma of impoverishment and exploitation in a global neo-colonial system lived on.

Only in the 1990s was there a move toward greater democracy in many Sub-Saharan African nations. The end of apartheid in South Africa in 1994 and the fashioning of a progressive constitution assuring racial and gender equality and ethnic diversity gave a boost to reform across the continent. This included environmental protection. The Bill of Rights of the South African Constitution declares: "Everyone has a right to an environment which is not harmful to their health and well-being and to have the environment protected for the benefit of present and future generations, …to prevent pollution and ecological degradation, promote conservation and secure ecologically sustainable development…"[1]

12.2.1. Wangari Maathai, Kenya's Colonization, and the Green Belt Movement

The prophetic leader of environmental protection in Kenya and through all Africa is Wangari Maathai, founder of the Kenyan Green Belt

---

1. Bill of Rights of the South African Constitution, Section 24.

Movement.[2] Maathai was born in 1940 and grew up in a rural area of the central highlands of Kenya. In her early years she experienced the land as still lush and green, with abundant clear waters on which families grew their own food of healthful fruits and vegetables. Hunger was unknown and the soil was "rich, dark brown and moist." Her mother taught her to respect and care for the trees which held the soil intact and facilitated the rising of abundant streams of water. In their area the iconic Mount Kenya, or *Kirinyaga*, the "place of Brightness" could be seen, viewed as a sacred mountain from which came all gifts.

Yet this abundant world was already being destroyed before she was born. The British had colonized the land at the beginning of the 20th century, giving the best land to white settlers, and assigning poor land as "native reserves" to the indigenous Africans. Her father worked as a mechanic on a farm of a White settler. The lush valleys were being cleared of their trees and brush to plant coffee and tea plantations for export and to grow foreign trees for lumber. This caused the streams to dry up and the soil to wash down hillsides.

Although Maathai's family was of modest means, she was lucky to receive a good education. Contrary to expectations, her mother agreed with her brother to send her along to primary school with her brothers. She then was accepted into a Catholic girls' school for later primary and secondary education. In 1960 the Kennedy family offered an "airlift" to six hundred Kenyan youth to go to college in the United States as Kenya looked forward to its independence. Maathai flourished at Mount St. Scholastica College in Atkinson, Kansas and then went on to get her MA in biology at the University of Pittsburgh. After six years away in the U.S. from 1960-1966, she returned home to Kenya for a job at the newly founded University in Nairobi, where, together with universities in Germany, she completed a Ph.D. in 1971 in veterinary science, making her one of the most educated women in Kenya. She married in that year and produced three children over the next five years, while continuing as a lecturer at the University.

12.2. Impoverishing Kenya's Environment and People, Particularly Kenyan Women

Meanwhile Maathai was becoming aware of the environmental issues that were impoverishing Kenya. She was invited to join the board of the Environmental Liaison Centre established in 1974 by international environmental organizations to link local NGOs in Nairobi to the United

---

2. Wangari Maathai, *The Green Belt Movement: Sharing the Approach and the Experience* (New York: Lantern Books, 2003).

Nations Environment Programme. Through this group, and also from her post-doctoral research on a parasite affecting cattle, Maathai became aware of the environmental degradation affecting Kenya. She was able to observe the deforestation and soil erosion devastating the rural area where she had grown up and the malnourishment of both the livestock and the people. Maathai began to see the relationship of environmental degradation and the poverty of the people. She was also a member of the National Council of Women of Kenya linking women's groups throughout the nation. A seminar given by a woman researcher for this group discussed the malnutrition of Kenyan children and its links with the "cash crop" economy that grew coffee and tea for export and no longer the nutritious local foods.

As Maathai studied these social problems, she became aware that they were all linked to environmental impoverishment. What was needed was a campaign to plant trees to restore the land and water. She also shared this concern with the NCWK (National Council of Women of Kenya) who had elected her both to the executive committee and the Standing Committee on Environment and Habitat. From this there emerged in 1977 the Green Belt Movement that developed networks of women to create tree nurseries and to plant trees all over the country. The tree planting program quickly spread through the NCWK networks and soon farmers, schools and churches were setting up their own programs. The Green Belt program also received funds to pay poor women a small fee for each tree planted that stayed alive six months, so this allowed these women to make a small income through their work in planting trees and caring for them.

Maathai also became increasingly aware of how women were discriminated against and the relation between ethnic injustice and women's rights. In her younger years she had been deeply nurtured by her mother and also by her teachers during her educational trajectory. But when she returned to Kenya, with her MA in biology, she was at first passed over for a job she had been promised, because of her ethnicity (as a Kikuyu) and her being a woman. She had to fight to get another job. Once she was married and also continuing to teach, she was aware of how she was seen as "out of place" because of her education and leadership. This came to a head when her husband left her in 1977 and sued for a divorce. The media took up the attack on her and reported that she was "too educated, too strong, too successful, too stubborn and too hard to control."[3]

This was followed by further disasters. Her questioning of the judge's treatment of her brought a charge of contempt of court and she was briefly jailed. Kenyan jails are quite oppressive, so this was no easy experience.

---

3. Wangari Maathai, *Unbowed: A Memoir* (New York: Anchor Books, 2006), 146.

She resigned her job at the University in order to run for Parliament, but was refused this opportunity, and then was not reinstated at the University; she was also evicted from her university housing. Thus, after sixteen years of service she found herself without a job or a salary, no pension, no house and few savings. However, she quickly picked herself up and found ways to continue. Free from university teaching, she became the full-time organizer of the Green Belt Movement. Funds from Norway and the UN arrived to help support the Green Belt Movement. The movement itself began to expand its focus. Although it centered on planting trees, it developed seminars to analyze larger implications of environmental degradation in the misuse of political power, economic domination, and human and gender rights.

12.3. Green Belt Responses to Food Insecurity and Political Repression in Kenya

As the Green Belt Movement grew, conflict with political power grew more volatile. President Daniel arap Moi, who had succeeded Jomo Kenyatta as President, had become increasingly violent as head of a one-party dictatorship. Maathai became aware that he planned to seize part of Uhuru Park in central Nairobi to build a sixty-story skyscraper and a huge statue to himself, thus destroying an important natural area enjoyed by ordinary people. Maathai and the Green Belt Movement led the struggle to prevent this and suffered much harassment from the police as a result. She was beaten and knocked unconscious at one point, when she supported a group of mothers fighting for the freedom of their sons from wrongful political imprisonment.

Planting trees became only one aspect of the Green Belt Movement. Equally important are food security, water harvesting and civic advocacy in the face of land grabbing of state land by the government to give to favorite supporters and the repeated violations of human rights by the powerful in league with outside corporations. Local people were taught sustainable agriculture to restore the growing of local nutritious food crops for consumption, rather than growing cash crops for export, for which Kenyan farmers are often poorly paid. Rural women learned to cultivate tree nurseries near their homes, planting trees that alleviated the need for long walks to gather firewood, fencing and building materials. Planting fruit trees provided both food as well as wood. The restoration of forest cover brought the return of animals and birds, protected and restored eroded soils and cleaned water resources. The women also learned to conserve water through mulching and harvesting water through metal roofs that drained into storage tanks.

Maathai's work also moved toward political organizing. She founded the Green Party of Kenya that allied itself with other Green Parties in Africa and beyond. In 2002, when President Moi finally agreed to step down and allow a multi-party election, she ran for Parliament and won a seat as an MP. Her gifts were recognized and she was appointed Assistant Minister of Environment and Natural Resources for the Kenyan Government. She also led the movement for cancellation of debts owed by poor countries around the world, including Kenya, that was part of the Jubilee 2000 movement.

12.4. Africa, Land, and Power

The impact of the Green Belt Movement went beyond Kenya. Training courses were developed that drew groups from across Africa, with people from more than fifteen African countries taking the training and programs back to their own nations. In 2009 Maathai published her book, *Challenge for Africa*, to spell out the implications of her thirty years of organizing to address the difficulties of Africa.[4] In this book she asks why post-independence Africa has suffered such poor leadership and its bright promise of freedom from colonialism in the 1960s has been so largely betrayed.

Maathai sees much of this problem as residing in the distortions of land and power that were imposed by colonialism and were continued by those trained in this system after independence. She sees the ongoing poor quality of leadership as the result of the way the colonialists socialized Africans to distrust themselves, to despise their own traditions and culture and to assume that the Western way of doing things was superior to their own. Dependency on outside aid also fosters a culture of dependency, as well as a quest to emulate the wealth and power of the former masters, rather than cultivating an ethic of service and responsibility to their own people.

For her, Africa needs a deep cultural revolution that both reclaims some pre-colonial cultural and social patterns of accountability of leaders to their own people and fosters grass roots initiatives of leadership and applies these to the new realities of Africa's place in the World of the 21st century. One of the issues that needs to be addressed is dealing with environmental degradation and climate change from which Africa is disproportionately suffering, even though it contributes little to the global carbon emissions that are causing this climate change. Environmental destruction must be understood in relation to poverty and to systems of injustice, rather than regarded as an isolated problem.

---

4. Wangari Maathai, *The Challenge for Africa* (New York: Pantheon Books, 2009).

12.5. Prophetic Leadership Makes History: Maathai's Nobel Peace Prize

On October 8, 2004, when Wangari Maathai was still an MP and was on her way to meet with her parliamentary constituency, she received a phone call from Norway informing her that she had been awarded the Nobel Peace Prize. This recognition was by no means the first of such awards she has received. She has received international recognition literally dozens of times from all over the world, but the Nobel Peace Prize was undoubtedly the most outstanding. The decision to give the Nobel Peace Prize to Maathai says several things. First of all, it recognizes the reality that environmental renewal is an integral part of creating peace in Kenya and in the world in general. Secondly, it recognizes Africa as a continent that is emerging as central to bringing peace and justice to the world after long having been victimized by colonial and neocolonial oppression. Finally, it salutes African women represented by the courageous leadership of Wangari Maathai as central to the prophetic leadership that imagined and led this transformative movement, the Green Belt Movement, that has knit together environmental renewal with issues of democratization, gender and human rights, and peace and justice.

CHAPTER 13

ENVIRONMENTAL RACISM AND REFLECTIVE DEMOCRACY: LOUISIANA AND CANCER ALLEY

Rosalind Flynn Hinton

13.1. Introduction

I have been thinking a lot about mutuality and interconnectedness in activism — perhaps, not so much as thinking, but as taking the time to fully understand its implications. At a section on Indigenous Religions at the Parliament of the World Religions, Douglas George-Kanentiio commented, and I paraphrase, "We don't need advocacy, we need mutuality. If people are not ready to join you, hold the space for them until they are ready."[1] As an activist working from a matrix of advocacy, this comment surprised me. What would the directive of mutuality look like in my geographic context: South Louisiana and the American South? Yet another petrochemical plant is going to be built on top of the town of Welcome, Louisiana, just north of New Orleans. The towns of Welcome, Freetown, Burton Lane, Chatman Town, and other historically African American hamlets pre-date the Civil War and comprise the 5th District of St. James Parish, where the Formosa Plastics Complex will locate. These towns were purchased from portions of plantations by ex-slaves and free people of color after the Civil War and have been passed on intergenerationally. There are currently six petrochemical facilities already in the 5th District and five more are planned.[2]

13.2. Grounding Our Understandings

In talking with me about her book *Gaia and God*, Rosemary Radford Ruether said that sometimes liberal activists complained to her that they give attention to numerous causes — education, women's rights, criminal justice — and they just don't have time for environmental causes. Ruether

---

1. Douglas George-Kanentiio, "The Twisted Roots of the Doctrines of Discovery" (Lecture, Parliament of the World Religions, Toronto, Canada November 2018).
2. Louisiana Bucket Brigade. Grant by Rosalind Hinton and Anne Rolfes (New Orleans, Louisiana, 2018).

noted the wrong-headedness of this thinking. She claimed, and I agree, that all justice is derived from earth justice. It was her assertion that humans must strive to live in harmony with earth's rhythms and teachings. It is never a matter of this cause or that, but a matter of right relations within life systems as a whole. In *Gaia and God*, Ruether states, "To believe in a divine being means to believe that those qualities in ourselves are rooted in and respond to the life power from which the universe itself arises."[3] All justice flows from earth justice. The term *Gaia*, an ancient Greek Earth Goddess, recovers the divinity that pulses within earth's lifesystems and, at the same time, describes how humans are dependent upon, in communion with, and are bound to these life systems. But Ruether also observed that humans are latecomers to earth systems, yet we are the major cause for the destruction of Earth's systems. We are living in an age of species extinction, including humans. Our over-reach has finally threatened the very bases of life upon which we as humans depend.[4]

Human overreach is hidden in plain sight on an 85-mile stretch of land on which I live and work between New Orleans and Baton Rouge, an area long known as Cancer Alley where there are more than two hundred petrochemical plants. This one section of the earth is responsible for 19% of the world's carbon emissions.[5] As you travel up the River Road, you pass the remaining plantation homes from slavery. It is no accident that plantations and petrochemical plants share the same geography: cheap land, a cheap water source in the Mississippi River, cheap labor, and ports along the Gulf of Mexico that give access to global markets. What is not advertised in the tourist guidebooks are the freetowns, unincorporated African American communities that came into being 130 years ago when ex-slaves purchased the land they worked. These towns have been removed from municipal land-use maps by local and state governments eagerly courting polluting industries. One of my colleagues, resigned to the fact that these industries are the backbone of the Louisiana economy, commented that we should just move everyone out and leave this area to the chemical companies — as if the wind doesn't blow southeast to New Orleans and the spills don't enter our wetlands. Perimetered toxic wastelands in already vulnerable communities sound more like targeted racial genocide, rather than holding a space of mutuality. Under these conditions, who is holding the space of mutuality? African American women leaders who are now standing up to dirty industries along the Mississippi River are hoping we will enter their space.

    3. Rosemary Radford Ruether. *Gaia and God: An Ecofeminist Theology of Earth Healing* (San Francisco: HarperCollins Publishers, Ltd., 1992), 4.
    4. Ibid., 5.
    5. Louisiana Bucket Brigade. Grant by Anne Rolfes (n.d).

13.3. Sharon Lavigne

Meet Sharon Lavigne and her daughter Shamell whose family has been in Welcome, Louisiana, in St. James Parish for five generations. Welcome is another unincorporated African American town founded by ex-slaves. Her grandparents, Valmond and Clara Reid Calvey, passed 40 acres of land on to her family. Sharon's father, Milton Calyette, Sr., fought for the integration of public schools during the Civil Rights movement in the 1960s and he welcomed a fertilizer plant thinking it would bring good salaries for black people that included medical insurance and retirement. But promises never met expectations. While in college, Sharon's entire family came down with an unexplainable rash that could only be cured with Clorox, which was painfully rubbed on their bodies. Her mother developed an autoimmune hepatitis and Sharon has a chronic sinus condition. As a child, Sharon played in the woods and the surrounding land along the river, but now she worries for her children: what is being pumped into the river, soil, and air?

Sharon Lavigne and the community of RISE St. James, a grassroots organization founded by Sharon to fight the Formosa Complex, invite us into a space of mutuality that very few have entered. Sharon Lavigne's story produced on video in a StoryCenter workshop in St. James Parish[6] shows us how to position ourselves in the logic of life-giving systems that counters the logic of the marketplace. Refusing to be uprooted or cast aside, she is rooted in the land, rooted in her ancestors' legacy dating back to slavery, rooted in the love of family and in community. It is Sharon Lavigne and RISE who are fighting for our right to clean air and water by confronting industries like Formosa, a Taiwanese petrochemical giant. She is determined, like her father before her, to claim her right to live in a healthy and prosperous community where her children and grandchildren can safely play outside.

13.4. Formosa Plastics Complex

If not stopped, Formosa will reside on 2400 acres of sugar cane fields adjacent to Sharon Lavigne's hometown. The plant, touted as a big win for Louisiana, will "operate 24/7, emitting over 26 million tons annually of cancer-causing compounds, particulates, and nitrogen oxides that cause respiratory problems."[7] Sharon Lavigne and her community by any

---

6. Sharon and Shamell Lavigne. "Our Town — Our Fight." (St. James, Louisiana, December 2018), mp4.
7. David J Mitchell. "St. James Parish Council, Planning Commission to Hold Hearings on Proposed $9.4 Billion Formosa Chemical Complex," *The Advocate*, July 2018, bit.ly/2OxrxXN.

account are discarded in this scenario. And for what purpose? Formosa will create plastic bags and bottles, "with no plan to handle the increased waste or pollution it will cause."[8] The World Economics Forum notes that there are 8.3 billion tons of plastic on the planet since manufacturing began in the 1950s and that 6.3 billion of these tons will end up as waste.[9] This waste is a problem for our oceans, our Gulf of Mexico, and our drinking water. In the Sportsman's Paradise, much of the livelihoods, foodways, music, and crafts built upon fishing, hunting, and farming are displaced now by oil and plastics. Only the twisted logic of economic progress can call this a *win*.

Formosa represents the horrors of global capitalism in which dirty industries create wealth for their investors with no attention paid to local communities who become collateral damage in an economy of perpetual growth built upon consumption. Government does not curb the excess of corporations like Formosa, but, on the contrary, these multinational corporations work through governments to achieve their financial aspirations. It is an old story of manifest destiny in which "a people without land," in this case multinational corporations, are lured to a land without people: communities deemed expendable by governments. Louisiana subsidies include a $12-million grant for infrastructure plus the Louisiana Economic Development FastStart state workforce development program, as well as access to Louisiana's Quality Jobs and Industrial Tax Exemption programs.[10]

Quality jobs are promised. The Formosa project promises 1200 new direct jobs at $84,500 per job and 8000 indirect jobs,[11] undoubtedly good jobs if they materialize in a stable local community. But jobs seldom materialize for the African American communities with the longest history in the area. In fact, global industries have taken to creating "man camps," fabricated housing complexes for itinerate workers who must leave their families to earn these salaries. Formosa is planning on taking over a remote

---

8. Anne Rolfes. "Six bright Orange Lies the Petro-Energy Crowd Wants You To Believe." *The Lens Nola*, November 24, 2018. https://thelensnola.org/2018/11/24/six-bright-orange-lies-the-petro-energy-crowd-wants-you-to-believe/.

9. John McKenna. "Picture this all the plastic we have produced weighs the same as 25,000 Empire State Buildings." *World Economic Forum*, July 2017, https://www.weforum.org/agenda/2017/07/picture-this-all-the-plastic-we-have-produced-weighs-the-same-as-25-000-empire-state-buildings/.

10. Robert Brelsford. "Taiwan's Formosa Advances $9.4-billion Louisiana Petrochemical Project." *Oil and Gas Journal,* April 2018.

11. Sam Karlin and Timothy Boone. "This Is a Big One: Formosa Picks St. James Parish for $9.4 Billion Chemical Complex." *The New Orleans Advocate,* April 23, 2018, https://www.theadvocate.com/new_orleans/news/business/article_4ee148fa-4715-11e8-a53b-2b350073db9d.html.

juvenile detention center for housing.¹² These self-contained dormitories bring few revenues, supermarkets or area stores and restaurants to established communities. Not even the workers love them. Jaime Portillo, a truck driver hauling fracked sand in Midland County, Texas, says, "It's very lonely… but you don't have to pay rent or stuff like that. I just want to give a better life for my kids."¹³ *Bloomberg* notes that man camps cost industry an average of $36 per night compared to steeper hotel prices or any type of housing in which workers can live with their families.¹⁴ License plates on other projects in the area, such as the Bayou Bridge Pipeline, reveal that workers are recruited from out-of-state. One friend commented that recruiting from out-of-state is the product of full employment, but Pastor Joseph, a long-time leader of Humanitarian Enterprise of Loving People (H.E.L.P.), also in St. James Parish, has called on industry for years to hire local truck drivers to no avail. Who then benefits from Formosa or Shell, or Dupont, all located in St. James Parish? Most of the wealth will not stay in Louisiana, and most of the investors live far from Welcome, Louisiana or New Orleans. Environmentalist Anne Rolfes notes that, "An analysis of the industrial tax exemption program by Together Baton Rouge found that in East Baton Rouge Parish, companies like Exxon, Georgia Pacific, and Honeywell have harvested tax breaks of more than $1 million per job created."¹⁵

The Formosa Project creates wealth for a global elite, separates families, destroys the health and the wealth of locals, and creates a need for consumer products that are destroying the environment. Formosa, like most of the petrochemical plants on the River Road, is a government subsidized death factory, one of the newest death factories that affect Sharon's hometown of Welcome, an area where "tank farms" (oil holding tanks), pipeline oil spills, and carcinogen emissions are a regular occurrence. Anne Rolfes, whose organization the Louisiana Bucket Brigade tracks and publicizes the accidents of nearby petrochemical plants, notes that, according to federal data, "The Mosaic Ammonia" plant, Plains pipeline company, and seven other facilities in the area have had 51 accidents since January 2017 to september 2018."¹⁶

---

12. Ibid.
13. Rachel Adams-Heard. "Welcome to the 'Man Camps' of West Texas." *Bloomberg Businessweek*. August 7, 2018. https://www.bloomberg.com/news/articles/2018-08-07/welcome-to-the-man-camps-of-west-texas.
14. Ibid.
15. Anne Rolfes, "Six bright Orange Lies." https://thelensnola.org/2018/11/24/six-bright-orange-lies-the-petro-energy-crowd-wants-you-to-believe/#.
16. Anne Rolfes, "Black communities in St. James on the losing end of Louisiana's 'big win.'" *The Lens Nola*. September 17, 2018. https://thelensnola.org/2018/09/17/black-communities-in-st-james-on-the-losing-end-of-louisianas-big-win/.

The 5th district of St. James Parish, Louisiana, where the freetowns reside, is paradigmatic for the racism involved in placing dirty industries in poor communities of color. A concentration of pollution goes with, to paraphrase Ta-Nehisi Coates, a concentration of poverty and a concentration of Melanin.[17] Communities of color bear a disproportionate burden for a global economy addicted to oil, plastics, and other unsustainable products. According to the U.S. Census, 84% of those living adjacent to petrochemical plants are African American. The poverty rate is five percent higher than the state average. The child poverty rates range from 25% to 40%. Cancer, auto-immune diseases, and respiratory problems abound. Anne Rolfes again notes that the median income is $29,840–$37,000 lower than a majority white 3rd District, just across the River.[18] Shamell Lavigne says, "I feel it is environmental racism. I love it here and I care about what happens. This is a place I want to retire to and it won't be a place to live and raise a family."[19]

Vandana Shiva calls this current extraction economy "ecoimperialist," noting that in economies that assume limitless growth in a world with limited resources, "It is the poor and other species that lose their share of the resources. Instead of restraint and limits, the imperialist project seeks to increase corporate control over resources."[20] Another feature of the current global economy that is visible in Louisiana (and the U.S.) is the erosion of democracy. Vandana Shiva continues, "Ecoimperialism is intolerant of the freedom and sovereignty of the other, be it other communities, other countries, or other species."[21]

The Women's Donor Network (WDN), in their Reflective Democracy Project, ranks Louisiana as 51 of 50 states and Washington D.C. in having a state government that represents the diversity of its residents. While white males are 26% of the population, they are 67% of the elected officials, and African American men and women represent 42% of the population but are 23% of the elected officials. When we take a gendered lens, white women are 30% of the population but only 10% of the elected officials, and African American women, representing 21% of the population are a mere 5% of the representatives.[22] Not only is democracy askew,

---

17. Ta-Nehisi Coates. "The Case for Reparations." *The Atlantic*, volume 313, no. 5 (June 2014), 60.
18. Anne Rolfes. "Black Communities."
19. Shamell Lavigne. Interview by Rosalind Hinton. Telephone. January 7, 2019.
20. Vandana Shiva. *Soil Not Oil: Environmental Justice in an Age of Climate Change*. 2nd ed. (Berkley, CA: North Atlantic Books, 2015).
21. Ibid.
22. Rebecca Carter. *Women's Donor Network Presentation*. New Orleans, LA: Ashé Power House, April 24, 2018. https://wholeads.us.

WDN notes that, "A full 70% of Americans are being relegated to the status of special interest groups, forced to lobby mostly white male legislators to look out for their concerns."[23] Government is no longer a check on corporations, but a check on democracy as corporate and financial institutions work through the government to increase profits for their investors. With the staggering amount of independent consultants, temp workers, and the assault on collective bargaining, we have stagnant wages. According to Oxfam, the world's eight richest billionaires control the same wealth between them as the poorest half of the globe's population.[24]

The path to "reflective democracy," or more representative government, at the state level in Louisiana, where the large sweep of policy is made, is difficult. I would like to discuss two obstacles that I see: the cultivation of white privilege and the institutional Catholic Church in South Louisiana.

13.5. The Shaping of White Privilege

I was facilitating a discussion among African American public school students in New Orleans and girls from a private school, Louise S. McGhee. The African American girls had a sharp critical analysis of race and economic realities, and, while the more privileged young girls were catching on fast, one girl I will paraphrase said, "Every time I bring these issues up in class, the teachers say not now, or comment that I am off topic, or tell me not to be disruptive." I thought, Ahhh, this is how it starts, the politeness that generates the ignorance that underlies a culture of privilege. Unless these young girls cross the color-line and stay in relationship to one another, they will not overcome this ignorance or break down the power differential into which they are born.

Thinking back on my own childhood in Mobile, Alabama, I realize that the demand for conformity and polite behavior is one way that young girls lose confidence in their own questions and instincts by the age of 13 or 14. Their questions are not appropriate: their anger at injustice is deemed too out of character for young (white) girls. Their questions are buried. The girls begin to disassociate from their own intellects because familial, cultural, and societal frameworks do not honor their questions. Yet these girls I met saw that the "emperor has no clothes!" At the moment I met them, the public school girls, black and white, were in a rare space

---

23. "Reflective Democracy Campaign," *Reflective Democracy 2017 Research Summary*, October 2017, https://wholeads.us/wp-content/uploads/2018/09/reflective-democracy-2017-research-summary.pdf.

24. Larry Elliot. "World's Eight Richest People Have Same Wealth as Poorest 50%." *The Guardian*, January 15, 2017.

of mutual understanding, but it will not be held for long before the logic of the market overtakes them and turns their heads from this rare space of intimacy and story sharing to a life, for white women, of discomfort with tough questions as the privilege starts to be a second skin.

Yet resources in the age of climate change are becoming scarcer. And we are at the moment of tough questions and really understanding those who are not like us. Industry has brought us to the forcible end of earth's life systems with extraction policies and economic growth philosophies that do not allow life systems to renew and rejuvenate. And the winds really do blow both ways, as late industrial cancers and diseases are experienced by all above and below the line of privilege and race, though certainly not equally or with the same access to health care.

13.6. The Catholic Church in South Louisiana

Unfortunately, I do not find spiritual direction in my own Catholic Church (a driving force in South Louisiana). This church embroiled in sexual abuse scandals since the 1960s (or before) is entrenched and protective of its male authority, rather than visionary. The New Orleans diocese, the only diocese in Louisiana to release the numbers of sexual predators, has implicated "57 Roman Catholic clergy members (who are) credibly accused of abusing minors over many decades in southeast Louisiana."[25] Jason Berry, in an interview around his book *Render unto Rome: The Secret Life of Money in the Catholic Church,* stated, "It became clear to me in writing this book, that, as Catholics, we really are shaped by a culture of passivity. It's not just 'pray, pay, obey,' as the old slogan goes. It's deeper than that. The biggest benefit the bishops have at this time is the apathy of the average Catholic."[26] If apathy exists in the pews, it does not exist in the Diocese's attacks against Planned Parenthood and those serving on the front lines of women's reproductive health.

In 2014, the Archdiocese of New Orleans, in alliance with Evangelical and Catholic antiabortion activists, staged a holy war against building a Planned Parenthood facility, one of the only clinics in New Orleans actively serving poor and rich, young and old, men and women, and LGBTQ holistically and compassionately. Apparently not getting the missive from Pope Francis to avoid witch hunts around abortion, contractors and

---

25. Here are the 57 clergy 'credibly accused' of abuse in the Archdiocese of New Orleans *nola.com*. November 2, 2018, https://expo.nola.com/news/erry-2018/11/6965b1c0328337/here-are-the-57-clergy-credibl.html.

26. Judy Ball, "Jason Berry: Church Whistleblower," *Franciscan Media.* https://www.franciscanmedia.org/jason-berry-church-whistleblower/.

subcontractors were cast as "cooperating with evil" by the current Bishop, Gregory Aymond, in a letter read from the pulpits of all Catholic Churches declaring anyone building the facility as morally blind and "cooperating with evil."[27] The contractor and subcontractors were intimidated by phone and email before starting work and threatened with future economic sanctions. Many subcontractors quit. At the Archdiocese's direction, the contractor was called into his daughter's Catholic high school and told that his work with Planned Parenthood may negatively affect his daughter's future at the school. Pictures of his daughter cheerleading were posted online with a request to call the school and say her tuition was paid for with "blood money."[28] The FBI was called in at this point. While many of these tactics are standard procedure in Planned Parenthood clinic construction, seldom do they have the weight of an Archdiocese that is one of the wealthiest entities and largest employers in the city.

The Catholic Church's anti-choice hyper-focus from the pulpit and behind the scenes creates a divide between women of faith that is difficult to overcome. Abortion becomes a wedge issue that sustains the status quo which is pro-petrochemical and plastics, the industries that fossil fuels are betting their future on, racist, and anti-woman. To be elected statewide, politicians must be anti-abortion. Legislators deliver the abortion issue along with other laws hostile to women and their constituents to prove their worth. The 2019 legislative session was a roster of enmity to women:

- Equal Rights Amendment ERA ratification - failed
- Sales tax exemption for feminine hygiene products and diapers - failed
- Stopping pay secrecy to achieve equal pay - failed
- Raising the minimum wage – failed
- Unleash Local — restoring local freedom to set the standards for wages and family leave that are right for local communities -failed
- Paid family and sick leave – withdrawn (it was not going to pass)
- Abortion ban — A six-week ban, a State Constitutional Amendment against Abortion (to go on the ballot November 2020) and other anti-abortion TRAP bills – passed[29]

Yet women in Louisiana advance their communities when they come together. Coming together in the 1960s, women strategized and changed

---

27. "Planned Parenthood abortion clinic: We cannot cooperate with evil." Monday, 27 January, 2014 21:10 | Written by Archbishop Gregory M. Aymond. https://abitadeacon.blogspot.com/2014/01/archbishop-aymond-urges-truly-catholic.html.

28. Pamela Steeg email to author July 8, 2019 with attachment "Planned Parenthood — Actions of Extremist During Health Center Construction," (n.d.).

29. Julie Schwam Harris email to author June 21, 2019.

Louisiana's oppressive family law statutes from head and master in which husbands controlled even a wife's separate property to a community property state. After Katrina, The Women of the Storm, a coalition of wealthier Republican and Democratic women, brought almost every member of Congress to the area to push for resources, and after the BP Oil Spill, they coalesced with other Gulf states to hold BP accountable. The Catholic Church refuses to see the moral agency of women who they cannot deploy on this one issue, keeping women in Louisiana in need of healthcare. In 2011, 58% of pregnancies were unwanted, 8% higher than the national average, and 43.5% of AIDS cases were newly diagnosed per every 100,000 African American women versus 3.3% per every 100,000 white women.[30] This is not a woman-centered institutional church, or state. Annually enormous resources (human and financial) are used to protect women's meager health resources, rather than addressing other pressing issues. Again, we also see that the greatest burden is on women of color.

Rosemary Radford Ruether observed, "Domination of women has provided a key link, both socially and symbolically, to the domination of earth."[31] Perhaps Sharon Lavigne's situation 85 miles north of New Orleans seems disconnected from the Catholic Church and Planned Parenthood, but both situations dismiss women's moral agency and marginalize their voices and needs. Control and intimidation replace mutuality and actual solutions to pressing problems. The treatment of the earth and the treatment of women are two grave and intertwined problems in Louisiana that deliver power into the hands of a patriarchal white ruling class, whether religious or corporate.

As we move forward, what resource can we draw upon? All of life's systems — socio-political, religious, economic, cultural, and environmental — are distorted by the logic of patriarchy and the global marketplace. Yet how do we walk away from systems in which we are so deeply embedded? Can we fix one problem — say, violence against women — while living inside the privilege (dependence on fossil fuel and throw-away consumer plastics and all of the other corrupted systems that bring advantage to the few at the expense of the many)? Can we play the fiddle in one system while our neighbors in Cancer Alley are choking on our consumptive lifestyles?

I return to the Native American speaker, Douglas George-Kanentiio, an Akwesasne Mohawk, whose call for mutuality opened this essay. The logic of the market can only be overcome by the deeper logic of mutuality

---

30. L.B. Finer and K. Kost. "Unintended Pregnancy Rates at the State Level." *Perspectives on Sexual and Reproductive Health*, 43: 2 (2011), 78-87 (Guttmacher); Kaiser Family Foundation. "Putting Women's Health Care Disparities on the Map: Examining Racial and Ethnic Disparities at the State Level." (June 2009).

31. Rosemary Radford Ruether, *Gaia and God*, 3.

within communities of resistance and with the earth. Our energies and resources, as late arriving settlers and conquerors of the Americas, must be redirected away from the mechanistic logic that sees both people and the earth as usable then discarded resources, and toward communities that have the logic and the spiritual resources to lead us forward, not back, into healthy relationship with earth's systems and its people. But, in Kanentiio's invitation to mutual existence is also a warning that appropriation of culture, spirituality and land are not relational actions. I turn once again to Rosemary Radford Ruether and Sharon Lavigne who are rooted in my own Judeo-Christian traditions.

13.7. Building A Future Together

I once asked Rosemary Radford Ruether how she could stay in relationship with a church in which she found so much fault. She pointed me toward Wisdom traditions and embodied sacramental traditions in Catholicism that recognize divinity deep within the human experience rather than a dualistic spiritualizing of divinity that is alienated from the body, nature and earth's processes. Sharon Lavigne also derives her wisdom and her truth-centeredness from her Catholicism.

Rosemary Radford Ruether has never abandoned Christianity. She spent her career deconstructing authoritarian directions while unearthing liberating strains within Christianity. In *Gaia and God,* Ruether resurrects the symbol of Gaia to rediscover the sentience of, and divinity within, earth's life systems and our inextricable dependence upon these systems. This notion of Gaia contrasts with a hierarchical notion of God that was codified in classical western traditions "from 500 B.C. to 800 C.E." that justifies and sacralizes relationships of domination.[32] Ruether continues, "In particular, the way these cultures have construed the idea of the male monotheistic God, and the relation of this God to the cosmos as its Creator, have reinforced symbolically the relations of domination of men over women, masters over slaves and (male ruling-class) humans over animals and over the earth."[33] Ruether worked to reconcile the ecofeminist Gaia with the Judeo-Christian God of justice and mercy, noting that Christianity has always been syncretistic and borrowed from the cultures within which it has taken root.

In *Gaia and God,* Ruether wanted "not only to deconstruct harmful systems" but also to point to a "vision of a source of life that is 'yet more' than what presently exists, continually bringing forth both new life and

32. Ibid., 3
33. Idem.

new visions of how life should be more just and more caring."[34] Embodied traditions that place the prophetic vision of women like Sharon Lavigne and the RISE St. James community at the center of consideration can bring forth life and a space of mutuality within current economic systems.

Sharon Lavigne founded RISE St. James after the city council voted 5 to 2 to allow Formosa to come in on October 30, 2018. Sheryl Lavigne commented, "A lot of the plants that come in here like Formosa want the Riverfront so they can put their filth in the River. We will put a stop to this and, Formosa, *you are the stop*. You will not come in and destroy what we have." Eve Butler said, "And we are here at RISE St. James to tell industry that we are going to fight for our neighborhood. The people that work at the plant and people that come in that don't live here, they don't buy homes here, their children don't go (to school) here, their wives do not shop here. We deserve to be treated just like everybody else."[35] These voices pierce through the logic of Louisiana prosperity politicians and economic development projects. Like the prophets of the Hebrew Bible, RISE St. James' voices are an octave too high and their words burn as Abraham Heschel describes the prophet's words, "where our conscience ends."[36] What is our moral answer to Sharon Lavigne, Eve Butler, Sharon's daughter Shamell, and RISE St. James?

Entering the space held by RISE St. James and other groups on the frontlines of climate change and supporting their leadership opens life up to possibilities we have not imagined. They are not just the prophetic voices sounding the alarm, but have the practical strategies and practice of confronting multinational corporations. They have a commitment to the earth and to community that is needed at this moment. RISE is involved in human rights litigation, storytelling, historical research, door to door advocacy, and education. Sharon's prophetic voice has touched her parish priest, who is bringing her church onboard in the RISE campaigns. They are extending a web of life, not a reign of terror. We think these powers are not strong enough to topple the power of multinational exploitation or patriarchy, but turning toward, acknowledging, and becoming part of this larger web of life is a powerful moral force that has toppled governments. One of the greatest obstacles is our own doubt that one voice joined with others can make a difference.

---

34. Ibid., 4-5.
35. Amy Hill, "Women of Cancer Alley Compilation" (St. James Parish, Louisiana, December 18, 2018), mp4.
36. Abraham Joshua Heschel. *The Prophets*. 1st ed. (Philadelphia: Jewish Publication Society of America, 1962).

CHAPTER 14

INDIGENOUS WOMEN ACT TO DEFEND MOTHER EARTH: EMPOWERMENT AND SOLIDARITY

Pamela K. Brubaker

COPINH[1], walking with other peoples for emancipation, confirms our commitment to defend the water, rivers and our common goods and nature, as well as our rights as peoples. ... Our Mother Earth — militarized, fenced-in, poisoned, a place where basic human rights are systematically violated — demands that we take action.
   Berta Cáceres, 2015 Goldman Environmental Prize Acceptance Speech

14.1.

Indigenous peoples, *campesinos*, unions and social movements from around the world came together "to defend the rights of the people and of Mother Earth" at The People's Climate Summit. They met in Exposition Park, Lima, Peru, from December 8-11, 2014. "The Summit is necessary," said Lourdes Huanca, president of the National Federation of Female Peasants, Artisans, Indigenous, Native and Salaried Workers of Peru, "because it allows the expression of civil society based on a much broader and more inclusive base than the official COP," the Conference of Parties, an annual meeting of all nations that have signed on to the United Nations Framework Convention on Climate Change.[2]

COP 20 was meeting on a military base near Lima. Official governmental delegates were expected to produce a draft text for negotiations at COP 21 in Paris, the following year.[3] It was crucial that COP 21 adopt an accord that would obligate *all* countries to combat climate change, to prevent a dangerous rise in temperature of more than two degrees Celsius.[4]

---

1. Civic Council of Popular and Indigenous Organizations of Honduras.
2. "The Peoples Summit will be a massive public expression against climate change," on Servindi — *Servicios en comunicación* Intercultural, November 19, 2014. http://www.servindi.org/actualidad/118277. Rarely are representatives from social movements granted access.
3. "The Summit differs from the COP on how to address climate change, how to determine responsibility and ensure accountability, and who should decide what programs to implement." https://nacla.org/blog/2015/05/27/perspectives-people%E2%80%99s-summit.
4. "Nations aim to chart a course while ensuring that developing nation goals are not derailed." Betwa Sharma, "Ahead of Peru climate summit, cautious hope for strong draft

The December 10th Global March in Defense of Mother Earth in Lima put pressure on COP 20. Huanca called "for the repeal of laws that criminalize social protest, attention to the impacts of climate change on women, and the urgent need for governments to take binding measures."[5] Tens of thousands of people participated in the March. The "Lima Declaration of the People's Summit" saw this as "a clear indication of the position of peoples in favor of a fair, democratic world, which guarantees harmony between the human being and the rights of Nature and Mother Earth."[6]

The Alliance for Global Justice (AfGJ) brought the largest U.S. delegation to the People's Summit. We participated in the March, carrying a banner that said "Alliance for Global Justice — For Earth, Against Imperialism." The groups marching near us included a Peruvian evangelical Christian group, an association of indigenous groups from the Amazon, and international ecofeminists. Their sign said "Revolutionary Ecofeminism — Si, Oui, Yes; Fossil Capitalism — No Non No." Several signs declared "Change the system, not the climate."

14.2. Defense of Mother Earth in Peru, Guatemala, and Honduras

In my 1993 essay "Sisterhood, Solidarity, and Feminist Ethics," I wrote "third world women who suffer and struggle in these webs of oppression ask that we in the first world hear their cries for justice, consider their analysis and vision, and struggle in solidarity with them."[7] This essay focuseD on delegations to these three countries. I write about them so that the reader might engage in this process.

text," Al Jazeera America, November 29, 2014, http://america.aljazeera.com/articles/2014/11/29/climate-change-summitperu.html. President Trump removed the U.S. from the agreement shortly after he took office.

5. "Indigenous peoples call for a global march against climate change," on Servindi, Ibid. https://www.servindi.org/actualidad/117966. See FENMUCARINAP founded on August 18, 2006. President Lourdes Huanca states "Our main goals ... [are] control and defense of the territory of the female body which is often violated... we are the ones that sustain society and yet our work and contributions are not recognized. We also defend the land, water and seeds ... It's been a hard-fought struggle for recognition because . . . it comes up against patriarchy, *machismo* and sexism." George Ygarza, in an interview with Lourdes Huanca, "Peru: In Defense of Land, Culture and the Female Body," June 1, 2016. https://nacla.org/news/2016/06/03/peru-defense-land-culture-and-female-body.

6. "The Lima Declaration — People's Summit on Climate Change," Lima, December 11, 2014. Available at https://www.foei.org/news/the-lima-declaration.

7. Pamela Brubaker, "Sisterhood, Solidarity, and Feminist Ethics." In *Journal of Feminist Studies in Religion,* Spring/Fall 1993, no. 9, 1-2, 53-66, 62. This was a "Special Issue In honor of Beverly Wildung Harrison," my advisor at Union Theological Seminary. Also see Rebecca Todd Peters, *Solidarity Ethics: Transformation in a Globalized World,* Fortress Press, 2014. Elsa Támez asked how can Third-World women be sisters with First-World women? The answer: "when you withdraw from the social reality in which you live and which drains our life blood."

14.2.1. Peru: Cajamarca and Lima

The AfGJ delegation arrived in Lima a few days before the start of the People's Summit. We were welcomed and given an orientation to Peru by the Forum *Solidarida* Peru, which was committed to building international solidarity to develop a more inclusive society. We then traveled overnight on a commercial bus to the region of Cajamara, to meet with peasant farmers and indigenous peoples who had been fighting the development of a huge gold mine for several years.

Minera Yanacocha, owned by U.S. giant Newmont Mining Corporation (51.3%) and Peru's *Compañia de Minas Buenaventura* (43.65%), campaigned aggressively for the development of the Conga Mine. They had operated the Yanococha mine, the second largest gold mine in the world, for over twenty years. Its output was diminishing, and they wanted to replace its production with gold from the Conga Mine. The government approved the project in 2010, and the next year 7,400 acres of land were turned over to the Newmont Mining Corporation.

The main point of contention for local communities "is that mining activity, which includes the use of cyanide and mercury, adversely affects the high-altitude lakes from which the nearby communities and cities get their water." This contaminates and diminishes their water supply and also harms animal life and medicinal plants. The people organized municipal and provincial *consultas* (popular referendums), created provincial and local defense groups, and "marched and shut down parts of the region with strikes and highway blockades."[8] The state and mining corporations responded with repression and violence.

Máxima Acuña, an indigenous *campesina*, brought international attention to the struggle through her fight to remain on land wanted for the Conga mine. The project would destroy four mountain lakes — two would be drained for exploration and extraction, and the other two made into "tailings ponds" for mining waste. In a 2012 interview, Acuña said "I may be poor. I may be illiterate, but I know that our mountain lakes are our real treasure.... Yet, are we expected to sacrifice our water and our land so that the Yanacocha people can take gold back to their country?"[9]

In 2011, Minera Yanacocha made several attempts to forcibly remove her from her land. Mining engineers beat her and her daughter. "And, the

---

8. Raúl Zibechi, "Community Resistance Against Extraction," North American Congress on Latin America (NACLA), Fall 2014, https://nacla.org/article/community-resistance-against-extraction.
9. "LIFE YES, GOLD NO!," Roxana Olivera, November 21, 2012, *New Internationalist*, https://newint.org/features/web-exclusive/2012/11/21/peru-gold-rush-threatens-indigenous-communities/.

police had their machine guns pointed at the heads of my husband and small son." Protests began to spread. On July 3, 2012, Peruvian soldiers and police fired on crowds protesting the mine, killing four in one area, one in another, and seriously injuring dozens. On October 21, 2012, "more than 200 *campesinos* — many of them with infant children — mobilized to defend their mountain lakes. Acuña welcomed the protesters to stay on her land." This led to ongoing legal battles between Acuña and the company.[10]

Our delegation traveled via bus to the mountainous lake region (12,000+ feet altitude), accompanied by local organizers. We first stopped at the site of the huge Yanococha open pit mine. The devastation was shocking, and such a contrast to the beauty of the mountains. Mother Earth desolated — acres of bleak soil poisoned by mining chemicals! We drove on to Mamacocha Lake, the deepest in the area, and one of the lakes to be drained. Our guide talked about the cosmovision of the people, how *Pachamama* (Mother Earth) and *Mamacocha* (Sea Mother) are sacred to the people, and must be protected.[11]

We also stopped at an indigenous community whose members were *Ronderos* (community patrols). We learned that traditionally the *Ronderos* were men, but now some women had joined their ranks. This community controls road access to the lakes area. Large groups of *Ronderos* camp out near the lakes, to guard and hinder any work from the company. They are called "guardians of the lakes."[12] The *Ronderos* and community protests contributed to halting the mining project earlier in 2014. However, the people were still on guard as it might be restarted.[13]

Our delegation returned to Lima for the People's Summit on December 8th. The next day, we participated in The People's March to Protect

---

10. Ibid. "On 3 May 2017, the Supreme Court of Peru acquitted the Quechua defender Máxima Acuña de Chaupe, charged with illegally occupying land. Due to her opposition to the Yanacocha mining company, she has been the victim of attacks, intimidation, attempted evictions and judicial harassment. On appeal, she was acquitted of all charges and her land rights were recognized." Report of the Special Rapporteur on the rights of indigenous peoples, United Nations, September 2018. She received the Goldman Environmental Prize in 2016.

11. Drawing on notes from my trip and an article by George Ygarza, a member of our delegation. "Cumbre de Los Pu Zibechi" and "Community Resistance Against Extraction," ibid., a Truthout original, December 23, 2014.

12. Raúl Zibechi, "Community Resistance Against Extraction," ibid.

13. They were right to be cautious. The 2014 decision was based in part on the decline in prices for gold and copper. Some hoped it would restart in 2018. However, in 2016 "Newmont Mining announced abandoning a $US 4.8 billion copper and gold mine in Peru 'for the foreseeable future.'" Brett Walton, "Conga Mine in Peru Halted By Water Concerns," Civic Opposition, April 21, 2016.

Mother Earth, Air, Water, and Seeds.[14] Some indigenous women brought flowers, produce, and seeds to create a *mística*, "a ceremony of gratitude and offering to Mother Earth for her soil and food that nourishes us." At the top of the *circular mística*, it said "Welcome;" at the bottom "Globalize the struggle." A banner above the *mística* said "Indigenous Women — the Good Life."[15] When the march started, we helped carry a beautiful block-long ecological banner above our heads. On it were drawings and signatures of people who wanted to protect Mother Earth.

On December 11th, the Summit Declaration was approved through a participatory process. It was presented to officials at COP 20, demanding that governments "respect our territories, rights and ways of life, our cultures, customs and cosmovisions about life and the world we inhabit." It ended with this pledge: "Now the social movements of the world prepare to give continuity to the struggles from our territories in defense of life, until our demands are met. We will continue in the struggle to change the system... Not the climate."[16]

14.2.2. Guatemala: La Puya and Santa Maria Xalapan

"We are part of a struggle in defense of water, life, and Mother Earth," people from the Peaceful Resistance Movement of La Puya told us. La Puya is a campsite at the entrance of the El Tambor gold mine in Guatemala, built by local people in 2012, after Kappes, Cassiday and Associates (KCA) — a U.S.-based company — tried to bring in mining equipment. Protesters had notified government officials that the Ministry of Energy and Mining granted a license for its operation without community consultation, and that the Environmental Impact Assessment was inadequate. But the government had not taken any action.

This was the first community visit for the Presbyterian Church USA Travel Study Seminar on "Peacemaking, Climate Justice and Faith in Guatemala and Costa Rica" (August 7-18, 2017). Our host in Guatemala was CEDEPCA — The Protestant Center for Pastoral Studies in Central America.[17] As we entered La Puya, we saw a sign saying "Water is more valuable than gold" and a platform with an altar and posters of Archbishop Romero

---

14. Seeds are important because the campesinos save seeds for future plantings. Monsanto seeds do not reproduce. Their use has been resisted by indigenous peoples and farmers in the U.S. and Europe.
15. A *Mística* is "a ceremony of gratitude and offering to Mother Earth for her soil and food that nourishes us." Good Life is the English term for *Buen Vivir*. For an explanation and illustration *see* https://thousandcurrents.org/decolonizing-the-conference/.
16. There were also workshops on various topics during the Summit.
17. See cedepca.org/en.

from El Salvador (d. 1980) and Bishop Juan José Gerardi Conedera of Guatemala (d. 1998) — both murdered for their defense of the rights of the people.[18] Several murals along one wall of the camp depicted women in action. Welcomed by La Puya women, men, and children, we listened to their stories and shared a meal.

Despite opposition and harassment, they successfully blockaded the mine for two years, until May 23, 2014. On that day about 500 national police came with tear gas, rubber bullets, and smoke grenades to evict them. Several people were sickened by the gas, others were dragged and beaten. The blockade was broken and mining began. Many trees were cut down, they said, and then the butterflies disappeared. Their groundwater was contaminated by the mining chemicals used, causing skin problems. Their water supplies have also dramatically diminished. They know that drought in the area brought by climate change has contributed to this. But the mining process uses in an hour what a family would use in 20 years!

From the beginning, women have been leaders in the resistance. Two women told us that supporters of the mines attempted to humiliate them, calling them "whores." Women, better able than men to tolerate harassment, were on the front lines when the national police came. They would kneel or stand, praying and singing religious songs or the national anthem. The men were crudely taunted by the police, accused of hiding behind the skirts of women.

After the opening of the mine, the resistance allied with non-governmental organizations in an advocacy campaign and legal battle to stop it. CALAS, The Center for Legal-Environmental and Social Action in Guatemala, filed a legal case for La Puya.[19] In February 2016, a preliminary injunction from the Supreme Court voided the mining license, based on lack of consultation as required by the International Labor Organization's Indigenous and Tribal People's Convention 169. Its protections include the local community's right to prior, free and informed consultation for any development project in their territory. The Guatemalan government is a signatory.[20] On May 5, 2016, the Supreme Court made the preliminary injunction permanent and suspended KCA's mining license. Since the original mining license was for twenty years, the peaceful resistance movement

---

18. To this day, Masses are celebrated there on some Sundays, although only a few priests come, as their Bishop is not supportive.

19. CEDEPCA is a partner of CALAS.

20. "C169 — Indigenous and Tribal Peoples Convention, 1989 (No. 169)," *Convention concerning Indigenous and Tribal Peoples in Independent Countries* (Entry into force: 05 Sep 1991). http://www.ilo.org/dyn/normlex/en/f?p=NORMLEXPUB:12100:0::NO::P12100_INSTRUMENT_ID:312314.

continues their presence at the campsite. "We do not follow persons; we follow ideals: the defense of the Mother Earth."[21]

From La Puya, we went to the departments of Jalapa and Santa Rosa, to meet with several communities that joined together to resist El Escobar mine, the third largest silver mine in the world. It is operated by Minera San Rafael SA, a subsidiary of Tahoe Resources, a Canadian mining company. Communities there are experiencing the same issues as the communities in La Puya and Cajamarca — contaminated water, diminished water supply, health effects. One community is uninhabitable because of the collapse of housing from underground explosions. We learned that although most local municipalities voted against mining projects, in 2014 the construction of El Escobar started anyway — under martial law.[22]

The Xinka communities of Santa Maria Xalapan are part of this resistance. CALAS arranged for us to meet with the Association of Indigenous Women of Santa Maria Xalapan, who struggle to protect their land from mining and deforestation. We met at their community building, and they welcomed us with a Xinka Invocation Ceremony. Women and children brought flowers, grasses, fruits, and vegetables, which they used to make a beautiful *mística*. There were five colors to it — green for nature, yellow for dawn, red for humanity, and black for night. White represented the ancestors, balance and wisdom.[23]

---

21. I am primarily drawing on my notes. The people there were mostly Catholics, but there were indigenous aspects to their spirituality. My blog for the World Council of Churches, November 9, 2017, has photos from La Puya, http://blog.oikoumene.org/posts/solidarity-with-peaceful-eco-resistance-movements. I also draw on a draft of "The Indispensible Ones: A Story of Mining Resistance from La Puya," by Raquel Aldana. It is included in *From Extraction to Emancipation: Development Reimagined*, coedited by Raquel Aldana and Steven Bender, Carolina Academic Press, 2018. She elaborates on stories we heard about the children learning to dance, as a distraction to the military presence, and the creativity of the people in their resistance.

22. The people's struggle against El Escobar is similar to that of the Peruvian people's struggle against the Conga Mine. I am not discussing it in detail as I want to focus on women-led groups in Guatemala.

23. The Xinca people are a non-Mayan indigenous people located in southeastern Guatemala, near the border with El Salvador. Their language, not known to be like any other language, is near extinction, but there are efforts to revive it. https://www.revolvy.com/page/Xinca-people. I am drawing on my notes from our meeting. I am grateful to Leslie Vogel, our CEDEPCA host, for her excellent translation throughout our time in Guatemala. I learned more from interviews of Lorena Cabnal, co-founder of AMISMAXAJ. "We believe that in our bodies exists the potential energetically, cosmically and politically for us to emancipate ourselves. Our body is an energetic source that permits us to reinterpret life and the world, knowing that we want to live with the right to life and happiness." In "*Latinas Feministas*: Lorena Cabnal," Juliana Britto Schwartz, 2013, http://feministing.com/2013/12/20/latinas-feministas-lorena-cabnal/. In a 2010 interview, she talks about the founding and history of AMISMAXAJ. The political training the women participated in "gives us an approach from a feminist viewpoint for the defense of our territory, our bodies, and our land. I think that

The women began organizing in 2004, but their work was difficult because of *machismo*. They were called witches; participation of women in political campaigns was criticized. "We work on changing the way we think," they told us, "so we won't be afraid." Women came to share the rights and values of women — right to life, freedom to make decisions, to speak, and about defense of our lives, bodies, territories. "If we don't defend our bodies, we won't defend earth."

Mothers brought daughters to their meetings when they were little. The daughters went to school, learned to read and write, and took notes for their mothers' meetings. They formed their own organization — to help young girls talk about their concerns and questions. They also participated in political training where they learned to have a voice, to vote and organize.

The women are part of the Wholistic Agriculture Association, which is working on the recovery of traditional and ancestral foods and practices, such as yucca, bananas, sweet potatoes, corn, beans, fruit, and herbs for natural medicine. They are bringing back bees so that they have honey. To have *buen vivir* (good life) — we women have the right to have healthy lives.[24]

The Xinka women are recovering their identity and learning about their cosmovision. "We learn from the whole universe," they told us, "it frees women." The ceremonies they perform were prohibited from the colonial period until recent years. Before Christianity, there were no images to pray to. We had sacred places, they said. Where there are trees, there is water, there is life!

A member of the Navajo Nation from our delegation talked about the history and resistance of Native Americans in the U.S. She shared the ongoing struggle of the Standing Rock Sioux against the Dakota Access Pipeline, to protect their water, sacred places and all living beings. They too declare that water is life!

14.2.3. *Honduras: La Esperanza, San Francisco Lempira, Tegucigalpa*

Berta Cáceres, Lenca leader, cofounder of COPINH (Civic Council of Popular and Indigenous Organizations of Honduras), and a 2015 Goldman

---

we indigenous women have to make important contributions based on the historic oppression, of our bodies and of our territories." "In Her Own Words," Lorena Cabnal, https://peacebrigades.org.uk/in-their-own-words/lorena-cabnal-indigenous-womens-association.

24. The concept of *buen vivir* means to live well. It "has been incorporated in the new constitutions of Bolivia and Ecuador, and provides a policy space for the articulation of indigenous movements with policy debates and struggles." See Marcelo Saguier and Zoe Brent, "Regional Policy Frameworks of Social Solidarity Economy in South America," Occasional Paper 6, Potential and Limits of Social and Solidarity Economy, United Nations Research Institute for Social Development (UNRISD), June 2014.

Environmental Prize recipient, was murdered in her home in La Esperanza, on March 2, 2016.[25] She led the fight against the construction of the *Agua Zarca* dam, part of a hydroelectric project that would dry up the Gualcarque River, which is both sacred to Lenca communities and vital to their survival.[26] The project was stopped a few months later in response to pressure from public campaigns which caused its major financial investors — the Netherlands Development Finance Company-FMO, the Central American Bank for Economic Integration and Finnfund — to suspend funding.[27]

COPINH was launched in La Esperanza in 1993, to "improve the living conditions of the Lenca people of Honduras and ... to implement a model of development that is more just, more dignified for human beings and in harmony with the environment."[28] Berta[29] stated that, from its beginning, "the anti-patriarchal struggle is a vision that is expressed in all areas of COPINH's work." Women led vital struggles for the defense of the land. For instance, thousands of women, some carrying their children, marched multiple times between 2006 and 2007, to stop a dam on the Lempa River. As a result, construction was later suspended.[30] Berta was also committed to protecting women and children, and eventually established a shelter for victims of domestic violence. She expanded the meaning of territory to

---

25. The Lenca people are the largest indigenous group in Honduras, numbering about 100,000 people. There are also about 37,000 Lencans in neighboring El Salvador. Their language is considered to be extinct, but there are efforts to revive it. They have maintained elements of their traditional culture.

26. Some members of COPINH took us to the river one day. It was a very moving experience, and helped us understand its sacred character. The water was pure, and peaceful — even as it rippled over the stones.

27. Moira Birss, "A Year Without Berta," NACLA, March 2, 2017. https://nacla.org/news/2017/03/02/year-without-berta. This is an interview with Gustavo Castro, founder of Friends of the Earth Mexico. He and Berta collaborated with other frontline communities in Mesoamerica working against climate change, damming, logging and mining. In this interview, he highlights the role of financial institutions in perpetuating continued violence and land grabbing in Honduras, and calls out the U.S. for contributing to a culture of impunity in Honduras.

28. Its early actions stopped at least 16 harmful lodging projects. "In July 1994, tens of thousands of indigenous Lenca people ... join[ed] the first and historic *Indigenous and Black Pilgrimage for Life, for Justice and for Liberty*." This "marked a watershed moment for the organization and the struggle of the people's movements in Honduras, resurrecting the marginalized who despite impoverishment and exclusion, raised their voice and assumed protagonism in Honduras and Central America. ... The contribution of COPINH to the national struggles led to recognition of the role of the indigenous people in the construction of a new society." "Civic Council of Popular and Indigenous Organizations of Honduras: 25 years of struggle and Revolution," http://copinhenglish.blogspot.com/2018/03/civic-council-of-popular-and indigenous.html.

29. I am using Berta's first name, as all the people who spoke to us addressed her in that way.

30. Ibid., "Civic Council of Popular and Indigenous Organizations of Honduras." They were accompanied by Berta and COPINH women from other areas.

include women's bodies. COPINH artists portrayed this on some large public murals in La Esperanza. One said "Our bodies and territories are not merchandise!"

In a 2014 interview, Berta was asked about her vision for Honduras. "First, we dream of a Honduras in which we have the right to be happy." She then spoke of its deep meaning. "It has to do with peace with justice, it has to do with the end of impunity, it has to do with the respect of spiritual and territorial rights, to have the right to walk without feeling assaulted. To live in a demilitarized society." She added, "we dream of a Honduras where women aren't just present, but where we also make decisions." This dream includes "black and indigenous people, sexual diversity, and people who work in the streets, the women of the *maquinas*. Everyone, no? So that we be respected, listened to, and this country be ours." "It may seem like a small thing to say," she said, "but it's a monumental act of defiance."[31]

Berta helped convene many regional and international meetings. In 2000, the U.S. based Agricultural Missions (AMI) met Berta at a meeting of COMPA, the Convergence of Movements of the Peoples of the Americas. Since then, they have been a partner with COPINH. Shortly after Berta's death, AMI organized a Solidarity Delegation to Honduras (April 28-May 6, 2016). I was one of nine participants — one Canadian and eight from the U.S. On April 29th, we traveled in a van from Tegucigalpa (the capital) to La Esperanza. Our first meeting with some members of COPINH was in their offices. One of several posters on the walls was of Tomas Garcia (COPINH cofounder), who had been killed by Honduran military on July 21, 2013.[32] Another poster is of Berta, kneeling with corn in her hands and around her feet. It reads, "Berta lives, the struggle continues." A third poster marked 100 years of International Women's Day, and proclaimed "March 8 Women's March — We are free women!"

We were told repression had intensified in the two months since Berta's death. COPINH leaders had been interrogated by the police, accused of being involved in her death. Nelson Garcia was murdered by unknown

---

31. "In May 2014, during a protest outside the Honduran National Congress in Tegucigalpa, freelance journalist Chris Lewis spoke with Cáceres about her work, the persecution she experienced, and the global victims of U.S. foreign policy. In her memory, *Jacobin* presents a translated and lightly edited transcription of the conversation." "They Want to Prohibit Us From Dreaming" by Berta Cáceres & Chris Lewis, https://www.jacobinmag.com/2016/03/berta-caceres-murder-honduras-agua-zarca-dam/.

32. He was leading a nonviolent delegation of 200-300 people, "who had come to deliver a message to the companies constructing dam on Rio Blanco." Brigitte Gynther, "The Murder of Tomas Garcia by the Honduran Military, SOA Watch," August 7, 2013, http://upsidedownworld.org/archives/honduras/the-murder-of-tomas-garcia-by-the-honduran-military/.

gunmen just 12 days after Berta. One member was detained for quite a while.[33] Berta was killed, they charged, because she proposed a project of life against a project of death.[34] They suspected (correctly, it turned out) that DESA, the hydroelectric company carrying out the *Agua Zarca* project, was behind her murder. The U.S. government "also bears some blame in Cáceres' death," said Al Gedicks "in its complacency with the 2009 coup and its continued military funding despite reports of human rights abuses."[35] Two of the men charged with her murder on February 28, 2017 had received military training from the U.S.[36]

COPINH asked our delegation to accompany them to a community forum on April 30th in San Francisco, Lempira (several hours away). They hoped that with our presence, the national police would be less likely to disrupt the meeting.[37] *La Casa Común* (Our Common Home), based upon Pope Francis' Encyclical *Laudato si'*, was the theme of the forum — held in the town square in front of the Catholic Church and broadcast on a local radio station. The local priest said that the role of the church is to raise consciousness, to care for the earth as Pope Francis claims. The Honduran government had recently granted concessions for five hydroelectric dams on the San Juan River, as well as concessions for mining, and a U.S. military base — all in Lempira Province. Each speaker focused on the need to resist these projects that would harm the water, land, and air.

Alberto Salamando and Heather Milton Lightening, members of our delegation representing the Indigenous Environmental Network, had been asked to speak, "to let the people know that the community was not alone, that the world is watching." Then Tomás Gómez, who took over coordination of COPINH after Berta's death, spoke powerfully about fear. Berta was not afraid, he said, she fought for liberation for all. "She was

---

33. This article in The Guardian gives more details about this repression. Nina Lakhani, "Fellow Honduran activist Nelson García murdered days after Berta Cáceres," March 16, 2016.

34. They also thought that her killing was meant to "cut off the head of COPINH, so it would no longer be a force of resistance." The COPINH: 25 Years of Struggle and Revolution blog from March 2018 shows that this effort failed!

35. Gedicks is "an environmental sociologist and expert on indigenous resistance to the extractive industry," quoted by Sarah Blaskey, "Murder of Indigenous Activist Berta Cáceres Exposes Reality of War on Honduran Social Justice Movements," March 4, 2016, *Upside Down World*, http://upsidedownworld.org/main/honduras-archives-46/5591-2016-03-04-18-12-04

36. See Nina Lakhani, "Berta Cáceres court papers show murder suspects' links to US-trained elite troops," *The Guardian*, February 28, 2017, https://www.theguardian.com/world/2017/feb/28/berta-caceres-honduras-military-intelligence-us-trained-special-forces.

37. Not too long after the forum started, two national police cars did arrive and looked over the crowd. After a while they left. I'm not sure if it was because of us, but we did stand out as *gringos/gringas* in the crowd. During the meal after the event was over, we were thanked several times for coming to the forum and being present in Honduras at this time.

not religious, but died like Jesus — who denounced injustice." Those who were afraid, he asked to mobilize, to struggle against these projects which come at the expense of the people. We propose, he said, a development that respects rights, does not give concessions; people must have land to work in our common home. He called for an open hearing to come together to make decisions. Marleny Reyes, also from COPINH, spoke about the importance of women taking part in community decisions. All need to come together to protect what is ours, she said. "There is no border on our common home — *Pachamama*."[38]

Our last event with COPINH was on May 2nd, at Utopia – their center outside La Esperanza. We met with Lenca and Garifuna women and men for dinner and conversation. The Garifuna women traveled for nine hours, to meet with COPINH women for two days. The evening closed with a sacred ceremony around a fire. These people had suffered repression, evictions, and the recent assassination of two of their leaders. They thanked us for our solidarity. The evening ended with all of us chanting "Berta *vive*! *La lucha sigue*! — Berta lives! The struggle continues!"

We traveled back to Tegucigalpa, met with some human rights organizations, and prepared our press release. On May 5th, our press conference was held at the offices of *Via Campesino*. The director asked us to do this, as it would bring some protection for them. Our last meeting was with staff at the U.S. Embassy. We called for (1) "an independent and thorough investigation of Bertha Cáceres assassination by the Inter-American Commission for Human Rights;[39] (2) upholding respect for the international conventions concerning the rights of Indigenous peoples including Free, Prior, and Informed consent; and (3) the demilitarization of Honduras and US-Honduras relations." Although "our delegation voiced passionate, articulate analyses and testimonies of the situation faced by Honduran people," wrote AMI staff Stephen Bartlett, "the embassy representatives' most salient response was, literally, 'This is above our pay grade.'"

---

38. Heather Milton Lightening, from the Indigenous Environmental Network, said that a lot of indigenous movements to protect the people, land and way of life in Canada were led by women. She added that it was an honor to be there, and that she would take their stories home. I'm drawing on my notes from the Forum and a Facebook post by Alberto.

39. On May 2, the news came that 4 persons had been arrested for Bertha's murder. They were said to be the head of DESA Security, the triggerman, a Major in the Honduran army and an environmental engineer, employed by the Agua Zarca dam, that Bertha had struggled so much against. See Nina Lakhani, "Berta Cáceres' murder: four men arrested over Honduran activist's death," *The Guardian*, May 2, 2016,). https://www.theguardian.com/world/2016/may/02/berta-caceres-murder-four-men-arrested-honduras). See Nina Lakhani's book, *Who Killed Berta Caceres? Dams, Death Squads, and an Indigenous Defenders's Battle for the Planet*," Verso, 2020.

We insisted "that the U.S. and embassy officials should be exerting greater pressure upon the Honduran government."[40]

14.3. Empowerment and Solidarity

These three delegations brought into life the horrific human and environmental impact of chemical mining, deforestation, and hydroelectric projects, as well as the courage, persistence, and faith of communities engaged in peaceful resistance in the face of repression, criminalization and violence. The communities we visited all thanked us for our solidarity. However, the experience at the U.S. Embassy in Honduras caused me to question the possibilities and limitations of solidarity in such precarious circumstances. The power of governments, corporations, and financial institutions seems overwhelming. Is our solidarity enough? Lorena Cabnal, cofounder of the Association of Indigenous Women of Santa Maria Xalapan, said in an interview that "It's hugely important for us to feel supported not just with solidarity, but also with political support," in order "to strengthen our political work more efficiently, while remaining aware of the risks that accompany the defense of human rights in the region."[41]

14.3.1. What Is at Stake?: Valuing Life, Defending Rights

"I've been alerted to hundreds of criminalization cases from nearly every corner of the world," said Victoria Tauli-Corpuz, the United Nations Special Rapporteur on the Rights of Indigenous Peoples in an interview after the release of her U.N. Report in August of 2018. "The rapid expansion of development projects on indigenous lands without their consent is driving a global crisis." Peru, Guatemala, and Honduras are three of the ten countries she names in her Report as "of grave concern," due to the "drastic escalation" of violent attacks while the people seek to defend their lands. In 2017, 207 land and environmental activists were assassinated; a fourth were from indigenous communities. Authorities in these countries have failed "to improve the protection of indigenous peoples," even though they have "repeatedly been urged to do so."[42]

---

40. "Solidarity Delegation Analysis Above US Embassy Pay Grade," Posted on May 6, 2016 by Sustainable Age of Louisville (SAL). Stephen was a long time staff member of Agricultural Missions (AMI) and leader of our delegation. He also was an excellent translator for those of us who did not speak fluent Spanish.
41. "*Latinas Feministas*: Lorena Cabnal," ibid.
42. The others are Brazil, Colombia, Ecuador, India, Kenya, Mexico, and the Philippines. (42) "These violations are occurring in the context of intensified competition for and exploitation of natural resources.... In several countries, increased militarization adds to

Tauli-Corpuz has been an indigenous activist and environmental defender in the Philippines for over 40 years. After President Rodrigo Duterte took power in June 2016, she was identified as a terrorist in a legal petition, along with six hundred other people. She thinks this was in retaliation for her part in an action to resist coal mining in Mindanao. "Going through this experience gave even more meaning to this report I was making," she said. "I experienced, myself, what those who are criminalized felt and feared." Her name was removed from the list shortly before the release of the U.N. Report, but others remain on it.[43]

One of her concerns is especially relevant to what we heard in our delegations. Tauli-Corpuz charges that "companies will still plough ahead with projects in disregard of judicial orders to suspend them," after "indigenous peoples have successfully challenged a project in court." She is also very concerned that in some recent cases, "high courts have ordered consultations to take place after the initiation of large-scale projects in an attempt to claim, *ex post facto*, that international norms have been complied with." However, this in not in accord "with international standards on consultation and consent."[44]

Our solidarity and political support is needed for movements and peoples who are criminalized and who persist in their peaceful resistance. As Beverly W. Harrison charges, "genuine solidarity requires concrete answerability to oppressed people, not just subjective identification with them." Pressure on governments, corporations, financial institutions, and international organizations is essential. We may come to see that our mutual survival is at stake.[45]

14.3.2. *What Is at Stake?: Healing and Defending Mother Earth*

"A crucial underlying cause of the current intensified attacks," Tauli-Corpuz says in her Report, "is the lack of respect for indigenous peoples' collective land rights and the failure to provide indigenous communities with secure land tenure." This "undermines their ability to effectively

---

the threats against indigenous peoples." (4) "Report of the Special Rapporteur on the Rights of Indigenous Peoples," Advance Edited Version, Released August 10, 2018. The data for 2017 is from Global Witness, "At What Cost: Irresponsible business and the murder of land and environmental defenders," https://www.globalwitness.org/en/campaigns/environmental-activists/at-what-cost/.

43. "Indigenous People Fight For Their Rights: Governments And Businesses Call Them Terrorists," Jeremy Hance, Huffington Post, 09/07/2018, https://www.huffingtonpost.com/entry/indigenous-people-terrorists-criminals-land-human-rights_us_5b8fab75e4b0511db3ddcdac.

44. "Report of the Special Rapporteur," ibid., 39.

45. I discuss this in more depth in "Sisterhood, Solidarity, and Feminist Ethics," ibid.

defend their lands, territories and resources from the damage caused by large-scale projects." The protection of their traditional lands, territories and natural resources is their priority. "They reject 'development' models which have been imposed on them without their participation and undermine their rights to self-determination and their right to set their own priorities for the development of their lands, territories and resources."[46]

We heard indigenous women speak about the relationship between geographical territory and women's bodies as territory. In her article "Is there a war 'on' the body of women?" Verónica Gago discusses an ongoing "crisis that focuses on the body of women as a territory under dispute." Diverse struggles use "the concept of body-territory to talk about the communities that resist neo-extractive attacks, a resistance largely led by women." She points to "the case of Berta Cáceres, whose murder the movement has named as a 'territorial femicide.' It is important to realize that the term "connects a notion of the body that not only goes beyond the human." It also refers to what Gago calls "the question of nature from a non-liberal point of view."[47] It challenges the "dispossession of material possibilities of life" — land, forests, water — that "shape the antagonism between multinational companies and states against populations that are being looted and displaced."[48]

At the time of Cáceres' murder, Tauli-Corpuz declared "that indigenous peoples are contributing to climate change solutions by continuing their traditional ways of forest and ecosystem management." Hydropower projects are not necessarily a climate change solution, as "they destroy forests and produce methane, which is more damaging to the atmosphere than carbon."[49] A global study of 28 nations released in June of 2018 found that

---

46. "Report of the Special Rapporteur," Ibid., 30, 33, 90. Recognition that indigenous peoples are the owners of the land "is a global demand." In "'Indigenous Peoples Are the Owners of the Land' Say Activists at COP20," Milagros Salazar, IPS, December 2014, http://www.ipsnews.net/2014/12/indigenous-peoples-are-the-owners-of-the-land-say-activists-at-cop20/. For a critical discussion of development models, with some attention to indigenous peoples and the role of finance and investment in dispossession and criminalization, see my chapter "Neoliberalism & Economic Development," in *Globalization and Economic Justice: From Terrorism to Global Peace*, ed. Karikottuchira Kuriakose, Gorgias Press, 2017, 243-87.

47. Ibid. The liberal is "abstract conservationism."

48. In this context, women are able "to bring all the blurred borders into play ... that have been elaborated for years between domestic, reproductive, productive, affective, and care labor." Veronica Gago, "Is there a war "on" the body of women?: Finance, territory, and violence," *Viewpoint Magazine*, March 7, 2018, 5, 7. https://www.viewpointmag.com/2018/03/07/war-body-women-finance-territory-violence/.

49. Tauli-Corpuz also said that "(The land) is the source of their identities, their cultures and their livelihoods," "Justice for Berta Cáceres Incomplete Without Land Rights: UN Rapporteur," Lyndal Rowlands, May 13, 2016, IPS Interpress News Service.

"the best way to save forests and curb biodiversity loss is to recognize the claims of indigenous peoples to their territories."[50]

14.4. Conclusion

We learned from women in Peru, Guatemala and Honduras how central the cosmovisions of indigenous peoples are to their defense of Mother Earth. Berta Cáceres' daughters, Berta Zuñiga Cáceres and Laura Zuñiga Cáceres, spoke eloquently about their mother's cosmovision in an interview a year after her death. Berta Zuñiga said that the way her mother "was able to recover identity, culture, spirituality and cosmovision for Indigenous peoples, specifically the Lenca people, stood out for her." This embraces "relations between people that are much more communitarian and collective, and that also have a strong relationship to the global commons and to nature, defying the dominant anthropocentric vision. They relate to spirituality and the relationships we have with all living beings — a holistic vision of life." This cosmovision, Laura Zuñiga said, "allows us to imagine another world." She added that "the struggle of Indigenous peoples," and other movements, "is a struggle for life. We're protecting the possibility that we may continue living in this world." It is possible, she said, "to have harmony for all people and not just for a few."[51]

Some Christian feminists are rethinking our understanding of our connection to the earth. In this respect, Rosemary Radford Ruether is a trailblazer in this work. Women have contributed their perspectives to the Poverty, Wealth, and Ecology project of the World Council of Churches (2007-13). African women challenged "the inadequacy of existing dominant theologies couched in patriarchal systems of domination and power." They are constructing their own feminist theologies, drawing on African spiritualities and religio-cultures. Among their learnings are "the sacredness of life and all creation," "our interconnectedness with each other and with mother earth," and "the need to redefine wealth as community and ecologically-centered such that wealth is shared equitably and used for the wellbeing of the community."[52] The "Call to Action"

---

50. Cory Rogers, "Investing in indigenous communities is the most efficient way to protect forests, report finds," July 2, 2018, Mongabay. For the report, see Rights and Resources Initiative, Cornered by Protected Areas, June 2018, https://www.corneredbypas.com/brief. Tauli-Corpuz is a coauthor of this report.

51. Beverly Bell, "The Vision and Legacy of Berta Cáceres Lives On," Otherworld, March 3, 2017. https://www.nationofchange.org/2017/03/03/vision-legacy-berta-caceres/. Berta Zuñiga took a leadership position in COPINH, in spite of ongoing death threats.

52. "African Women's Statement on Poverty, Wealth and Ecology," *African Women's Hearing on Poverty, Wealth and Ecology*, 05-06 November 2007, Dar es Salaam, Tanzania, available at www.oikumene.org.

from the Global Forum in Indonesia — June 2012 — includes these words: "We must challenge ourselves and overcome structures and cultures of domination and self-destruction that are rending the social and ecological fabric of life. Transformation must be guided by the mission to heal and renew the whole creation."[53]

May our solidarity contribute to our mutual survival and the healing of Mother Earth.

---

53. This project continued the AGAPE (Alternative Globalization Addressing People and Earth) process, which began in the early 2000's. Indigenous peoples were participants in this process. An Ecuadorian economist also participated, focusing on the understanding of *buen vivir* that was incorporated into Ecuador's constitution. For a discussion of this process, see my chapter "Alternatives to Globalization Addressing People and Earth: A Feminist Theological Reflection on Women, Economy, and Creation," in *Reimagining with Christian Doctrines Responding to Global Gender Injustices*, eds, Grace Ji-Sun Kim and Jenny Daggers, Palgrave Macmillan, 2014, 10-25.

IV

FOOD

CHAPTER 15

HUMANS AND HONEY BEES: BEE-HUMAN RELATIONS, SACRED SPACE, AND ENVIRONMENTAL SUSTAINABILITY AT SHORESH JEWISH ENVIRONMENTAL PROGRAMS

Adrienne Krone

15.1. Introduction

The hand painted sign at the entrance to the Bela Farm Apiary reads "Shema" in Hebrew letters and "Listen" is written below in English. It is a request that serves a dual purpose. It encourages the visitors to the farm to open their ears and hear the buzzing of the bees. It also allows the bees to continue their work without disruption. This sign is meaningful to most of the Canadian Jews that visit the farm because "Shema" is the first word of the central prayer in Judaism. The first line of the Shema in translation is "Hear, O Israel, the Lord is Our God, the Lord is One." However, the word takes on new meaning in this space. Here, it calls for the attention of humans to God's creation, and one creature in particular: the bee. And, just as the Shema is a central prayer in Judaism, bees are central to the mission and actions of Shoresh Jewish Environmental Programs, one of the organizations that runs Bela Farm.[1]

Figure 1: Shema Sign at Bela Farm Grand Opening[2]

1. Participant Observation, Bela Farm, a project of Shoresh Jewish Environmental Programs, June 26, 2016.
2. All images included here were taken by the author.

Shoresh is part of a larger movement of Jewish community farms and farming organizations. The Jewish community farming movement grew from one farm in 2004 to over twenty in 2017. The Jewish community farming organizations offer spaces for North American Jews to reconnect with ancient agricultural aspects of Jewish tradition and enact their environmental values. The founders of these organizations were often motivated by concerns about climate change, environmental degradation, food insecurity, and animal welfare. The farming organizations were all set up based on the needs of the local communities that they serve. They share a commitment to environmental and food justice as they have developed methods, models, and goals for addressing injustices independently so the organizations vary widely. Shoresh is one of just four Jewish Community Farming organizations that was founded and is run primarily by women. The women-led organizations tend to prioritize sustainability and community engagement over land ownership and use. This has been the approach of the Shoresh team led by Executive Director Risa Alyson Cooper and Director of Engagement Sabrina Malach. Jewish environmental programming began in Toronto with the establishment of Torat HaTeva in 2002, which was relaunched as Shoresh Jewish Environmental Programs in 2011.[3] Shoresh manages Kavannah Garden at the Lebovic Jewish Community Campus in suburban Toronto, where they offer educational programs and work with Jewish private schools in the surrounding suburbs, Maxie's Garden in downtown Toronto in partnership with Jewish Family and Child, and Bela Farm outside Toronto in Erin, Ontario, in partnership with local educators, artists, and an activist group focused on water sovereignty.[4]

Shoresh means "root" in Hebrew and the staff aspire to reconnect community members in Toronto to their Jewish roots.[5] The mission statement of Shoresh appears on their website: "To inspire our community to act as responsible stewards of the earth by nurturing a sense of awe and connection through Jewish experiential education and action."[6] They set their work in the context of three challenges they have identified in the Toronto community, including environmental crisis, poverty and hunger, and Jewish disengagement.[7] Shoresh staff addresses these challenges in all of their

---

3. "History," Shoresh Jewish Environmental Programs Website, Accessed March 8, 2018, http://shoresh.ca/history/.
4. Participant Observation, Shoresh Jewish Environmental Programs, June 2016.
5. "Introducing Shoresh," Shoresh Jewish Environmental Programs Website, Accessed March 8, 2018, http://shoresh.ca/introducing/.
6. Idem.
7. Idem.

physical spaces and programs. In this essay, I will utilize the example of the Shoresh beekeeping program to demonstrate the innovative blending of Jewish ethical teachings and sustainable environmental practices that Shoresh staff uses to address the challenge of an environmental crisis. Staff at Shoresh fosters Jewish engagement by introducing the Toronto Jewish community to creative rituals based on ancient teachings that engage and include bees as partners in their religious community. The Shoresh apiary and bee sanctuary serves as a sacred space where bees and humans encounter each other in service to their shared Creator as they pursue sustainability for creation.

15.2. Honey Bees in Crisis

Sabrina Malach is the head pollinator-protector at Shoresh. She focused on pollinator protection in urban centres in her graduate work in environmental studies and brought that knowledge and passion with her to Shoresh. Concerned about the declining local pollinator population, Malach wanted to do what she could to include bees in the mission of Shoresh. In a Toronto Star article titled "Ring in a Sweet Rosh Hashanah with Jewish Honey" from 2014, Malach describes the process by which Jews in Toronto came to care about the bees: "They fell in love with the honey. But bees dying made people care."[8] Malach continued, "They saw us as an outlet to express their concern."[9] The bees are dying, and as Sabrina indicates, once people learn about it, it is hard not to care.

Figure 2: European Honeybee at Bela Farm

8. Michele Henry, "Sourced: Ring in a Sweet Rosh Hashanah with Jewish Honey," *The Toronto Star*, September 24, 2014, accessed March 8, 2018, https://www.thestar.com/life/sourced/2014/09/24/sourced_ring_in_a_sweet_rosh_hashanah_with_jewish_honey.html.

9. Idem.

The bees at Shoresh are *Apis mellifera*, also known as European honeybees. This species of bees pollinates more than one-third of global produce.[10] Most grains do not rely on insect pollination but many fruits, nuts, spices, and vegetables require cross-pollination. Alfalfa, which is one of the main sources of livestock forage, is also pollinator dependent so meat production similarly requires pollinator participation. In their book *Vanishing Bees*, scholars Sainath Suryanarayanan and Daniel Lee Kleinman point out that growers are increasingly dependent on managed honeybees, rather than wild honeybees, to pollinate their crops.[11] They suggest that the transformation of agriculture post-World War II and "the increasing dominance of genetically narrow crops" is to blame for what they describe as "the uneven disappearance of endemic 'native' pollinator species."[12] Without native wild pollinators, growers require outside help. They find this in commercial beekeepers, who travel from farm to farm renting out their beehives to growers to pollinate their crops when they are in bloom. Suryanarayanan and Kleinman note that the common practice is to place the beehives at or near the crops, which exposes honeybees to grower practices, such as insecticides.[13] In recent years, commercial beekeepers in the US, Canada, and Europe have dealt with Colony Collapse Disorder, or CCD. Suryanarayanan and Kleinman explain that CCD-affected hives are considered collapsed after a sudden loss of their adult population. This often involves bees leaving the hive in droves abandoning their queen, her immature offspring, and their honey and pollen behind. They explain that the piece that has perplexed researchers is that the abandoned honey, which would normally be "robbed" by other bees or animals, remains untouched in cases of CCD.[14] In the U.S., beekeepers face an annual honey bee mortality rate averaging 30% due to CCD.[15]

CCD is complicated, and two geographers, Kelly Watson and J. Anthony Stallins argue that there are three main narratives about the causes and consequences of CCD. The first is a regulatory narrative that focuses on finding a single cause for CCD and seeks to alleviate pollinator shortages by eliminating the identified problem. This has been the approach of the

---

10. Kelly Watson and J. Anthony Stallins, "Honey Bees and Colony Collapse Disorder: A Pluralistic Reframing," *Geography Compass* 10, no. 5 (2016): 224, accessed March 6, 2018, doi:10.1111/gec3.12266.
11. Sainath Suryanarayanan and Daniel Lee Kleinman, *Vanishing Bees: Science, Politics, and Honeybee Health* (New Brunswick: Rutgers University Press, 2017), 10.
12. Idem.
13. Idem.
14. Ibid., 2.
15. Kelly Watson and J. Anthony Stallins, "Honey Bees and Colony Collapse Disorder: A Pluralistic Reframing," 225.

US government.[16] In 2015, President Obama created a Pollinator Task Force, a partnership between the Environmental Protection Agency and the United States Department of Agriculture, which called for $82 million in funding to address pollinator health.[17] The main potential causes identified are neonicotinoids, the largest group of pesticides currently used in agriculture, the invasive parasitic varroa mite, which arrived in North America from Asia in the 1980s, and a variety of viruses and fungal parasites.[18]

A second narrative suggests that CCD is a complex problem that likely has many causes and argues for attention to context as causes and solutions are identified.[19] The final narrative is an ecological conservation narrative that highlights the importance of wild pollinators and suggests that honeybee decline is a symptom of a much larger problem. This approach seeks to understand the relationships between humans, domesticated honey bees, other animal pollinators, and wild and domesticated plants.[20] Watson and Stallins suggest that a pluralistic approach to understanding Colony Collapse Disorder can aid the identification of causes and the implementation of solutions. Suryanarayanan and Kleinman identify an emerging alliance between sustainable growers and beekeepers, which has resulted in collaborations seeking to shift towards "truly sustainable and pollinator-friendly cropping practices."[21] At Shoresh, Malach considers a multiplicity of potential contributors to CCD and adheres to the ecological conservation model in her beekeeping vision. She serves as both a grower and a beekeeper, which ensures that their gardens and farms are set up with native plants to attract both honeybees and wild pollinators.

15.3. Pollinator Restoration at Shoresh

In June 2016, I attended the grand opening of Bela Farm. Risa Alyson Cooper explains that Bela Farm is organized through a partnership model and that Shoresh is one of the main partners in "animating and stewarding Bela Farm."[22] On that sunny afternoon, Cooper welcomed the hundreds of people in attendance who shared her vision for Shoresh's work at

---

16. Ibid., 223.
17. Ibid., 224.
18. Ibid., 225.
19. Idem.
20. Ibid., 226.
21. Suryanarayanan and Kleinman, *Vanishing Bees: Science, Politics, and Honeybee Health*, 10-11.
22. Participant Observation, Bela Farm, June 14, 2018.

the farm, where they planned to enact a "sustainable land-based Judaism."[23] After Cooper's welcome, we joined a procession to the 114-acre site that was about to become Bela Farm. A lively band led the way but as we approached the apiary the band stopped playing so we could do as the "Shema" sign commanded. We listened to bees buzz as they went about their work as volunteers in beekeeping suits waved. Then we headed into the field next to the apiary and were shown the 20 acres that would be set-aside as a bee sanctuary where they will plant 20 million native wildflowers and trees by 2021 in order to nourish the bees and other wild pollinators. We gathered in the field and Cooper led the crowd in a blessing of thanks for reaching this moment as seed balls were passed out. We walked in silence to a fence at the edge of the field and threw our seed balls. The seed balls flying onto the land were the first of the wildflowers that would be planted on the Bela Farm bee sanctuary. When all the seeds balls had been thrown, the band played a hora and the crowd began to dance.[24]

Figure 3: Bee Sanctuary Sign at Bela Farm Grand Opening

As mentioned above, Sabrina Malach adopted a pluralistic approach to addressing CCD at Shoresh. In a conversation I had with her in 2017, she identified multiple causes of CCD including pesticides, invasive pests, and wild habitat loss because of industrial agriculture. Climate change has also become a factor, and this affected Shoresh's bees that year. Malach explained to me that bees rely on a balanced relationship between rain,

23. Participant Observation, Bela Farm Grand Opening, June 26, 2016.
24. Ibid.

light, and flowers. In 2017, in Ontario they had more rain and less sun than usual. Flower blooms were shorter and bees had less access to nectar. Today, Malach is concerned that climate change will continue to adversely affect pollinators, which would eventually affect food supply.[25]

Malach started her work around bees at Shoresh by selling the honey produced by a Jewish beekeeper in Toronto. She felt that this gave people a space to embody their newfound care for bees. In the article about her work in the *Toronto Star*, Malach explained: "the narrative of the Jewish bees garnered donations from community members, including a 13-year old boy who donated $1,000 of his "bar mitzvah" money."[26] The Shoresh staff decided they wanted to continue to offer people Jewish honey from Jewish bees. The money they raised selling other beekeeper's honey and educating Toronto Jews about the bee population decline allowed them to build their apiary up to nine hives. Their current goal is to have thirty hives by 2021. Shoresh refers to their work as "community supported beekeeping," and they ensure that the Toronto Jewish community has plenty of opportunities to learn about bees, Colony Collapse Disorder, and other local pollinators. Every garden that Shoresh runs around the city of Toronto has a section of plants to support wild pollinators and at Bela Farm they have dedicated a significant portion of their land to the bees.

Sabrina and her coworkers continue to update their practices based on the information they gather from the beekeeping community in Toronto and their ongoing research on the subject. During a visit in the summer of 2018, I visited hives with Sabrina that were now located in a new area on the farm that she called "the bowl" because it was a lowland area tucked in between Bela's rolling hills. After the aforementioned difficult year of 2017, during which Shoresh lost 60% of their bees, Sabrina moved the hives and found that they made it through the winter at a higher rate. She thought this was partially due to the fact that the hives were now somewhat shielded from the wind. She also showed me experiments that she was doing with different types of hives. Most of the hives Shoresh builds are Langstroth hives, which are comprised of stacked boxes with removable rectangle frames. In 2018, Sabrina built one Warre hive, which is a box with removable bars that are designed so that bees can build their own comb in a manner that is closer to what they would build in trees. Sabrina was excited by the results and planned to continue to research and experiment with Warre hives.[27]

---

25. Participant Observation, Honey Harvest at Bela Farm, September 9, 2017.
26. Michele Henry, "Sourced: Ring in a Sweet Rosh Hashanah with Jewish Honey."
27. Ibid.

Malach was interviewed recently for an article about Jewish women farmers and she stressed the Jewish imperative to act: "If we destroy our world it will be disappointing to our Creator."[28] But Malach suggests it is more than just a desire to please but instead a duty. She continued, "we're commanded to guard and protect our planet."[29] At Shoresh, beekeeping is understood as an integral piece of their mission to do as they were commanded.

15.4. Bees in Judaism

In September 2017, I attended a Honey Harvest event at Shoresh. This time, we spent about thirty minutes in the apiary. Malach, wearing a shirt with a bee on it, took questions and offered information about the honeybees. One of the things she mentioned was that honeycombs have the same hexagon shape that appears inside the Star of David, a common Jewish symbol. She passed around some honeycomb so we could see the hexagon pattern that the Bela bees had crafted with precision.

Figure 4: Bela's Bees Sign at Bela Farm Grand Opening

Though Bees and Jews share a symbol, bees actually occupy a liminal space in Judaism. They are not a kosher animal, and according to Jewish law anything produced by a non-kosher animal is impure. However, the rabbis determined that a bee's body does not produce honey. Instead, they

---

28. Rahel Musleah, "My Daughter, the Farmer," *Hadassah Magazine*, January 2018, http://www.hadassahmagazine.org/2018/01/11/my-daughter-the-farmer/.
29. Ibid.

determined that bees store nectar in their mouths and then transfer it to honeycomb. So, bees are not kosher, but their honey is. The honey described in the Bible is often honey made from dates and in texts refers to as honey from wild beehives. Beekeeping is not mentioned in Jewish texts until the first century of the Common Era. When bee honey begins to appear in the Bible and in rabbinic texts, it is often described as an extraordinary substance, which may help to explain its curious kosher status.

In one biblical story, Saul's troops are preparing for battle and he makes them swear an oath that they will not eat any food until Saul takes revenge on his enemies.[30] The troops then happen upon a "stack of beehives where some honey had spilled on the ground."[31] The men, fearing the oath, restrain themselves. However, Jonathan, Saul's son, was not there when his father addressed the troops. So, Jonathan "put out the stick he had with him, dipped it into the beehive of honey, and brought his hand back to his mouth; and his eyes lit up."[32] One of the soldiers tells Jonathan that they had taken the oath and suggests that the soldiers are now faint because they are cursed for breaking the oath. Jonathan argues the point: "My father has brought trouble on the people. See for yourselves how my eyes lit up when I had tasted that bit of honey."[33] Jonathan goes on to suggest that the soldiers would have fared better in their battle had they eaten the honey. When Saul finds out that Jonathan ate, he suggests that Jonathan should lose his life for this. The soldiers protest and say he saved the day. Jonathan is punished, but his life is spared.[34]

The rabbis raise this story in their discussion of exceptions for the required fast on Yom Kippur. The rabbis discuss people with *bulmos*, which is described as a life-threatening illness that causes unbearable hunger pangs and impaired vision.[35] The rabbis suggest that people seized with *bulmos* eat "honey and all types of sweet foods, as the honey and all types of sweet foods restore the sight of his eyes."[36] The rabbis caution that there is "no clear proof for the matter" but that there is "allusion to the matter" and they reference Jonathan saying his eyes were brightened when

---

30. *The Jewish Study Bible*: Jewish Publication Society Tanakh Translation (Oxford: Oxford University Press, 2004), I Samuel 14:24.
31. Ibid., I Samuel 14:25.
32. Ibid., I Samuel 14:27.
33. Ibid., I Samuel 14:29.
34. Ibid., I Samuel 14:43-46.
35. *Koren Talmud Bavli*, Hebrew/English Edition (Jerusalem: Shefa Foundation, 2012), Yoma 83a, 415.
36. *Koren Talmud Bavl*, ibid., Yoma 83b, 417.

he ate the honey.[37] Some of the rabbis add their own honey remedies to the conversation. Rabbi Nahman says that Shmuel said that one should feed a person seized with *bulmos* a sheep's tail with honey "since the combination of the fatty meat and the honey helps greatly."[38] Rabbi Huna, son of Rabbi Yehoshua says, "fine wheat flour with honey is a remedy."[39] Then Rabbi Pappa says, "even barley flour with honey is good for curing *bulmos.*"[40] The conversation goes on to offer other remedies and stories about *bulmos*, but it is clear from this discussion that the rabbis understood honey as a food with distinctive properties.

A discussion of some of the special talents of bees also shows up in a medieval text centered on the unsustainable aspects of the human-animal relationship. In the fourteenth century, the Christian King Charles of Anjou requested a Latin translation of a Hebrew tale. Rabbi Kalonymus ben Kalonymus translated *The Letter of the Animals*, which is actually a Sufi Muslim story that originated in tenth century Iraq, in a mere seven days. This act of translation exposed Medieval Christians to the story of a lawsuit brought against humanity by the animals they had enslaved. A parrot uses bees as a counterexample to prove that humans are not superior because bees also gather as a community to choose their leaders and they divide their workforce into nurses, gatherers, soldiers, and builders.[41] The Queen bee then represents the winged swarming things and offers an evaluation of how bees are getting along with humans. She describes the human tendency to destroy bee homes and rob bee storehouses to eat their provisions. She ends her testimony with a grave warning.

> And they excuse all the cruelty they do because they believe everything is for their benefit alone; because they are our masters and we their slaves. They often can't see beyond their own appetites, beyond their own greed, and the whole world suffers for it.[42]

The Queen Bee's words foreshadow CCD and other hardships that modern honeybees face.

Despite the rather curious history and understanding of bee honey, it has become a key component of a Jewish dietary ritual. On Rosh Hashanah, the Jewish New Year, Jews dip apples in honey to bring in a sweet new year.

---

37. Biblical texts usually constitute proof, so the rabbis clarify that the example of Jonathan is not clear proof because he was not seized with *bulmos*, he was just very hungry. Idem.
38. Idem.
39. Idem.
40. Idem.
41. Rabbi Anson Laytner and Rabbi Dan Bridge, *The Animals' Lawsuit Against Humanity: A Modern Adaptation of an Ancient Animal Rights Tale* (Louisville: Fons Vitae, 2005), 54.
42. Ibid., 55.

This is where Shoresh started when they decided to include bees in their Jewish environmental vision. The Shoresh staff regularly refers to the bees as "Jewish bees," and they embrace the fact that the honey harvest coincides with Rosh Hashanah. They sell the bees' honey, and everywhere they give credit to the bees that made it. The page on their website with information about purchasing honey opens with the following statement: "Since 2014, Shoresh has been tending to and learning from our magnificent honey bees at Bela Farm. With deep gratitude to our partners, the bees and flowers, we are honoured to be able to offer local, raw, kosher honey for purchase just in time for Rosh Hashanah."

15.5. Bees and Humans in Sacred Community

In September 2017, I attended a Shoresh Honey Harvest event. We gathered at noon in the outdoor sanctuary of Bela Farm. Risa Alyson Cooper opened with a shofar call and a short D'var Torah. She talked about how we were in the Hebrew month of Elul and explained that one understanding of the meaning behind Elul is that it is an anagram. The four letters of Elul in Hebrew — *aleph lamed vav lamed* — are thought to correspond to the first letter of the first four words of a verse of the Song of Songs — Ani L'dodi V'dodi Li — which means "I am my Beloved's and my Beloved is mine."[43] Elul is the month just before the High Holy Days, so this is commonly understood to mean that God is drawing Jews closer in preparation for the holidays to come. Cooper offered a different interpretation as we prepared for an afternoon of harvesting honey. She described the relationship between the Shoresh staff and the bees as one befitting of this verse. She explained that we were about to take from the bees. We were going to spend the next few hours scraping the wax off their honeycombs, removing the honey tucked inside, and bottling it to sell to Jews all around Toronto. Cooper asked us to think about what we give the bees in return.[44]

Sabrina Malach then led us into the apiary. As we talked, she described some of the things Shoresh does to show their love for the bees and other pollinators. They check the hives regularly to make sure the queen is healthy and that there are no invasive mites or signs of disease. After the harvest they wrap the hives so the bees can survive the cold Canadian winter. Most importantly, they have planted flowers. After time in the apiary spent viewing honeycombs and listening to bees, we headed into the field that had been filled with grasses the year before when I visited. It was now filled from waist to shoulder high goldenrod

---

43. *The Jewish Study Bible*, Song of Songs 6:3.
44. Participant Observation, Honey Harvest at Bela Farm, September 9, 2017.

198   CHAPTER 15

Figure 5: Bela Farm Apiary

and other wild flowers. Malach explained that they plant native species that flower at different points during the year so the pollinators have a diverse and plentiful diet. We were given a few moments to walk around and observe the bees before Cooper called us back with the shofar. As we walked to the honey house, Malach pointed out monarch caterpillars resting on milkweed leaves. When they become butterflies, they will join the bees in pollinating the area.[45]

Figure 6: Honey House Sign at Bela Farm Grand Opening

We arrived at the honey house and we were given instructions to enter and exit the honey house quickly and carefully, so the bees would not get inside.

45. Idem.

They enjoy the honey, and it becomes difficult to harvest it with them present. By the time we started harvesting honey, we had already been at Bela Farm for about an hour. Everything about the honey harvest, and the Shoresh approach to beekeeping is intentional. The Shoresh staff center on Jewish and environmental education, so we could not harvest honey until they felt we understood the Jewish framework of the relationship between bees and humans and the needs and concerns of the bees.[46]

Bees are vulnerable in the modern world and marginal in the Jewish world, but at Shoresh they are considered part of the sustainable land-based Jewish community the staff is building. The humans that enter this community are asked to consider their relationship with bees and pollinators more broadly. They are encouraged to learn more about the dangers that pollinators face and to do everything they can to support pollinators. The Shoresh website includes resources to help people select and plant native wildflowers in order to establish pollinator gardens at their homes.[47]

When we finished bottling honey for the day, we gathered and were asked by Cooper to reflect on our experience and our gratitude for the bees. Only then could we enjoy the honey they worked so hard to make. Malach has described working with the bees as a religious practice: "It's spiritual for me. It's more than walking into synagogue. It's how it all feels, how it sounds, how it smells."[48] All participants at Shoresh are encouraged to engage their senses in this way and be in community with the bees. We listened to the buzzing as we approached the apiary, we observed them flying, feeding, and pollinating in the bee pasture, we got sticky during the harvest, and finally, we enjoyed the sweet taste of the honey.

15.6. Conclusion

The education about pollinators is not limited to those who participate in Shoresh's programs. Shoresh sells their honey at Jewish organizations around Toronto for $15-20 per jar. When they do, they educate their customers with information about what they call the "Bela's Bees Honey Pricing Philosophy."[49] The policy reads:

> Shoresh's Bela's Bees Honey is more than just a product — it is the delicious result of our deep commitment to supporting our pollinator friends through hands on education and activism (for example, we planted 4-acres of bee

---

46. Idem.
47. "The Beet," Shoresh Jewish Environmental Programs Blog, accessed March 8, 2018, http://shoresh.ca/blog/.
48. Michele Henry, "Sourced: Ring in a Sweet Rosh Hashanah with Jewish Honey."
49. "Honey and Candles," accessed March 7, 2018, http://shoresh.ca/products/.

pasture at Bela farm and will expand that to 20-acres of habitat to nurture and feed our bees). The cost of each jar of this liquid gold reflects the time and resources that go into creating meaningful experiences for community members around the vital role pollinators play in supporting sustainable food systems, ecosystems and Jewish life.[50]

Even the language in this simple statement centers on bees. They refer to the bees as their "pollinator friends" and describe their bee pasture as an example of their activist work in Toronto. They refer to the honey as "liquid gold" and make sure those who purchase it understand the true cost of the honey the bees spent a year producing. They highlight the role of bees in the food system, ecosystem, and Jewish life. They remind Jews that the honey they enjoy during Rosh Hashanah reflects a meaningful relationship between bees and humans.

Figure 7: Shoresh Honey

The labels on the actual jars of honey that Shoresh sells also identify the bees as the primary agent. The labels read "Pure Honey by Bela's Bees" followed by a disclaimer, which this year read "Limited Edition 5777." At the bottom in a smaller font, it says "shoresh.ca" — a simple reference to the Shoresh website. A small tag attached on the side also explains the mission of Shoresh — to help community members get back to their Jewish roots.[51] Shoresh also sells beeswax Shabbat candles and Rosh Hashanah tribute cards with their honey.

The Shoresh staff are working to return their community to their Jewish roots and to move them towards sustainability. This includes planting seeds, repairing the ecosystem, selling honey, and educating their community about sustainable land-based Judaism. They consider and involve the bees in every step of this process because they truly see the bees as

50. Idem.
51. Participant Observation, Honey Harvest at Bela Farm, September 9, 2017.

their friends and partners. As a result, Bela Farm serves as a sustainable sanctuary and a sacred Jewish space for the bees and humans that dwell there together.

CHAPTER 16

TANGIBLE ACTIONS TOWARD SOLIDARITY: AN ECOFEMINIST ANALYSIS OF WOMEN'S PARTICIPATION IN FOOD JUSTICE

Kelsey Ryan-Simkins and Elaine Nogueira-Godsey

16.1. Introduction

Research shows that in developing countries women are more dependent on agriculture to earn a living and are important agricultural producers, making up a large portion of farm labor force.[1] Consequently, rural women in developing countries are disproportionately harmed by the effects of anthropogenic climate change, such as food shortages, drought, flooding, illness, and natural disasters, as demonstrated by the Intergovernmental Panel on Climate Change's (IPCC) Fourth Assessment Report.[2] Thus, women's contributions are critical to agricultural productivity in these countries and consequently to climate change mitigation.[3] However, as ecofeminist philosopher Chris Cuomo argues, most political debates about anthropogenic climate change and mitigation fail to adequately address gender dynamics and women's experiences.[4] And, when they do address gender, generalizations about women's vulnerability tend to be made, reinforcing stereotypes by rendering invisible women's knowledge.

Ecofeminist scholars have investigated why women are in such positions of vulnerability. Research shows that women's vulnerability to

---

1. Bina Agarwal, "Food Crises and Gender Inequality," UN Department of Economic and Social Affairs Working Paper No. 107, New York, NY, June 2011, https://www.un.org/esa/desa/papers/2011/wp107_2011.pdf.
2. IPCC, *Climate Change 2007: Impacts, Adaptation and Vulnerability. Contribution of Working Group II to the Fourth Assessment Report of the Intergovernmental Panel on Climate Change* (Cambridge, UK: Cambridge University Press, 2007). https://www.ipcc.ch/site/assets/uploads/2018/03/ar4_wg2_full_report.pdf.
3. Agarwal, "Food Crises and Gender Inequality;" Cheryl Doss, "If Women Hold Up Half the Sky, How Much of the World's Food Do They Produce?," in *Gender in Agriculture: Closing the Knowledge Gap*, ed. Agnes R. Quisumbing et al. (Springer and the Food and Agriculture Organization of the United Nations, 2014), 69–88.
4. Chris Cuomo, "Gender and Climate Change," in *Encyclopedia of Global Warming and Climate Change*, ed. George Philander (Los Angeles, CA: SAGE Publications, 2012), 609–11.

climate change depends in part on gender roles and relations. However, as Cuomo explains, generalizations about women's vulnerability do not always tell the entire story — women's vulnerability to climate change results from an entire range of intersecting social forces.[5] Vandana Shiva argues that environmental hardships run along racial and gender lines by highlighting the particular experiences and challenges of agrarian Indian women whose livelihoods and survival are threatened when water is privatized, food economies are globalized, and common lands are enclosed.[6]

In light of this background and from an ecofeminist perspective, this chapter examines the key roles that women involved in sustainable agriculture play by resisting globalized industrial agriculture and promoting an alternative food system. It demonstrates how sustainable agriculture provides a foundation for women in North America to build transnational solidarity in response to the day-to-day effects of anthropogenic climate change and colonization. North American women have diverse experiences of food injustice that are shaped not only by gender but also race, class, and education. Based on qualitative research that we conducted with three small sustainable agricultural projects in the Columbus, Ohio area, we found that women from a variety of backgrounds use sustainable agriculture as a way to resist the dominant industrial agriculture system and the harm it causes locally and globally.[7] We interviewed staff, board members, AmeriCorps VISTA volunteers[8] and interns of two sustainable farms: Franklinton Farms (FF),[9] a nonprofit urban farm, and Seminary Hill Farm (SHF),[10] an organic peri-urban farm on the campus of the Methodist Theological School in Ohio. Through field research observations, we contrasted our findings with the Charles Madison Nabrit Memo-

---

5. Cuomo, "Gender and Climate Change."
6. Vandana Shiva, *Earth Democracy: Justice, Sustainability, and Peace* (Berkeley, CA: North Atlantic Books, 2015), 26-54.
7. This study was reviewed and approved as exempt by the Human Subject Review board at the Methodist Theological School in Ohio. Informed consent was obtained from all individual participants included in the study, including written informed consent to use first names of participants in publications of research results. For more information on the research methodology and questions used in the interviews please contact the authors (ryan-simkins.1@osu.edu and egodsey@mtso.edu).
8. AmeriCorps VISTA is a national service program that supports organizations working to alleviate poverty. VISTA members serve at an approved nonprofit and receive federally funded stipends to cover living expenses and a monetary award upon completion that can be put toward further education or student loans. Franklinton Farms hosted five VISTA volunteers at the time of the interviews.
9. See https://franklintonfarms.org/.
10. See https://www.seminaryhillfarm.org/.

rial Garden (CMNMG), a community garden that was founded and led by a predominantly African-American church in Columbus.[11]

We investigated how this work by women to build more sustainable food systems represents a form of solidarity with women in developing nations. We approached solidarity from an ecofeminist perspective, keeping in the forefront of our minds the challenge posed by Brazilian ecofeminist liberation theologian Ivone Gebara. Gebara asked "How can we act politically in our countries for the common good of all?"[12] Gebara writes that solidarity requires a deep realization of interconnection along with a response to the ways the social, political, and economic systems that connect us allow some to flourish at the expense of others' survival.[13]

We argue that one path toward solidarity is promoting an awareness of the moral ripples of our choices. Have we, as humans, sufficiently grappled with the responsibilities we accept by partaking in a globalized food system, which is characterized by large-scale industrial agriculture and neoliberal policies? This paper argues that this reality beckons a moral and ethical responsibility to understand the real impact of our choices. Sustainable food production has become a matter of survival and a moral imperative. For our participants, food justice is a moral question and requires a moral — and tangible — action.

We divided this paper into three parts. We first offer a background on the intersection of women, agriculture, and climate change, using an ecofeminist perspective to situate food justice and gender oppression within the larger environmental justice movement. Subsequently, we draw on themes from semi-structured interviews with FF and SHF to demonstrate three interconnected outcomes: 1) how participation in sustainable agricultural projects expanded participants' notion of justice; 2) how food justice work served as an entry into other social and environmental movements, providing a way for participants to resist oppression outside of the food system; and 3) how food justice was presented as a moral question in which the urban and sustainable agriculture work became a tangible way to act morally and show solidarity. We bring particular attention to how our participants from the three researched projects engage religion and spirituality to support a commitment to food justice. We contrasted our findings at FF and SHF with field research observations from

---

11. See https://telosinc.org/.
12. Ivone Gebara, "Radical Hope in Daily Life: An Ecofeminist Perspective from Latin America" (paper presented at the conference: "Dawning of a New Story, Radical Hope," Seattle, WA, May 2009).
13. Ivone Gebara, *Out of Depths: Women's Experience of Evil and Salvation*, trans. Ann Patrick Ware (Minneapolis, MN: Fortress Press, 2002).

CMNMG in order to highlight issues of race and economic privilege. We conclude by arguing that food and sustainable agriculture become a foundation for solidarity by providing tangible localized actions for those in North America to resist injustice caused by the dominant global food system, which is characterized by large-scale industrial agriculture, enforced worldwide by the policies of the United States and other developed nations. The sustainable projects profiled here revealed responses to food injustice that foster solidarity across geographic and social inequality caused or exacerbated by anthropogenic climate change. This form of solidarity promotes nature's wellbeing and human flourishing.

16.2. Women, Agriculture and Climate Change

Sustainable agriculture is a crucial response to the threats of climate change. Agriculture is a major contributor to greenhouse gas emissions, accounting, along with forestry and other land use, for 24% of total greenhouse gas emissions.[14] These emissions include not only those produced by industrial machinery but also the production and use of nitrogen fertilizers and pesticides necessary to sustain large-scale monoculture farming. While industrial agriculture contributes to climate change, climate change is causing altered precipitation patterns and severe weather events that threaten agricultural production and food security for millions of people.[15] However, biodiverse agriculture, such as agroecology which incorporates ecology into the design of agricultural systems, has been shown to be more resilient to impacts of climate change, such as severe weather events.[16] In addition, agroecology and other sustainable agroforestry methods have been proposed as strategies to sequester carbon and produce lower greenhouse gas emissions.[17] Thus, a shift towards ecologi-

---

14. IPCC, *Climate Change 2014: Mitigation of Climate Change. Contribution of Working Group III to the Fifth Assessment Report of the Intergovernmental Panel on Climate Change* (Cambridge and New York: Cambridge University Press, 2014), 9, https://www.ipcc.ch/site/assets/uploads/2018/02/ipcc_wg3_ar5_full.pdf.

15. IPCC, *Global Warming of 1.5°C. An IPCC Special Report on the Impacts of Global Warming of 1.5°C above Pre-Industrial Levels and Related Global Greenhouse Gas Emission Pathways, in the Context of Strengthening the Global Response to the Threat of Climate Change* (In press, 2018), accessed on December 15, 2018, https://www.ipcc.ch/sr15/; Agarwal, "Food Crises and Gender Inequality," 5; FAO, *The State of Food and Agriculture 2018: Migration, Agriculture, and Rural Development* (Rome: FAO, 2018), 11, http://www.fao.org/3/I9549EN/i9549en.pdf.

16. Miguel A. Altieri, Clara I. Nicholls, Alejandro Henao, and Marcos A. Lana, "Agroecology and the Design of Climate Change-Resilient Farming Systems," *Agronomy for Sustainable Development* 35, no. 3 (2015): 869–90.

17. Elliott Campell, "The Agroecostyem Role in Climate Change Mitigation and Adaptation," *Carbon Management* 2, no. 5 (2011); Eric Toensmeier, *The Carbon Farming*

cally sustainable agriculture is central to climate change mitigation and adaptation.

Patricia Allen argues that this globalized food system is dependent on unequal material and social relations, epitomized by starvation wages and sparse living conditions of farmworkers, who often work for large agribusiness corporations with huge reserves of wealth.[18] For Vandana Shiva, the reductive assumptions of the dominant global food systems are patriarchal and displace the reproductive role of women in social processes and agricultural practices such as traditional methods of seed saving in India.[19] The reductive assumption that herbicides, pesticides, and synthetic fertilizers can replace the complex ecological relationships of healthy soil, regionally adapted seed varieties, and other agroecological techniques, disrupts "the essential links between forestry, animal husbandry, and agriculture, which have been the basis of the sustainable model."[20] By disrupting this link, the productivity of both women and nature are obfuscated "when agricultural development becomes a project of western capitalist patriarchy."[21]

Ecofeminist scholars have investigated socio-economic gender inequality by analyzing how certain aspects of human life, those culturally linked to female work and the female body, have been marginalized due to a connection with the Earth. Ecofeminist theologian Rosemary Radford Ruether explains this connection on two levels: cultural-symbolic and socio-economic. The former is an "ideological superstructure that reflects and ratifies the second."[22] Dominant systems of privilege and patriarchal views have historically defined women as "'naturally' closer to the material world and lack[ing] the capacity for intellectual and leadership roles."[23]

Solution: A Global Toolkit of Perennial Crops and Regenerative Agricultural Practices for Climate Change Mitigation and Food Security (White River Junction, VT: Chelsea Green Publishing, 2016).

18. Patricia Allen, *Together at the Table* (University Park, PA: Pennsylvania University Press, 2004), 27.

19. Vandana Shiva, *Staying Alive: Women, Eoclogy, and Development* (Berkeley, CA: North Atlantic Books, 2016). The same argument can be found in reports generated by women working on farms in South Africa, for example. See Fatima Shabodien's "Livelihoods Struggles of Women Farm Workers in South Africa." http://www.wfp.org.za/publications/general-reports.html.

20. Shiva, *Staying Alive*, 93.

21. Ibid., 106.

22. Rosemary Radford Ruether, "Ecofeminist Thea/logies and Ethics: A Post-Christian Movement?," in *Post-Christian Feminisms: A Critical Approach*, ed. Lisa Isherwood and Kathleen MacPhillips (Burlington, VT: Ashgate Publishing Company, 2008), 39.

23. Rosemary Radford Ruether, "Ecofeminist Philosophy, Theology, and Ethics: A Comparative View," in *Ecospirit: Religions and Philosophies for the Earth*, ed. Laurel Kearns and Catherine Keller (New York: Fordham University Press, 2007), 77.

Defining women as naturally closer to the material world has resulted in ideologies that normalize and justify relegating women to a "devalued sphere of material work [that supports male elites] and excluding them from higher education and public life."[24]

One of the results of women doing most of the domestic and agricultural work is that this role placed them in integral relation with environmental questions about health, food safety, and water quality.[25] Movements, such as *La Via Campesina*, an international organization leading the global movement for food sovereignty and the rights of peasants, prioritizes the participation and leadership of women as it seeks to revalue their role in traditional and emerging food economies.[26] For this movement, food sovereignty, food security, and food justice require gender justice and the inclusion of agricultural wisdom acquired by women throughout centuries of patriarchal history.

Women are important agricultural producers, particularly in developing countries. They make up a substantial portion of farm labor force in developing countries and their contributions are critical to agricultural productivity in these countries.[27] Globally, 48% of economically active women report agriculture as their primary activity; however, in the developing countries this figure rises to 79%.[28] Despite women's involvement in agriculture, gender inequality in land ownership and access to credit, technical resources, and agricultural inputs remain pervasive.[29] Barriers within and outside of the agricultural sector contribute to the dependence of women in developing countries on agriculture for their survival — meaning women are disproportionately harmed by the ecological destruction and economic deprivation resulting from industrial agriculture. Women are also particularly vulnerable as climate change threatens agriculture and food security.[30]

---

24. Ibid.

25. Noël Sturgeon, *Environmentalism in Popular Culture: Gender, Race, Sexuality, and the Politics of the Natural* (Tucson, AZ: University of Arizona Press, 2009), 9.

26. Mark Navin, "Food Sovereignty and Gender Justice," in *Just Food: Philosophy, Justice, and Food*, ed. J.M. Dieterle (London: Rowman and Littlefield, 2015).

27. Agarwal, "Food Crises and Gender Inequality," 8; Cheryl Doss, "If Women Hold Up Half the Sky."

28. Doss, "If Women Hold Up Half the Sky," 84.

29. Agarwal, "Food Crises and Gender Inequality," 11–12; World Bank, Food and Agriculture Organization and International Fund for Agricultural Development, *Gender in Agriculture Sourcebook* (Washington, D.C.: World Bank, 2009), https://doi.org/10.1596/978-0-8213-7587-7.

30. Sam Sellers, *Gender and Climate Change: A Closer Look at Existing Evidence* (WEDO and Global Gender and Climate Alliance, 2016), https://wedo.org/wp-content/uploads/2016/11/GGCA-RP-FINAL.pdf.

Despite the vulnerability faced by women in developing countries, sustainable agriculture can also be a method of adaptation and community resilience driven by women. For example, throughout Latin America, women cultivate home gardens that produce diverse nutritious, medicinal, and culturally important foods. These foods play a vital role in family subsistence and generate additional income, both of which provide a buffer against environmental and economic crises that threaten the commercial crop production typically managed by men.[31]

Although women in the United States are in the minority of farmers and also face gender-based disparities in land ownership and access to resources, a higher proportion of U.S. women choose small-scale, less-industrialized farms than do men.[32] Women in the U.S. have greater representation in sustainable agriculture organizations than in conventional agriculture and are more prominent in leadership of urban agriculture and community gardening projects in marginalized communities.[33] The following sections of this chapter explore the key roles that women involved in sustainable agriculture in the U.S. are playing by resisting globalized and dominant industrial agriculture and promoting an alternative food system. We investigated how this work of women in the U.S. to build sustainable food systems represents a form of solidarity with women in developing nations, especially when these sustainable food projects are oriented toward food justice.

16.3. Bringing Justice to the Food System

The term 'food justice' has arisen within the alternative food movement in the United States to emphasize that constructing an ecologically sustainable food system requires addressing social justice issues. The New York organization *Just Food*, an early incorporator of justice into their organization's identity, defined food justice in 2010 as "communities exercising their right to grow, sell, and eat [food that is] fresh, nutritious,

---

31. P.L. Howard, "Gender and Social Dynamics in Swidden and Homegardens in Latin America," in *Tropical Homegardens: A Time-tested Example of Sustainable Agroforestry*, ed. B.M. Kumar and P.K.R. Nair, Advances in Agroforestry, vol. 3 (Dordrecht: Springer, 2006), 179.

32. Patricia Allen and Carolyn Sachs, "Women and Food Chains: The Gendered Politics of Food," *International Journal of Sociology of Food and Agriculture* 15, no.1 (2007): 6; Megan Horst and Amy Marion, "Racial, Ethnic and Gender Inequities in Farmland Ownership and Farming in the U.S," *Agriculture and Human Values* 36 (2019): 9–11.

33. Gregory Peter, Michael Mayerfeld Bell, and Susan Jarnagin, "Coming Back Across the Fence: Masculinity and the Transition to Sustainable Agriculture," *Rural Sociology* 65, no. 2 (2000): 231–2; H. Patricia Hynes, *A Patch of Eden: America's Inner-City Gardeners* (White River Junction, VT: Chelsea Green Publishing Company, 1996).

affordable, culturally appropriate, and grown locally with care for the well-being of the land, workers, and animals."[34] This all-encompassing definition of food justice understands that the food system as a whole reflects deeply interconnected concerns of justice, bringing together local and global concerns that focus on environmental health, treatment of agricultural animals, and the nourishment of human beings. Food justice requires the recognition that the act of eating is tied to the well-being of the environment and other human communities. With this recognition, food justice demands that justice pervade every part of the food system. The question, then, raised by this definition is, "What constitutes justice?"

Justice, as it is understood within the food justice movement, has roots in the Environmental Justice (EJ) movement. The EJ movement draws attention to the disproportional location of toxic waste facilities and other pollutants in communities of color and low-income communities.[35] Justice is partially related to equitable distribution, requiring that benefits, such as access to fresh healthy food, and detriments, such as agricultural pollution, are shared equally.[36] However, justice is also related to equitable power and participation in decision-making. Feminist political theorist Iris Marion Young critiques distributive justice approaches for not adequately dealing with the causes of maldistribution and instead suggests a focus on the "recognition of group difference."[37] Young argues that "where social group differences exist and some groups are privileged while others are oppressed, social justice requires explicitly acknowledging and attending to those group differences in order to undermine oppression."[38] Food justice, like EJ, requires attentiveness to the intersection of gender, race, and class, and justice highlights the need to address gendered, racial, and economic inequalities in the food system.

---

34. Quoted in Alison Hope Alkon and Julian Agyeman, eds., *Cultivating Food Justice: Race, Class, and Sustainability* (Cambridge, MA: MIT Press, 2011), 5.

35. See Robert D. Bullard, *Toxic Waste and Race at Twenty 1987-2007: A Report Prepared for the United Church of Christ Justice and Witness Ministries* (Cleveland, OH: United Church of Christ, 2007), https://www.nrdc.org/sites/default/files/toxic-wastes-and-race-at-twenty-1987-2007.pdf.

36. Richard R. II Bohannon and Kevin J. O'Brien, "Justice," in *Grounding Religion: A Field Guide to the Study of Religion and Ecology*, ed. Whitney A. Bauman, Richard II Bohannon, and Kevin J. O'Brien (London: Routledge, 2017), 217; David Schlosberg, *Defining Environmental Justice: Theories, Movements, and Nature* (Oxford: Oxford University Press, 2007), 3.

37. Iris Young, *Justice and the Politics of Difference* (Princeton, NJ: Princeton University Press, 1990), 22.

38. Young, *Justice and the Politics of Difference*, 3.

Justice, according to Gebara, operates within a framework of interconnection and interdependence. Gebara's understanding of justice requires that we "realize the connection between the destruction of living beings, among them human beings, and the degradation of living condition on the planet," showing us the "intimate correlations between social justice and ecological justice."[39] The day-to-day experiences of women, especially the barriers poor women of color face in their daily struggles to survive, "enlarge our perspective on the problem of evil," by contextualizing evil as multipronged and interconnected with colonization, neoliberal capitalism, patriarchal theologies that glorify suffering, and the destruction of the earth.[40] In this context, justice requires that we resist structural evil by finding ways to live that do not come at the expense of others' survival, as Nam Kim has argued.[41] Of the food system we might ask, how can we eat in ways that do not come at the expense of others' survival or flourishing?

Food justice recognizes our shared dependence on food that comes from the earth and on the human labor that provides this sustenance, bringing together concerns about "health, the environment, food quality, globalization, worker's rights and working conditions, access to fresh and affordable food, and more sustainable land use."[42] The growing food justice movement in the United States responds to critiques of the alternative food movement in the United States, which has prioritized organic agriculture but has given less attention to social justice and creating equity. Food justice highlights the need to address racial, gendered and economic inequalities in the food system. Thus, food justice aligns with an ecofeminist perspective, which emphasizes that justice requires addressing intersecting forms of oppression.[43]

16.4. Food Justice at Franklinton Farms and Seminary Hill Farm

Franklinton Farms (FF) is a nonprofit urban farm in the Franklinton neighborhood of Columbus, Ohio, dedicated to transforming the food

---

39. Ivone Gebara, "A Reform That Includes Eco-Justice," *Dialog: A Journal of Theology* 55 (2016), 118.
40. Gebara, *Out of Depths*, 41.
41. Nam Kim, "Survival at No One's Expense: Forging an Intersectional Coalition (@ theTable: Intersectionality & Political Action)," *Feminist Studies in Religion*, March 7, 2017. http://www.fsrinc.org/survival-no-ones-expense/.
42. Robert Gottlieb and Anupama Joshi, *Food Justice* (Cambridge, MA: MIT Press, 2010), 5.
43. See Val Plumwood's *Feminism and the Mastery of Nature* (London: Routledge, 1993) for more on intersecting forms of human oppression and abuse of the earth.

system by "growing and sharing food, creating beauty, and building community with [their] neighbors."[44] Franklinton Farms grows food on 27 small parcels of land scattered throughout the Franklinton neighborhood, including winter production in ten high tunnels. In 2017, the farm produced $50,000 of food in sales, distributing produce through a seasonal CSA[45] program, weekly Mobile Market online order and delivery program, and a Columbus farmers' market. Franklinton Farms offers subsidized prices for the CSA and Mobile Market programs, allowing those who self-identify as low-income to receive a 50% discount on a typical market price. During the summer of 2018, FF enrolled 60 CSA members, half of which received a subsidized share. In addition to addressing food security through offering subsidized prices and local delivery, FF also seeks to increase economic opportunity. The farm has worked with The Refuge Ministries[46] addiction recovery program to employ participants in the recovery program and provide training related to urban agriculture.

Seminary Hill Farm (SHF) is a four-hectare organic market farm on the campus of the Methodist Theological School in Ohio (MTSO) located in the periphery of Columbus' metropolitan area. The farm is part of MTSO's commitment to placing sustainability and social justice at the core of its seminary education. In 2017, Seminary Hill Farm produced 20,865 kg of produce, which primarily fed members of the farm's CSA program and faculty, staff, and students that ate lunch in MTSO's dining hall.[47] By partnering with other small-scale sustainable Ohio farms, Seminary Hill Farm provides its CSA members and MTSO diners with non-GMO pastured-proteins and fresh bread baked in-house and made with locally grown heritage grains. As part of its mission statement, Seminary Hill Farm has taken steps toward making its produce and the sustainable products of other farms available to Columbus neighborhoods with limited access to fresh food.[48] During the late summer and fall of 2018, Seminary Hill Farm participated in the inaugural farmers market in Linden, a low-income Columbus neighborhood that has faced challenges around

---

44. "About Us," Franklinton Farms, accessed December 15, 2018, https://franklintonfarms.org/about-us/.

45. Community Supported Agriculture (CSA) programs allow customers to support and share risk with a local farm by agreeing to purchase allotted amount of food from the farm weekly. Typically, this includes an upfront payment for an entire season and weekly shares of the farm's produce. Franklinton Farms offers flexible payment options.

46. See https://therefugeohio.org/.

47. Nancy McKibben, "Theology Meets Ecology," *Edible Columbus*, November 25, 2018, http://ediblecolumbus.ediblecommunities.com/food-thought/theology-meets-ecology.

48. See https://www.mtso.edu/ecotheology/seminary-hill-farm/.

fresh food access, exacerbated by the closing of the neighborhood's remaining supermarket in 2018.[49]

Women represent an important segment of both Franklinton Farms' and Seminary Hill Farm's operations, reflecting larger trends of women's increasing participation in sustainable agriculture compared to conventional agriculture.[50] Slightly over half of FF and SHF team members interviewed were women and gender nonbinary individuals. The contributions of women were recognized by those involved with the farms. Kate, a Franklinton Farms intern, shared, "Recently, it seems like just women in the food justice movement. It's a lot of women that are heading this up and making it known and being very active."[51] Seminary Hill Farm also relies heavily on the work of women, including its Farm Supervisor, fulltime farmworkers, apprentices, and student workers. Noel, the Farm Supervisor, shared that at times the female ratio within her team is higher than males or equal, but never lower. She also recognized that the same work opportunities and level of responsibilities would never be offered to her among those doing conventional agriculture. Although Noel has ten years of experience and various college degrees and certifications, she stated, "Those outside the food justice movement normally see women as incapable of farming or lacking in knowledge." Noel uses her photography and Instagram as an advertising strategy for Seminary Hill Farm and proudly tags her posts with "#womenwhofarm," connecting her work with the large and growing community of women farming sustainably in the U.S.

Based on semi-structured interviews and field observations,[52] we argue that those involved with sustainable agriculture at Franklinton Farms and Seminary Hill Farm promote food justice in a way that resists the dominant industrial food system and provides tangible ways for those living in the U.S. to build transnational solidarity. This was illustrated in three ways: 1) participation in sustainable agricultural projects expanded participants' notion of justice; 2) food justice served as an entry into other

---

49. See https://www.dispatch.com/news/20180121/kroger-closing-creates-food-desert-in-north-linden-frustrates-officials; https://www.dispatch.com/news/20180610/city-backed-farmers-market-will-bring-fresh-food-to-linden.

50. Allen and Sachs, "Women and Food Chains," 12–14.

51. All quotations from interview transcripts are cited in the text with the participant's first name, title, and organization. The authors conducted interviews with Franklinton Farms team members between November 2017 and February 2018 and with Seminary Hill Farm's farm team members in December of 2018.

52. Kelsey Ryan-Simkins was a part-time student worker at Seminary Hill Farm from April 2016 to June 2018 and an intern at Franklinton Farms from August 2017 to May 2018. Both positions were held as part of her master's education at MTSO.

social and environmental movements, providing a way for participants to resist oppression outside of the food system; and 3) food justice was presented as a moral question in which the urban and sustainable agriculture work became a tangible way to act morally, find spiritual fulfillment, and show solidarity.

16.4.1. *Learning About Justice*

The mission and vision of Franklinton Farms and Seminary Hill Farm articulate an orientation toward food justice; however, not all FF and SHF team members identified with this terminology. Other motivations for becoming involved with sustainable farming included a desire to do good, to share and build communities, to have a purpose, to be connected with the earth, to live up to religious commitments, and a concern for urban communities and future generations of living beings. Though food justice as a concept was new to some, involvement with FF and SHF prompted team members to think about structural oppression beyond these farms. For example, Kate, an intern at FF, articulated growth in her understanding of food justice when she began working with another urban farm. Kate explained, "I knew [our work] was to increase food access…I thought I was just going to grow food. I thought I was just learning farming, but now I think farming was the least of it that I learned." Jenny, an apprentice at SHF shared, "It was only after I started working on a small-scale sustainable farm that I realized what was wrong with big scale animal production farming… Quicker does not mean good… You can't treat nature as a factory." Jenny's desire to be part of alternative food production increased as she realized how the dominant economic global system regards the earth as objects of consumption and exploitation.

Others involved with FF and SHF offered systemic global critiques of the food system and cited these as the primary motivators for their involvement with these farms. Em, an AmeriCorps VISTA volunteer, acknowledged that food "has the potential to heal, but that is often used as an agent of harm as well." Historically and today, food is distributed inequitably. Em recognized this, explaining, "We were always taught that [the Irish potato famine] was a crisis of not having enough food, but really it was a crisis of capitalism not distributing food equitably. There was food. And, I just see so much of that playing out everywhere, all around… [food is] often used as a weapon against marginalized folks, communities of color, people who are different socioeconomic classes." The ways that industrial food systems have contributed to modern day famines, such as the famines in Ethiopia and Bangladesh in the 1970s, and to the inaccessibility of fresh food in low-income communities, especially low-income communities of color, in North America are well documented.[53]

Another VISTA volunteer, Sarah, explicitly connected oppression within the food system to the oppression of nature, acknowledging that the environment has been "neglected and oppressed under this capitalist society." Food justice pushes "against the industrial food system," she explained, "so that we're not destroying the environment or oppressing people." Sarah, Em, and others involved with these projects recognize that neoliberal capitalism drives both the destruction of nature and the oppression of people through food insecurity and unjust working conditions, leading them to embrace food justice as a solution.

Food justice work and the community that forms around that work shape emerging understandings of food justice and help those involved take actions toward justice and express solidarity. For example, Aisha, a volunteer, explained, "I'm learning from people at the farms ... about farmworkers' rights." These interactions are expanding participants' understanding of the role of sustainable urban agriculture in a broader context than organic food production or food movements do. Aisha learned from Em and others at Franklinton Farms that growing food in an urban neighborhood is connected to a broader movement addressing economic and social injustices within and outside the food system. Similarly, at SHF Jenny shared that she learned from another apprentice at SHF to think about race, food deserts, and who has access to healthy food in developed countries. The interactions between FF and SHF team members led to a more comprehensive understanding of food justice and the intersecting forms of oppression running throughout the global food system. Aisha, Em, and Jenny spoke about making connections between local justice issues — access to fresh food, urban land use, environmentally friendly farming practices — and larger movements for farmworkers' rights that explicitly resist the capitalist structure of the food system and its implications on a global scale.

---

53. See Amartya Sen's *Poverty and Famines: An Essay on Entitlement and Deprivation* (Oxford: Clarendon Press, 1981) for more on the famines of the 1970s. For more on racial inequality in food distribution see Isabelle Anguelovski's "Alternative Food Provision Conflicts in Cities: Contesting Food Privilege, Injustice, and Whiteness in Jamaica Plain, Boston," *Geoforum* 58 (2015): 184–94; "Healthy Food Stores, Greenlining and Food Gentrification: Contesting New Forms of Privilege, Displacement and Locally Unwanted Land Uses in Racially Mixed Neighborhoods," *International Journal of Urban and Regional Research* 39, no. 6 (2015): 1209–30.

16.4.2. *Entry into Other Justice Work*

Food justice is an entry point to resisting other forms of oppression and injustice. As Michelle, a former board member of FF, explained, "food is really just one lens by which we can see every inequality that exists." Noel, SHF's farm supervisor, shared that SHF's apprentice program[54] seems to attract many young adults who want to start over in a career connected with larger, global issues: "Sustainable local farming means to have this global connection." For FF and SHF team members, involvement with these organizations supported the desire to contribute toward broader change. This broader change included transformation of the food system, shifts towards environmental well-being, and large scale social and economic change.

Food justice work at FF and SHF and the broader scope of change that it embodies includes connections to a global narrative. Sarah, Jenny and Em understand their work with the farm as connected to a global and historical narrative of change. Sarah explained that the work of Franklinton Farms reminds her that she is "participating in this tradition of humans trying to cultivate the earth and feed themselves." "It makes me feel like I'm a part of something bigger," she shared. Jenny, stated "Farming allows me to connect with people through the land. It allows me to be connected with like-minded people." Similarly, Em chose to work with Franklinton Farms partly because of previous involvement with the food justice activism of the Coalition of Immokalee Workers.[55] Em participated in a week-long fast in solidarity with Florida farmworkers, which was a "powerful tool of resistance and revolution and powerful spiritual connection" that connected Em with the legacies of farmworker justice movements, including the fasts of United Farm Workers during the 1960 to 1980s. Em's participation in the fast contributed to a desire to "never treat food like a commodity again," and to identify and reject neoliberal food policies. The narrative of food justice connects the work of those at Franklinton Farms to the resistance movements of others seeking justice.

---

54. See https://www.seminaryhillfarm.org/apprentice-program/.

55. The Coalition of Immokalee Workers and Alliance for Fair Food organize for the rights and fair wages of farmworkers in Immokalee, Florida. Their campaigns draw on the support of students and communities of faith to boycott and lobby restaurants and grocery stores to join the Fair Food Program. Three of Franklinton Farms team members participated in a week-long fast as part of an organizing tactic for the Boycott Wendy's campaign. For more information see CIW Blog, "Here we are in Columbus, Ohio, which puts all of us at ground zero for farmworker justice..." (March 25, 2017), https://ciw-online.org/blog/2017/03/osu-meeting-vigil/.

16.4.3. Tangible Moral Action

Franklinton Farms and Seminary Hill Farm team members also find spiritual meaning in their work. For them, food justice work is moral action that is tied to systemic changemaking and solidarity. Mara, for example, described that becoming involved with social justice disrupted her religious belief that "everything happens for a reason." "I can't justify anymore my belief that everything happens for a reason because I know of my privilege," she explained. Mara's previous involvement with justice work like the Real Food Challenge[56] and the Coalition of Immokalee Workers also contributed to disrupting her Christian theology and her understanding of morality and moral actions in the context of recognized privilege. Food justice work offers the opportunity for moral action and spiritual fulfillment. Working with Franklinton Farms has given Mara a "renewed sense of optimism," she shared. It offered her the opportunity to reengage with hope and spirituality as she takes moral actions towards the creation of a more just and sustainable food system.

In addition to its moral and spiritual saliency, sustainable agriculture provides tangible action toward change and solidarity. While studying climate change at university, Em felt overwhelmed and hopeless by the immensity of global environmental issues. However, food justice work gave Em a "hopeful avenue" for contributing to change because "if we do it well, we can see it changing the world around us." Jenny graduated in animal science at The Ohio State University and worked as a veterinary technician in the emergency room of animal hospitals. She shared often feeling resentful towards the ways humans mistreated non-human animals. "It was eating my soul," described Jenny. Sustainable farming provided Jenny with purpose: "Working in the farm, it puts your energy towards good." Sarah started a potluck series to connect more deeply with Franklinton neighbors. She reflected, "I think that food and justice and everyone being able to eat good food is a way of communicating worth. And a way of extending hospitality to people in a way that Jesus would." For these farms, food justice work is a way of transforming the larger food system and being in solidarity with their neighbors and larger global community. Ultimately, these tangible moral actions move participants toward increased solidarity with those most affected by the industrial food system and by other forms of environmental and social injustice.

---

56. Real Food Challenge is a national campaign in the United States that organizes university students to demand that their university purchase food from local, sustainable, and ethical sources. See https://www.realfoodchallenge.org/.

16.4.4. Food Justice and Solidarity

Franklinton Farms and Seminary Hill Farm create spaces in which team members can expand their understanding of justice, contextualize local issues within the global movement for food justice, and engage in agriculture as a tangible action of solidarity. However, FF and SHF also face challenges in the ability to be a platform for solidarity within the U.S. context, where racial discrimination and economic disparity are often overlooked in climate change discussions. Scholars working in Critical Food Studies question the effectiveness of the alternative food movement in the United States, including urban agriculture projects, CSA farms, and organic labeling by pointing out the whiteness of alternative food spaces and how neoliberal strategies that emphasize individual choices rather than systemic change perpetuate economic inequality.[57] These critiques and the work of ecofeminist scholars, such as Nöel Sturgeon, point out how the well-meaning individuals who initiate alternative food projects fail to achieve justice due to their own embeddedness within dominant social, economic, and political systems.[58] All the Franklinton Farms and Seminary Hill Farm team members interviewed were white, college-educated individuals, representing the majority of those involved with both farms.[59]

The food justice mission of urban agriculture projects like Franklinton Farms, for example, is challenged by the process of gentrification in which wealthy residents move into and redevelop urban communities while displacing long-term residents. Urban agriculture has become fashionable in some social circles and is increasingly associated with an idealized urban living. This makes neighborhoods with conspicuous urban agriculture more desirable and results in city policy that promotes urban agriculture as part of a redevelopment plan for low-income

---

57. Alkon and Agyeman, *Cultivating Food Justice*; Alison Hope Alkon and Julie Guthman, eds., *The New Food Activism: Opposition, Cooperation, and Collective Action* (Berkeley, CA: University of California Press, 2017); Patricia Allen, "Realizing Justice in Local Food Systems," *Cambridge Journal of Regions, Economy and Society* 3 (2010): 295–308; Debra Davidson, "Is Urban Agriculture a Game Changer or Window Dressing? A Critical Analysis of Its Potential to Disrupt Conventional Agri-Food Systems," *International Journal of Sociology of Agriculture & Food* 23, no. 2 (2017): 63–76; Gottlieb and Joshi, *Food Justice*; Rachel Slocum and Arun Saldanha, eds., *Geographies of Race and Food: Fields, Bodies, Markets* (Abingdon: Ashgate, 2013).

58. Sturgeon, *Environmentalism in Popular Culture*.

59. It is important to note that SHF has intentionally changed the racial demographics of its staff. As of 2019, 40% of those working on the farm and food team were people of color, including a newly hired Community Food and Wellness Initiative Organizer.

neighborhoods.⁶⁰ Redevelopment, of which urban agriculture is only a part, leads to increasing property values and rent costs that displace low-income residents and attract wealthier residents. Though urban agriculture alone does not cause gentrification, several studies identify the close association between rising property values, changing neighborhood demographics, and urban agriculture.⁶¹ Further, urban agriculture projects like FF (the same goes for SHF) are in a position to benefit financially from city investment, partnership with private development, and an increasing pool of higher-income customers, sometimes in contradiction to food justice-oriented goals.

In Franklinton, residents express concern about redevelopment and gentrification, and team members at FF as well as SHF recognize that the fresh local food they produce is often easier to sell to the young professionals moving into the neighborhood or those who have access to farmers markets. However, these challenges are not only economic but also reflect wider questions about participatory justice. Gentrification, in addition to being a problem of middle-class consumption, also has racial dimensions. Trendy urban agriculture projects led by white individuals are often more publicly visible and receive greater funding support, while the longstanding practice of urban agriculture to supplement food needs in communities of color is overlooked.⁶² Additionally, the revitalization efforts led by the Black middle-class and elites more often serve as "defensive development" or a form of resistance and community-building that strengthens a community of color rather than contributing to gentrification.⁶³

Those involved with Franklinton Farms recognize the need for greater involvement of a diverse segment of Franklinton residents. "If the right

---

60. Nathan McClintock, "Cultivating (a) Sustainability Capital: Urban Agriculture, Ecogentrification, and the Uneven Valorization of Social Reproduction," *Annals of the American Association of Geographers* 108, no. 2 (2018): 580–82; John G. Stehlin and Alexander R. Tarr, "Think Regionally, Act Locally?: Gardening, Cycling, and the Horizon of Urban Spatial Politics," *Urban Geography* 38, no. 9 (2017): 1330–37.

61. Taylor Harris Braswell, "Fresh Food, New Faces: Community Gardening as Ecological Gentrification in St. Louis, Missouri," *Agriculture and Human Values* 35, no. 4 (2018): 1–14; Pascale Joassart-Marcelli and Fernando J. Bosco, "Alternative Food and Gentrification: Farmers' Markets, Community Gardens and the Transformation of Urban Neighborhoods," in *Just Green Enough: Urban Development and Environmental Gentrification*, ed. Winifred Curran and Trina Hamilton (London: Routledge, 2018).

62. Megan Horst, Nathan McClintock, and Lesli Hoey, "The Intersection of Planning, Urban Agriculture, and Food Justice: A Review of the Literature," *Journal of the American Planning Association* 83, no. 3 (2017): 277–95; Teresa M. Mares and Devon G. Peña, "Environmental and Food Justice: Toward Local, Slow, and Deep Food Systems," in Alkon and Agyeman, *Cultivating Food Justice*, 197–220.

63. Michelle Boyd, "Defensive Development: The Role of Racial Conflict in Gentrification," *Urban Affairs Review* 43, no. 6 (2008): 752.

people aren't at the table," emphasized Em, "[the farm is] not going to be the solution that we're trying to make it out to be." The desire to invest in the Franklinton community also resulted in eight of those interviewed relocating to the Franklinton neighborhood, though they acknowledge the tension of their own position in the gentrification process. While these concerns do challenge the work of Franklinton Farms, those involved expressed an ongoing commitment to challenge broader economic and systemic oppression within the food system and beyond.

16.5.1. *The Charles Madison Nabrit Memorial Garden*

The Charles Madison Nabrit Memorial Garden (CMNMG) offers a different perspective on food justice and solidarity than Franklinton Farms or Seminary Hill Farm. CMNMG is located on the property of The Church of Christ of the Apostolic Faith in the Linden neighborhood, which has few sources of fresh food located nearby. Just as the experiences of women globally differ by race, ethnicity, class, sexuality, and religion, within Columbus the experiences of women vary. CMNMG offers a contrasting example of solidarity from the perspective of women engaging in urban agriculture and food justice work from different social and economic locations within the food system and power structures of U.S. society. While the white individuals at Franklinton Farms are learning about food justice through their exposure to the experiences of others, those at CMNMG more closely share the experience of women across the globe who rely on agriculture as a tool of survival and resistance to injustice.

Paula Penn-Nabrit started the community garden in honor of her late husband, Charles Madison Nabrit, and received inspiration from "past generations of Mothers, Grandmothers, and Great-grandmothers."[64] This garden taps into a long history of agriculture as a strategy for resistance and resilience in the U.S. African-American community. When African people were enslaved and brought to the Americas, they brought African seeds braided in their hair and maintained 'slave gardens' that contributed to the nutrition, cultural heritage, and economic resources of the community.[65] Sociologist Monica White identifies this history as the foundation of

---

64. "About the Garden: The Charles Madison Nabrit Memorial Garden," Telos Training Inc., accessed January 10, 2019, https://telosinc.org/.

65. B. J. Barickman, "'A Bit of Land, Which They Call Roça': Slave Provision Grounds in the Bahian Recôncavo, 1780-1860," *The Hispanic American Historical Review* 74, no. 4 (1994): 649–87; Judith A. Carney, "'With Grains in Her Hair': Rice in Colonial Brazil," *Slavery & Abolition* 25, no. 1 (2004): 1–27.

contemporary community agriculture projects of the African-American community, which not only provides food but also increase community resilience and build collective agency.[66]

Paula and other church members active at the CMNMG use the social media tag "#wewerebroughttheretocultivate" to acknowledge African-Americans' complex relationship with agriculture.[67] The garden is a space to lament the enslavement of African people for agricultural work, but also to "increase awareness of the spiritual and cultural connections to gardening within black and brown communities."[68] By hosting events that celebrate African-American culture, acknowledge historic and present-day challenges, and invest in the future of the community's youth, CMNMG is not only resisting the industrial agriculture and food system but also the legacy of racism and economic disenfranchisement experienced by the African-American community in the United States.

White also argues that urban agriculture is a form a resistance that allows African-Americans to "enact human rights for themselves."[69] Black women, in particular, are able to resist the triple oppression of being low-income, women, and Black by creating a safe space in the garden.[70] Drawing on the tradition of African-American women's agricultural work, Paula explained that "growing your own food is like printing your own money and preserving food is like a savings account."[71] This is especially important for women who are responsible for providing and preparing a family's meals. Additionally, Paula emphasizes the importance of beauty in the CMNMG, which includes plants to attract pollinators and a certified Monarch Waystation to protect the migratory patterns of monarch butterflies. The CMNMG, according to Paula, reminds the community that they are worthy of beauty, even when spaces of aesthetic value are so often reserved for those with more privilege. In this way urban agriculture

---

66. Isaac Sohn Leslie and Monica M. White, "Race and Food: Agricultural Resistance in U.S. History," in *Handbook of the Sociology of Racial and Ethnic Relations*, ed. Pinar Batur and Joe R. Feagin, 2nd ed. (Cham, Switzerland: Springer, 2018), 347.

67. Paula Penn Nabrit, "Charles Madison Nabrit Memorial Garden," Urban Farming breakout session, Midwest Symposium on Ecologically Informed Theological Education at the Methodist Theological School in Ohio, Delaware, OH, October 18, 2017.

68. "About the Garden: The Charles Madison Nabrit Memorial Garden," Telos Training Inc., accessed January 10, 2019, https://telosinc.org/.

69. Monica M. White, "Shouldering Responsibility for the Delivery of Human Rights: A Case Study of the D-Town Farmers of Detroit," *Race/Ethnicity* 3, no. 2 (2010): 190.

70. Monica M. White, "Sisters of the Soil: Urban Gardening as Resistance in Detroit," *Race/Ethnicity* 5, no. 1 (2011): 18; 22–24.

71. Paula Penn Nabrit, "Charles Madison Nabrit Memorial Garden," Urban Farming breakout session, Midwest Symposium on Ecologically Informed Theological Education at the Methodist Theological School in Ohio, Delaware, OH, October 18, 2017.

becomes an important way to affirm one's own dignity through the cultivation of good food and community.

16.6. Conclusion

Women in North America, such as those involved with Franklinton Farms, Seminary Hill Farm, and the Charles Madison Nabrit Memorial Garden resist the dominant industrial agriculture system enforced worldwide by the policies of the United States and other developed nations. Though women at these farms experience the injustices of the food system in ways that reflect their diverse backgrounds (i.e. race and class), caused by particular forms of intersectionalities, they share recognition of the harm this dominant agricultural system does to ecological system health and to human communities. They respond with their commitment to alternative forms of agriculture that resist the social and environmental harm of the globalized food industry and work towards food justice. Acknowledging this shared commitment, all three farms currently partner with one another and participate in a larger network of food system change in Ohio.

The actions of North American women involved in sustainable agriculture projects are tangible responses to food injustice, fostering solidarity across geographic and social disparities caused or exacerbated by climate change. The prospect of responding to global environmental problems, like climate change, and global social injustices often feels distant and overwhelming. However, these local actions allow women to create positive social and sustainable changes. In both developed and developing nations, food security and adequate access to fresh, healthy foods remain a privilege for the few. This and other injustices of the globalized industrial food system persist along lines drawn by race, class, and gender. In response, the food justice work of Franklinton Farms, Seminary Hill Farm, and the Charles Madison Nabrit Memorial Garden, becomes not only a tangible action but also a moral imperative grounded in spirituality and religious beliefs.

Participation in food justice as a form of solidarity is not only open to women. However, in our research, this form of solidarity accompanied the women's work. Globally, women contribute significantly to food production, especially production focused on day-to-day subsistence. Women's involvement with sustainable agriculture and food justice as a tangible act of solidarity offers an example of how to learn from women's work across the Earth to promote nature's wellbeing and human flourishing.

CHAPTER 17

THE *TIANGUIS*: A MEXICAN MODEL OF A GREEN IDEOLOGY AND PHILOSOPHY

Juan A. Tavárez

17.1. Introduction

In the fifteenth-century, Western conquistadors imposed the Modern Era on much of the New World. Consequently, Pre-Hispanic ecological sensibilities that were rooted in the sacrality of the land would have been forgotten in post-conquest Mexico, if not for the Vice-Royalty of New Spain. The Kingdom of New Spain rose from the ruins of the Mexica Triple Alliance Empire. And from the ashes of the great ecological Nahua city of Tenochtitlan, the Castilian metropolis of Mexico City would be born. Hernán Cortés, founding father of this Spanish inland city, had an ambitious vision for his Renaissance capital. He wanted to "...create something which would make even Venice seem a village."[1] His vision would come to pass. Today, Modern-Mexico City is one of the largest urban centers of the world. As a global mega-metropolis it faces grave ecological challenges as it tries to reconcile its ecological pre-Hispanic heritage with Modernity.

Henri Lefebvre, the French philosopher and sociologist, states that the pre-Hispanic marketplace, the *tianquiztli*, commonly known by its Hispanicized name *tianguis*, represents the temporal continuity between Tenochtitlan and Mexico City. It is also a "representational space" with coded biological symbolism."[2] Unfortunately for pre-Hispanic markets, on January 1, 1999, Mexico made its grand entry into Modernity with the North American Free Trade Agreement (NAFTA). This neo-liberal trade agreement has been detrimental to Mexico's *tianguises*. Since NAFTA, *tianguises* are under constant threat, as they are becoming post-NAFTA wastelands. In the 20th and 21st centuries, post-NAFTA Mexico has failed to preserve the environmental symbols embedded in

---

1. Hugh Thomas, *Conquest: Montezuma, Cortes, and the Fall of Old Mexico* (New York: Touchstone, 1993), 560.
2. Barbara E. Mundy, *The Death of Aztec Tenochtitlan: The Life of Mexico City* (Austin, Texas: University of Texas Press, 2015), 12-13.

its *tianguises*. Mexico must defend its marketplaces from the onslaught of neoliberal policies if it is to value lives, heal the earth, and restore equilibrium to the world.

17.2. Tenochtitlan, Xochitlalpan, and the Sacred City of Gods

If Modern-Mexico is to succeed in forging an ecological consciousness, it must preserve and protect the "lived space" of its *tianguises*, vestiges of the ecological sensitivities of Tenochtitlan, the great garden city of the Valley of Mexico and the capital of the Triple-Alliance Empire. At the time of the arrival of the Europeans, the Nahua capital was *par excellence* the greenest city in the world. Almost every home had its own agricultural fields and gardens to cultivate. From the abundance of its flowery gardens that dangled from the city's rooftops, the capital resembled a rainbow forest painted by the vibrant colors of its flora. And from Lake *Texcoco*, the flowery misty scent would rise and enclose the city in a cloud with a tantalizing aroma of heavenly dimensions. Perhaps, St. Augustine of Hippo, in his description of the heavenly city in his formidable tome *The City of God*, could well have been the first European describing Tenochtitlan. Like Yahweh for the Jews, *Huitzilopochtli*, the chief Mexica god, guided the Mexica/Nahua through the arid deserts of North America and into their promised land, the Valley of Mexico. In this valley, the Mexica constructed their City of God.

> Tenochtitlan roughly means "next to the nopal cactus fruit of the rock," from the Nahuatl *nochtli*, for "nopal cactus fruit," and *tetl*, for "rock." Residents of the city held that their great migration of the eleventh and twelfth centuries were brought to a close by their tribal deity, Huitzilopochtli (hummingbird of the south), in 1325, when he sent the Mexica tribal leaders a potent sign. Taking on the form of an eagle, he flew to a perch on top of a nopal cactus where the exhausted and harried tribe was resting, on a rocky outcrop in the center of the great lake of Tetzcoco. These leaders founded their island city on this spot and gave it the name Tenochtitlan, a name drawn from the topography of the site of this miraculous event. Thus the name is not just a descriptive toponym but the location where Huitzilopochtli, a powerful warrior deity, chose Tenochtitlan as the island home for the Mexica, confirming their sense of themselves as his chosen people.[3]

Though they were the last major northern group to settle in the Valley of Mexico, the Nahua people were not merely northern migrants to the region. Rather, they were pilgrims who finally arrived at the Promised Land. The Nahua were inherently spiritual beings who knew that life was

---

3. Ibid., 1-2.

a passing moment and that their true and final destination was not Tenochtitlan, but instead the metaphysical flowery ecological realm of *Xochitlalpan*, the land of flowers.

17.3. A People of Flower and Song

For the Nahua, the flowery people of the Valley of Mexico, the goal of the earthly pilgrimage was the paradisiacal *Xochitlalpan*. To arrive at this highest state, knowledge of the infinite was required. It was achieved through *flor y canto*, or poetry and song. Nahua thought used poetic and symbolic language to interpret and express the apotheosis of truth and beauty. And from "flower and song" or "truth and beauty" Mexico's art of aesthetics and transcendental religious beliefs came into existence. Through the potent poetic imagery of flowers, symbols of a visual language, the Nahua were able to decipher divine revelation. And an important part of their divine truth demanded human sacrifice. Consequently, the Nahua initiated ritual wars or "flower wars" as a way to obtain captives to please the Mesoamerican gods.

> Blood was not only valued as a symbol of life but as a divine element we carry within us – "precious water" (*chalchíhuatl*) that could serve as food for the gods. As such, flower petals – ethereal as bird feathers or a butterfly's wings – were closely linked to blood, fire, the sun and holy wars.[4]

From their ancient floral mythology, the Nahua gave Nature anthropomorphic forms and qualities. Thus, Nature became a living entity. Flowers metamorphosed into *Xochipilli*, the flower prince; the hummingbird was now *Huitzilopochtli*; the quetzal bird embodied *Quetzalcoatl*, and Mother Earth came to be known as *Tonantzin*, Our Great Mother. These Nature gods and goddesses were carved into stone sculptures, which adorned the city's temples and marketplaces. And countless oral stories of their benevolence were kept in the Nahua's cosmogonic myth narratives, in which flowers sustained the whole of existence.

> The world was conceptualized as an enormous terrestrial platform that took the shape of a four-petal flower upon which lived humans and animals, surrounded by mountains, caves, rivers and lakes, grasses and trees.[5]

The four-petal flower might as well be the *Nahui Ollin* flower. The *Nahui Ollin* was the most important symbol in Nahua cosmology. In it, the

---

4. Dominique Dufétel, "Revelation of War: Reaping Flowers for Huitzilopochtli." In *Flores: Artes de México*, Number 47 (México: Reproducciones Fotomecánicas, 1999), 84.
5. Xavier Lozoya, "Cosmic Revelation: Flowers of the Soul." In *Flores: Artes de México*, Number 47 (México: Reproducciones Fotomecánicas, 1999), 85.

whole Nahua universe was contained. The *Nahui Ollin* not only denoted the four cardinal points but also denoted the sign of *Teotl*, the true god. Hence the garden city of *Huitzilopochtli*, the flowery sanctuary of *Teotl*, and thus the City of God, Tenochtitlan, was predestined to flourish as a world power.

17.4. Tenochtitlan: An Urbanistic Engineering Marvel

Construction of Tenochtitlan, the celestial city above the salty waters of Lake *Texcoco*, became the most ambitious and ecofriendly industrial enterprise ever undertaken in the Pre-Hispanic world. And the frontrunners of such an industrialized achievement were the Nahua people, the most accomplished environmental engineers in North America who mastered the eco-technology of *chinampas*, aquatic infrastructures that revolutionized and altered the landscape and lifestyle of the Mesoamerican people. The artificial islands allowed the Nahua people to transition from a nomadic existence to the greatest North America Native Empire. The *chinampa* system allowed for greater crop cultivation, human settlement, and population growth. Upon the arrival of the Europeans, Tenochtitlan had roughly over 200,000 residents making it one of the most urbanized and populated cities in the world.

> When we saw so many cities and towns built in the water, and other great towns on dry land, and that causeway so straight and level as it went to Mexico, we were amazed. We said it looked like the enchanted things they tell of in the book of Amadís because of the great towers and cues and buildings that are in the water, all built on stonemasonry. Some of our soldiers even asked if what we saw was not a dream, and it is not to be wondered at that I write here in this way, because there is so much to ponder that I do not know how to describe it; seeing things never heard or not even dreamed of as we were seeing...[6]

The city's great stonemasonry architecture was built on soft ground in a region prone to strong seismic movement. Yet, Tenochtitlan was relatively earthquake proof since the city was one of the first world capitals to use roller bearings or earthquake protective building buffers. The *chinampas*, or raised fields allowed the city to withstand the damaging effects of seismic movement as they served as earthquake isolators. With their island capital, the first nations of *Cemanahuac*, reached the height of their technology and engineering power. Today, the *chinampas* of *Xochimilco* are

---

6. Bernal Díaz del Castillo, *The True History of the Conquest of New Spain*. Translated, with an Introduction and Notes, by Janet Burke and Ted Humphrey (Indianapolis/Cambridge: Hackett Publishing Company, Inc., 2012), 189.

the sole remainder of this Native American eco-engineering knowledge of integrating both ecology and urban planning.

> González Aparicio posited that the pre-Hispanic builders of the valley cities consciously connected the urban nuclei — the urban network clustered around the lake — with great visual axes that tied together the built environment and in turn connected urban dwellers to the sacred mountain peaks that surrounded the valley. In doing so, he underscored both the genius of indigenous hydraulic engineers as well as the ideological drives behind their great urbanistic feats, as they created and built environment in harmony with the natural one, particularly the mountains and bodies and currents of water.[7]

As the city's urban prestige, power and dominance expanded across Lake *Texcoco*, the lake's eco-systems were carefully safeguarded and integrated into the city's landscape. The environmental inclusion in the urban setting had twofold purposefulness. It preserved vital eco-systems and created natural sacred sanctuaries. For Mesoamericans, Nature with her rivers, lakes, mountains and caves were dwelling places of their deities. Lake *Xochimilco*, the last enduring groundwork of Tenochtitlan, was and is the sacred home of the *Axolotl*, the amphibious Mesoamerican god with the power to regenerate itself. Currently, due to foreign invasive predatory species and the city's lack of effort to properly treat its wastewater, the *Axolotl* is now a threatened deity. According to *National Geographic*: After a three-month survey, Mexican biologists spotted Axolotls in the wild after fearing it was extinct in its natural habit, Lake *Xochimilco*.[8] David B. Wake, a biologist and curator of the Museum of Vertebrate Zoology at the University of California, Berkeley continues "At one time, Mexico City was really an aquatic city, and over time [Lake *Xochimilco*] has been drained and reduced in size and gotten polluted."[9] By its ancestral culture, history and to heal the Earth, Mexico City is obligated to do more in order to rescue Lake *Xochimilco*, the *Axolotl* and the Mesoamerican worldview of a waste-free society.

17.5. The Waste-free Capital City

The Nahua capital of Mexico-Tenochtitlan, ancient wonder of the New World, had an emphasis on cleanliness and personal hygiene that surpassed that of any European city. Unlike its European counterparts, Mexico-Tenochtitlan

---

7. Mundy, *The Death of Aztec Tenochtitlan*, 15.
8. Sonia Harmon, "The Mexican "Water Monster" Resurfaces: Freshwater Species of the Week." In *National Geographic* online at https://blog.nationalgeographic.org/2014/03/01/the-mexican-water-monster-resurfaces-freshwater-species-of-the-week/; March 1, 2014; accessed May 7, 2019.
9. Ibid.

was not beset by plagues or infectious-disease outbreaks. With an abundant supply of fresh and potable water from the *Chapultepec* aqueduct, crystal clean air from its elevation of 3000 meters above sea level and free from any major diseases, the city's population thrived and was once one of the healthiest in the world. Plus, the Nahua people happened to be a highly hygienic society. It had a zero tolerance for waste and littering. As a result, Martin Medina claims that a waste-free civilization arose.

> No descriptions or records have been found of Aztec garbage dumps. Instead they developed a system that is similar to a sustainable materials management system, considered today as the most desirable way to manage solid wastes, conserve resources and protect the environment. The Aztecs maximized recycling, burned some materials and disposed of the remainder in their *chinampas*. From what we know about Aztec society, they found productive uses for all wastes.[10]

Predominantly, Western historians have written the history of Native Americans. Beginning with Christopher Columbus's letters, the Conquistador's re-telling of the Natives and their ways of life eventually gave way to a negative understanding of their culture that has endured to the present day. For Western historians, the Nahua civilization is marred by their practice of human sacrifice. Yet, in many ways, this great Native nation was more ecologically advanced than its European counterparts. Medina's evidence demonstrates that Tenochtitlan developed and implemented a sustainable agrarian urbanism that allowed it to have a resource-efficient culture. It was this civilization that discovered the fine line between preserving and protecting the environment while building a first-class world city. Yet, this part of their civilization is hardly mentioned in Western historical texts. Besides constructing an ecological urban metropolis, in the midst of their cities they built the temple-*tianquiztli* complex, the origin of Mexico's ecological sensibilities and sacred commerce.

17.6. Mesoamerican Markets: The Temple-*Tianquiztli* Complex

The temple-*tianquiztli*, the sacred commerce complex consisted of a ceremonial and sacrificial temple, the marketplace, and the *momoxtli*, a sort of public altar composed of a round base that dominated the marketplace's center. Perhaps the idol *Yacatecuhtli*, the Nahua god of commerce, was mounted on the *momoxtli*. According to Pascale Villegas, the Spanish friar Diego Durán

---

10. Martin Medina, "The Aztecs of Mexico: A Zero Waste Society" in Our World online sponsored by the United Nations University at https://ourworld.unu.edu/en/the-aztecs-of-mexico-a-zero-waste-society, accessed May 7, 2020.

documented that a Native deity adorned the shrine and the Nahua would bring offerings of all sorts of things that were sold at the marketplace, including maize, tomatoes and fruits.[11] Therefore, to Villegas, the *tianquiztli* represented the ideal place or "lived space" for the exchange of physical and spiritual goods. Furthermore, Native marketplaces operated under the protective gaze of the great pyramid-temples. Therefore, the temple-*tianquiztli* complex materialized into a dimension not limited to space and time.

> The physical space of the market itself is the third sphere. Created out of the actions of urban dwellers, its meaning and character inflected by the ideologies encoded in the symbol, the market was not a mere physical expanse, a void in the urban fabric, but what Lefebvre would call "representational space," and what we will call "lived space," given how it carried in it the larger ideologies of the marketplace as well as the traces of its own historical creation and existence.[12]

Modern-Mexico has alienated the "representational space" of the *tianquiztli* to the margins of the urban metropolis. As a result, the ecological message embedded in the pre-Hispanic marketplace is being forgotten and drowned in post-NAFTA Mexico, hindering the country from rediscovering and fostering an ecological philosophy around its ancestral "lived spaces." As Mexico continues on its perilous transition from an undeveloped nation into an industrialized one, it must retain its pre-Hispanic environmental ideologies to safeguard the nation's natural resources and ecosystems from neo-liberal exploitive trading policies. Mexico has the potential to be a leading nation in healing the earth with its pre-Hispanic ancestral knowledge once it rediscovers the environmental and spiritual legacy and symbolism of the *tianquiztli*, the Native marketplace.

> This symbol, one representation of space, is itself significant. It is composed of concentric circles, one of them filled with smaller disks. These disks connoted preciousness: when colored blue-green, they are the symbol for "jade," the most valuable gemstone of the Americas; appearing on the entablature of a building, disks representing jade marked it as the dwelling of a lord. Inflecting the sphere of lived space, this symbol conveyed ideas of the market as being a place of preciousness (indeed, precious items were for sale in indigenous markets) and a space of lordly authority; its concentric circles also connoted origin and order (we find them also in symbols of navels, that biological sign of origins).[13]

---

11. Pascale Villegas, *Del tianguis prehispánico al tianguis colonial: Lugar de intercambio y predicación* (Siglo XVI). (Estudios Mesoamericanos: Nueva época, Enero-Junio, 2010), 94. Online at http://iifilologicas.unam.mx/estmesoam/uploads/Volúmenes/Volumen%208/Villegas-tianguis-prehispanico.pdf, accessed May 7, 2020.
12. Mundy, *The Death of Aztec Tenochtitlan*, 12.
13. Idem.

Mexico's *tianquiztli* or marketplace represents the cosmic order and existence of the Universe itself. As said by Barbara E. Mundy for the residents of Tenochtitlan, the *tianquiztli* was understood to represent the constellation Pleiades.[14] Therefore, from these marketplaces, the Nahua looked up to the firmament to map the origins of their myth narratives, ecological equilibrium, divine truth and social justice. Fortunately, the great pre-Hispanic *tianquiztli* survived the Fall of Tenochtitlan and thus they became New Spain's marketplaces.

17.7. From *Tianquiztli* to the *Tianguis* of New Spain

With the fall of Tenochtitlan in 1521, the city's great temples were razed to the ground and their deities smashed into pieces. The waste- and disease-free city, now found itself under siege by war and smallpox. After the fall, the Spaniards eventually would drain the once clear Lake *Texcoco* dry. As Mexico's largest lake turned to dust, the *chinampas* were abandoned and the fragile eco-systems of the Valley of Mexico were forever altered. It was an ecological conquest. Bernal Díaz Del Castillo, an eyewitness to the environmental destruction and who took part in the city's siege and invasion penned his own personal interpretation of the city's death. In a nostalgic and almost repentant tone, Díaz Del Castillo describes the life and death of the flowery city of Tenochtitlan.

> After having looked carefully at all that we went to the orchard and garden, which was such a wonderful thing to see and to pass through that I never grew tired of experiencing the variety of trees and the scent each one had, the terraces full of roses and flowers, the many fruit trees and native rose gardens, a pond of fresh water, and something else worth seeing: that, through an opening they had made, large canoes could enter the garden from the lake without landing, everything very whitened and bright with all kinds of stone and pictures on it that gave much to ponder, and birds of many kinds and species that came into the pond. I say again that I was there looking at it, and I believed that never in the world had lands like these been discovered, because at the time there was no Peru, nor any idea of it. Now all this is fallen down, ruined; there is nothing.[15]

In post-Conquest Mexico, Native ecological symbols, religious centers, and the *tianquiztli* survived by metamorphosing into Catholic temples and in the Hispanic marketplace. For example, some of the original brickwork of

---
14. Idem.
15. Bernal Díaz del Castillo, *The True History of the Conquest of New Spain*, 190.

Mexico City's Grand Metropolitan Cathedral came from the stonemasonry of the dismantled *Templo Mayor*. Also, the Native marketplaces survived and retained their sacred dimensions as they were transformed into Catholic and Hispanicized marketplaces: the *tianguises* of New Spain. For instance, since the sixteenth century, the marketplace in Mexico City's *La Lagunilla* neighborhood continues to operate next to the Santa Catarina Church. Since then, New Spain's marketplaces have retained the sacred space of its pre-Hispanic past, but now under the religious auspices of Catholicism. As a result, the visible structural ground of pre-Hispanic marketplaces were reassigned to serve a Catholic and Hispanic population. To Pascale Villegas, the Spanish friars reflected continuity and preservation of the pre-Hispanic market as they utilized the *momoxtli* to evangelize New Spain's multiracial society. In the process, they were also transferring the religious presence of the pre-Hispanic marketplaces over to New Spain's *tianguises*.

Hispanicized marketplaces were the ideal place for religious orders to bring Catholic doctrine, first to the Mesoamerican people and then to Novohispanos of New Spain. Therefore, the *tianguises* were an important forum for various racial communities to interact, to socialize and to be evangelized. And an important piece for this new evangelization was the *momoxtli*. For Villegas, the *momoxtli* was a public pulpit for Catholic priests to preach the Christian 'good news.' Consequently, the *momoxtli* gave way to a permanent Catholic shrine in the now Church-*tianguis* complex. Today, Mexican marketplaces still conserve a sacred space inside the Church-*tianguis* complex. In almost every Mexican marketplace there are public altars dedicated to Our Lady of Guadalupe. With the four-petal flower, the *Nahui Ollin* found in Our Lady's *tilma*, the floral cosmology and the idea of the paradisiacal *Xochitlalpan* are still present in Mexico's marketplaces.

17.8. Mexico and the Shadow Market

Most of Mexico's traditional marketplaces no longer are seen as paradisiacal or ecological havens of "valuable gemstones." NAFTA has turned these last ecological centers into sanctuaries of pirated merchandise making them the ideal destination for the black market underground economy to flourish. According to a 2015 study of *Piratería — Entendiendo el mercado "sombra" en México* ("Piracy — Understanding the Shadow Market in Mexico) found that 70 percent of Mexicans acquire counterfeit products from the traditional *tianguises*. Also, it showed that the *tianguises* represent 70 percent of the localities where the counterfeit products are purchased.[16] In the 2014 U.S. Embassy and Consulates in Mexico report: "Piracy — Understanding the Shadow Market in Mexico," concurs that "music, movies, clothing and footwear are the most pirated and counterfeited goods in Mexico." It states, "There is widespread social acceptance of purchasing counterfeit and pirated goods despite the fact that most know it is illegal and the health and safety implications of substandard goods."[17] Post-NAFTA studies have clearly proven that the abandonment of the traditional *tianguises* and their ecological origins coincides with NAFTA's dominant presence in Mexico's retail sectors. In their study, *La rápida expansión de los supermercados en América Latina: desafíos y oportunidades para el desarrollo*, Thomas Reardon and Julio A. Berdegué state: "During the nineties, supermarkets stopped being a niche for rich consumers in Latin America, and their participation in the retail sector went from an average of around 10% to 20% in 1990 to between 50% and 60% in the year 2000."[18] As the supermarkets spread across Mexico, they were perceived positively as a sign of Modernity, progress and Mexico's full integration into a Neo-liberal market. As a byproduct, Mexico's middle and upper classes saw their purchasing power increase. As a result, the Americanized sectors of Mexican society rejected the *tianguises* and the *ixtle* bag, a handbag made of maguey fiber. Unfortunately, the *ixtle* bag, an emblematic symbol of Mexico's Native and Novohispano societies, has been abandoned for the single-use plastic bag. The neglect and rejection of *tianguises* have resulted in the abandonment of Mexico's pre-Hispanic ecological heritage.

17.9. Conclusion

With the pending expiration of NAFTA in 2018, Mexico has the potential to value lives and heal the earth by exporting its ancient ecological culture. It can heal the earth because its ecological philosophy is rooted in the ancient wisdom of the *tianguises*. Today, in southern Mexico, pre-Hispanic

---

16. *Piratería — Entendiendo el mercado "sombra" en México*. Centro de Investigación para el Desarrollo, A.C. 2015, published by the American Chamber of Commerce of Mexico, published at https://www.scribd.com/document/319300705/PIRATERIA-Entendiendo-el-mercado-sombra-en-Mexico-1-pdf, accessed May 7, 2020.

17. "Piracy — Understanding she Shadow Market in Mexico," on the website for U.S. Embassy & Consulates in Mexico U.S. Mission to Mexico 30 June, 2015, published at https://mx.usembassy.gov/piracy-understanding-the-shadow-market-in-mexico/, accessed May 7, 2020.

18. Thomas Reardon and Julio A. Berdegué, *La rápida expansión de los supermercados en América Latina: desafíos y oportunidades para el desarrollo*, in *Economía*. 25.49 (June 2002), 87+ Pontificia Universidad Católica del Peru. Published at http://revistas.pucp.edu.pe/index.php/economia/article/view/943, accessed May 7, 2020.

and Spanish vice-regal marketplaces are still very visible in Chiapas and Oaxaca, the most Native states in the region. Both have held onto their ecological traditions rooted in the *tianguises*. To heal the earth, Mexico must reclaim the ecological sensitivities of these Native marketplaces and export them to the rest of the country, and world. It also must rehabilitate the cultural value of the Native *ixtle* bag in order to minimize the use of plastic bags that are creating havoc on the environment. And most importantly, the *tianguises* should defend its floral belief of the paradisiacal *Xochitlalpan* that represents beauty and truth, against a shadow market culture. In addition, to value lives, Mexico's *tianguises* should be *par excellence*, the 'representative space' for all Mexicans. In his poem, *México está en los mercados,* the great Chilean poet Pablo Neruda said: *Lo recorrí por años enteros de mercado a mercado. Por que México está en los mercados.*[19] An informal interpretation of Neruda's verse is that an ecological Mexico and its people are found in its marketplaces.

---

19. Pablo Neruda, "México está en los mercados," https://permanecerenlamerced.wordpress.com/2016/04/07/pablo-neruda-y-los-mercados-de-mexico/ accessed May 7, 2020.

CHAPTER 18

CAMPESINA SCHOOL: POPULAR AGROECOLOGICAL EDUCATION IN ECCLESIAL BASE COMMUNITIES IN EL SALVADOR[1]

Laurel Marshall Potter

> "Neither Jesus nor Monseñor Romero did 'pastoral care.' What they did was the true praxis of the Good News preached in the Gospels."
> Gustavo, a member of the Base Ecclesial Communities of El Salvador

18.1.

In Cacaopera, Morazán, El Salvador,[2] farmers plant the last of their food in the ground every May and wait for the rain. They reserve the fattest kernels of corn and offer them to the Earth under the blazing sun, waiting for the clouds to come. There is no irrigation in Cacaopera, and by the end of the dry season, last year's rainwater is long gone. I reread *The Grapes of Wrath* one year, and as the men in the first chapter watched the dust roll in to bury the wheat and push their families west, I looked up to see Juan watching the clouds dissipate around the mountain's crest, [an] empty bag of seed flapping in his hand. The rain didn't come that year. The year before, a tropical depression hit right before the harvest, and mature corn rotted in the fields as farmers looked on helplessly from their doorframes.

Young people growing up in Cacaopera watch their parents struggle with debt, watch their land get tired and thin, and watch their siblings' and children's skinny kid hipbones struggle to hold up the elastic waist of their shorts. Despite millions of dollars' worth of post-war reconstruction

---

1. The use of the feminine "Campesina" reflects the grammatical feminine gender of the word *escuela* (school) in Spanish, not the gender of participants. *Campesina* was not translated to "peasant" or "farmworker" or some other English-language word because it signifies a way of life inclusive of but beyond economic status or explicit work tasks such that no adequate English translation was found.
2. El Salvador is divided into 14 "departments," which are each divided into municipalities. Cacaopera is a municipality in the rural department of Morazán, comprised of dispersed communities organized around a central town which houses the mayor's office, a Catholic church, and commercial centers.

projects,[3] Cacaopera continues to be one of the most impoverished municipalities in El Salvador.[4] In Central America, social violence and family reunification are quickly becoming the biggest push factors for undocumented migration,[5] but young people in Cacaopera continue to leave because of the infeasibility of their local economy. When the rain doesn't come, young men head North without papers, women move into the city to clean houses, and families buy imported corn in increasing quantities every year.[6]

Cacaopera is one of many small rural communities facing similar issues. After the revolutionary conflicts of the 1970s and 1980s in Central America, neoliberal policies that characterized international repatriation and reconstruction assistance "undermined the markets, economic support, and return for small farmers... The national development model shifted from export agriculture to one based on industrial and banking services, even as half the population remained rural."[7] In Morazán, over 9,000 refugees returned from camps in Colomoncagua, Honduras to burned crops and seeds, slaughtered livestock, and demolished homes, schools, and chapels.[8] People rebuilt their communities throughout the nineties from materials the United Nations proffered from its member countries: sheet metal, tarps,

---

3. The World Bank alone loaned El Salvador $125 million in the two years immediately after the war, as detailed in the report by Alcira Kreimer, et al., "*La reconstrucción en los países en etapa de posguerra: El Salvador.*" *Précis* 172 (1998): 2, https://studylib.es/doc/5011451/la-reconstrucci%C3%B3n-en-los-pa%C3%ADses-en-etapa-de-posguerra. — Individual countries also contributed millions of dollars of aid money, earmarked by special interest groups. For more, see Chris Van Der Borgh. *Cooperación externa, gobierno local y reconstrucción posguerra: La experiencia de Chalatenango* (Amsterdam: Rozenberg Publishers, 2004).

4. Briones, Carlos Roberto, Mauricio Castro, and Oscar Alejandro López. "Mapa de Pobreza: Tomo I. Política Social y Focalización" (San Salvador: FISDL, 2005), http://www.fisdl.gob.sv/temas-543/mapa-de-pobreza.

5. Cohn, D'Vera, Jeffrey S. Passel and Ana Gonzalez-Barrera. "Rise in U.S. Immigrants from El Salvador Guatemala and Honduras Outpaces Growth from Elsewhere." Pew Research Center, Hispanic Trends (2017), accessed July 19, 2019, http://www.pewhispanic.org/2017/12/07/rise-in-u-s-immigrants-from-el-salvador-guatemala-and-honduras-outpaces-growth-from-elsewhere/. See also, Center for Migration Studies and Cristosal, "Point of No Return: The Fear and Criminalization of Central American Refugees." *The Central American Humanitarian Crisis and US Policy Responses* (2017), http://cmsny.org/publications/cms-cristosal-report.

6. "*El Salvador: Importaciones y exportaciones de cultivos seleccionados.*" Observatorio del Derecho Humano la Alimentación en Centroamérica (2017), http://www.odhac.org/index.php/estadisticas/por-pais/el-salvador/127-el-salvador-importaciones-y-exportaciones-de-cultivos-seleccionados.

7. Hecht, Susana B. and Sassan S. Saatchi. "Globalization and Forest Resurgence: Changes in Forest Cover in El Salvador." *BioScience* 57, no. 8 (2007), https://www.jstor.org/stable/10.1641/b570806?seq=2#metadata_info_tab_contents.

8. Cagan, Steve. "Salvadoran Refugees in the Camp at Colomoncagua, Honduras, 1980-1991." *ReVista: Harvard Review of Latin America* (Spring 2016), https://revista.drclas.harvard.edu/book/salvadoran-refugees-camp-colomoncagua-honduras-1980-1991.

and eventually cinder block for homes, commercial seeds and imported foods, and donated clothing, shoes, and school supplies. Almost 30 years later, it remains difficult for people in Cacaopera to pursue formal education beyond the sixth grade,[9] to receive healthcare beyond wildly overprescribed antibiotics,[10] or to access basic food items sufficient for a balanced diet as the cost has almost doubled since 2001.[11]

In contrast to war and continued impoverishment, life in Cacaopera is also characterized by the story of the Christian Ecclesial Base Communities, or CEBs, by their initials in Spanish. The CEBs grew out of an increase in biblical literacy in the late 1960s through which impoverished and marginalized Salvadorans became convinced that the Jesus of the Gospels does not will injustice or suffering but rather in word and deed announces a reign of full and dignified life for all God's children. The nascent CEBs were encouraged by the writings of the Latin American Bishops' Conference (CELAM) after the Second Vatican Council and by priests who accompanied marginal communities in their context of extreme poverty, structural injustice, and war. In the period after the Salvadoran Civil War (1980-1992), the Salvadoran CEBs lost institutional support that had helped them access theological formation, liturgical and sacramental practice, and physical spaces in which to meet. In Cacaopera, however, the CEBs' identity remained stronger than it did in other parts of the country, and present-day CEBs in Cacaopera remain committed to their organizational principles of prophetic memory, liturgy, and *diakonia*.[12] These principles are manifested today when the CEBs remember their martyrs and denounce social injustice (prophetic memory), in their liturgical celebrations, songwriting and artwork (liturgy), and in their faithful commitments to social and political justice (*diakonia*).[13] For the team members from Cacaopera and for the students, the Campesina School has been part of our *diakonia* as faithful Christians.

---

9. "*Estadísticas educativas por municipio: del año 2017.*" Ministry of Education, Republic of El Salvador (2018), https://www.mined.gob.sv/index.php/estadisticas-educativas/item/7153-estadisticas-educativas-por-municipio.

10. "*Antibióticos inyectables con receta médica.*" National Department of Medicine (2015), http://www.medicamentos.gob.sv/index.php/es/secciones-m/noticias-dnm/23-noticia-30062015.

11. "*Índice de precios al consumidor (IPC) Canasta Básica Alimentaria Rural (2001-2018).*" Department of Statistics and Census (2018), http://www.digestyc.gob.sv/index.php/servicios/en-linea/canasta-basica-alimentaria.html.

12. Gregorio Iriarte. ¿*Qué es una Comunidad Eclesial de Base?* (Bogota: Ediciones Paulinas, 1991), 107.

13. For more on the CEBs' current practices of prophetic memory, liturgy, and *diakonia* and connections to decolonial praxis, see Elizabeth Gandolfo. "Decolonial Ecclesiology in the Base Communities of El Salvador," unpublished conference presentation in the Ecclesiology Section of the College Theology Society annual convention (2018).

As the epigraph at the beginning of this chapter suggests, the CEBs do not see pastoral care and social action merely as a service that church leadership offers. Rather, actions that make justice real in our communities and societies are inseparable from the call to all of the faithful to continue Jesus' earthly mission of proclaiming and working towards the reign of God.

This chapter intends to describe the process of structuring, executing, and evaluating Campesina School (2014-present), which we describe as an agroecological curriculum for students from the post-war generations in Cacaopera who have discontinued their formal education. The orienting principles for this chapter are the leadership of marginal voices and the use of non-standardized popular methodologies. Often, the project goals, structure, and success indicators of development projects that seek to improve conditions in places like Cacaopera are articulated by granting agencies or large development organizations whose perspective is squarely situated in the literate, Western, Global North. An overrepresentation of these methods leaves little room in project planning and project execution for the radical protagonism of dynamic local leadership and popular insights from folks who live the target problems in their daily lives.[14] The vignettes explored in this chapter will demonstrate how fundamental trust in local people's ways of knowing and learning is indispensable for projects like Campesina School to be truly transformative.

18.2. Coming Together as a Team

In the 1996 precursor to the current volume, Janet W. May describes a multicultural dialogue in which she and other women at the *Seminario Bíblico Latinoamericano* in Costa Rica tried to make sense of what it means to be a foreigner.[15] Implicit in her decision to bring diverse voices to the table is the popular affirmation that two heads are better than one. Particularly when shared in friendship and mutual trust, diverse perspectives widen the scope of reality that a group will be able to describe. Different points of view help a group prevent historically and socially dominant norms from drowning out traditionally marginalized voices and make it more difficult for the assembly to share incomplete or unexamined assumptions. In the creation of Campesina School, we discovered that working as a team resulted in better outcomes for our shared project;

---

14. "Overrepresentation" as in Sylvia Wynter. "Unsettling the Coloniality of Being/Power/Truth/Freedom: Towards the Human, After Man, Its Overrepresentation — An Argument." *The New Centennial Review* 3, no. 3 (2003): 257-337.

15. Janet W. May. "Foreigners." In *Women Healing Earth: Third World Women on Ecology, Feminism, and Justice*, ed. Rosemary Radford Ruether (New York: Orbis Books, 1996), 39-50.

the contributions of each member of the team were uniquely foundational. The members of the core team throughout the most intense period of curriculum planning and adjustment were:

Name	Gender	National Origin	Level of Education	Urban/Rural Roots	Field
José Gómez	Male	Salvadoran	Some college	Urban	Nonprofit administration
Angel Cruz	Female	U.S.	Ph.D.	Rural	Agroecology
Estela Pérez	Female	Salvadoran	Some elementary school	Rural	Community leader
Daniel Pérez	Male	Salvadoran	Some elementary school	Rural	Young farmer
Laurel Marshall	Female	U.S.	Master's degree	Semi-urban	Theology, nonprofit sector
Agustín Luna	Male	Salvadoran	High school	Rural	Organic farmer

As formally-educated, White U.S. citizens,[16] Angel and I struggled to take a back seat as we identified with common values of a "White supremacy[ist] culture."[17] In particular, we struggled to admit that lecture-style lessons or reading assignments were not effective learning tools for our group of students. We would trudge through background information about soil composition all morning, but as soon as students *felt* the difference between their soil and the fertilizer we made as a school, they understood the importance of organic material and micronutrients. Though being called out was uncomfortable at the time, when Angel and I were able to resist insisting on what we thought were the best ways to learn, the lessons created by the whole team were ones that most of the students remembered as most impactful.

Estela's contributions to our teamwork were key factors for the school's design. Looking at the above table, Estela consistently falls on the disadvantaged side of the listed social categories. She has been a logistical support for many projects in Cacaopera, but she had never had a leadership role in project formation. Estela cannot read or write, so she is excluded from

---

16. By identifying as White, Angel and I do not wish to reify race as biologically or ultimately real. Rather, we wish to recognize the privileges, especially material benefits, that social and historical constructions of whiteness afford us.

17. The values of "White supremacy culture" are articulated in Kenneth Jones and Tema Okun. "Dismantling Racism: A Workbook for Social Change Groups." *ChangeWork* (2001), http://www.cwsworkshop.org/PARC_site_B/dr-culture.html.

implementing or contributing to written, manual-based projects. She has four kids and an elderly mother-in-law, so she is often cooking or watching the house when project teams facilitated by a salaried nonprofit employee normally meet. Estela is not the sole head of her household, so asking her to join a team instead of asking her husband could have put our project out of favor with him and could compromise an organization's reputation in her tight-knit, patriarchal community. However, Estela's intelligence for municipal politics, community dynamics, and personal contexts has helped the rest of the team understand how to structure the school around students' daily lives and responsibilities. Her presence on the team is an example for women who want to participate and permission for parents to let their daughters learn more about agriculture. Estela and Daniel both demonstrate the most effective methods for teaching students whose learning is hands-on and practical. In this way, each person's contributions, specifically from the marginal or disadvantaged perspectives of their complex identities, made the school more inclusive and more effective for our students.

18.3. Learning through Ritual

Throughout the seven months of the curriculum, some lessons stand out as poignant examples of how ways of knowing from marginalized and nondominant perspectives surpass the potential for dominant methodologies to teach the same lesson. One kind of activity that has a profound impact on students' understanding of their relationship to the earth is ritual celebration. Most sessions begin and end with prayer, including an altar made from natural flowers, grasses, food, photos of loved ones, and the didactic materials we use in that session, as well as traditional Catholic prayers combined with indigenous and popular names for God. These group prayers help the students to not only become aware of what their ancestors may have called God or be able to explain how their ancestors fused Catholic and indigenous spiritualities, but also to enact these practices. We feel what it is to pray to the "Creator and Former of the Earth," or to commence and bless our study by meditating on the visual of a textbook next to almost-extinct and culturally significant varieties of gourds.

In May, the Kakawira people have a ritual practice called *el pago de la tierra*.[18] Grandparents who lived in Cacaopera before the war remember

---

18. Kakawira refers to both the indigenous people who originally populated in Cacaopera and the language spoken by them. Cacaopera is designated to become a UNESCO global heritage site as the "sole surviving representative" of Kakawira culture and language. See "Cacaopera," United Nations Educational, Scientific, and Cultural Organization (1992), http://whc.unesco.org/en/tentativelists/211/.

burying cacao, beans, sweet breads, and corn in a hole on the same part of their land every year and blessing the sacrifice with chicken blood. They remember lighting candles and praying a litany to the saints listed in their almanacs before passing around homemade corn alcohol and sharing a meal. It is a ritual sign of the spiritual significance of planting seeds to grow food. In 2016, our students had heard of this ritual but had never celebrated it themselves. As part of our lessons in May about planting, we reinstated the practice in the sparse woods adjacent to the land we were working as a demonstration parcel. Capirio, an elder from the neighboring community of Yancolo, led the ceremony, and students' families came to participate. Our students, men and women, prepared elaborate bouquets of flowers and palm fronds, and each person brought some of their stored seed and foods. It was a dark, pungent, literally intoxicating experience. In a reflection afterwards, our students were on fire. They questioned Capirio endlessly about the history and significance of the ritual and its symbols and referenced the celebration throughout the rest of the season.

Another important ritual that we celebrate is the *atolada* at harvest time. In August, when corn reaches maturity but before it dries out on the stalks, folks harvest a small portion to make traditional foods like *atol*, *tortas*, and *tamales de elote* and to eat it off the cob. Like the *pago de la tierra*, it is customary to invite neighbors and family to share in the harvest and to give thanks for the crop. In our August session, we harvest from our organic, native seed demonstration parcel to make the traditional foods and share them with the wider community. After a few months learning about agrochemicals, food security, and nutrition, our students have felt proud to be able to host an *atolada* and give their friends and family products that they know are healthy, sustainable, free from commercial pesticides, and produced in harmony with their land. New techniques do not have to mean a break with tradition, and recovering ancestral practices does not have to result in the poverty and hunger that agrochemical advertisements predict.

In celebrating ritual and tradition as part of our curriculum, we are able to more effectively promote the three axes of our curriculum: sustainable agriculture, indigenous and *campesina* history and culture, and liberative spirituality. Experiencing the *pago de la tierra* and the organic *atolada* helps the students identify the value of their own indigenous and cultural practices as an alternative to the dominant, totalizing values of modernity. They are then able to articulate this value in a cost-benefit analysis of using sustainable agriculture techniques versus commercial agrochemicals. Commercial agrochemicals make farming a lot easier, which is a real concern when tractors are unavailable and there might not be enough water for a shower — let alone refrigeration for a cold drink — after a day's work. The experience of participating in their history and culture and feeling pride in their work gives students a more complete grasp of the factors at play in making informed decisions about their family's plots and food production and in collectively seeking higher levels of food security in Cacaopera.

18.4. Learning through Activism

Another significant knowledge source for our students is participating in political activism. In addition to individual and familial choices about how to produce food in rural El Salvador, national policies and international programs also control what is possible for rural producers. The years of Campesina School's formation were particularly dynamic times for agricultural policy in El Salvador. In 2009, the government responded to civil organizations by beginning to transition from buying seed from Monsanto to buying nearly 50% of its seed from national farmer cooperatives and associations in 2015.[19] A Food Sovereignty law was proposed by a coalition of civil society organizations and published in a popular format for community groups to read and understand.[20] As a school, we discussed the main contents of these political decisions and boarded a bus to San Salvador to participate in the National Ecological March in June 2014.

At the march, students were exposed to other hyperlocal groups and national organizations similarly struggling with the effects of the climate crisis, low levels of food security, and pollution caused by modern agrochemicals. They marched together with high schools, feminist and LGBTIQ collectives, explicitly environmental organizations, war veterans, labor unions, small entrepreneurial associations, and religious orders and churches, including the National CEBs. In talking with other activists during the march, students learned about issues they did not encounter every day, like potable water in cities contaminated by sewage. They also had the chance to share where they were from and how conventional agriculture practices and environmental degradation affect them. For some students, it was their first trip to San Salvador, and for all of us, it was a

---

19. Nathan Weller. "Farmer Cooperatives, Not Monsanto, supply El Salvador with seed." *EcoViva* (2015), https://ecoviva.org/farmer-cooperatives-not-monsanto-supply-el-salvador-with-seed/>.

20. Manuel Portillo Recinos. "*Anteproyecto de: Ley de soberanía y seguridad alimentaria y nutricional.*" Fundación Salvadoreña para la Reconstrucción y el Desarrollo (San Salvador: Equipo Maíz, 2016), https://redes.org.sv/media/uploads/documents/ley-soberania-alimentaria-vp.pdf.

chance to find comfort and energy marching in solidarity with others. We sang catchy slogans: "¡*Amemos al planeta, el agua y la vida se respeta!*" We stopped traffic; we taped our signs to the doors of the Legislative Assembly. We returned to Cacaopera invigorated and recommitted to our own daily work and lives.

Another reason that learning through activism is important for our students is the opportunity to express themselves creatively. For the march, we painted a banner that said, "Defend Mother Earth! Let's care for *Pachamama*!" The students painted the river, the trees, their houses, fields with terraced contour ditches and harvest baskets with multicolored ears of corn. They defined themselves through the natural world that surrounds them. They defined their experience through their own creativity, over and against statistics or census categories that define them to development agencies and international assessors.

Since 2018, the CEBs have been active in the fight against a water privatization law poised to pass the Legislative Assembly.[21] At the forefront of this struggle among the CEBs in Cacaopera are some of the students who have participated in Campesina School. They maintain an awareness of their connection to the wider national struggle for environmental justice and continue to contribute to their communities' analyses of the national reality during liturgy and community meetings. They participate in creative movements at the local and national levels to educate other young people, painting murals on public walls and picking up trash from stretches of the river with organized youth groups in their communities. They have come to understand that, in addition to personal responsibility for their own farming decisions, they are affected by and responsible for affecting policy decisions at the national level about agriculture, natural resources, and the environment.

18.5. Food as a Didactic Category

A third way in which Campesina School engages non-dominant knowledge is through the category of food, specifically by bringing men and women together as students and future community leaders. Crops and

---

21. Salvadoran civil society organizations published a press release summarizing their demands in the struggle against water privatization, accessible here: "*Apoyamos el NO a la privatización del agua en El Salvador*." Movimiento Mesoamericano contra el Modelo extractivo Minero (2018), http://movimientom4.org/2018/06/apoyamos-el-no-a-la-privatizacion-del-agua-en-el-salvador/. The Salvadoran bishop's conference has also issued a statement available here: "*No permitamos que los pobres mueran de sed*." Conferencia Episcopal de El Salvador (2018), https://www.iglesia.org.sv/wp-content/uploads/2018/06/Comunicado-Derecho-humano-al-agua.pdf.

food are opposite poles of the gendered division of labor in Cacaopera, and focusing on both food and corps has helped us begin to recognize that this division is arbitrary, that it negatively affects women, and that discussing it openly need not be taboo. For example, during our day-long workshops, we need to eat. At first, we divided the students up into shifts responsible for cooking for the group, but this quickly fell apart. First, a meal is not a meal in Morazán without a tortilla, and it takes all morning to sort, boil, clean, grind, form, and cook corn to make tortillas. Households usually do this once per day, and it is always a woman's job. Because of this, most of our male students did not know how to make tortillas, and the cooking teams were effectively reduced to either the female student on the shift or the female head of household whose kitchen we were borrowing. After we had campaigned in the communities to recruit female students, within the first month a pattern formed of the female students making tortillas for everybody's lunch most of the morning while the male students and the team discussed fertilizers and colonial history.

After the first session, we sat down as a team with the students to discuss what was going on. The female students shared that they were happy to help but felt that they had missed out on the lesson. The male students shared that they felt silly trying to make tortillas but also awkward that their female peers were doing the cooking while they participated fully in the school. We ultimately decided to use a larger-than-anticipated share of the economic resources we had to pay local women who were not students to prepare meals. This allowed our male and female students to participate fully in the curriculum and drew more community members into the school community. While not a perfect fix — we still relied upon the domestic labor of women and used financial resources not available to the average rural family — we reflected later that if we try to be perfect, we will never do anything! This fix allowed us to include our female students in a meaningful and equitable way, and we hope that our students' experiences learning and working together can be meaningful for them and other young people in the communities. We further reflected that it was a community effort for the school to happen, and the students shared a feeling of responsibility for sharing their knowledge with the wider community. Now, the women who help prepare meals often sit in on our lessons in the afternoon, too, and participate in activities like the *pago de la tierra* and the *atolada*.

In addition to this experience of restructuring practical aspects of the school for greater food justice, we also make conscious efforts to work food preparation into the curriculum. Specifically, in August, we learn about cultivating soybeans. In 2016, we invited a nutritionist from the public university in San Salvador to teach us how to cook with soy. She brought ingredients that were largely accessible to folks in the communities and taught the students, the team, and the women who made meals to prepare soy patties, soy milk and cheese, and soy doughnuts. Female and male students learned the new cooking techniques side-by-side. Male students described feeling satisfied eating something they had prepared. For our celebration and graduation ceremony in October that year, the students decided to prepare soy patties and soy milk for the attendees. In subsequent years, this workshop has become a student favorite and is now facilitated entirely by both male and female alumni of Campesina School.

Food is elemental for human life, and food production and preparation are the principal daily activities for folks in Cacaopera. By insisting on the category of "food" as intrinsically tied to sustainable (agri)culture and culture and by considering food justice from a religious or spiritual conviction, we make it more difficult to separate male and female work or to think of men and women as working toward different goals. In a similar way to practicing ritual or participating in activism, centering food justice in our agricultural and identity work helps Campesina School transcend damaging patterns that frequently limit community projects.

18.6. Looking Forward

In the experience of creating and bringing Campesina School to life, we as a team have witnessed the effective power of non-dominant ways of learning and the importance of incorporating diverse and marginalized voices into the structuring team. The above examples are our best of times. Obviously, Campesina School is not the arrival of the definitive eschaton, and we struggle to keep going every year because of financial duress, the team's own personal and familial responsibilities, and the harsh reality of life in Cacaopera, including the war trauma, infeasibility of local economics, and push factors for international migration described at the beginning of this chapter. We consistently refer to Campesina School as a "small initiative," an "attempt," and a work-in-progress.

In a Central America now forty years beyond the revolutionary wars of the 1970s and 1980s, revolutionary fervor and hope for a totalizing alternative to neoliberal capitalism has changed. Where the revolutions succeeded, flawed revolutionary governments have yet to enact the ultimate solutions for their countries' troubles. Where the leftist struggle for justice has been enfeebled by the ceaseless, violent imposition of Western modernity, revolutionary movements have had to adjust their energy and practices to survive the long haul. There has been no concrete proposal for a positive, ultimate utopia — no declaration of a *victoria final* — that has not fallen towards either totalitarianism or impossibility.

In a Christian worldview, this utopia is the "reign of God" as proclaimed by Jesus in the Gospels, and faithful Christians name themselves as such to proclaim their continued hope in this reality that is already but not yet among us.[22] For the CEBs, their *diakonia*, concretized in "small initiatives" like Campesina School, is what Christian theologian Edward Schillebeeckx calls *orthopraxis*, a right-doing that approaches "a historical form of what is already growing in this world."[23] The "what" is the ineffable, indescribable, un-imposable reign of God, and initiatives like Campesina School are "plural, fragmentary and mutually contradictory positive"[24] projects that keep it dynamically though imperfectly alive in salvation history. As the prayer inspired by Salvadoran St. Oscar Romero says, "No program accomplishes the Church's mission. No set of goals and objectives includes everything… We cannot do everything, and there is a sense of liberation in realizing that. This enables us to do something, and to do it very well."[25] Our attempts to improve the world are neither complete nor final — but we are responsible to keep trying.

The "something" that the Campesina School does well is demonstrate positive proof for strength in diversity and value in historically marginalized methods and praxis. 1970s and 1980s Central American revolutionary marches clamored for *otro mundo posible*, for another kind of possible world, for a definitive alternative. In the early nineties, the Mexican Zapatistas made a small addition: *otros mundos posibles*.[26] The clamor for many alternative worlds, for a plurality of explicit paths towards the ever-expanding horizon of the reign of God, is a more appropriate object for

---

22. This sense of what it means to be Christian is explored profoundly in the theology of Edward Schillebeeckx. Language cited here was taken from Schillebeeckx's critique of Karl Rahner's description of the "anonymous Christian," found in Edward Schillebeeckx, *The Understanding of Faith* (New York: The Seabury Press, 1974), 100.

23. Ibid., 66.

24. Ibid., 65.

25. "Prophets of a Future Not Our Own." United States' Conference of Catholic Bishops, http://www.usccb.org/prayer-and-worship/prayers-and-devotions/prayers/prophets-of-a-future-not-our-own.cfm.

26. This is alternatively expressed as "a world that contains many worlds." A few accessible sources for this idea include: Subcomandante Insurgente Moisés and Subcomandante Insurgente Galeano. "Una casa, otros mundos." *Enlace Zapatista* (2016), http://enlacezapatista.ezln.org.mx/2016/09/12/una-casa-otros-mundos. See also, "*Un mundo donde quepan muchos mundos: arte zapatista en la Casa de las Américas*." Art exhibit presented at the 3rd International Colloquium for the Study of the Indigenous Cultures of America. October 9-12, 2018, http://www.casadelasamericas.org/pecoa/2018/programa.html. See also, Alfonso Insuasty Rodríguez. "To think by building other possible worlds." *El Ágora USB* 18, no. 1 (2018): 16-19, http://dx.doi.org/10.21500/16578031.3441.

today's hope. Campesina School is one possible, evolving alternative for young people on our mountainside and an invitation for other communities to create their own paths. We are a voice in a growing choir of possibilities for a more just and humane world, a voice without which the song would reach fewer ears.

Adelante.

BIBLIOGRAPHY

"About the Garden." The Charles Madison Nabrit Memorial Garden. Telos Training Inc. https://telosinc.org/.
Acserald, Henri. "Environmental Justice and the Dynamics of Socio-environmental Struggles in Brazil: An Introduction." In *Justiça Ambiental e Cidadania*. Edited by Henri Acserald, S. Herculano and J. Padua. Rio de Janeiro: Relume-Dumará, 2004.
"Actualizing the Vision of *Laudato Si*': On Care for Our Common Home." The Pontifical Academy of Sciences, Nov. 2016. https://pas.va/content/accademia/en/events/2016/roundtable.html.
Adams-Heard, Rachel. "Welcome to the 'Man Camps' of West Texas." *Bloomberg Businessweek*. https://bloomberg.com/news/articles/2018-08-07/welcome-to-the-man-camps-of-west-texas.
Advrudra. "Environmental Laws and Constitutional Provisions in India." Legal Services India. https://legalservicesindia.com/article/1926/Environmental-Laws-and-Constitutional-Provisions-In-India.html.
Agarwal, Bina. "Food Crises and Gender Inequality." In the UN Department of Economic and Social Affairs Working Paper No. 107, New York, NY, June 2011. https://un.org/esa/desa/papers/2011/wp107_2011.pdf.
—. "Food Crises and Gender Inequality." World Bank, Food and Agriculture Organization and International Fund for Agricultural Development. In *Gender in Agriculture Sourcebook*. Washington D.C.: World Bank, 2009. https://doi.org/10.1596/978-0-8213-7587-7.
Aguirre Beltrán, Gonzalo. *Medicina y Magia*. México: Instituto Nacional Indigenista-SEP, 1980.
Alkon, Alison Hope, and Julie Guthman, editors. *The New Food Activism: Opposition, Cooperation, and Collective Action*. Berkeley, CA: University of California Press, 2017.
—, editors. *Cultivating Food Justice: Race, Class, and Sustainability*. Cambridge, MA: Massachusetts Institute of Technology Press, 2011.
Allen, Patricia. "Realizing Justice in Local Food Systems." In *Cambridge Journal of Regions, Economy and Society*, vol. 3, no. 2, July 2010, 295-308.
—. *Together at the Table*. University Park, PA: Pennsylvania University Press, 2004.
Allen, Patricia, and Carolyn Sachs. "Women and Food Chains: The Gendered Politics of Food." In *International Journal of Sociology of Food and Agriculture* 15, no. 1, 2007.
Altieri, Miguel A., Clara I. Nicholls, Alejandro Henao, and Marcos A. Lana. "Agroecology and the Design of Climate Change-Resilient Farming Systems." In *Agronomy for Sustainable Development* 35, no. 3, May 2015.
Anguelovski, Isabelle. "Alternative Food Provision Conflicts in Cities: Contesting Food Privilege, Injustice, and Whiteness in Jamaica Plain, Boston." In *Geoforum* 58, 2015.
—. "Healthy Food Stores, Greenlining and Food Gentrification: Contesting New Forms of Privilege, Displacement and Locally Unwanted Land Uses in

Racially Mixed Neighborhoods." In *International Journal of Urban and Regional Research* 39, no. 6, 2015.

Anthony, Carl. *The Earth the City and the Hidden Narrative of Race*. New York: New Village Press, 2017.

"Antibióticos inyectables con receta médica." In the National Department of Medicine, 2015. http://medicamentos.gob.sv/index.php/es/secciones-m/noticias-dnm/23-noticia-3006201.

Apffel-Marglin, Frédérique. *Subversive Spiritualities: How Rituals Enact the World*. New York: Oxford University Press, 2011.

Apffel-Marglin, Frédérique, and Stefano Varese, editors. *Contemporary Voices from Anima Mundi: A Reappraisal*. New York: Peter Lang Academic Press, 2020.

"Apoyamos el NO a la privatización del agua en El Salvador." In *Movimiento Mesoamericano contra el Modelo extractivo Minero*, 2018. https://movimientom4.org/2018/06/apoyamos-el-no-a-la-privatizacion-del-agua-en-el-salvador/.

"Apprentice Program." Seminary Hill Farm. https://seminaryhillfarm.org/apprentice-program/.

Aquino, María Pilar and Maria José Rosado-Nuñes, editors. *Feminist Intercultural Theology: Latina Explorations for a Just World*. New York: Orbis Books, 2007.

Archibald, J. A. *Indigenous Storywork: Educating the Heart, Mind, Body, and Spirit*. Vancouver: UBC Press, 2008.

Attias, Isabel Lagarriga. *Medicina Tradicional y Espiritismo*. México: Sep-Setentas No. 191, 1975.

Austin, Alfredo López. *Cuerpo Humano e Ideología*, 2 volumes. México: UNAM IIA, 1984.

Aymond, Archbishop Gregory M. "Planned Parenthood Abortion Clinic: We Cannot Cooperate with Evil." Monday, 27 January, 2014. https://abitadeacon.blogspot.com/2014/01/archbishop-aymond-urges-truly-catholic.html.

Ball, Judy. "Jason Berry: Church Whistleblower." In *Franciscan Media*. https://www.franciscanmedia.org/jason-berry-church-whistleblower/.

Barickman, B. J. "'A Bit of Land, Which They Call Roça': Slave Provision Grounds in the Bahian Recôncavo, 1780-1860." In *The Hispanic American Historical Review* 74, no. 4, 1994.

Bastide, Roger. *The African Religions of Brazil*. London: Johns Hopkins University Press, 1978.

Battiste, Marie. "Maintaining Aboriginal Identity, Language, and Culture in Modern Society." In *Reclaiming Indigenous Voice and Vision*. Edited by M. Battiste. Vancouver: University of British Columbia Press. 2000.

Bauman, Whitney A. *Religion and Ecology: Developing a Planetary Ethic*. New York, NY: Columbia University Press, 2014.

Baytelman, B. Jardin. *Etnobotánico en el Estado de Morelos*. México: SEP-INAH, 1986.

Beauregard, Mario, Larry Dossey and Lisa Miller. "Manifesto for a Post-Materialist Science." http://opensciences.org/about/manifesto-for-a-post-materialist-science.

Berlin, Adele, Marc Zvi Brettler, and Michael Fishbane, editors. *The Jewish Study Bible*: Jewish Publication Society Tanakh Translation. Oxford: Oxford University Press, 2004.

Berry, Thomas. *Evening Thoughts: Reflecting on Earth as Sacred Community*. Collection of writings edited by Mary Evelyn Tucker. San Francisco: Sierra Club. 2009.

Bingemer, Maria Clara. *Latin American Theology: Roots and Branches*. New York, Orbis Books, 2016.
Bohannon, Richard R. II, and Kevin J. O'Brien. "Justice." In *Grounding Religion: A Field Guide to the Study of Religion and Ecology*. Edited by Whitney A. Bauman, Richard II Bohannon, and Kevin J. O'Brien. London: Routledge, 2017.
Bonfil, Guillermo. "*Lo propio y lo Ajeno.*" In *La Cultura Popular*. Edited by A. Colombres. México: Red. Jonas-Premia Editora, 1984.
Boff, Leonardo and Virgilio P. Elizondo, Editors. *Ecology and Poverty Cry of the Earth, Cry of the Poor*. London: SCM Press, 1995.
Boyd, Brian. *On the Origin of Stories: Evolution, Cognition, and Fiction*. New York: Harvard University Press, 2009.
Boyd, Michelle. "Defensive Development: The Role of Racial Conflict in Gentrification." In *Urban Affairs Review* 43, no. 6, 2008.
Braswell, Taylor Harris. "Fresh Food, New Faces: Community Gardening as Ecological Gentrification in St. Louis, Missouri." In *Agriculture and Human Values* 35, no. 4, 2018.
Brave Heart, Maria Yellow Horse and Lemyra DeBruyn. "The American Indian Holocaust: Healing Historical Unresolved Grief." In *American Indian and Alaska Native Mental Health Research*, 1998. https://search.proquest.com/docview/236003962.
Brave Heart, Maria Yellow Horse, et al. "Historical Trauma Among Indigenous Peoples of the Americas: Concepts, Research, and Clinical Considerations." In *Journal of Psychoactive Drugs* 43, no 4: Growing Roots: Native American Evidence-Based Practices, 2011.
Brelsford, Robert. "Taiwan's Formosa Advances $9.4-billion Louisiana Petrochemical Project." In *Oil and Gas Journal*, April 2018.
"Bring Back Our Heroes." *The Patriot*. 3 March, 2020: https://www.thepatriot.co.zw/old_posts/bring-back-our-heroes/.
Briones, Carlos Roberto, Mauricio Castro, and Oscar Alejandro López. "*Mapa de Pobreza: Tomo I. Política Social y Focalización.*" San Salvador: FISDL, 2005. https://fisdl.gob.sv/temas-543/mapa-de-pobreza.
Brown, Karen McCarthy. "'The Other' Revisited." In *Personal Knowledge and Beyond: Reshaping the Ethnography of Religion*. Edited by James V. Spickard, et al. New York: New York University Press, 2002.
Brubaker, Pamela. "Neoliberalism & Economic Development." In *Globalization and Economic Justice: From Terrorism to Global Peace*. Edited by Karikottuchira Kuriakose. Piscataway, NJ: Gorgias Press, 2017.
—. "Alternatives to Globalization Addressing People and Earth: A Feminist Theological Reflection on Women, Economy, and Creation." In *Reimagining with Christian Doctrines Responding to Global Gender Injustices*. Edited by Grace Ji-Sun Kim and Jenny Daggers. London: Palgrave Macmillan, 2014.
Bullard, Robert D. *Toxic Waste and Race at Twenty 1987-2007: A Report Prepared for the United Church of Christ Justice and Witness Ministries*. Cleveland, OH: United Church of Christ, 2007. https://nrdc.org/sites/default/files/toxic-wastes-and-race-at-twenty-1987-2007.pdf.
Butler, Judith. *Pictures of War: When Life Is Mournful*. Rio de Janeiro: Civilização Brasileira, 2015.
"Cacaopera." In the United *Nations Educational, Scientific, and Cultural Organization*, 1992. https://whc.unesco.org/en/tentativelists/211/.

Cagan, Steve, "Salvadoran Refugees in the Camp at Colomoncagua, Honduras, 1980-1991." In *ReVista: Harvard Review of Latin America*, Spring 2016. https://revista.drclas.harvard.edu/book/salvadoran-refugees-camp-colomoncagua-honduras-1980-1991.
Cajete, Gregory A. "American Indian Epistemologies." In *New Directions for Student Services*, Issue 109. Edited by Mary Jo Tippeconnic Fox (Comanche), Shelly C. Lowe (Navajo), and George S. McClellan. Wiley Online Press, 2005.
—. *Native Science: Natural Laws of Interdependence*. Santa Fe, NM: Clear Light Publishers, 2000.
Campell, Elliott. "The Agroecostyem Role in Climate Change Mitigation and Adaptation." In *Carbon Management* 2, no. 5, 2011.
Carmody, John. *Ecology and Religion*: *Toward a New Christian Theology of Nature*. New York: Paulist Press, 1983.
Carney, Judith A. "'With Grains in Her Hair': Rice in Colonial Brazil." In *Slavery & Abolition* 25, no. 1, 2004.
Carroll, John E., Paul Brockelman et al. *The Greening of Faith*. Hanover and London: University of New Hampshire, 1997.
Catechism of the Catholic Church. Libreria Editrice Vaticana: Citta del Vaticano, 1993.
Capobianco, Laura. *Community Safety and Indigenous Peoples: Sharing Knowledge, Insights and Action*. Montreal: International Centre for the Prevention of Crime, 2010.
Castellano, Marlene B. "Updating Aboriginal Traditions of Knowledge." In *Indigenous Knowledges in Global Contexts*. Edited by George J. S. Dei, B. L. Hall, and D. G. Rosenburg. Toronto: University of Toronto Press, 2000.
Castellano, Marlene B. "Indigenous Research." In *The Sage Encyclopedia of Qualitative Research Methods*. Edited by Lisa M. Given. London: SAGE Publications, Ltd., 2008.
Caxaj, C. Susana. "Indigenous Storytelling and Participatory Action Research: Allies Toward Decolonization? Reflections from the Peoples' International Health Tribunal." In *Global Qualitative Nursing Research*, vol. 2, 2015.
Ceballos, Gerardo, et al. "Biological Annihilation via the Ongoing Sixth Mass Extinction Signaled by Vertebrate Population Losses and Declines." In *Proceedings of the National Academy of Sciences*. 10 July, 2017, doi:10.1073/pnas.1704949114.
Center for Migration Studies and Cristosal. "Point of No Return: The Fear and Criminalization of Central American Refugees." In *The Central American Humanitarian Crisis and US Policy Responses*, 2017. https://cmsny.org/publications/cms-cristosal-report.
Chan, Wingtsit. *A Source Book in Chinese Philosophy*. Princeton, N.J.: Princeton University Press, 1963.
"City Backed Farmers Market Will Bring Fresh Food to Linden," Dispatch, 10 June 2018. https://dispatch.com/news/20180610/city-backed-farmers-market-will-bring-fresh-food-to-linden.
Charumbira, Ruramisai. "Nehanda and Gender Victimhood in the Central Mashonaland 1896-97 Rebellions: Revisiting the Evidence." *History in Africa* 35, 2008, 103-131.
Coalition of Immokalee Worker (CIW), "Here we are in Columbus, Ohio, which puts all of us at ground zero for farmworker justice...," March 25, 2017. https://ciw-online.org/blog/2017/03/osu-meeting-vigil/.

Coates, Ta-Nehisi. "The Case for Reparations." In *Atlantic,* vol. 313, no. 5, June 2014.
Cohn, D'Vera, Jeffrey S. Passel and Ana Gonzalez-Barrera. "Rise in U.S. Immigrants from El Salvador Guatemala and Honduras Outpaces Growth from Elsewhere." In Pew Research Center, Hispanic Trends, 2017. https://pewhispanic.org/2017/12/07/rise-in-u-s-immigrants-from-el-salvador-guatemala-and-honduras-outpaces-growth-from-elsewhere/.
Cone, James. *The Cross and the Lynching Tree.* Maryknoll, N.Y.: Orbis Press, 2011.
Con-spirando: Revista Latinoamericana de Ecofeminismo, Espiritualidad y Teología. Santiago de Chile, no. 1. March 1992. https://conspirando.cl.
Cordero, Verónica, et al. *Vírgenes y Diosas en América Latina: La Resignificación de lo Sagrado.* Santiago de Chile: *Con-spirando* y *Red Latinoamericana de Católicas por el Derecho de Decidir,* 2004.
Cortina, Adela. "Aporophobia, the Rejection of the Poor." Barcelona-Buenos Aires-México: Paidós Estado y Sociedad, 2017.
Crenshaw, Kimberlé. "Demarginalizing the Intersection of Race and Sex: A Black Feminist Critique of Antidiscrimination Doctrine, Feminist Theory and Antiracist Politics." In *University of Chicago Legal Forum,* Vol. 1989: Issue 1, Article 8.
Cuomo, Chris. "Gender and Climate Change." In *Encyclopedia of Global Warming and Climate Change.* Edited by George Philander. London: SAGE Publications, Ltd., 2012.
Daneel, Marthinus L. *African Earthkeepers, Volume 1. Interfaith Mission in Earth-Care.* Pretoria: University of South Africa Press, 1998.
—. *African Earthkeepers. Volume 2. Environmental Mission and Liberation in Christian Perspective.* Pretoria: University of South Africa Press, 1999.
Datta, Ranjan. "Traditional Storytelling: An Effective Indigenous Research Methodology and Its Implications for Environmental Research." In *AlterNative: An International Journal of Indigenous Peoples,* 14, no. 1, March 2018.
Davidson, Debra. "Is Urban Agriculture a Game Changer or Window Dressing? A Critical Analysis of Its Potential To Disrupt Conventional Agri-Food Systems." In *International Journal of Sociology of Agriculture & Food* 23, no. 2, 2017.
Dei, George J. S., B. L. Hall, & D. G. Rosenberg, editors. *Indigenous Knowledges in Global Contexts: Multiple Readings of our World.* Toronto: University of Toronto Press, 2000.
Deloria Jr., Vine. *God Is Red: A Native View of Religion.* 30th Anniversary Edition. Golden, CO: Fulcrum Publishing, 2003.
—. *Custer Died for Your Sins: An Indian Manifesto.* Norman, OK: University of Oklahoma Press, 1969.
Denzin, Norman K., and Yvonna S. Lincoln, editors. *The Sage Handbook of Qualitative Research.* Fifth Edition. London: SAGE Publications Ltd., 2017.
De Pádua Bosi, Antônio. "Urban Reform and Class Struggle." São Paulo: Ed. Xamã, 2004.
Derrida, Jacques. "Faith and Knowledge: The Two Sources of 'Religion' at the Limits of Reason Alone." In *Religion,* edited by Jacques Derrida and Gianni Vattimo. Stanford, CA: Stanford University Press, 1998.
de Sahagún, Fray Bernardino. *Historia de las Cosas de la Nueva España.* México: Porrua, 1982.
Dhar, Damayantee. "The Tall Price That Gujarats Tribals Are Paying for the 'Tallest' Statue." *Sabrang India.* 31 October, 2018. https://sabrangindia.in/article/tall-price-gujarats-tribals-are-paying-tallest-statue.

Díaz del Castillo, Bernal. *The True History of the Conquest of New Spain.* Translated, with an Introduction and Notes, by Janet Burke and Ted Humphrey. Indianapolis/Cambridge: Hackett Publishing Company, Inc., 2012.

Doi, Sr. Joanne, M.M. *Bridge to Compassion: Theological Pilgrimage to Tule Lake and Manzanar.* Unpublished Dissertation: Graduate Theological Union, Berkeley, CA, 2007.

Doss, Cheryl. "If Women Hold Up Half the Sky, How Much of the World's Food Do They Produce?." In *Gender in Agriculture: Closing the Knowledge Gap.* Edited by Agnes R. Quisumbing et al. Springer and the Food and Agriculture Organization of the United Nations, 2014.

Edinger, Edward F. *Anatomy of the Psyche: Alchemical Symbolism in Psychotherapy.* Peru, IL: Open Court Publishing Company, 1985.

"El Salvador: Importaciones y exportaciones de cultivos seleccionados." Observatorio del Derecho Humano la Alimentación en Centroamérica, 2017. https://odhac.org/index.php/estadisticas/por-pais/el-salvador/127-el-salvador-importaciones-y-exportaciones-de-cultivos-seleccionados.

Elliot, Larry. "World's Eight Richest People Have Same Wealth as Poorest 50%." In *The Guardian*, January 15, 2017.

"Estadísticas educativas por municipio: del año 2017." Ministry of Education, Republic of El Salvador, 2018. https://mined.gob.sv/index.php/estadisticas-educativas/item/7153-estadisticas-educativas-por-municipio.

European Union Agency for Fundamental Rights. *Violence against Women: An EU-Wide Survey.* Vienna, 2015. https://fra.europa.eu/sites/default/files/fra-2014-vaw-survey-main-results-apr14_en.pdf.

Feldman, John. A film: *Symbiotic Earth: How Lynn Margulis Rocked the Boat and Started a Scientific Revolution.* From Bullfrog and Hummingbird Films, 2018.

"Feminine Force of Recycling, The." Associação Brasileira Eng Sanitária, São Paulo. ABES-SP Bulletin (Portuguese), March 2014.

Fernandes, Maira. "*Mulheres são a entre catadores e catadoras de materiais recicláveis.*" In *Centro de Estudios e Apoio ao Desenvolvimento, Emprego, e Cidadania.* 17 October, 2016. https://ceadec.org.br/noticias/mulheres-sao-a-maioria-entre-catadores-e-catadoras-de-materiais-reciclaveis.

Fernández-Llamazares, Á. and Cabeza, M. "Rediscovering the Potential of Indigenous Storytelling for Conservation Practice." In *Conservation Letters*, 11: e12398. doi:10.1111/conl.12398.

Finer, Lawrence B. and Kathryn Kost. "Unintended Pregnancy Rates at the State Level." In *Perspectives on Sexual and Reproductive Health*, 43, no. 78-87. San Francisco: Kaiser Family Foundation, 2011.

Finkler, Kaja. *Spiritualist Healers in Mexico.* Amherst: Bergin and Garvey, 1985.

Fisher, J. L. *Pioneers, Settlers, Aliens, Exiles: The Decolonisation of White Identity in Zimbabwe.* Canberra: Australian National University Press, 2010.

Fitzgerald, Rachel. *Feminine Archetypes: Patterns of Relationships.* Translated into Spanish. In: *Con-spirando*, no. 36, June 2001.

Freire, Paolo. *Pedagogy of the Oppressed.* New York: Herder & Herder, 1970.

Friedman, Thomas. "The People We Have Been Waiting For." In *The New York Times.* 2 December, 2007: https://www.nytimes.com/2007/12/02/opinion/02friedman.html?_r=1.

García-Rivera, Alejandro. *A Wounded Innocence: Sketches for a Theology of Art.* Collegeville, MN: The Liturgical Press, 2003.

Gebara, Ivone. "A Reform That Includes Eco-Justice." In *Dialog: A Journal of Theology* 55, 2016.
—. "Radical Hope in Daily Life: An Ecofeminist Perspective from Latin America." Paper presented at the conference: "Dawning of a New Story, Radical Hope." Seattle, WA, May 2009.
—. *Out of the Depths: Women's Experience of Evil and Salvation*. Translated by Ann Patrick Ware. Minneapolis: Fortress Press, 2002.
—. *Longing for Running Water: Ecofeminism and Liberation*. Minneapolis: Fortress Press, 1999.
—. 'Women Doing Theology in Latin America." In *Through Her Eyes: Women's Theology from Latin America*. Edited by Elsa Támez. Maryknoll, NY: Orbis Books, 1989.
—. "Option for the Poor as an Option for the Poor Women." In *Concilium 194 Women, Work, and Poverty*. Edited by Elisabeth Schüssler-Fiorenza. Edinburgh: T&T Clark, 1987.
Gelfand, Michael. *Shona Religion*. Cape Town: Juta, 1962.
Gnanadason, Aruna. *Listen to the Women: Listen to the Earth*. Geneva: Risk Book, World Council of Churches Publications, 2005.
—. "Toward a Feminist Eco-theology for India." In *Women Healing Earth, Third World Women on Ecology, Feminism and Religion*. New York: Orbis Books, 1996.
Gottlieb, Robert, and Anupama Joshi. *Food Justice*. Cambridge, MA: MIT Press, 2010.
Gunnar, Myrdal. *An American Dilemma*. New York: Harper and Brothers, 1944.
Hall, Gillette H. and Harry Anthony Patrinos. *Indigenous Peoples, Poverty and Development*. New York: Cambridge University Press, 2012.
Hall, Stuart, Jessica Evans, Sean Nixon, editors. *Representation: Cultural Representations and Signifying Practices*. London: SAGE Publications, Ltd., 1997.
Hecht, Susana B. and Sassan S. Saatchi, "Globalization and Forest Resurgence: Changes in Forest Cover in El Salvador." In *BioScience* 57, no. 8, 2007. https://jstor.org/stable/10.1641/b570806?seq=2#metadata_info_tab_contents.
Heidegger, Martin. "Letter on Humanism." In *Basic Writings*. New York: Harper & Row, 1977.
—. "Words." *On the Way to Language*. Translated by Joan Stambaugh. New York: Harper and Row, 1971.
Henry, Michele. "Sourced: Ring in a Sweet Rosh Hashanah with Jewish Honey." *The Toronto Star*. September 24, 2014. https://thestar.com/life/sourced/2014/09/24/sourced_ring_in_a_sweet_rosh_hashanah_with_jewish_honey.html.
Heschel, Abraham Joshua. *The Prophets*. 1st ed. Philadelphia: Jewish Publication Society of America, 1962.
Hillman, James. *The Thought of the Heart & the Soul of the World*. Dallas, Texas: Spring Publications, Inc., 1996.
Hindu, The. https://thehindu.com.
Hinga, Teresia. "The Gikuyu Theology of Land and Environmental Justice." In *Women Healing Earth: Third World Women on Ecology, Feminism, and Religion*. Maryknoll, N.Y.: Orbis Press, 1996.
Ho, Wan-Li. *Ecofamilism: Women, Religion, and Environmental Protection in Taiwan*. St. Petersburg: Three Pines Press, 2016.

Hodge, F. S., Pasqua, A., Marquez, C. A., and Geishirt-Cantrell, B. "Utilizing Traditional Storytelling to Promote Wellness in American Indian Communities." In *Journal of Transcultural Nursing* 13, no. 1, 2002.
Holiday, Billie. "Strange Fruit," song recorded in 1939, written by Abel Meeropol, 1937.
"Homepage." Franklinton Farms. https://franklintonfarms.org/.
"Homepage." Real Food Challenge. https://realfoodchallenge.org/.
"Homepage." Seminary Hill Farm. https://seminaryhillfarm.org/.
Horst, Megan and Amy Marion, "Racial, Ethnic and Gender Inequities in Farmland Ownership and Farming in the U.S." In *Agriculture and Human Values* 36, no. 2, 2019.
Horst, Megan, Nathan McClintock, and Lesli Hoey. "The Intersection of Planning, Urban Agriculture, and Food Justice: A Review of the Literature." In *Journal of the American Planning Association* 83, no. 3, 2017.
Howard, Patricia L. "Gender and Social Dynamics in Swidden and Homegardens in Latin America." In *Tropical Homegardens: A Time-Tested Example of Sustainable Agroforestry*. Edited by B.M. Kumar and P.K.R. Nair. Advances in Agroforestry, vol. 3. Dordrecht: Springer, 2006.
Hynes, H. Patricia. *A Patch of Eden: America's Inner-City Gardeners*. White River Junction, VT: Chelsea Green Publishing Company, 1996.
"Índice de precios al consumidor (IPC) Canasta Básica Alimentaria Rural (2001-2018)." In the Department of Statistics and Census, 2018. https://digestyc.gob.sv/index.php/servicios/en-linea/canasta-basica-alimentaria.html.
Inter-Agency Support Group on Indigenous Peoples' Issues. *The Health of Indigenous Peoples*. Thematic Paper towards the preparation of the 2014 World Conference on Indigenous Peoples. New York: United Nations, 2014. https://un.org/en/ga/president/68/pdf/wcip/IASG%20Thematic%20 Paper%2.
IPCC, *Global Warming of 1.5°C. An IPCC Special Report on the Impacts of Global Warming of 1.5°C above Pre-Industrial Levels and Related Global Greenhouse Gas Emission Pathways, in the Context of Strengthening the Global Response to the Threat of Climate Change* (In press, 2018). https://ipcc.ch/sr15/. Agarwal, "Food Crises and Gender Inequality," 5; FAO, *The State of Food and Agriculture 2018: Migration, Agriculture, and Rural Development*. Rome: FAO, 2018. https://fao.org/3/I9549EN/i9549en.pdf.
IPCC, *Climate Change 2014: Mitigation of Climate Change. Contribution of Working Group III to the Fifth Assessment Report of the Intergovernmental Panel on Climate Change*. Cambridge and New York: Cambridge University Press, 2014. https://ipcc.ch/site/assets/uploads/2018/02/ipcc_wg3_ ar5_full.pdf.
IPCC, *Climate Change 2007: Impacts, Adaptation and Vulnerability. Contribution of Working Group II to the Fourth Assessment Report of the Intergovernmental Panel on Climate Change* (Cambridge, UK: Cambridge University Press, 2007. https://ipcc.ch/site/assets/uploads/2018/03/ar4_wg2_full_ report.pdf.
Iriarte, Gregorio. "¿Qué es una Comunidad Eclesial de Base?" Bogota: Ediciones Paulinas, 1991.
Isasi-Díaz, Ada María. *En La Lucha: Elaborating a Mujerista Theology*. Minneapolis: Fortress Press, 1993.

Iseke, Judy. "Indigenous Storytelling as Research." In *International Review of Qualitative Research* 6, no. 4, 2013.

Iseke, Judy, and Brennus, B. "Learning Life Lessons from Indigenous Storytelling with Tom McCallum." In *Indigenous Philosophies and Critical Education*. Edited by George J. Sefa Dei. New York: Peter Lang, 2011.

Iwanka Raya, Mairin. *New Beginnings — Indigenous Women Stand against Violence*. FIMI Companion Report to the UN Secretary General's Study on Violence against Women. Executive Summary. New York: International Indigenous Women's Forum (IIWF), 2006. https://fimi-iiwf.org/archivos 7ffd8ee2807b42a0df93d25d70c9cfdb.pdf.

James, Cara V., et al. "Putting Women's Health Care Disparities on the Map: Examining Racial and Ethnic Disparities at the State Level." In *the Kaiser Family Foundation*. June 2009.

Jewish Study Bible, The. Jewish Publication Society Tanakh Translation. Oxford: Oxford University Press, 2004.

Joassart-Marcelli, Pascale, and Fernando J. Bosco. "Alternative Food and Gentrification: Farmers' Markets, Community Gardens and the Transformation of Urban Neighborhoods." In *Just Green Enough: Urban Development and Environmental Gentrification*. Edited by Winifred Curran and Trina Hamilton. London: Routledge, 2018.

Johnson, Bart and Kristina Hill, editors. *Ecology and Design: Frameworks for Learning*. Washington, D.C.: Island Press, 2002.

Jones, Kenneth, and Tema Okun, "Dismantling Racism: A Workbook for Social Change Groups." In *ChangeWork*, 2001. https://cwsworkshop.org/PARC_site_B/dr-culture.html.

Josselson, Ruthellen. "On Becoming the Narrator of One's Own Life." In *Healing Plots: The Narrative Basis of Psychotherapy*. Edited by A. Lieblich, D. P. McAdams and R. Josselson. American Psychological Association, 2004.

Jung, Carl G. "The Transcendent Function." In *The Structure and Dynamics of the Psyche*, CW. Vol. 8. London: Routledge & Kegan Paul, 1960.

Jung, Carl G. et al. "Archetypes and the Collective Unconscious," Vol. 9, Part 1. In *The Collected Works of C.G. Jung: Complete Digital Edition*. Kindle Location 101391. Princeton, NJ: Princeton University Press, Kindle Edition, 2014.

—. "Conscious, Unconscious and Individuation." In *Archetypes and the Collective Unconscious*, Vol. 9, Part 1-IV. *The Collected Works of C.G. Jung: Complete Digital Edition*. Kindle Location 106443. Princeton, NJ: Princeton University Press, Kindle Edition, 2014.

—. "Psychological Types," Vol. 6 in *The Collected Works of C.G. Jung: Complete Digital Edition*. Princeton, NJ: Princeton University Press, 2014.

Karlin, Sam, and Timothy Boone. "This Is a Big One: Formosa Picks St. James Parish for $9.4 Billion Chemical Complex." In *The New Orleans Advocate*. April 23, 2018. https://theadvocate.com/new_orleans/news/business/article_4ee148fa-4715-11e8-a53b-2b350073db9d.html.

Kawagley, A. O., and Barnhardt, R. "Education Indigenous to Place: Western Science Meets Native Reality." In *Ecological Education in Action: On Weaving Education, Culture, and the Environment*. Edited by G. A. Smith and D. R. Williams. Albany: State University of New York Press, 1999.

Kearney, Michael. "Oral Performance by Mexican Spiritualists in Possession Trance." In *Journal of Latin American Lore* 3/2, 1977.

Kim, Nam. "Survival at No One's Expense: Forging an Intersectional Coalition (@theTable: Intersectionality & Political Action." In *Feminist Studies in Religion*. 7 March 2017. https://fsrinc.org/survival-no-ones-expense/.

Kleinman, Arthur. *Patients and Healers in the Context of Culture*. Berkeley: University of California Press, 1980.

Kopenawa, Davi & Bruce Albert. *The Falling Sky: Words of a Yanomami Shaman*. Translated by Nicholas Elliott and Alison Dundy. Cambridge, MA: The Belknap Press of Harvard University Press, 2013.

Kovach, Margaret. *Indigenous Methodologies: Characteristics, Conversations, and Contexts*. Toronto: University of Toronto Press, 2009.

—. "Doing Indigenous Methodologies: A Letter to a Research Class." In *The Sage Handbook of Qualitative Research*, 5th edition. Edited by Norman K. Denzin and Yvonna S. Lincoln. London: SAGE Publications, Inc., 2018.

Kraft, Siv Ellen. and G. Johnson. "Protective Occupation, Emergent Networks, Rituals of Solidarity: Comparing Alta (Sápmi), Mauna Kea (Hawaii), and Standing Rock (North Dakota)." In *The Bloomsbury Handbook of Religion and Nature*. Edited by Laura Hobgood and Whitney Bauman. London: Bloomsbury Academic Series, 2018.

Kreimer, Alcira, et al. "*La Reconstrucción en los Países en Etapa de Posguerra: El Salvador*." In *Précis* 172, 1998. https://studylib.es/doc/5011451/la-reconstrucci%C3%B3n-en-los-pa%C3%ADses-en-etapa-de-posguerra.-.

"Kroger Closing Creates Food Desert in North Linden Frustrates Officials," Dispatch, 21 January, 2018. https://dispatch.com/news/20180121/kroger-closing-creates-food-desert-in-north-linden-frustrates-officials.

Lakhani, Nina. *Who Killed Berta Caceres? Dams, Death Squads, and an Indigenous Defender's Battle for the Planet*." New York: Verso, 2020.

Lan, Kwok Pui. *Introducing Asian Feminist Theology*. Sheffield, England: Sheffield Academic Press, 2000.

Latour, Bruno. *We Have Never Been Modern*. Translated by Catherine Porter. Cambridge MA: Harvard University Press, 1995.

Lavigne, Sharon and Shamell "Our Town — Our Fight." St. James, Louisiana, December 2018. https://climatesofinequality.org/project/women-of-cancer-alley/.

Laytner, Rabbi Anson and Rabbi Dan Bridge. *The Animals' Lawsuit Against Humanity: A Modern Adaptation of an Ancient Animal Rights Tale*. Louisville: Fons Vitae, 2005.

Leeming, David A. *Creation Myths of the World: An Encyclopedia*.-Gale Virtual Reference Library. https://link.galegroup.com/apps/doc/CX2440800008/GVRL?u=carp39441&sid=GVRL&xid=1f8a9048.

Leslie, Isaac Sohn, and Monica M. White. "Race and Food: Agricultural Resistance in U.S. History." In *The Handbook of the Sociology of Racial and Ethnic Relations*. Edited by Pinar Batur and Joe R. Feagin. Cham, Switzerland: Springer, 2018.

Lessing, Doris. *The Grass is Singing*. New York: Thomas Y. Crowell Company, 1950.

Levi-Strauss, Claude. *The Elementary Structures of Kinship*. London: Eyre & Spottiswood, 1969.

"Lima Population." World Population Review. https://worldpopulationreview.com/world-cities/lima-population/.

"Lonely Struggle of India's Anti-nuclear Protestors." *The Guardian*, 06 June 2016. https://www.theguardian.com/global-development/2016/jun/06/lonely-struggle-india-anti-nuclear-protesters-tamil-nadu-kudankulam-idinthakarai.

Lonergan, Bernard. *Collected Works of Bernard Lonergan*. Toronto: University of Toronto Press, 1993.

Long, Charles H. "Cosmogony." In *Encyclopedia of Religion*. Edited by Lindsay Jones. London – New York: Macmillan Reference USA, 2005.

Longchar, Wati. "Indigenous Theology in Asia." In *Asian Theology on the Way: Christianity, Culture and Context*. Edited by Peniel Jesudason Rufus Rajkumar. London: SPCK, 2012.

López, Austin A. *Textos de Medicina Nahuatl*. México: Sep-Sententas, 1971.

—. *Cuerpo Humano e Ideología*. México: UNAM, 1984.

—. "*Cosmovisión y Salud entre las Méxicas*." In *Historia General de la Medicina en México*. Edited by Tomo I. Lopez Austin and C. Viesca. México: México Antiguo, 1984.

Lugar de la Memoria, la Tolerancia, y la Inclusion Social, Lima, Peru. https://lum.cultura.pe.

Maathai, Wangari. *The Challenge for Africa*. New York: Pantheon Books, 2009.

—. *Unbowed: A Memoir*. New York: Anchor Books, 2006.

—. *The Green Belt Movement: Sharing the Approach and the Experience*. New York: Lantern Books, 2003.

Marcos, Sylvia. "*Medicinas Paralelas: Potencial Popular para la Salud Mental.*" In *Manicomios y Prisiones*. Edited by Sylvia Marcos. México: Redediciones, 1983.

Mares, Teresa M., and Devon G. Peña. "Environmental and Food Justice: Toward Local, Slow, and Deep Food Systems." In Alkon and Agyeman, *Cultivating Food Justice*, 2011.

Margulis, M. "*La Cultura Popular.*" In *La Cultura Popular*. Edited by A. Colombres. México: Red Jonas-Premia Editores, 1984.

Marshall III, Joseph M. *The Lakota Way: Stories and Lessons for Living*. New York: Penguin Compass, 2002.

May, Janet W. "Foreigners." In *Women Healing Earth: Third World Women on Ecology, Feminism, and Justice*. Edited by Rosemary Radford Ruether. New York: Orbis Books, 1996.

McAdams, Dan P. *Stories We Live By: Personal Myths and the Making of the Self*. New York: William Morrow and Company, Inc., 1993.

—. *Unity and Purpose in Human Lives: The Emergence of Identity as a Life Story*. New York: Springer Publishing Company, 1992.

McClintock, Nathan. "Cultivating (a) Sustainability Capital: Urban Agriculture, Ecogentrification, and the Uneven Valorization of Social Reproduction." In *Annals of the American Association of Geographers* 108, no. 2, 2018.

McFague, Sallie. *Life Abundant: Rethinking Theology and Economy for a Planet in Peril*. Minneapolis: Fortress Press, 2000.

—. *Super, Natural Christians: How We Should Love Nature*. Minneapolis: Fortress Press, 1997.

McKenna, John. "Picture This: All the Plastic We Have Produced Weighs the Same as 25,000 Empire State Buildings." In *World Economic Forum*, July 2017. https://weforum.org/agenda/2017/07/picture-this-all-the-plastic-we-have-produced-weighs-the-same-as-25-000-empire-state-buildings/.

McKibben, Nancy. "Theology Meets Ecology." In *Edible Columbus*. 25 November, 2018, https://ediblecolumbus.ediblecommunities.com/food-thought/theology-meets-ecology.
McNeill, J.R., and Peter Engelke. *The Great Acceleration: An Environmental History of the Anthropocene since 1945*. Cambridge, MA: Harvard University Press, 2014.
Merchant, Carolyn. *The Death of Nature*. San Francisco: Harper and Row, 1980.
Michell, Herman J. "*Nehithawak* of Reindeer Lake, Canada: Worldview, Epistemology and Relationships with the Natural World." *Australian Journal of Indigenous Education*, 2005.
Mies, Maria, and Vandana Shiva, editors. *Ecofeminism*. London and New York: Zed Books, 2014.
Mignolo, Walter. *The Darker Side of Western Modernity: Global Future, Decolonial Options*. Durham, NC: Duke University Press, 2011.
Miller, Lisa. *The Spiritual Child: The New Science on Parenting for Health and Lifelong Thriving*. New York: St. Martin's Press, 2015.
Mitchell, David J. "St. James Parish Council, Planning Commission to Hold Hearings on Proposed $9.4 Billion Formosa Chemical Complex." *The Advocate*. July 2018.
Moisés, Subcomandante Insurgente, and Subcomandante Insurgente Galeano. "Una casa, otros mundos." In *Enlace Zapatista*, 2016. https://enlacezapatista.ezln.org.mx/2016/09/12/una-casa-otros-mundos.
Mora, Camilo, Derek P. Tittensor, Sina Adl, Alastair G. B. Simpson, Boris Worm. "Census of Marine Life: 'How Many Species Are There on Earth and in the Ocean?'" In *PLoS Biology* 9, no. 8, 2011. https://doi.org/10.1371/journal.pbio.1001127.
Mundy, Barbara E. *The Death of Aztec Tenochtitlan: The Life of Mexico City*. Austin, TX: University of Texas Press, 2015.
Musleah, Rahel. "My Daughter, the Farmer." In *Hadassah Magazine*. January 2018. https://hadassahmagazine.org/2018/01/11/my-daughter-the-farmer/.
Navin, Mark. "Food Sovereignty and Gender Justice." In *Just Food: Philosophy, Justice, and Food*. Edited by Jill Marie Dieterle. London: Rowman and Littlefield, 2015.
New Oxford Annotated Bible, The New Revised Standard Version. New York: Oxford University Press, 2010.
"Ndola Slave Tree." *Zambian Watchdog*. March 15, 2019. https://www.zambiawatchdog.com/the-ndola-slave-tree/.
"Ndola Slave Tree." *Atlas Obscura*. https://www.atlasobscura.com/places/ndola-slave-tree.
Nityanand Jayaraman, "Sterlite — here's the proof: Data on air pollution, and the case of the missing trees." *The News Minute*. 1 April. 2018. https://thenewsminute.com/article/sterlite-here-s-proof-data-air-pollution-and-case-missing-trees-78841.
"*No permitamos que los pobres mueran de sed*." Conferencia Episcopal de El Salvador, 2018. https://iglesia.org.sv/wp-content/uploads/2018/06/Comunicado-Derecho-humano-al-agua.pdf.
Noble, David. *A World Without Women: The Christian Clerical Culture of Western Science*. New York: A.A. Knopf, 1992.

Nyajeka, Tumani Mutasa. "Nyajeka, Shona Women and the Mutupo Principle" in *Women Healing Earth: Third World Women on Ecology, Feminism, and Religion*. Maryknoll, N.Y.: Orbis Press, 1996.
Oh, Jea Sophia. *A Postcolonial Theology of Life: Planetarity East and West*. Upland, CA: Sopher Press, 2011.
Olavarrieta, Marenco. *Magia en los Tuxtlas*. México: Institut Nacional Indigenista, 1977.
Palmer, Robin and Isobel Birch. *Zimbabwe: A Land Divided*. Oxford: Oxfam, 2010.
Parry, Alan. "Why We Tell Stories: The Narrative Construction of Reality." In *Transactional Analysis Journal* 27, no. 2, 1997.
Peter, Gregory, Michael Mayerfeld Bell, and Susan Jarnagin. "Coming Back Across the Fence: Masculinity and the Transition to Sustainable Agriculture." In *Rural Sociology* 65, no. 2, 2000.
Plato. *Phaedrus*. Translated by R. Hackforth. Cambridge: Cambridge University Press, 1972.
Plumwood, Val. *Feminism and the Mastery of Nature*. London: Routledge, 1993.
Pollan, Michael. *How To Change Your Mind: What the New Science of Psychedelics Teaches Us About Consciousness, Dying, Addiction, Depression, and Transcendence*. New York: Penguin Press, 2018.
Pongweni, A. C. *Songs that Won the Liberation War*. Harare: College Press, 1982.
Pope Francis. *Laudato Si': On Care for Our Common Home*. Rome: Vatican Press, 2015.
—. *Joy of the Gospel*. Dublin, Ireland: Veritas Publications, 2013.
"Pope Francis Warns the Poor Have Become Part of the Landscape." *BBC News*. 22 June, 2020: https://www.bbc.com/news/world-53055220.
Preston, Matthew. *Ending Civil War: Rhodesia and Lebanon in Perspective*. London: Tauris, 2004.
"Prophets of a Future Not Our Own." United States' Conference of Catholic Bishops, http://www.usccb.org/prayer-and-worship/prayers-and-devotions/prayers/prophets-of-a-future-not-our-own.cfm.
Puleo, Mev. *The Struggle Is One: Voices and Visions of Liberation*. Albany, N.Y.: State University of New York Press, 1994.
Rae, Eleanor. *Women, the Earth, the Divine*. Maryknoll, New York: Orbis Press, 1994.
Ratzinger, Joseph Cardinal, editor. *Catechism of the Catholic Church: With Modifications from the Editio Typica*. New York: Doubleday, 1997.
Recinos, Manuel Portillo. "*Anteproyecto de: Ley de soberanía y seguridad alimentaria y nutricional*." Fundación Salvadoreña para la Reconstrucción y el Desarrollo. San Salvador: Equipo Maíz, 2016. https://redes.org.sv/media/uploads/documents/ley-soberania-alimentaria-vp.pdf.
Reflective Democracy Campaign. *Reflective Democracy 2017 Research Summary*. October 2017. https://wholeads.us/wp-content/uploads/2018/09/reflective-democracy-2017-research-summary.pdf.
Rodriguez, Alfonso Insuasty. "To Think by Building Other Possible Worlds." In *El Ágora USB* 18, no. 1, 2018. https://dx.doi.org/10.21500/16578031.3441.
Rolfes, Anne. "Six Bright Orange Lies the Petro-Energy Crowd Wants You To Believe." In *The Lens Nola*. November 24, 2018. https://thelensnola.org/2018/11/24/six-bright-orange-lies-the-petro-energy-crowd-wants-you-to-believe/#.

—. "Black communities in St. James on the losing end of Louisiana's 'big win.'" In *The Lens Nola*. September 17, 2018. https://thelensnola.org/2018/09/17/black-communities-in-st-james-on-the-losing-end-of-louisianas-big-win/.

Ruether, Rosemary Radford. *America, Amerikkka: Elect Nation and Imperial Violence*. New York, NY: Routledge, 2014 edition.

—. *My Quests for Hope and Meaning: An Autobiography*. Eugene, OR: Wipf and Stock, 2013.

—. "Ecofeminist Thea/logies and Ethics: A Post-Christian Movement?." In *Post-Christian Feminisms: A Critical Approach*. Edited by Lisa Isherwood and Kathleen MacPhillips. Burlington, VT: Ashgate Publishing Company, 2008.

—. *America Amerikkka: Elect Nation and Imperial Violence*. New York: Acumen Publishing, 2007.

—. "Ecofeminist Philosophy, Theology, and Ethics: A Comparative View." In *Ecospirit: Religions and Philosophies for the Earth*. Edited by Laurel Kearnes and Catherine Keller. New York, NY: Fordham University Press, 2007.

—. *Integrating Ecofeminism, Globalization and World Religions*. Lanham, MD: Rowman and Littlefield, 2005.

—. *Christianity and the Making of the Modern Family*. Boston, MA: Beacon Press, 2000.

—. *Women Healing Earth: Third World Women on Ecology, Feminism, and Religion*. New York: Orbis Books, 1996.

—. *Gaia and God: An Ecofeminist Theology of Earth Healing*. San Francisco: Harper, 1992.

—. *Sexism and God-Talk*. Boston: Beacon Press, 1983.

Rasmussen, Larry. *Earth Community*. Maryknoll, NY: Orbis Books, 1996.

Ruiz de Alarcon, Hernando. *Treatise on the Heathen Superstition that Today Live Among the Indians Native to This New Spain, 1629*. Translated and Edited by J. Richard Andrews and Ross Hassig. Norman: University of Oklahoma Press, 1984.

Russell, Letty M. *Feminist Interpretation of the Bible*. Philadelphia: The Westminster Press, 1985.

Sahagun, Bernardino de. *Historia General de las Cosas de Nueva España*. México: Porrua, 1982. Originally published 1793.

—. *Florentine Codex: General History of the Things of New Spain*. Translated and Edited by A. Anderson and C. Dibble. No. 14. Salt Lake City: School of American Research and University of Utah, 1979. Originally published 1793.

"San Juan de Miraflores," City Population. DE. https://citypopulation.de/php/peru-limametro.php?cityid=150133.

Schillebeeckx, Edward. *The Understanding of Faith*. New York: The Seabury Press, 1974.

Schlosberg, David. *Defining Environmental Justice: Theories, Movements, and Nature*. Oxford: Oxford University Press, 2007.

Sellers, Sam. *Gender and Climate Change: A Closer Look at Existing Evidence*. WEDO and Global Gender and Climate Alliance, 2016. https://wedo.org/wp-content/uploads/2016/11/GGCA-RP-FINAL.pdf.

Sen, Amartya. *Poverty and Famines: An Essay on Entitlement and Deprivation*. Oxford: Clarendon Press, 1981.

Shabodien, Fatima. "Livelihoods Struggles of Women Farm Workers in South Africa." https://wfp.org.za/publications/general-reports.html.

"Six Bright Orange Lies the Petro Energy Crowd Wants You to Believe." *The Lens Nola.* 24 November 2018. https://thelensnola.org/2018/11/24/six-bright-orange-lies-the-petro-energy-crowd-wants-you-to-believe/https://therefugeohio.org/.
Shiva, Vandana. *Staying Alive: Women, Ecology, and Development.* Berkeley, CA: North Atlantic Books, 2016.
—. *Soil Not Oil: Environmental Justice in an Age of Climate Change.* 2nd ed. Berkeley, CA: North Atlantic Books, 2015.
—. *Earth Democracy: Justice, Sustainability, and Peace.* Berkeley, CA: North Atlantic Books, 2015.
—. *Staying Alive: Women, Ecology and Survival in India.* Delhi: Kali for Women, 1988.
Shoresh, "History," Shoresh Jewish Environmental Programs Website, accessed March 8, 2018, http://shoresh.ca/history/.
Shoresh, "Introducing Shoresh," Shoresh Jewish Environmental Programs Website, accessed March 8, 2018, http://shoresh.ca/introducing/.
Shoresh, "The Beet," Shoresh Jewish Environmental Programs Blog, accessed March 8, 2018, http://shoresh.ca/blog/.
Simpson, J. A., et al. "Nature." *Oxford English Dictionary*, 2018. https://.oed.com/.
Slocum, Rachel, and Arun Saldanha, editors. *Geographies of Race and Food: Fields, Bodies, Markets.* Abingdon: Ashgate, 2013.
Smith, L. T. *Decolonizing Methodologies: Research and Indigenous Peoples.* 2nd ed. London, England: Zed Books, 2013.
Sobrino, Jon. *Jesus the Liberator: A Historical-Theological Reading of Jesus of Nazareth.* Maryknoll: Orbis, 1993.
Spickard, James V. et al. *Personal Knowledge and Beyond: Reshaping the Ethnography of Religion: Reshaping the Ethnography of Religion.* New York: New York University Press, 2002.
Stehlin, John G., and Alexander R. Tarr. "Think Regionally, Act Locally?: Gardening, Cycling, and the Horizon of Urban Spatial Politics." In *Urban Geography* 38, no. 9, 2017.
Steinsaltz, Rabbi Adin. *Koren Talmud Bavli*, Noé Edition, vol 9: Yoma Hebrew/English. Jerusalem: Shefa Foundation, 2012.
Stengers, Isabelle. "Reclaiming Animism." In *e-flux Journal* 36, July 2012.
"Sterlite plant: Tamil Nadu rejects report on Tuticorin groundwater contamination citing prejudice" IB Times, 9 September, 2018. https://ibtimes.co.in/sterlite-plant-tamil-nadu-rejects-report-tuticorin-groundwater-contamination-citing-prejudice-780023.
Sturgeon, Nöel. *Environmentalism in Popular Culture: Gender, Race, Sexuality, and the Politics of the Natural.* Tucson, AZ: University of Arizona Press, 2009.
Swimme, Brian, and Thomas Berry. *The Universe Story.* New York: Harper Collins, 1992.
Swimme, Brian. *The Hidden Heart of the Cosmos: Humanity and the New Story.* New York: Orbis Books, 1996.
Swimme, Brian and Mary Evelyn Tucker. *Journey of the Universe.* New Haven CT: Yale University Press, 2011.
Suryanarayanan, Sainath and Daniel Lee Kleinman. *Vanishing Bees: Science, Politics, and Honeybee Health.* New Brunswick: Rutgers University Press, 2017.

Tagore, Proma. *Shapes of Silence: Writing by Women of Colour and the Politics of Testimony*. McGill-Queen's Press, 2009.
Taylor, Bron. *Dark Green Religion: Nature, Spirituality, and the Planetary Future*. Berkeley: University of California Press, 2010.
Thomas, Hugh. *Conquest: Montezuma, Cortes, and the Fall of Old Mexico*. New York: Touchstone, 1993.
Toensmeier, Eric. *The Carbon Farming Solution: A Global Toolkit of Perennial Crops and Regenerative Agricultural Practices for Climate Change Mitigation and Food Security*. White River Junction, VT: Chelsea Green Publishing, 2016.
"Top 10 Facts about Poverty in Lima, Peru." The Borgen Project. 24 May 2018. https://borgenproject.org/top-10-facts-about-poverty-in-lima-peru/.
"Truth Commission: Peru 01." U.S. Institute of Peace. 13 July 2001. https://usip.org/publications/2001/07/truth-commission-peru-01.
Tucker, Catherine, Editor. *Nature, Science, and Religion: Intersections Shaping Society and the Environment*. Santa Fe: SAR Press, 2012.
Turner, Denys. *The Darkness of God: Negativity in Christian Mysticism*. Cambridge, UK: Cambridge University Press, 1966.
"*Un mundo donde quepan muchos mundos: arte zapatista en la Casa de las Américas*." Art exhibit presented at the 3rd International Colloquium for the Study of the Indigenous Cultures of America. October 9-12, 2018; http://www.casadelasamericas.org/pecoa/2018/programa.html.
UNFPA, UNICEF and UN Women. "Indigenous Women's Maternal Health and Maternal Mortality." March 2018. *UNFPA*. https://unfpa.org/sites/default/files/resource-pdf/factsheet_digital_Apr15.pdf.
United Nations Women. "Facts and figures: Ending violence against women." In *UN Women*. United Nations. August 2017. https://unwomen.org/en/what-we-do/ending-violence-against-women/facts-and-figures.
United Nations Development Program. *Social Justice? The Challenge of Intersecting inequalities*. New York: United Nations, 2010.
UNICEF. *Female Genital Mutilation/Cutting: A Global Concern*. New York, 2016. https://unicef.org/media/files/FGMC_2016_brochure_final_UNICEF_SPREAD.pdf.
United Nations. *The Sustainable Development Goals Report 2017*. Annual. New York: United Nations, 2017.
United Nations, Economic and Social Council, Permanent Forum on Indigenous Issues. *Indigenous Speakers in Permanent Forum Decry Governmental Abuse of Traditional Lands, Natural Resources, Urge Respect for Self-Governing Systems*. 26 April 2017. https://un.org/press/en/2017/hr5353.doc.htm.
U.S. Central Intelligence Agency World Fact Book. https://www.cia.gov/library/publications/the-world-factbook/geos/pe.html.
Van Der Borgh, Chris. *Cooperación externa, gobierno local y reconstrucción posguerra: La experiencia de Chalatenango*. Amsterdam: Rozenberg Publishers, 2004.
—. *Informed Consent Critical to Protecting Survival, Human Rights of Indigenous Peoples, Speakers Tell Permanent Forum*. 1 May, 2017. 3 May, 2017. https://un.org/press/en/2017/hr5356.doc.htm.
Viesca C. EL "Tratamiento de las Enfermedades Mentales en el Códice Badiano." In *Estudios de Etnobotánica y Antropología Médica II*. Edited by C. Viesca. México: IMEPLAN, 1976.

—. "Prevención y Terapéuticas Méxicas." In *Historia General de la Medicina en México*. Edited by Tomo I. López Austin y Viesca C. México: México Antiguo, 1984a.

—. "El Médico Méxica." In *Historia General de la Medicina en México*. Tomo I. México: México Antiguo, 1984b.

—. "De la Medicina Indígena a la Medicina Tradicional." In *México Indígena* 9. México: Instituto Nacional Indigenista, 1986.

Watson, Kelly and J. Anthony Stallins. "Honey Bees and Colony Collapse Disorder: A Pluralistic Reframing." In *Geography Compass* 10/5, 2016.

"Welcome to Seminary Hill Farm." Methodist Theological School in Ohio. https://mtso.edu/ecotheology/seminary-hill-farm/.

Weller, Nathan. "Farmer Cooperatives, Not Monsanto, supply El Salvador with seed." In *EcoViva*, 2015. https://ecoviva.org/farmer-cooperatives-not-monsanto-supply-el-salvador-with-seed/.

White Jr., Lynn. "The Historical Roots of Our Ecological Crisis." In E*cology and Feminist Theology*. Edited by Mary Heather MacKinnon, and Moni McIntyre. Kansas City: Sheed and Ward, 1995.

White, Monica M. "Sisters of the Soil: Urban Gardening as Resistance in Detroit." In *Race/Ethnicity* 5, no. 1, 2011.

—. "Shouldering Responsibility for the Delivery of Human Rights: A Case Study of the D-Town Farmers of Detroit." In *Race/Ethnicity* 3, no. 2, 2010.

Wilson, Shawn. *Research Is Ceremony: Indigenous Research Methods*. Halifax, NS: Fernwood, 2008.

"Work on Mbuya Nehanda Memorial Statue Begins" in *The Herald*. 13 August 2020: https://www.herald.co.zw/work-on-mbuya-nehanda-memorial-statue-begins/.

World Bank Group. *Women, Business and the Law 2016*. 2016. https://wbl.banquemondiale.org/~/media/WBG/WBL/Documents/Reports/2016/Women-Business-and-the-Law-2016.pdf.

World Health Organization, "Naming the coronavirus disease (COVID-19) and the virus that causes it,"https://who.int/emergencies/diseases/novel-coronavirus-2019/technical-guidance/naming-the-coronavirus-disease-(covid-2019)-and-the-virus-that-causes-it.

Wynter, Sylvia. "Unsettling the Coloniality of Being/Power/Truth/Freedom: Towards the Human, After Man, Its Overrepresentation — An Argument." In *The New Centennial Review* 3, no. 3, 2003.

Young, Iris. *Justice and the Politics of Difference*. Princeton, NJ: Princeton University Press, 1990.

Zachariah, George. *Alternatives Incorporated: Earth Ethics from the Grassroots*. London: Equinox, 2011.

"Zimbabwe's Sacred 'Hanging Tree' is Felled" in *The Telegraph*. June 23, 2020: https://www.telegraph.co.uk/news/worldnews/africaandindianocean/zimbabwe/8944988/Zimbabwes-sacred-Hanging-Tree-is-felled.html.

Zolla, C. Terapeutas. "*Enfermedades y Recursos Vegetales.*" In *México Indígena* 9. México: Instituto Nacional Indigenista, 1986.

CONTRIBUTOR AND EDITOR BIOGRAPHIES

Frédérique Apffel-Marglin is Professor Emerita in the Department of Anthropology at Smith College. She has taught at Harvard, Wellesley, and Wesleyan University. She founded Sachamama Center in the Peruvian High Amazon in 2009, which she directs. She has spent years in India and Peru working with indigenous peoples and with farmers. She was a research associate at the World Institute for Development Economics Research (WIDER) in Helsinki, a part of the United Nations University. Along with the Harvard economist Stephen A. Marglin, she has directed several research projects questioning the dominance of the modern paradigm of knowledge. She has authored, as well as edited fifteen books and published some 70 articles and book chapters. In 1993, she decided for ethical reasons that she could no longer engage in classical anthropological fieldwork in Odisha, India, and ever since then has been invited to collaborate with activist/intellectual groups in Peru and Bolivia. Her recent books include *Subversive Spiritualities* (Oxford University Press, 2011), *Sacred Soil* (North Atlantic Books, 2017), and *Contemporary Voices from Anima Mundi*, edited with Stefano Varese (Peter Lang Academic Press, 2020). https://www.sachamacenter.org

Whitney A. Bauman is Associate Professor of Religious Studies at Florida International University in Miami, FL. He is also co-founder and co-director of *Counterpoint: Navigating Knowledge*, a non-profit based in Berlin, Germany that holds public discussions over social and ecological issues related to globalization and climate change. His areas of research interest fall under the theme of "religion, science, and globalization." He is the recipient of a Fulbright Fellowship and a Humboldt Fellowship. His publications include: *Religion and Ecology: Developing a Planetary Ethic* (Columbia University Press 2014), and co-authored with Kevin O'Brien, *Environmental Ethics and Uncertainty: Tackling Wicked Problems* (Routledge 2019). He is currently working on a manuscript about the 19th Century German, Romantic Scientist, Ernst Haeckel.

Pamela K. Brubaker is Professor of Religion Emerita at California Lutheran University. Her books include *Women Don't Count: The Challenge of Women's Poverty to Christian Ethics* (American Academy of

Religion Academy Series, Oxford University Press, 1994), *Globalization at What Price? Economic Change and Daily Life* (Pilgrim Press, 2001, 2007), *Justice not Greed*, co-edited with Rogate Mshana (World Council of Churches Publications, 2010), and *Justice in a Global Economy: Strategies for Home, Community, and World*, co-edited with Rebecca Todd Peters and Laura Stivers (Westminster/John Knox Press, 2006). She has also published numerous book chapters and articles on feminist ethics, economic ethics, and just peacemaking. Brubaker participated in several World Council of Churches consultations on women, economics, and alternatives to globalization (2002-13). Her Ph.D. is in Christian Social Ethics, Union Theological Seminary (New York, 1989). She is a mother, grandmother, advocate, and activist who currently lives in Austin, Texas.

Yuria Celidwen is of Indigenous Nahua and Maya descent from the highlands of Chiapas, Mexico. As a scholar, she works on the intersection of Indigenous studies, cultural psychology, and contemplative science. Her interests are the interdisciplinary approaches to how the experience of self-transcendence is embodied and enhances prosocial behavior (ethics and compassion) across ecstatic traditions. From this work, she uncovers Indigenous contemplative practices from the world and finds their place in contemplative studies. She developed her thesis on the earth-based ecological experience of the Ethics of Belonging, an ethos that engenders conscious social responsibility for self, community, and environment. Within this work, she examines how our personal stories relate to cultural accounts that can transform our identities and the social and racial injustices of our times. She brings the voices of Indigenous peoples of the world as equal holders of sophisticated systems of contemplative insight. She is committed to the reclamation, revitalization, and transmission of Indigenous wisdom, the advancement of Indigenous rights and the rights of the Earth for social and environmental justice.

Rebecca Berru Davis is currently an Assistant Professor of Theology at St. Catherine's University in St. Paul, MN. As a Hispanic Theological Initiative Fellow, she earned her degree in the area of Art and Religion at the Graduate Theological Union in Berkeley, California, in 2012 and subsequently completed a two-year Louisville Institute Post-Doctoral Fellowship at St. John's University in Collegeville, Minnesota. She is interested in the intersection of art, faith, and justice as a way to understand the spiritual and religious expressions of those located on the margins of society. Her writing appears in the *Wiley Blackwell Companion to Latino/a*

Theologies (Wiley Blackwell, 2015) and in *U.S. Catholic Historian* (Catholic University of America Press). She continues to pursue her activist research related to *Picturing Paradise,* a curatorial project launched in 2006, featuring the work of Peruvian women artists living in the shantytowns outside of Lima, Peru.

Lilian Dube is an Associate Professor and former chair of the Theology and Religious Studies Department at the University of San Francisco that she joined in 2006 after teaching at universities in the U.S.A. and U.K. and the University of Zimbabwe for a decade. In 1999, she made history as the first Black woman to earn a Doctor of Theology degree from Stellenbosch University, South Africa. She is the executive director of the film, *USF in Zambia: HIV/AIDS and Social Justice,* co-author of *African Initiatives in Healing Ministry* (Unisa Press, 2011), and co-editor of *Theology in the Context of Globalization: African Women's Response* (EATWOT, 2005). She has published several journal articles and book chapters. Dube received international fellowships and awards including the American Association of University Women Fellowship. She has served on the AAUW Research and Grants Awards Selection Pane as panelist and session chair. Courses she teaches include Feminist Theology from the Third World, African Theology and Religious Cosmologies, and Theology in HIV/AIDS Contexts. In 2009, she developed a month-long Service-Learning program in Zambia and became its sole faculty of record for five years (2010-2014). She has been a speaker at Harvard and Stanford Universities, a Visiting Associate Professor at Columbia University, and a Research Fellow at the University of South Africa.

Ivone Gebara is a Catholic nun, a Brazilian Sister of Our Lady (Canonesses of St. Augustine), and a pioneering Latin American ecofeminist philosopher and liberation theologian. She taught theology and philosophy at the Institute of Theology of Recife, Brazil. Presently, she is also invited by different universities and religious centers in Brazil and worldwide to lecture. She has authored books and articles from a feminist and ecological perspective, such as *Longing for Running Water: Ecofeminism and Liberation* (Fortress Press, 1999) and *Out of the Depths: Women's Experience of Evil and Salvation* (Fortress Press, 2002).

Aruna Gnanadason has a Doctorate in Ministries from San Francisco Theological Seminary in the U.S.A. She has directed the global programme on Women in Church and Society and the Justice, Peace and Creation work of the World Council of Churches in Geneva, Switzerland, from 1991 to 2009. She has a Master's degree in English Literature from the University of Bangalore, India. She has written or edited several books, including *No Longer a Secret: The Church and Violence Against Women* (World Council of Churches, 1997) and *Listen to the Women, Listen to the Earth* (World Council of Churches, 2005). Her work has been published in major books and journals globally. She now lives in Chennai, India, and resources the churches and the ecumenical movement in India and globally, reflecting on the role, the challenge, and the alternatives offered by the gospel in addressing the impact of patriarchy, caste, and global capitalism on the people and the earth.

Teresia Mbari Hinga was born in Kenya. Currently, she teaches in the Religious Studies Department at Santa Clara University in California, U.S.A. She received a B.Ed. in English Literature and Religious Studies from Kenyatta University and an M.A. in Religious Studies from Nairobi University, both in Nairobi, Kenya. She earned a Ph.D. in Religious Studies/African Christianity from the University of Lancaster, England. Her thesis on the role of women in African Christianity focused on women's power and liberation in the African Independent Church. Dr. Hinga's research focuses on religion and women's issues, particularly in Africa, African religious history, and expression in the global religious landscape, religion and public policy, and the ethics of globalization. She is a founding member of the "Circle of Concerned African Women Theologians," a pan-African association of women who study the role and impact of religion and culture on African women's lives. She is also a member of the Black Catholic Symposium of the AAR and of the Association for the Academic Study of Religion in Africa (AASR). As faculty at Santa Clara University, she teaches courses on women and religion, feminist theologies, African religions and society, and religion and contemporary moral issues. Recent publications include *African, Christian, Feminist: The Enduring Search for What Matters* (Orbis, 2017) and a chapter, entitled "Of Kente Cloth, Rainbow Nations, and the Virtue of Pluralism: Navigating the Beauty and Dignity of Difference in Search of a Livable Future in Africa" in *Finding Beauty in the Other: Theological Reflections Across Religious Differences* (Crossroads, 2019).

Rosalind Flynn Hinton is an independent scholar, oral historian and non-profit consultant with three decades of experience in educational and community settings. She has a "tricoastal" footprint in New York, New Orleans, and San Francisco, U.S.A. Focusing on African American religion and culture, music, visual arts, gender equality, and women and children's health, she has held positions in teaching, development, strategic planning, project design and management. As an oral historian and fellow at Newcomb College Institute in New Orleans, Louisiana, she created laoutloud and nolajewishwomen — websites and efforts dedicated to bringing forward the voices of progressive women activists in Louisiana. Skilled in cross-cultural discussions on ethics, values, culture and religious beliefs, she has a Ph.D. in Religious Studies from Northwestern University in Evanston, Illinois, and has taught multiculturalism, feminist global theologies, feminist history, African American history and religions at DePaul University in Chicago and at Tulane and Loyola Universities in New Orleans.

Adrienne Krone is an Assistant Professor of Religious Studies and Director of Jewish Life at Allegheny College in Pennsylvania, U.S.A. Her research focuses on religious food justice movements in North America. In her manuscript, "Free Range Religion: Religious Food Justice Movements in North America," she investigates the nature and complexity of contemporary religious food justice movements. She is a contributor to *Jewish Veganism and Vegetarianism: Studies and New Directions* (State University of New York Press, 2019) and *Feasting and Fasting: The History and Ethics of Jewish Food* (New York University Press, 2019). Her current research project is an ethnographic and historical study of the Jewish community farming movement.

Sylvia Marcos, Ph.D., is the founder and a senior researcher of the Seminario Permanente de Antropologia y Genero at the Institute for Anthropological Research (IIA), Universidad Nacional Autonóma de Mexico (UNAM). She is the author of many books, including: *Taken from the Lips: Gender and Eros in Mesoamerican Religions* (2006) the co-edited volume, *Dialogue and Difference: Feminisms Challenge Globalization* (2005); Indigenous Women and Decolonial Cosmovision (2014); and *Religion y Genero: Vol. III, Encyclopedia Iberoamericana de Religiones* (2004). Beside her publications she has been actively engaged with the Indigenous women's movements in Mexico and Latin America.

Alyssa Moore is a graduate student and lay Catholic from Santa Rosa, California, U.S.A. She received a Bachelor of Science degree in 2018 from the University of San Francisco, California, where she double majored in environmental science and theology/religious studies, and is pursuing her Master of Divinity degree at Santa Clara University's Jesuit School of Theology, Berkeley. Her work explores the vital connections between Christian faith and environmental and animal rights activism, promoting the practice of a loving pastoral care for all of creation, human and nonhuman.

Elaine Nogueira-Godsey is Assistant Professor of Theology, Ecology and Race at the Methodist Theological School in Ohio, U.S.A. Her research focuses on the development of ecological ethics and decolonial methods of research and teaching in relation to the study of religion and ecofeminist theology. Her published articles include "Towards a Decological Pedagogy" in *Religião, Gênero, Violências e Direitos Humanos* (Editora Unida, 2018). Her forthcoming book is entitled, The *Ecofeminism of Ivone Gebara*. She holds a doctorate in Religious Studies from the University of Cape Town in South Africa. She also received a fellowship for postdoctoral study from the University of Cape Town in religion and education and another postdoctoral fellowship from the University of Johannesburg studying the intersection of ecofeminism and postcolonial theory. She is a board member of the International Society for the Study of Religion, Nature and Culture, an Assistant Editor for the *Journal for the Study of Religion, Nature and Culture,* and co-chair of the American Academy of Religion-Society of Biblical Literature Women's Caucus.

Jea Sophia Oh is an Assistant Professor of Philosophy at West Chester University of Pennsylvania, U.S.A. She received a Master of Sacred Theology with a focus in feminist theology from Yale Divinity School and a Ph.D. in Philosophical and Theological Studies from Drew University in New Jersey with a concentration in Women's and Gender Studies. Her research primarily focuses on the fields of Asian philosophies, comparative ethics, ecofeminism, and postcolonial theory. Her first book *A Postcolonial Theology of Life: Planetarity East and West* (Sopher Press, 2011) is a path-making work in Korean ecofeminist theology and comparative philosophy. She is the editor and author of *Nature's Transcendence and Immanence: A Comparative Interdisciplinary Ecstatic Naturalism* (Lexington Press, 2018). She is a section chair of Comparative Religion and Ecology in the American Academy of Religion (AAR) and also a board member of the Women's Caucus. She serves as the chair of the Society of Study of Process Philosophy at both Central and Eastern divisions of the American Philosophical Association (APA).

Laurel Marshall Potter is pursuing a Ph.D. in Systematic Theology at Boston College, Massachusetts, U.S.A. She lived and worked among the ecclesial base communities of El Salvador from 2011-2017 while studying Latin American Theology at the Jesuit University of Central America in San Salvador. Her master's thesis, entitled "Actions Speak Louder than Words: Ecclesial Base Communities in El Salvador in the Construction of Eucharistic and Baptismal Celebrations," explores the communities' reflections on liturgy, the Sacraments, and other ecclesiological challenges, using participatory research methods. Her research continues to probe the constructive relationships between decolonial studies, ecclesiology, and grassroots theology in Latin America.

Mary Judith Ress, Ph.D., is a founding member of the *Con-spirando* Collective in Santiago, Chile. She is an Ecofeminist Theologian who is the author of *Ecofeminism in Latin America* (Orbis Books, 2006). Lately, she has taken to writing novels: *Blood Flowers* (IUniverse, 2010), dedicated to the four churchwomen murdered in El Salvador in 1980, and her recently released *Different Gods* (IUniverse, 2018).

Sarah E. Robinson is a U.S.-based critical-constructive scholar of religion, environment, and social justice. Her scholarship addresses ethical leadership in eco-food, sustainable agriculture, and climate change resilience among contemporary Muslim, Buddhist, and Christian community locations. She serves on the Steering Committee for the Religion and Food unit of the American Academy of Religion and has served as a unit chair of Ecology and Religion for the American Academy of Religion, Western Region. She has taught religious studies, experiential learning for social justice, women's and gender studies, and environmental studies at Santa Clara University (California) and Pacific Lutheran University (Washington). Her prior work in religious, arts, and environmental non-profit organizations include organizing events for Buddhist teacher Thich Nhat Hanh (2000), managing the first summer youth eco-jobs program for California Youth Energy Services (2001), and participating as a singer and administrator for the Oakland Interfaith Gospel Choir (1997-2005). Publications include chapters in *Religion, Food, and Eating in North America* (Columbia University Press, 2014), *Key Thinkers on the Environment* (Routledge, 2018), and *That All May Flourish: Comparative Religious Environmental Ethics* (Oxford University Press, 2018).

Rosemary Radford Ruether is an American feminist scholar and Catholic theologian. She is the Carpenter Emerita Professor of Feminist Theology at Pacific School of Religion and the Graduate Theological Union in Berkeley, California, as well as the Georgia Harkness Emerita Professor of Applied Theology at Garrett Evangelical Theological Seminary in Evanston, Illinois, U.S.A. She has enjoyed a long and distinguished career as a scholar, teacher, and activist in the Roman Catholic Church, and is well known for her groundbreaking work in Christian feminist theology.

Kelsey Ryan-Simkins is a Ph.D. student in the School of Environment and Natural Resources at Ohio State University in Columbus, Ohio, U.S.A. She is an environmental sociologist whose research focuses on food justice and the creation of environmentally sustainable and socially equitable food systems in the United States. Through her research, she aims to understand how urban agriculture projects in the U.S. vary and what characteristics contribute to an equitable urban food system. In addition, her master's research at the Methodist Theological School in Ohio continues to inspire an interest in the cultural and religious dimensions of the food justice movement. She is involved with several applied projects that aim to implement equitable food system transformation through the exploration and establishment of food hubs in marginalized neighborhoods in Columbus, Ohio.

Juan Antonio Tavárez is a tenured professor at Compton College in Compton, California. He earned his Master of Arts in Spanish from California State University, Fullerton. He is the co-author of "The Enlightened West: The Origins of Climate Change" for the *Journal of Feminist Studies in Religion*.

Theresa A. Yugar is a professor at California State University, Los Angeles, in the Chicana/o and Latina/o Studies department. She is a Latinx scholar in religion whose scholarly focus is on women and ecology in Latin America. She is a graduate of Harvard University with a Master's degree in Feminist Theology, and has a Ph.D. from Claremont Graduate University in the field of Women Studies in Religion. Her areas of specialization are Gender in Colonial Latin American History, ecofeminist theories and praxis, and transnational ecofeminist movements. She is the author of *Sor Juana Inés de la Cruz: Feminist Reconstruction of Biography and Text* (Wipf and Stock, 2014). Her current research reflects on transnational ecological movements with a focus particularly on issues that relate to border, migration, and climate justice, as well as incoming and outgoing migratory patterns along the Southern U.S. border, including Mexico, Central America, and Latin America.

INDEX

Acserald, Henri 20
activism
—, Black Lives Matter movement 6, 32
—, eco-justice 144
—, and epistemology 3, 141, 144
—, and food justice 199, 216, 242-245
—, against Formosa Plastics Complex 155, 157-159, 166
—, indigenous 136
—, against Sterlite Copper Smelting factory 137-138
—, against nuclear reactors, Tamil Nadu 139
—, RISE St. James 157, 166
—, Save the River Narmada 136
—, Standing Rock 76, 174
Adams-Heard, Rachel 159
addiction 116-117, 123, 212
African American communities 6, 155-164, 205, 220-221
Agarwal, Anil (see Vedanta) 138
Agarwal, Bina 203, 208
agriculture (see also animals; farming; gardens)
—, agroecology 206, 239
—, built environment 115
—, *chinampas* (raised fields) 226-228, 230
—, industrial 190, 192, 203-210, 218-222, 241
—, environmental and food justice 8, 243, 245
—, labor 203-210
—, myth 110
—, perennial plants 207
—, pesticide use 191
—, seasonal and climate change 88
—, sustainable 8, 42, 152, 204, 206-207, 209, 213-214, 217, 241
—, traditional forms of 174, 176, 188
—, urban 212, 215, 218-222
Aguirre Beltrán, Gonzalo 127
Albert, Bruce 113, 123

Alkon, Alison Hope 210, 218, 219
Allen, Patricia 207, 209
Altieri, Miguel A. 206
Amazon
—, Brazilian 113
—, feminine archetype 107
—, indigenous perspective 116, 118, 168
—, Peruvian 6, 120
AmeriCorps VISTA 204, 214
Anguelovski, Isabelle 215
Anima Mundi 118-119, 122
animals
—, agriculture and farming 188, 207, 210, 214, 217
—, bees (see also pollinators) 8, 69, 174, 187, 189, 190, 191, 192, 193, 194, 195, 196, 197, 198, 199, 200, 201
—, creation stories and dreams 51, 58, 60-65, 78, 90-93, 109-110, 142, 165, 196, 225
—, garbage 17-18
—, and Green Belt Movement 152
—, harm from mining 169
—, kosher 194
—, metaphors 129
—, poaching 43
—, as predators and prey 34
—, rights 58, 196
—, welfare xv, 188
animism 119, 142
Anthony, Carl 25
anthropocentrism xiii, xv, 53-54, 58, 102, 114, 143, 182
anthropology 22, 23, 86, 119, 123
—, medical 125
—, non-anthropocentric 143
Aquino, María Pilar 86
archetypes 72, 101, 107, 114
Archibald, J. A. 76
Austin, Alfredo López 127, 131
Aztec (see Nahua)

Barickman, B. J. 220
Barnhardt, R. 77
Battiste, Marie 77
Baytelman, B. Jardin 127
Bell, Michael Mayerfeld 209
Berry, Jason 162
Berry, Thomas 113, 116, 120
Bible 57, 61-64, 143, 166, 195, 197
biodiversity 3, 4, 9, 78, 182, 206
Bingemer, Maria Clara 86
Birch, Isobel 27
Black Lives Matter movement 6, 32
Bohannon, Richard R. II 210
Boff, Leonardo 45
Bosco, Fernando J. 219
Boyd, Brian 73
Boyd, Michelle 219
Braswell, Taylor Harris 219
Brazil 5, 16, 17, 18, 20n5, 21, 104, 106, 113, 179, 220
Brelsford, Robert 158
Brennus, B. 71
Bridge, Rabbi Dan 196
Briones, Carlos Roberto 236
Brockelman, Paul 143
Brown, Karen McCarthy 90
Bullard, Robert D. 210
Butler, Judith 17

Cabeza, M. 76
Caceres, Berta 167
Cagan, Steve 236
Cajete, Gregory A. 71
Campell, Elliott 206
"Cancer Alley" xvi, 7, 155, 156, 164
care, ethic of 2, 22, 54, 143, 144, 145, 147, 189
Carmody, John 45
Carney, Judith A. 220
Carroll, John E. 142
"cash crop" economy 151-152
Castellano, Marlene B. 71, 77
Castro, Gustavo 175
Caxaj, C. Susana 76
Catechism of the Catholic Church 6, 57-66
Chan, Wingtsit 53
Chile 106
Christianity 174

—, Ecclesial Base Communities (CEBs) 8, 235-238, 242-243, 246
—, in Latin America 7
—, and ecofeminism 168
—, and environment 142, 146, 165
—, ethical responsibility 22-23, 45
—, and gender 51, 102, 104
—, indigenous groups 168, 174
—, liberation 144
—, missions 140, 142, 143
—, *momoxtli* (public altar or pulpit) 228, 231
—, and nonhuman creation 58, 60, 63-64, 67
—, revolutionary community 246
—, and soul 128
—, Western cultures xiv
cleansing rituals 28, 30, 32, 34, 126
climate change
—, anthropogenic 203-204, 206
—, climate disruption 1, 3, 88
—, climate weirding xiv, xvi
—, United Nations Framework Convention on Climate Change 167
coalition building 2, 5, 164, 211
Coalition of Immokalee Workers (CIW) 216, 217
Coates, Ta-Nehisi 160
cognitive frameworks 125
collectivism
Colombia 179
colonialism (see also conquest) 5, 29, 80, 140
—, African continent 33, 36, 149-154
—, and missions 140
—, and non-European spirit worlds 119
—, resistance to 131
community 239-245
—, gardens 204-205, 219
—, planetary xv-xvi, 6, 50
Cone, James 32-33, 42
Confucian family 48, 53
Confucianism 48, 49
conquest 105-106, 119, 130, 140, 145, 223, 230
—, Columbus, Christopher 228
—, Ruiz de Alarcon, Hernando 128
conquistadors 228

Con-spirando Women's Collective 7, 101, 102, 103, 104, 108
Cordero, Verónica 106
Cortina, Adela 17
COVID-19 (see pandemics)
Creation narrative 59-60, 72, 75-76, 78, 105, 142-143, 182-183, 187, 189
Crenshaw, Kimberlé xiii
cuadros (fabric pictures) 6, 86-93
Cuomo, Chris 203, 204
cultural inheritance 5

dams 135-137
Daneel, Marthinus L. 32-34, 44, 45
Datta, Ranjan 76
Davidson, Debra 218
Deloria Jr., Vine 78
Democratic Republic of Congo 25
Denzin, Norman K. 75
Derrida, Jacques xiii-xiv
diaspora 6, 41, 43, 44, 138
Díaz del Castillo, Bernal 226, 230
dictatorship, one-party 149
diversity, human 3-4
Doi, Joanne 91
Doss, Cheryl 203, 208

ecofamilism 47, 53-55
ecofeminism xiv, 6, 23, 54, 55, 93, 101, 102, 140, 168
—, and anthropocentrism 54, 102, 143
—, and justice 6, 23, 102, 140
ecoimperialism 160
ecology 2, 3, 5, 45, 47, 50, 52, 54, 55, 85, 113, 114, 120, 123, 182, 227
—, integral 3, 113, 120
—, movements
economic empowerment 7, 78, 80, 167, 179
Ecuador 179
Edinger, Edward F. 74
ego, dissolution of 123-124
El Salvador 8, 172, 235-245
—, Cacaopera, Morazán agriculture 235-345
Elizondo, Virgilio P. 45
embodied spirituality x, 103, 117, 120, 165
enclosure movement 18

environment 227-228, 233, 243
—, destruction of ix, 16, 22, 116, 153, 177, 204, 222, 230
—, ecological degradation xv, 2, 16, 20, 25, 85, 149, 151-153, 188, 242
—, environmental justice 2, 7, 20, 21, 26, 205, 210 (EJ movement), 243
—, poverty 16, 19-22, 45, 85, 89, 150-153, 160-161
—, racism 7, 155-166, 204, 210, 222
equity, social 4, 211
eschatology 61
ethnography 127

family
farming 7, 38, 42-44, 158, 188, 206, 213-217, 241-243
—, *Shoresh* (Jewish community farm) 187-200
Feldman, John 114
feminine archetypes 107
Fernandes, Maira 16
Fernández-Llamazares, Á. 76
Finer, Lawrence B. 164
Fisher, J. L. 38
Fitzgerald, Rachel 107
Food (see also agriculture; farming)
—, activism 188, 200, 208, 216, 218, 242, 245
—, food desert 213, 215
—, justice 8, 41, 188, 203-222, 244-245
—, procurement 5
—, security 152, 206-208, 212, 222, 241, 242
Freire, Paolo 103

Gaia xiii, xv, xvi, 114, 155, 156, 165
garbage xv, 13-23, 228
García-Rivera, Alejandro 92
gardens 8, 34, 52, 66, 90, 96, 104 (Shared Garden), 188, 191, 199, 205, 207, 209, 219-222, 224, 226, 230
Gebara, Ivone xv, 5, 13, 88n9, 93, 104, 205
Geishirt-Cantrell, B. 76
Gelfand, Michael 29
gentrification 218-220
global capitalism 158
globalization 41, 211

—, "globalatinization" xiii-xvi
Gnanadason, Aruna xvi, 7, 135, 141, 146
goddess traditions 101, 105-107, 156, 225
Gonzalez-Barrera, Ana 236
Gottlieb, Robert 211, 218
Green Belt Movement (see Activism) 7, 149, 151, 152, 153, 154
greenhouse gas emissions 206
Guadalupe (Our Lady of; Virgin of)
—, *Nahui Ollin* (flower) 225, 226, 231
—, Our Lady of 231
—, *Tonantzin* (Title, Aztec goddess) 106, 225
—, Virgin of 121-122
Guatemala 106
Gunnar, Myrdal 30

Hall, B. L. 71, 77, 80
Hall, Stuart 74
healing ritual 29, 30, 33-34, 72, 126-128, 131, 225, 240, 241, 245
healthcare 39, 40, 164, 237
Hecht, Susana B. 236
Henao, Alejandro 206
Henry, Michele 189, 193, 199
Heschel, Abraham Joshua 166
Hill, Kristina 45
Hillman, James 114-116
Ho, Wan-Li 53-54
Hodge, F. S. 76
Hoey, Lesli 219
Holiday, Billie 29-30
Honduras 174
honey (see also pollinators) 8, 69, 159, 174, 187, 189, 190, 191, 193, 194, 195, 196, 197, 198, 199, 200
Horst, Megan 209, 219
household (*oikos*) 6, 18, 47-55, 240, 244
Howard, P. L. 209
Hynes, H. Patricia 209

images of the Sacred 102, 105, 108
Imago Dei 57, 59
Inanna 105
India 140-143, 179n41
—, Tamil Nadu anti-nuclear protests 139-140

indigenous
—, Earth-based narratives 78, 105-108
—, epistemologies, ways of knowing 3, 5, 7, 73, 75-76, 80, 141, 144, 227, 229, 240
—, green movements 35, 168-169, 172-173, 176-177
—, medicine 7, 120, 122, 125, 127, 130-131
—, methodologies 35, 71, 75-77, 103, 125, 136, 240, 241, 246
—, narratives and storytelling (personal, communal, cultural) 6, 71, 73, 75-78
—, people 3, 76, 80, 113, 135-136, 140-143, 167-169, 176-182
—, relationships to religion and the church 35, 105, 107, 140, 143, 155, 178, 182
—, women and gender 7, 79, 80, 136, 141, 144, 167, 171, 173, 179, 181
Intergovernmental Panel on Climate Change (IPCC) 203, 206
intersectionality xiii, xvi, 3, 7, 55, 211, 222
Iriarte, Gregorio 237
Isasi-Díaz, Ada María (*lo cotidiano*) 91n11
Iseke, Judy 71, 76
Iwanka Raya, Mairin 79

Jarnagin, Susan 209
Jesus 60, 86, 101, 106, 108, 178, 217, 235, 237, 238, 246
Joassart-Marcelli, Pascale
Johnson, Bart 45
Johnson, G. 76
Jones, Kenneth 239
Joshi, Anupama 211, 218
Josselson, Ruthellen 72
Judaism 187, 194, 200
—, Jewishness 8, 187-189, 193-201
Jung, Carl G. 72, 74, 107, 114, 115, 119

Kawagley, A. O. 77
Kenya 2, 7, 25, 149-154, 179n41
—, *Kirinyaga* (Mount Kenya) 150
Kim Hong-do 49
Kim, Nam 211

Kleinman, Daniel Lee 190-191
Kopenawa, Davi 113, 115-116, 118, 121-124
Korea
—, Confucian family in 48
—, *Hojujae* (patriarchal family system) 51-52
—, *Salim* ("enlivening") 47, 50-55
—, *Seo-ok-jae* (wedding custom) 48, 51
Kost, Kathryn 164
Kovach, Margaret (Maggie) 71, 75, 76
Kraft, Siv Ellen 76
Kreimer, Alcira 236

Lakhani, Nina 177, 178
Lan, Kwok Pui 146
Lana, Marcos A. 206
land wars 27
Latour, Bruno 119
Laudato Si' (see also Pope Francis) 22fn7, 85, 86*fn*3, 113, 177, 249, 251
Lavigne, Sharon and Shamell
Laytner, Rabbi Anson 196
Leeming, David A. 76, 78
Leslie, Isaac Sohn 221
Lessing, Doris 26
liberation ix, 5, 26, 27, 28, 33, 34, 37, 45, 143, 144, 145, 149, 205, 246
Lincoln, Yvonna S. 75
Lonergan, Bernard, SJ CC 58, 63
Longchar, Wati 142
López Austin, Alfredo 127, 131
Louisiana 155-166
—, Bucket Brigade 159
—, "Cancer Alley" xvi, 7, 155, 156, 164
—, St. James Parish 157-159, 166
Lovins, Amory xiv
lynching 6, 25, 27-30, 33

Maathai, Wangari xvi, 7, 32, 149-154, 259
Malach, Sabrina 188-189, 192-193, 197
"man camps" 158-159
Mares, Teresa M. 219
Margulis, Lynn 114
Marion, Amy 209
Marquez, C. A. 76
Marshall III, Joseph M. 75

masculinity 129, 145, 209
materialist science 119
May, Janet W. 238
McAdams, Dan P. 72, 73
McClintock, Nathan 219
McFague, Sallie 47, 50, 53
McKenna, John 158
McKibben, Nancy 212
medicine, traditional 6, 32, 70, 125-131, 169, 174
Merchant, Carolyn 142
mestizo 101, 104, 121
Mexico 179n41, 223, 227, 231
Michell, Herman J. 77
Mies, Maria 55
Mitchell, David J. 157
Mundy, Barbara E. 223, 227, 229-230
Musleah, Rahel 194
mutuality 143, 155, 156, 157, 164, 166
myth 69-79, 104-105, 108, 225, 230

Nabrit, Charles Madison, Memorial Garden 204, 220, 222
Namibia 149
Nahua
—, *Cemanahuac* (first nations) 226
—, floral mythology 225-226
—, *ixtle* bag 232-233
—, and Mexico City 223-233
—, *momoxtli* (public altar or pulpit) 228, 231
—, Tenochtitlan (city) 223, 224, 225, 226, 227, 228, 230
—, *tianguis* (*tianquiztli*, pre-Hispanic marketplace) xvi, 8, 223, 224, 225, 227, 229, 230, 231, 232, 233
—, *Tonantzin* (goddess) 106, 225
—, *Xochitlalpan* (paradise) 224-225, 231
—, *Yacatecuhtli* (god of commerce) 228
Native Americans
Navin, Mark 208
Ndola "slave trees" 31-33
neo-colonialism 149
neoliberalism
New Spain 223, 226fn6, 230-231
Nicholls, Clara I. 206
Noble, David 119
North American Free Trade Agreement (NAFTA) 8, 223, 229, 231-232

numinous powers 118
Nyajeka, Tumani Mutasa 26, 45
Nyakasikanda, Nehanda 26-28, 30-31, 33

O'Brien, Kevin J. 210
Oh, Jea Sophia 52
oikos (see household)
Okun, Tema 239

Pachamama 101, 103, 106, 108, 170, 178, 243
Pádua Bosi, Antônio De 21
Palmer, Robin 27
Pamplona Alta 6, 86-93
pandemics
—, COVID-19 xv, 1, 6, 35, 36, 39-41 (across African continent), 44
—, HIV/AIDS 35, 36
Parliament of the World Religions 155
Pasqua, A. 76
Passel, Jeffrey S. 236
Patrinos, Harry Anthony 79
Peter, Gregory 209
petrochemicals 155-160, 163
Philippines 179n41
Planned Parenthood 162-164
Plumwood, Val 211
Pollan, Michael 122-124
pollinators 8, 189, 190, 191, 193, 197, 198, 199, 200
—, colony collapse disorder 191
—, honey bees 174, 187, 189, 190, 191, 192, 193, 194, 195, 196, 197, 198, 199, 200, 201
—, honey 8, 69, 159, 174, 187, 189, 190, 191, 193, 194, 195, 196, 197, 198, 199, 200
Pope Francis 6, 22, 41, 42, 43, 45, 86, 92, 113, 162, 177
Pope Saint John Paul II 57
postcolonial
poverty 16, 21, 25, 26, 27, 35, 36, 41, 42, 43, 45, 79, 237, 241
—, "aporophobia" 17
—, poaching 43
pregnancy 93 (as metaphor), 105, 164
Preston, Matthew 38
prophets 140, 151, 153, 160, 166, 182, 188

psychedelics 121-124
—, *ayahuasca* 120-121
—, *yakoana* 121n27, 123-124
Pueblos Jóvenes 88
Puleo, Mev 86

racism xv, 7, 78, 80, 90, 155, 160, 221
Rae, Eleanor 45
Rasmussen, Larry 142
Ratzinger, Cardinal Joseph 58
real life 5, 13, 14, 15, 17, 19, 21, 23
Recinos, Manuel Portillo 242
recycling 13-16, 19-21, 52-53, 87, 228
Reflective Democracy Project 155, 160-161
relationality xv, xvi
reparation 33, 160
ritual (see healing ritual)
Rolfes, Anne 155
Rosado-Nuñes, Maria 86
Rosh Hashanah 189, 193, 196-197, 199-200
Rosenberg, D. G. 80
Ruether, Rosemary Radford ix-x, xiii-xvi, 2-9, 13, 23, 25, 26, 30, 45, 55, 142, 149, 155-156, 164-165, 182, 207, 238
rural life 8
Russell, Letty M. 143

Saatchi, Sassan S. 236
Sachs, Carolyn 209, 213
Sahagún, Fray Bernardino de 128, 130-131
Saldanha, Arun 218
Schillebeeckx, Edward 246
Schlosberg, David 210
Sellers, Sam 208
Sen, Amartya 215
Shabodien, Fatima 207
shamanism 6, 113, 118, 120-123
Shona 25-26, 29, 35
Shiva, Vandana 55, 145, 160, 204, 207
slavery 25, 29, 32, 36, 156, 157
Slocum, Rachel 218
Smith, L. T. 75
Sobrino, Jon 86
social justice 209-212
sorcery 122

soul 114-116, 118, 122, 127-129, 217
South Africa
—, Bill of Rights of South African Constitution 149
—, farms in 207
Spickard, James V. 90
spirits 29, 69, 71, 113-114, 118-124, 125
spirituality 46, 76, 101-104, 114, 117, 141, 144-145, 165, 182, 205, 217, 222, 241
Stallins, J. Anthony 190-191
Stehlin, John G. 219
Stengers, Isabelle 119
storytelling 70, 71, 75-77, 79, 80, 89 (visual), 166
Sturgeon, Nöel 208, 218
sustainable 8, 35, 42, 47, 52-55, 78, 92, 101, 228, 241, 245
—, agriculture 8, 206-209, 213-214, 217, 222, 241
Suryanarayanan, Sainath 190-191
Swimme, Brian 113, 114, 116, 118
Symbiotic Earth (film) 114

Tagore, Proma 80
Taiwan 53, 54, 158
Tarr, Alexander R. 219
Taylor, Bron (dark green religion) 53
Thomas, Hugh 224
Toensmeier, Eric 206
traditional ecological knowledge 4
trauma 27, 32, 33, 79, 80, 102, 104, 123, 149, 245
Trinity 60, 62
Truth and Reconciliation Commission (Peru) 88
Tucker, Catherine 35
Tucker, Mary Evelyn 113, 116
Turner, Denys 58

United Nations 170, 179, 203, 228, 236, 240
—, Conference of Parties (COP) 167
—, Development Program (UNDP) 79
—, Framework Convention on Climate Change (UNFCC) 167
—, Research Institute for Social Development (UNRISD) 174

Van Der Borgh, Chris 236
Vedanta mining company 137-138
Venezuela 106
Virgin Mary (see also Our Lady of Guadalupe) 105
vulnerability xv, 3, 79, 203, 204, 209

Wake, David B. 227
water
—, advocacy 167, 168, 175, 177
—, clean drinking water 16, 40-41, 136, 138, 157, 158, 169, 208, 228, 230, 242
—, dam 137
—, danger of mines and pipelines 88, 170-174, 181
—, harvesting 152
—, lakes and rivers 135, 150-151, 156, 236-237
—, myth 31, 142, 225
—, privatized 93, 204, 243
—, rainwater and irrigation 32, 235
—, ritual 126, 130
—, sovereignty 188
Watson, Kelly 190-191
Weller, Nathan 242
White Jr., Lynn 142
White, Monica M. 220, 221
Whiteness
—, and food justice 37, 150, 215, 218, 220
—, white privilege 161-162
Wisdom 6, 70, 75, 77, 85, 86, 92, 103, 117, 141, 144, 145, 146, 165, 173, 208, 232
Women
—, agricultural labor 203-210, 240
—, and Christianity 45, 51, 102, 104
—, Equal Rights Amendment (ERA) 163
—, exploitation of 22-23
—, female genital mutilation/cutting
—, feminism
—, indigenous 7, 79-80, 136, 141, 144, 167, 171, 173, 179, 181
—, Korean 48-51
—, maternal mortality
—, motherhood 141
—, poverty xv, 13, 15, 19, 22, 23, 140, 151, 211

—, stereotypes 48
—, and violence
—, Women's Donor Network (WDN) 160-161
World Council of Churches 22, 145, 173, 182
Wynter, Sylvia 238

Yanomami 6, 113, 121n27, 123, 124
Young, Iris 210

Zachariah, George 143, 145
Zambia 25, 30, 32, 43
Zapatistas 130, 131, 246
Zimbabwe (formerly Rhodesia) 6, 25-28, 30, 32-34, 36-38, 43-44, 149
—, Zimbabwean Institute for Religious Research and Ecological Conversation (ZIRRCON) 33-35, 45